The Big Book of Interiors

Design Ideas for Every Room

The Big Book of Interiors

Design Ideas for Every Room

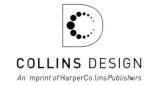

COLLINS DESIGN

An Imprint of HarperCollins Publishers

HarperCollins books may be purchased for educational, business, or sales promotional use.
For information, please write: Special Markets Department, HarperCollins*Publishers*,
10 East 53rd Street, New York, NY 10022

First Paperback Edition published in 2009

First Edition published in 2006 by:
Collins Design
An Imprint of HarperCollins*Publishers*
10 East 53rd Street
New York, NY 10022
Tel.: (212) 207-7000
Fax: (212) 207-7654
CollinsDesign@harpercollins.com
www.harpercollins.com

Distributed throughout the world by:
HarperCollins*Publishers*
10 East 53rd Street
New York, NY 10022
Fax: (212) 207-7654

Packaged by:
LOFT Publications
Via Laietana 32, 4° Of. 92
08003 Barcelona, Spain
Tel.: +34 932 688 088
Fax: +34 932 687 073
loft@loftpublications.com
www.loftpublications.com

Editor: Àgata Losantos

Texts: Eva Dallo

Translation: Matthew Clarke

Art Director: Mireia Casanovas Soley

Layout: Ignasi Gracia Blanco

Library of Congress Cataloging-in-Publication Data

ISBN-13: 978-0-06-114994-8 (paperback)

Losantos, Àgata.
  Big book of interiors / Àgata Losantos.— 1st ed.
    p. cm.
  ISBN-13: 978-0-06-083343-5 (hardcover)
  ISBN-10: 0-06-083343-2 (hardcover)
  1. Interior decoration. I. Title.

NK2110.D34 2006
747—dc22
                        2005031531

Printed in Spain

D.L: B-10861-06

First Paperback Printing, 2009

Contents

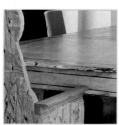
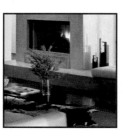
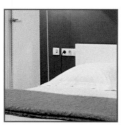
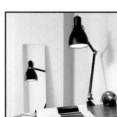
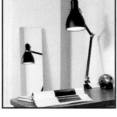
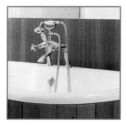

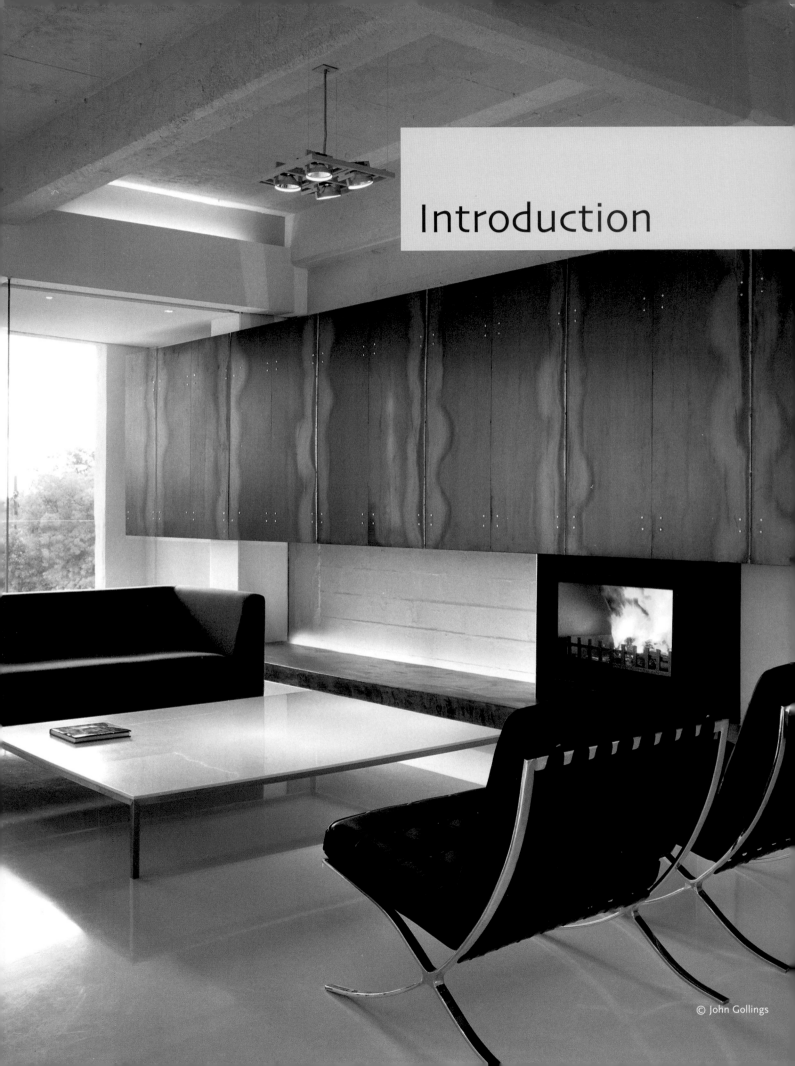

Introduction

This book explores and celebrates the world of today's interior architecture, offering innovative solutions to classical problems. All aspects of today's home are discussed and illustrated—halls, staircases, kitchens, dining rooms, living rooms, bedrooms, home offices, and bathrooms—and the selection features the best work of contemporary architects from around the world. You will find fresh ideas and new ways of making the best use of your budget and your imagination to maximize the potential of any space in your home.

This book does not only reflect the latest trends in interior design, including avant-garde styles such as minimalist, industrial, retro, neo-rural, and neo-rococo. It also emphasizes solutions based on the skillful selection of materials and the spatial distribution and aesthetic character of a space without adhering to any particular style. These solutions derive from the specific needs of people and the creativity of some of today's most interesting designers.

Interior architecture studies the way in which we relate to the space that surrounds us, identifying the spatial needs of a residence and providing us with the opportunity to create a personal space in which we can relax and feel at home. The growth of a global community has led to a constant exchange of cultural values, along with the weakening of traditional ones. The end result has been the growth of a more open-minded society and the emergence of a vast number of extraordinary cultural and artistic movements.

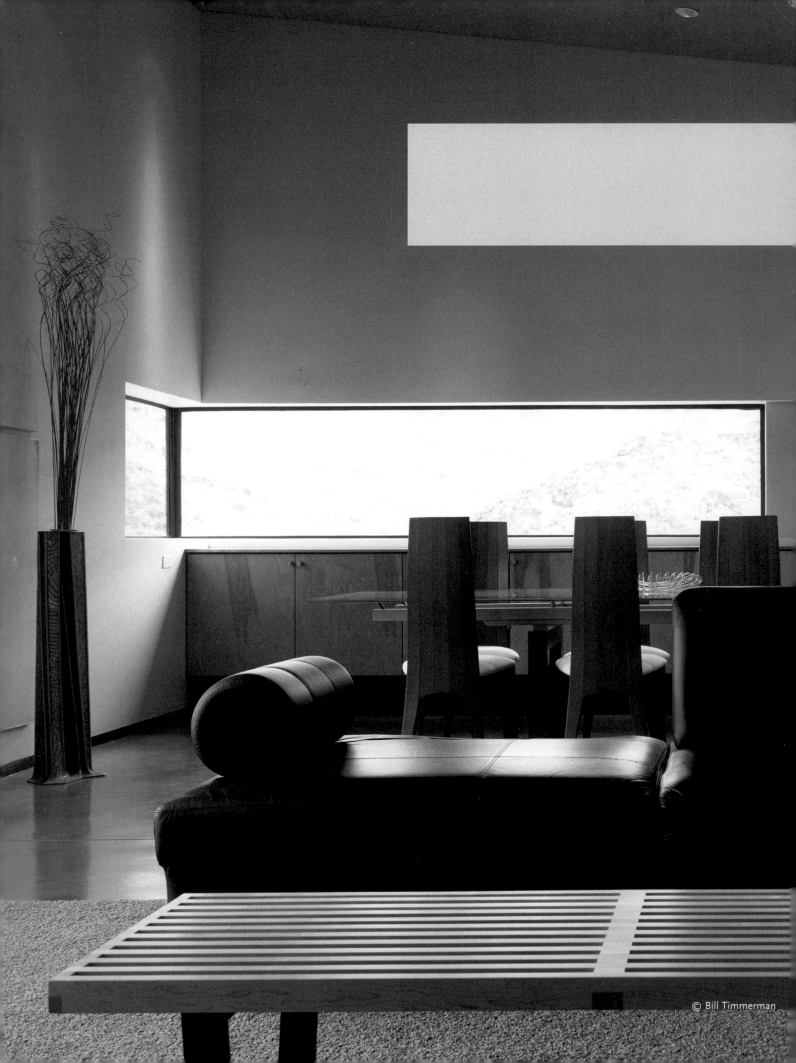

Contemporary interior architecture reflects the awakening of this new global culture, generating designs that exhibit Eastern and Western influences alike. It also expresses such values as ecological awareness and a concern for spiritual wellness as a source of happiness. In this way, design today not only pursues aesthetic harmony, but also aims to counter the negative effects of our fast-paced society.

With this in mind, today's interior design plays with both tangible and intangible elements. As many architects affirm about their own work, architecture not only consists of filling space, but manipulating it as well. Often furnished areas alternate with voids in which light and shadow accentuate the dialiogue between geometric forms and contrasting textures. Created are sensations rather than functions, atmosphere rather than decoration.

Our culture is increasingly individualistic, stimulating the examination of our own concerns and inclinations. Dwellings are designed to adapt to individuals, to the point of removing walls so that one's spirit may flow freely. From lofts without walls, to those that have half-height partitions, or those that use textile panels as room dividers, the possibilities are endless. The personality of each homeowner is no longer locked in by a rigid structure; instead, the residence adapts to each homeowner thanks to the tools and techniques offered by interior design.

Halls & Staircases

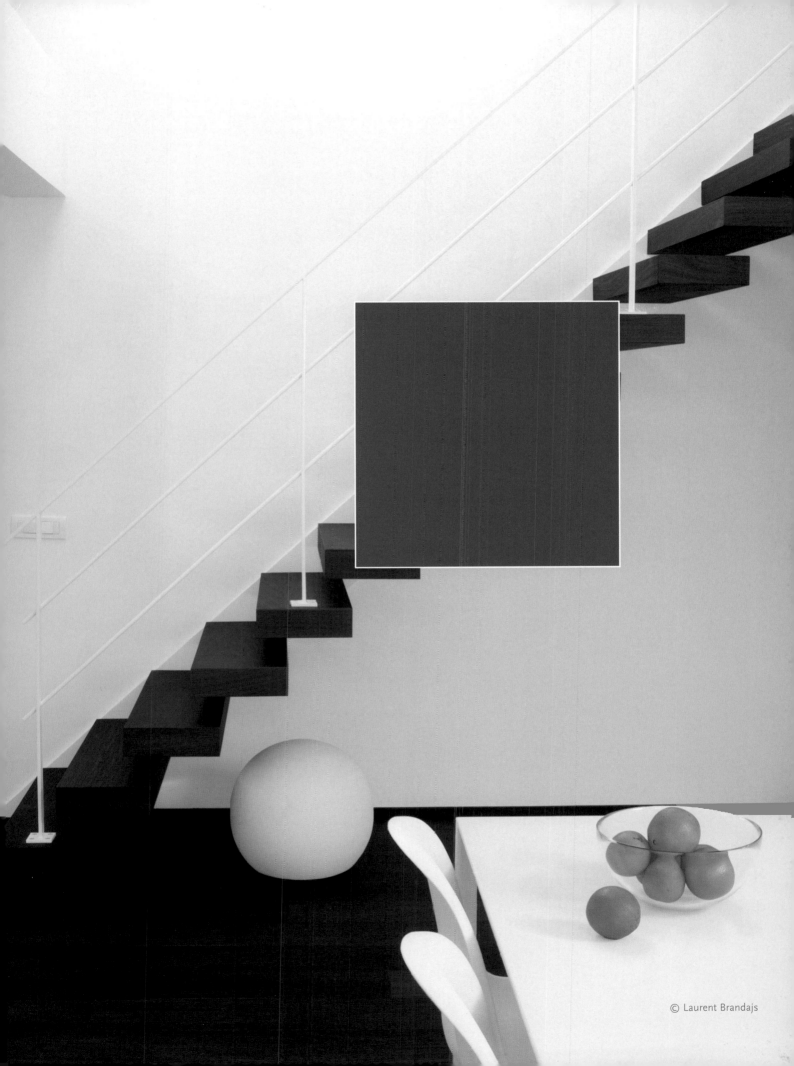

Halls & Staircases

The halls and staircases in a house are a part of its soul

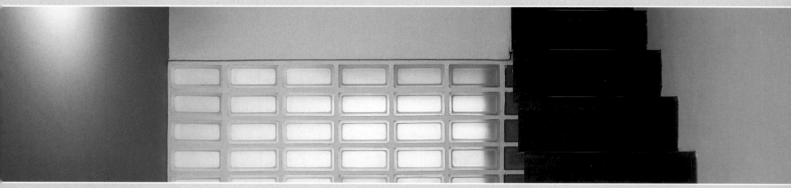

© Andrea Martiradonna

Just as the eyes are said to be the mirrors of the soul, halls and staircases in a house are part its soul. Although these elements are vital, in the past they were often unappreciated. Recently, the approach to these spaces has changed radically. Before, halls and staircases were nothing more than a formality resulting from the logic of construction. From a decorative viewpoint, many would have been better off if they didn't exist at all. Today they are conceived of as a continuation of the other spaces in the house, and they provide a chance to establish or change the atmosphere, create specific settings, and connect spaces. Once neutral and set apart from the rest of the house, they are now designed with the same materials used in other rooms. They can have uses other than those that are purely structural—staircases can be closets and corridors can be lit to provide ambient lighting for other areas in the home.

When they are designed as veritable sculptures, staircases can acquire an artistic dimension. In a process that could be called the sublimation of the staircase, it may no longer be strictly utilitarian, but also becomes a central element in a residential project. It defines its atmosphere and serves as an axis for spatial distribution.

Today there is a trend toward integrating both staircases and passageways closely into the rest of the house. Contributing elements include translucent walls, made of glass and other materials, and sliding doors, which make it possible to enlarge spaces, either physically or through lighting. Other options include turning these spaces into a gallery that reflects the tastes of a home's occupants or taking advantage of corners and nooks to create areas for storage or for activities that require little space, such as reading and writing.

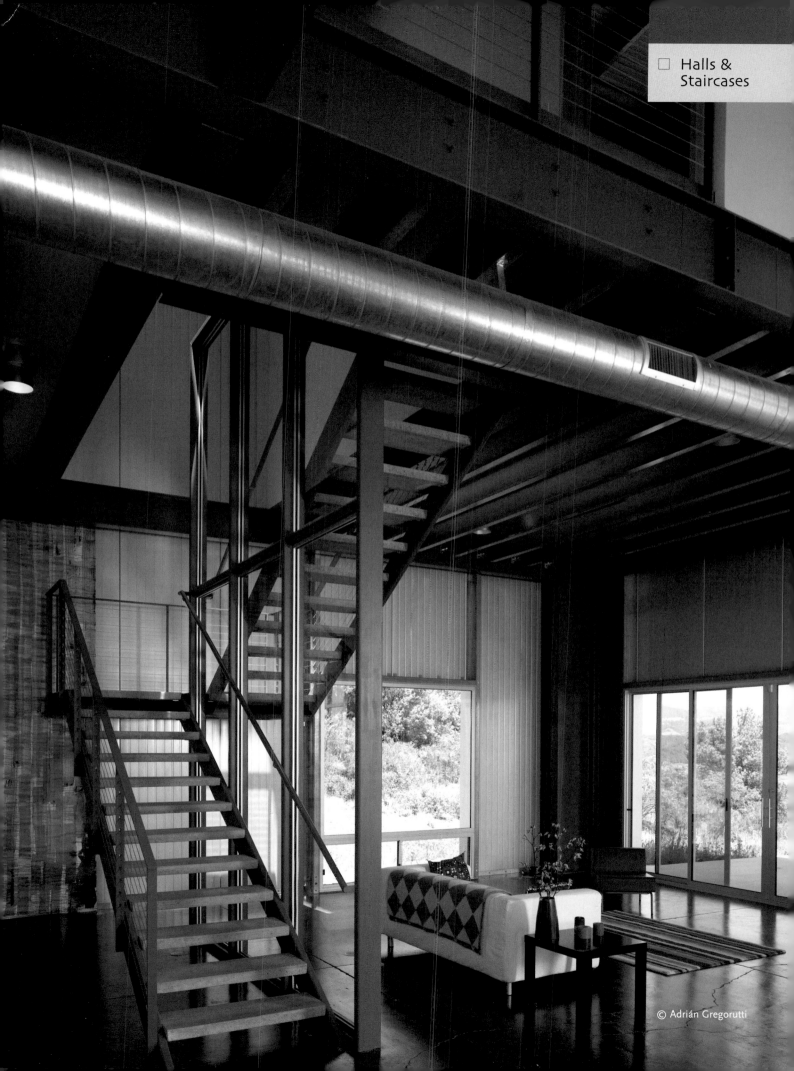

© Adrián Gregorutti

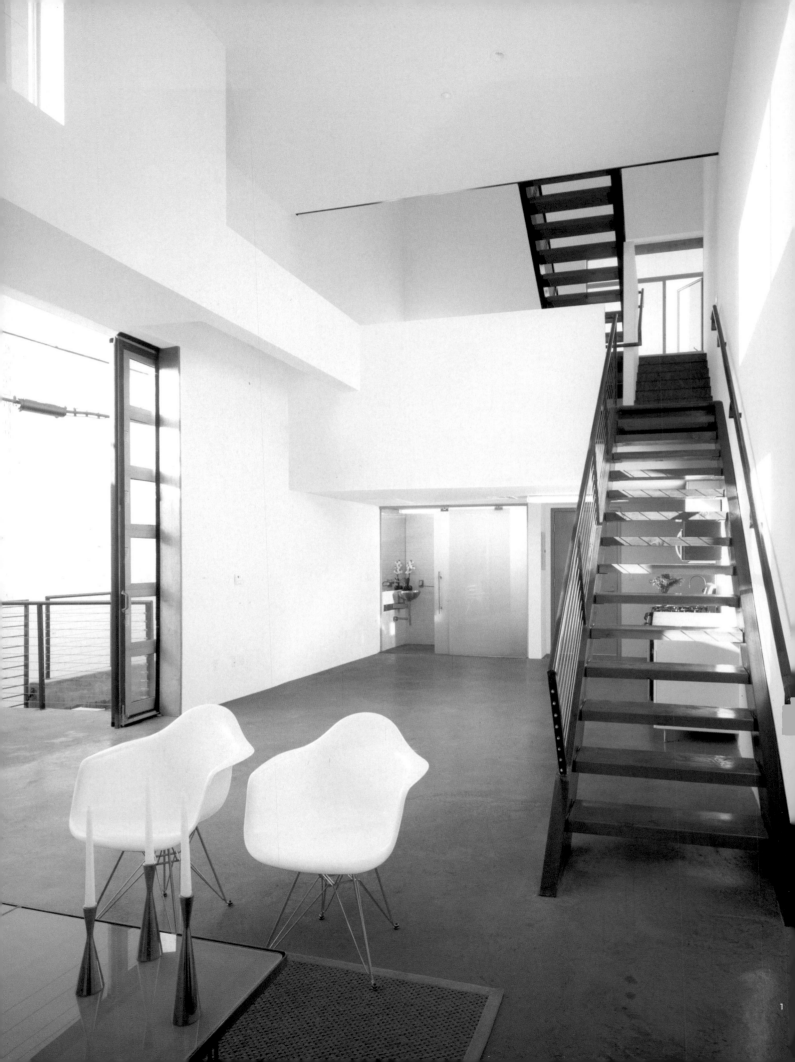

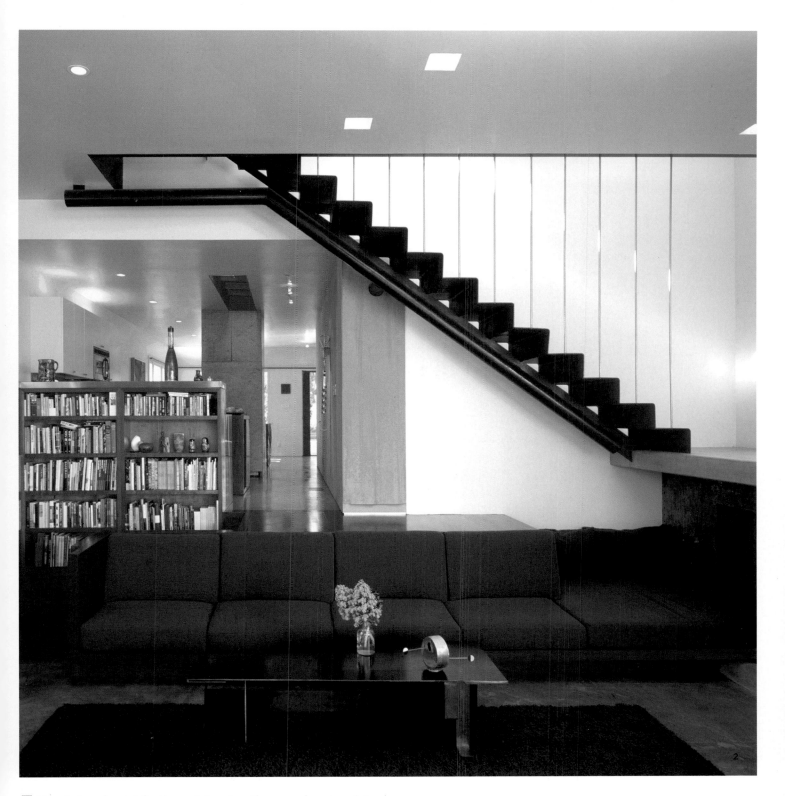

The choice of metal for these stairs gives them an almost sculptural prominence, especially if the setting is white, as in these two rooms. In open spaces like this, an element that is often difficult to integrate into a space has to be handled imaginatively to achieve a desirable aesthetic effect. Treating a stairway as a decorative element is frequently the best solution, and the design and materials can be selected on that basis.

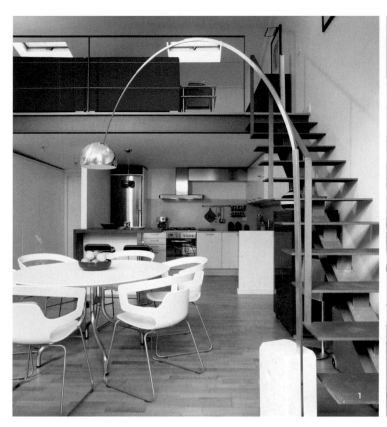 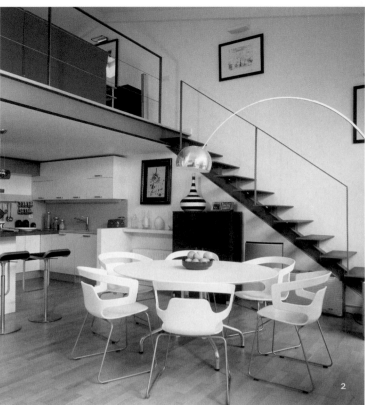

The image below shows a different approach to a staircase:
It has been integrated into the space since it is the same color
and material as the walls.

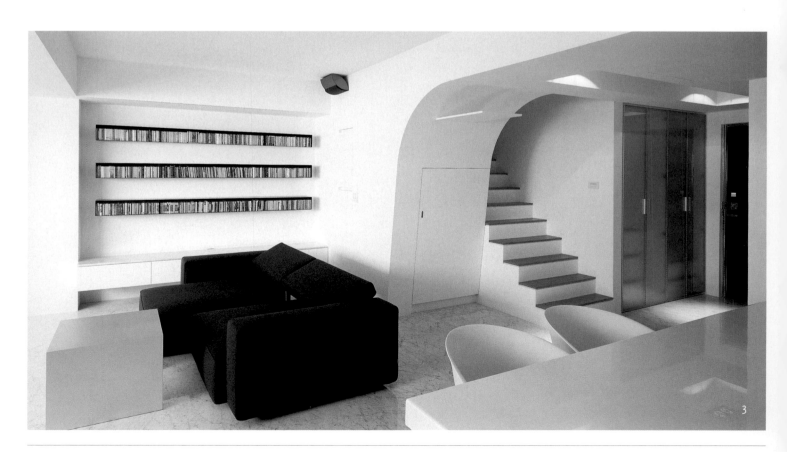

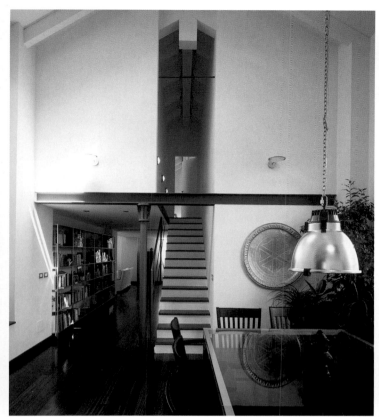

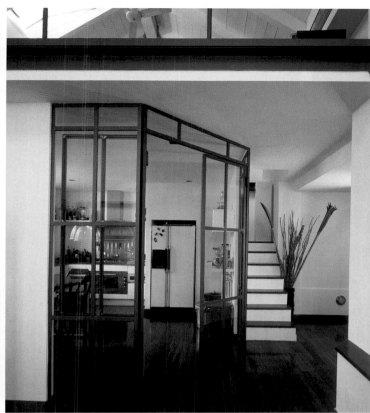

*The wood on the steps achieves a very interesting optical effect,
as the staircase appears much lighter visually.*

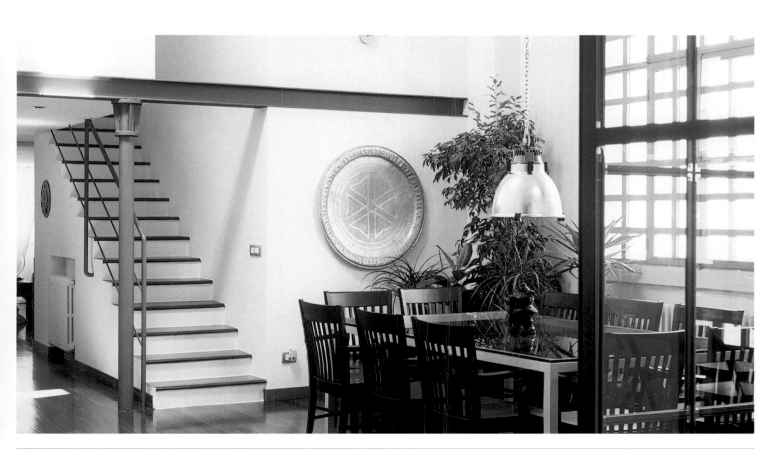

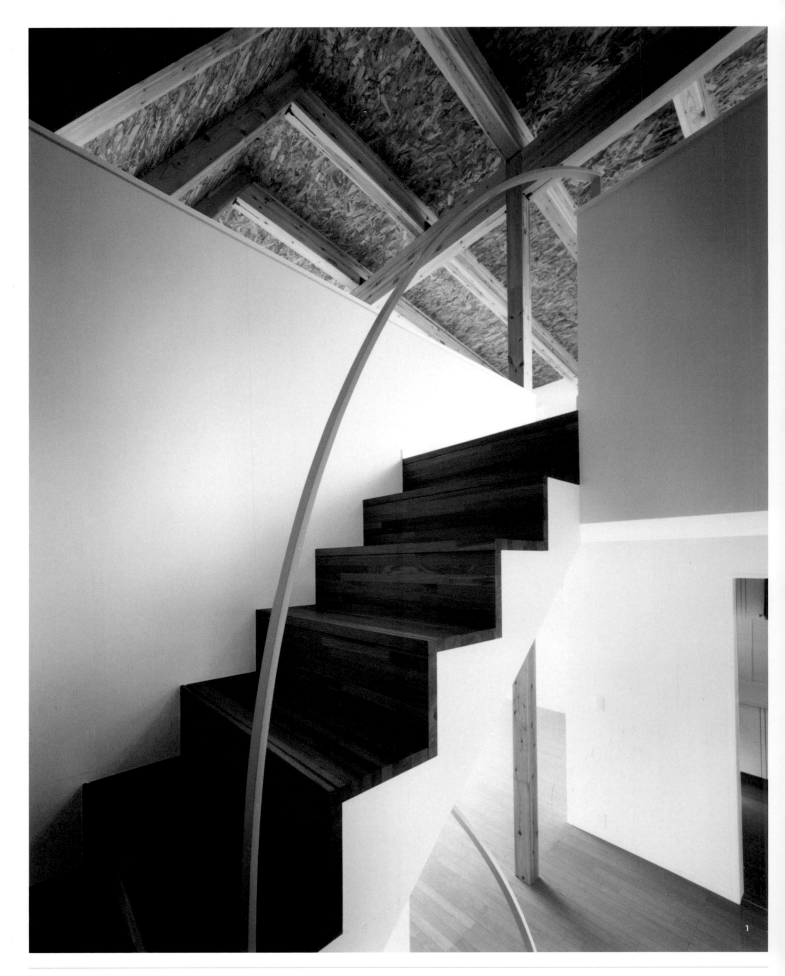

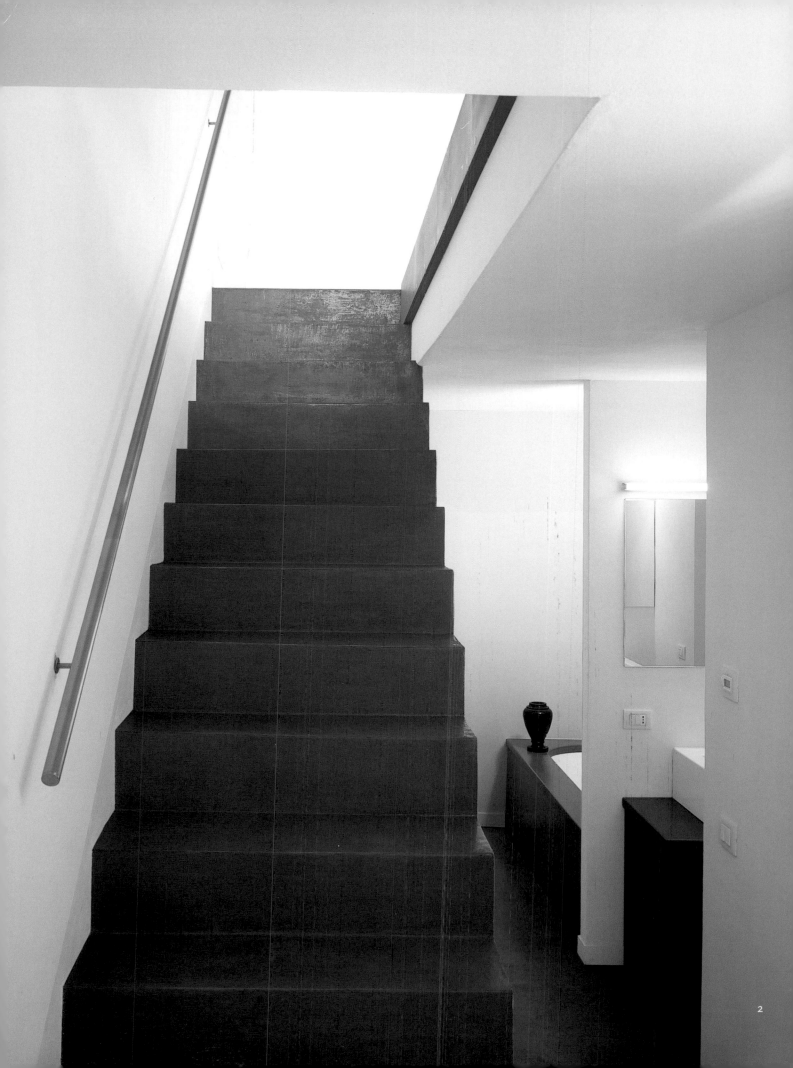

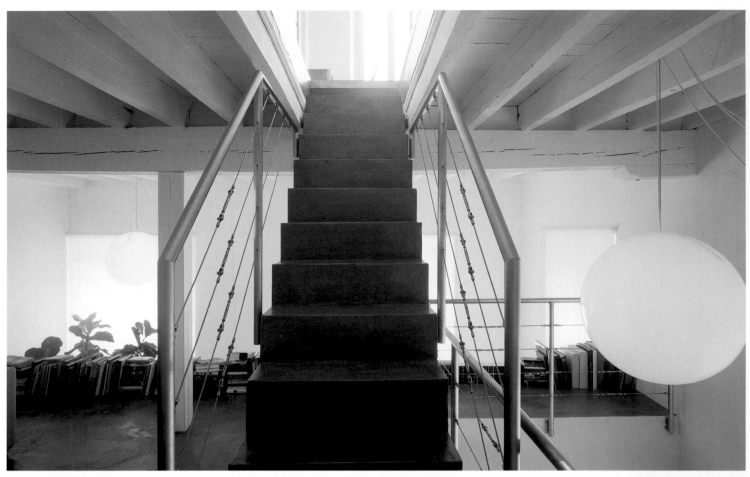

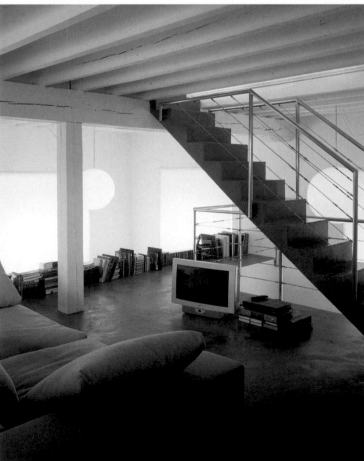

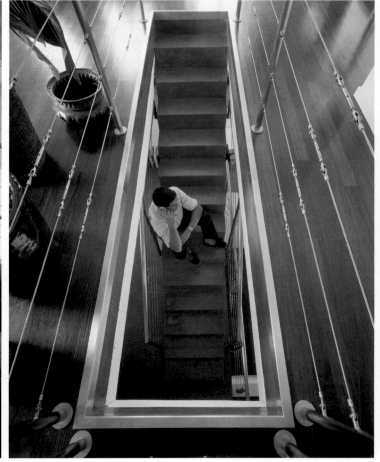

© Andrea Martiradonna

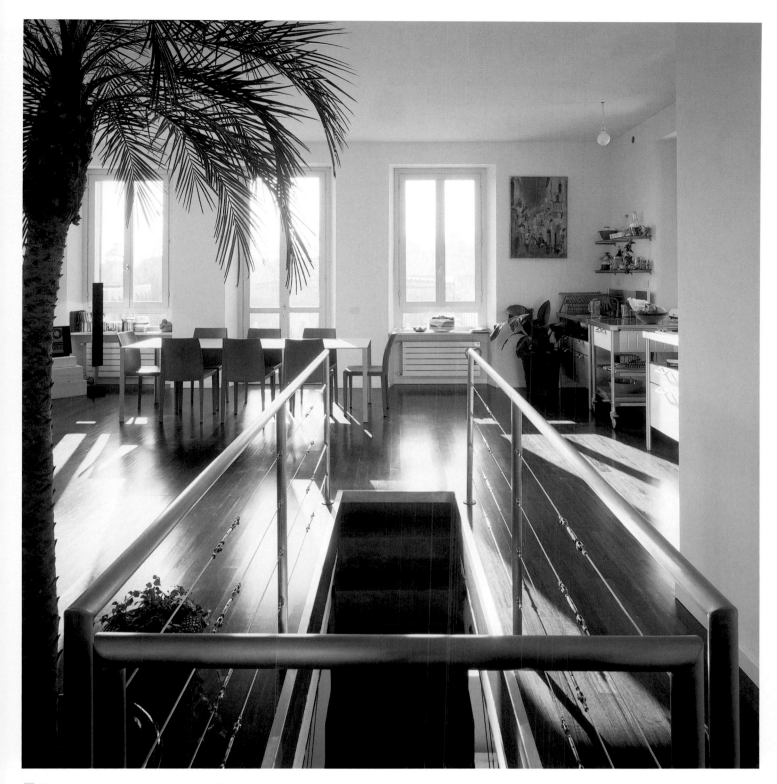

The stairs are the same color as the floor, creating the feeling that they are a continuation of it and setting up a dialogue between the floor, staircase, and ceiling.

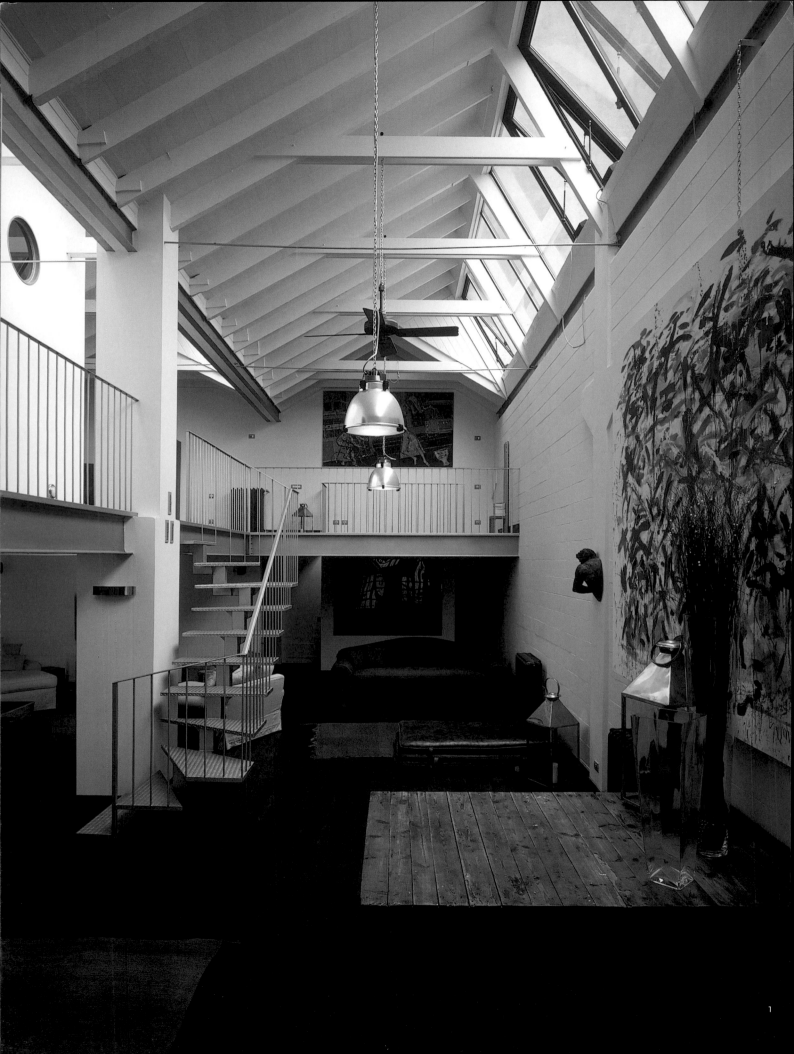

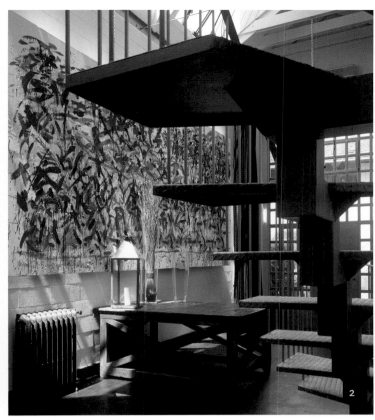

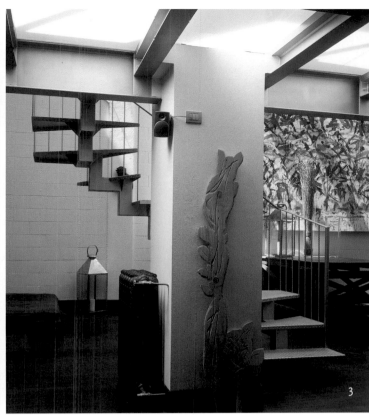

It is not only materials that provide the opportunity to play with aesthetic effects on staircases: variations in the size and form of the steps can also be visually striking.

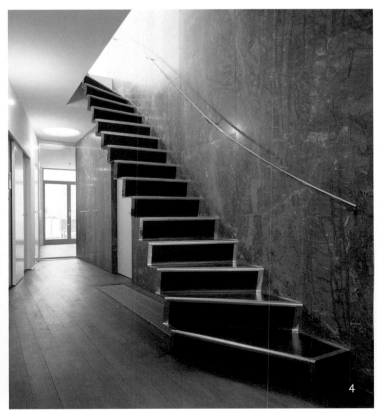

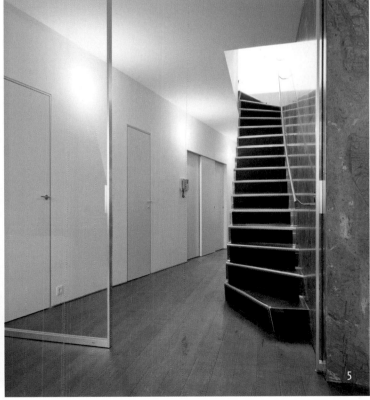

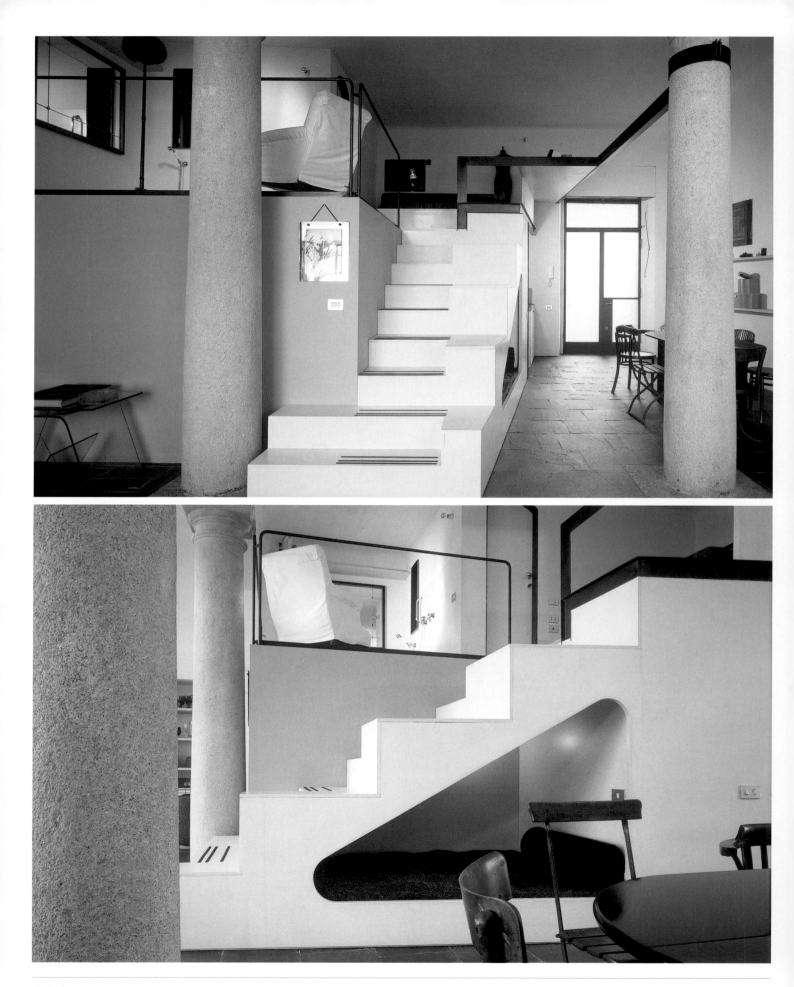

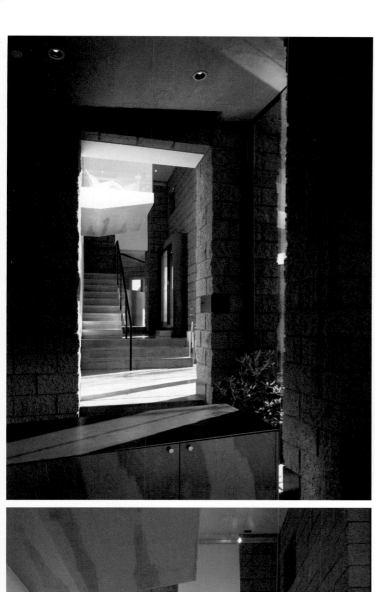
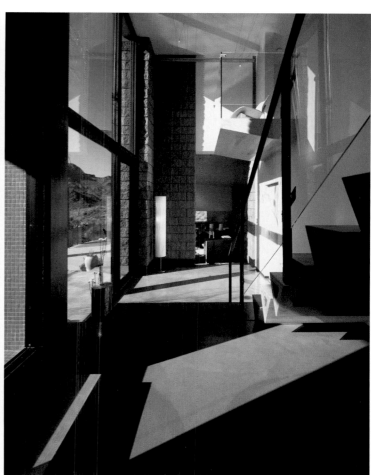
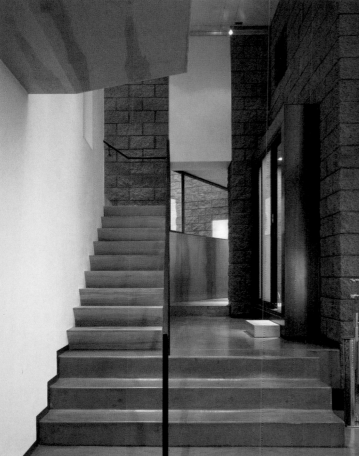
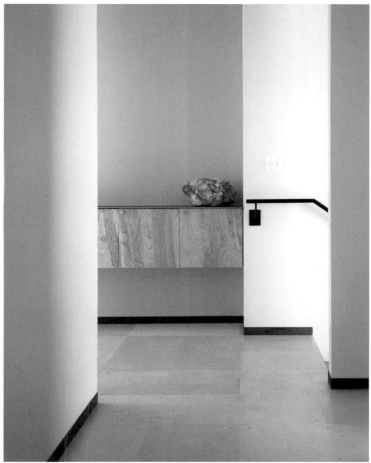

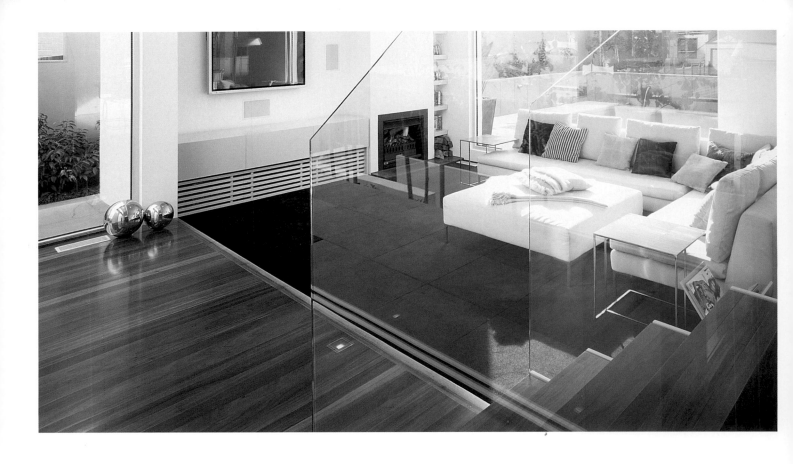

The staircase is "camouflaged" by the banister, which is made with glass and the same wood as the floor.

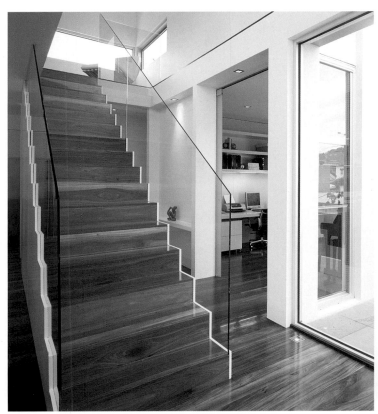

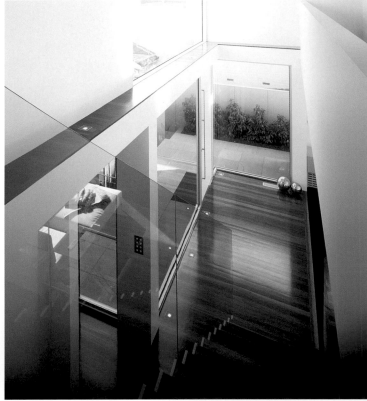

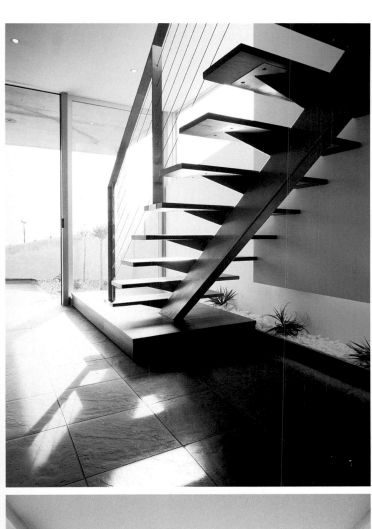

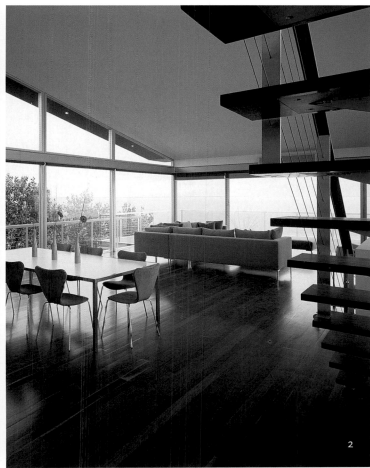

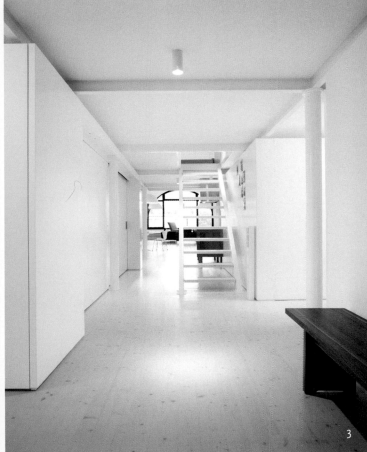

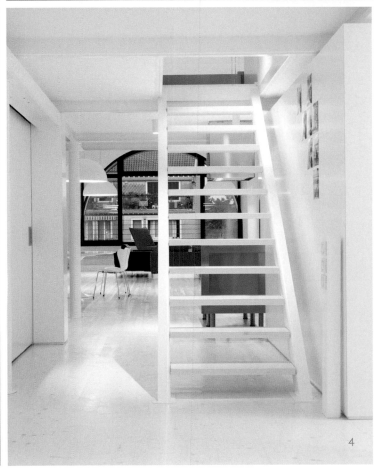

1, 2 © Christopher Ott   3, 4 © Matteo Piazza

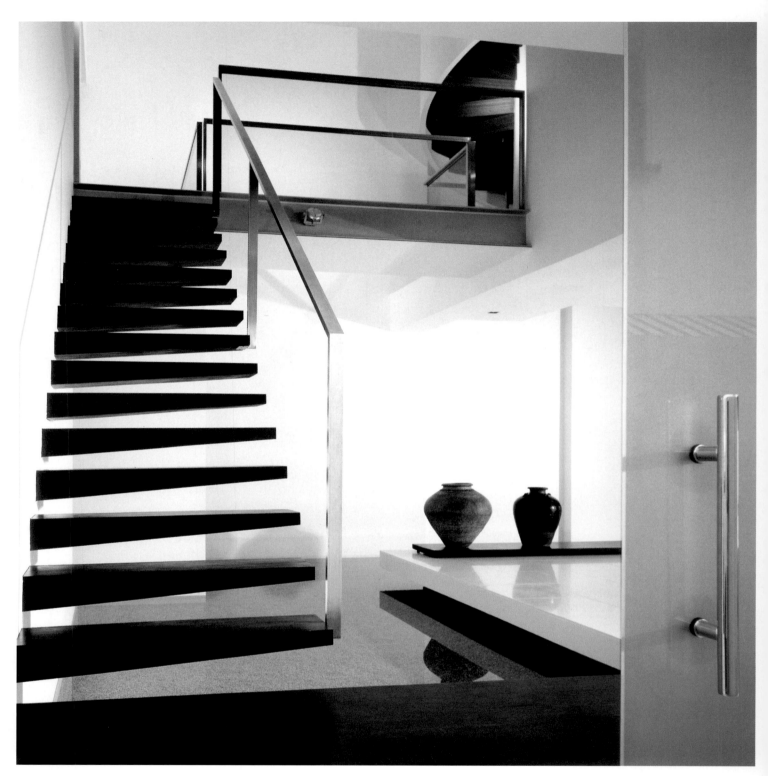

☐ Steps fixed to the wall not only add dynamism and occupy less space
visually, but they also allow light to pass through.

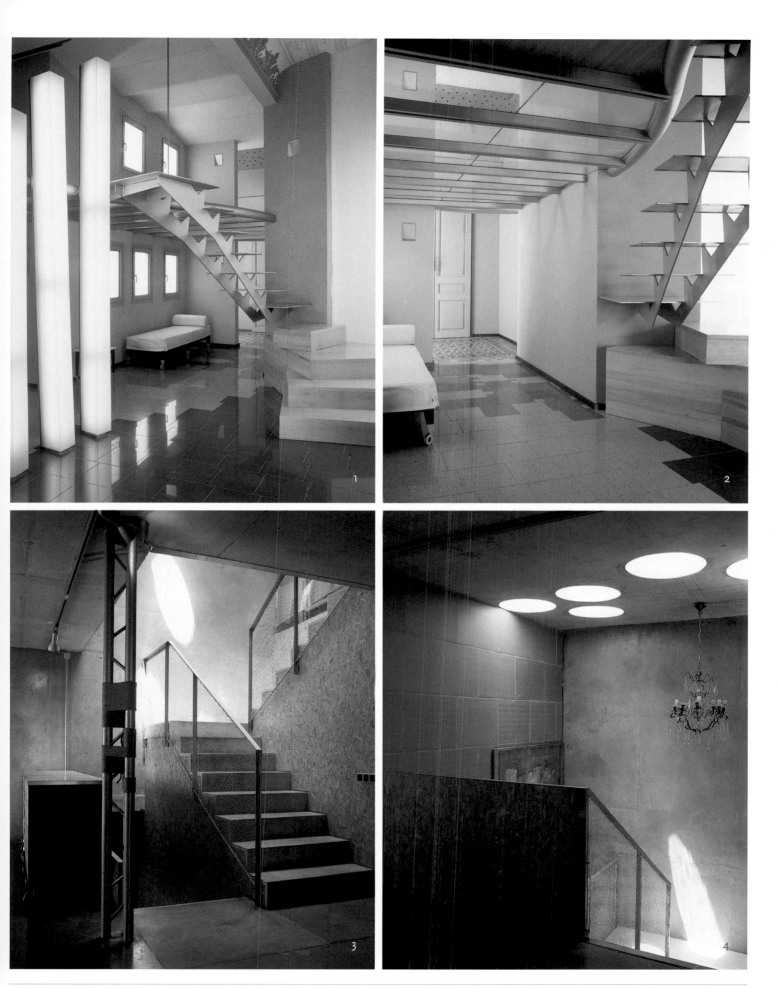

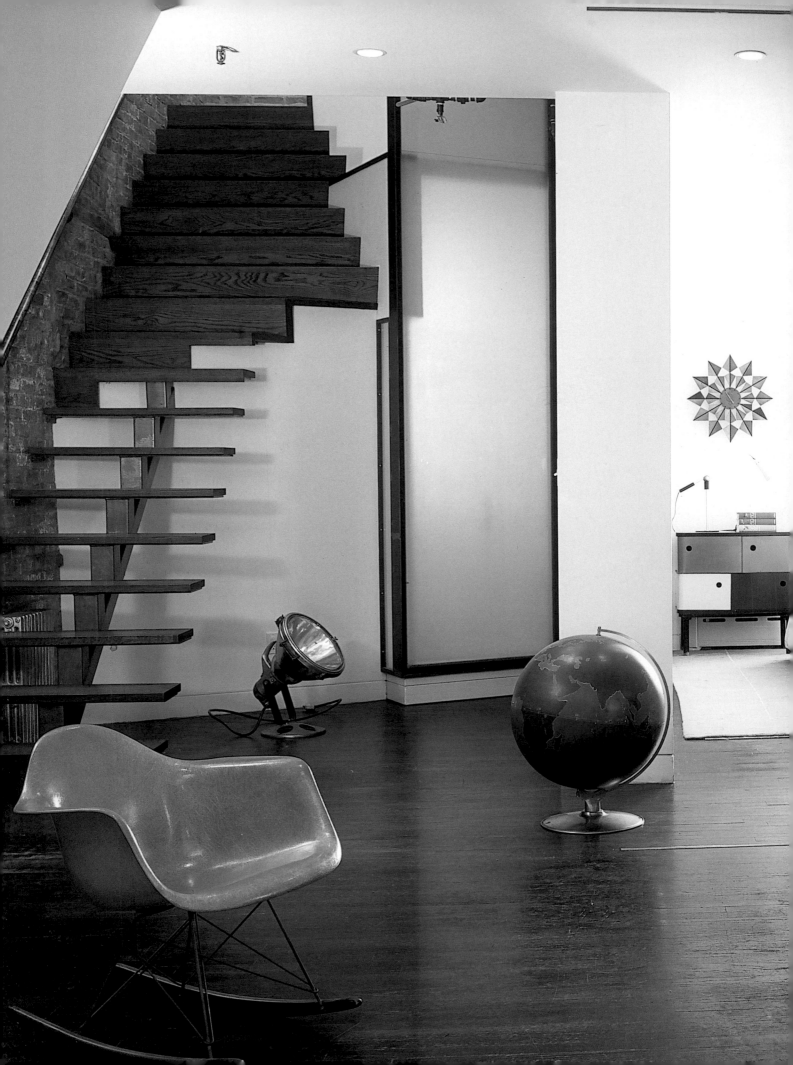

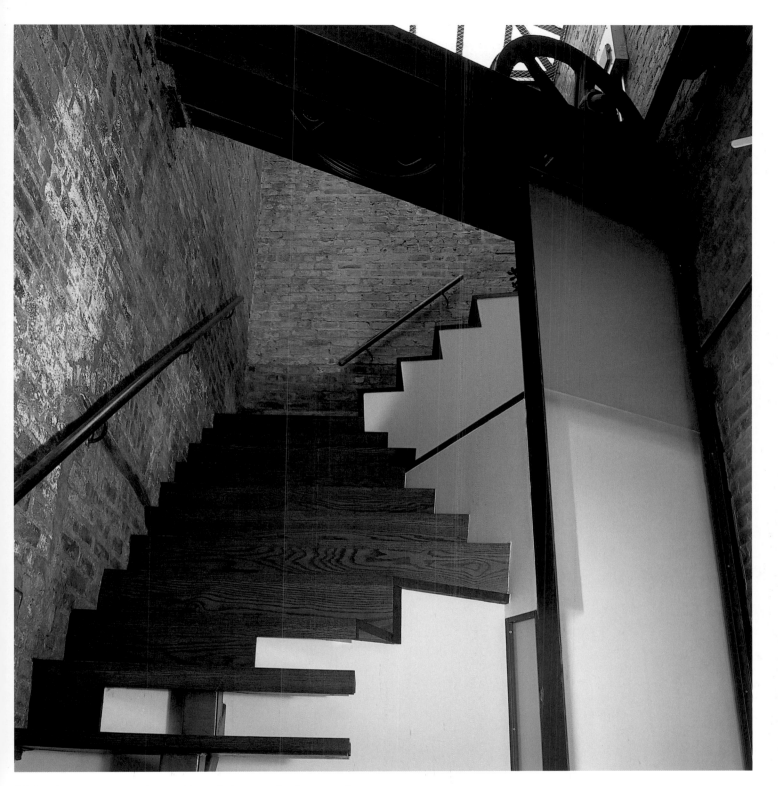

☐ Creating structures under a staircase helps to make the most of space when it is at a premium. The first flight of steps, set on a beam, converges with another one, which is integrated into the top of a closet.

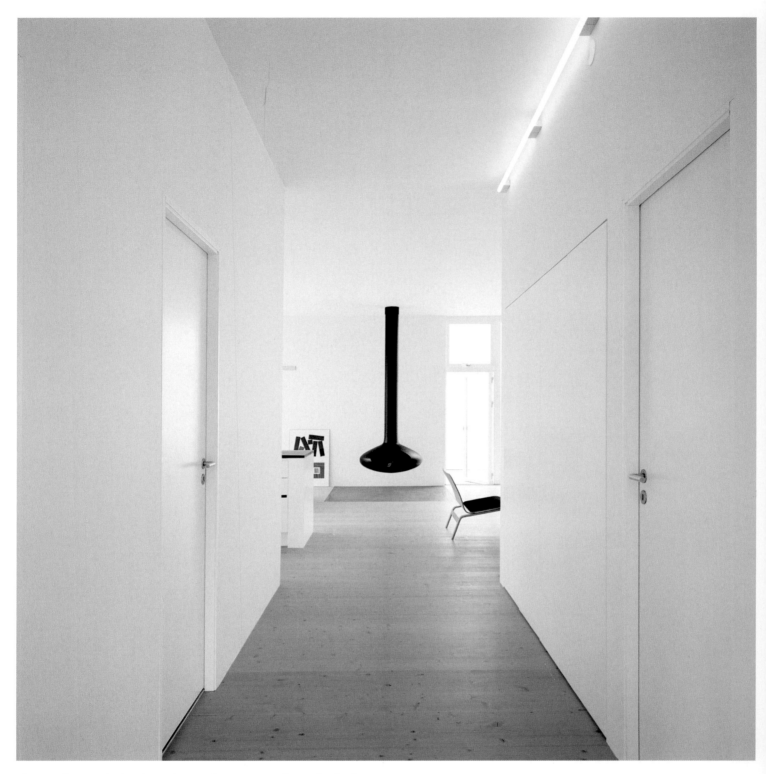

△ Here the corridor has been designed to serve as a frame for the fireplace in the lounge at one end.

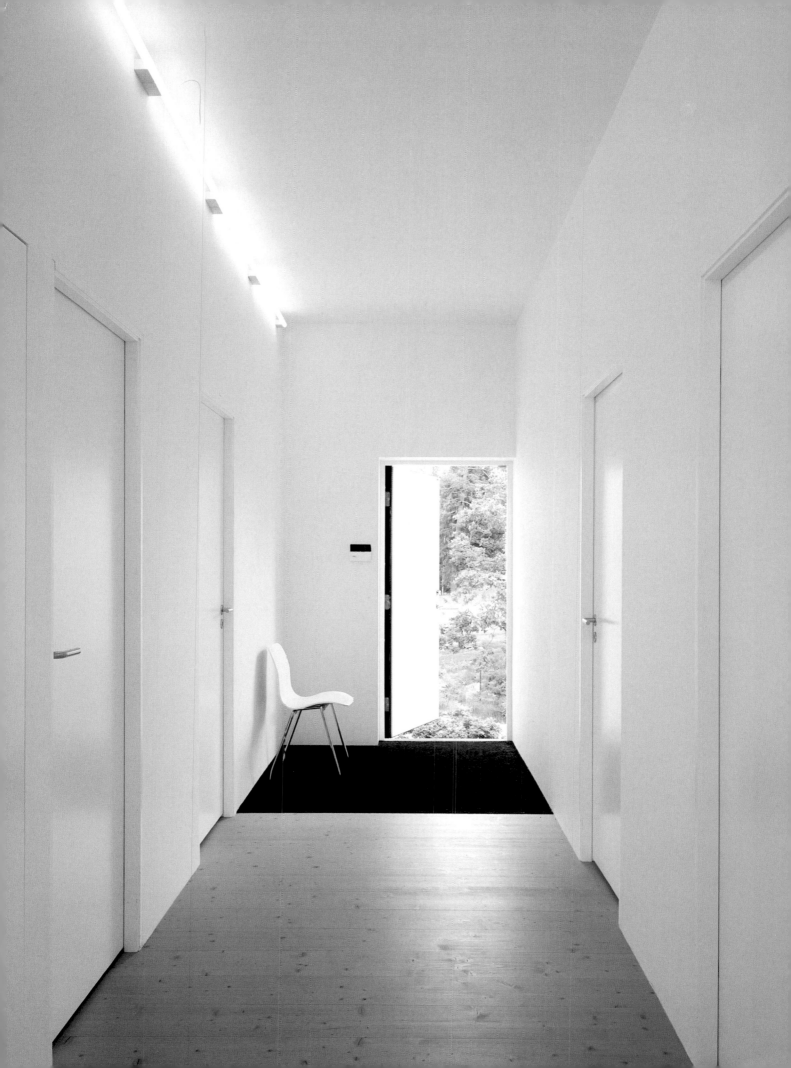

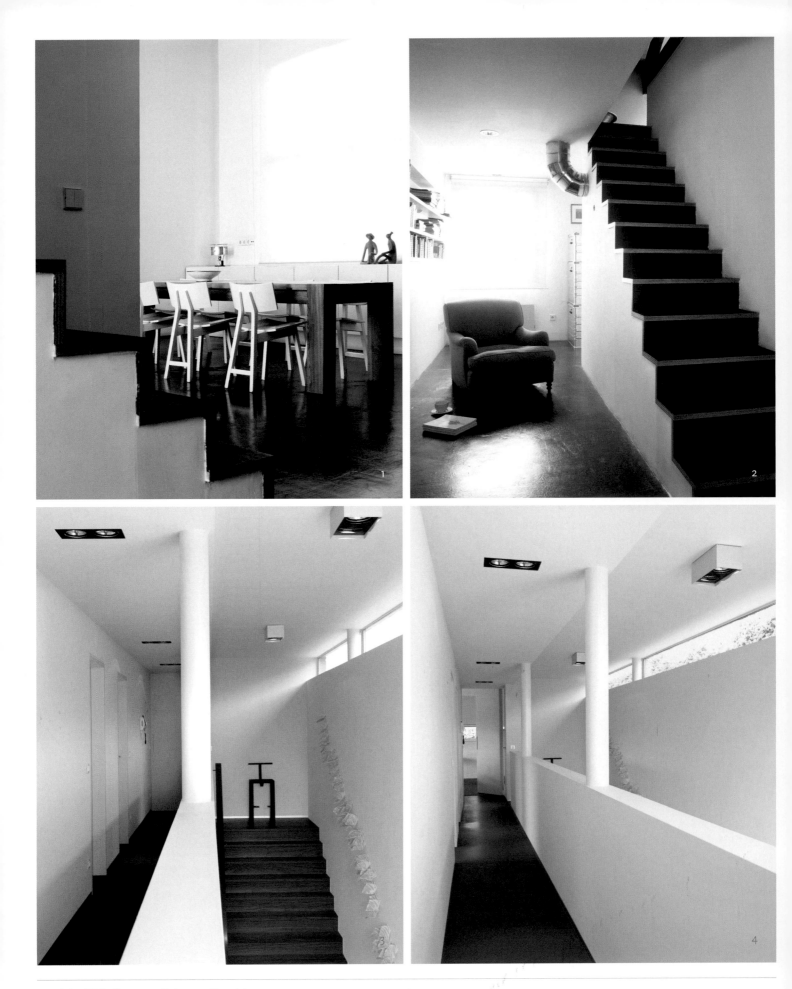

1, 2 © Jordi Miralles   3, 4 © Laurent Brandajs

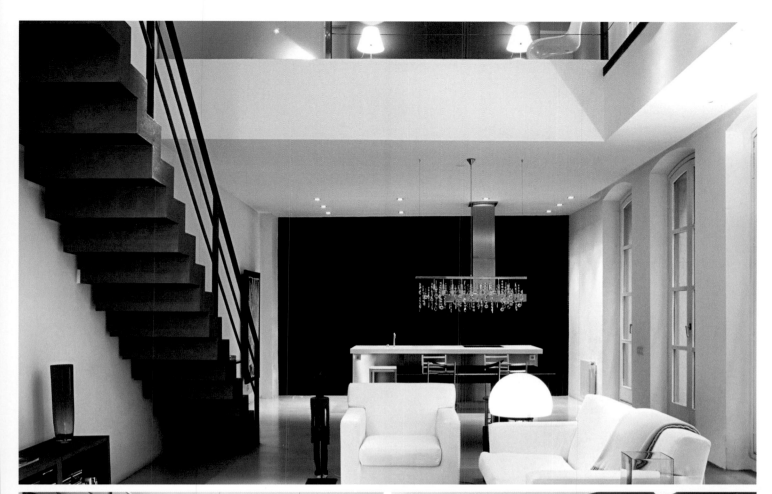

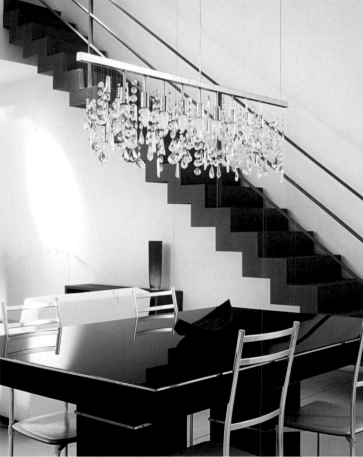

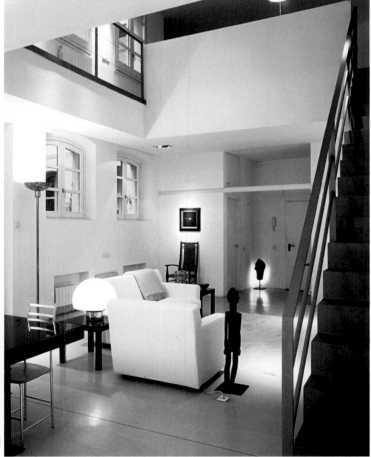

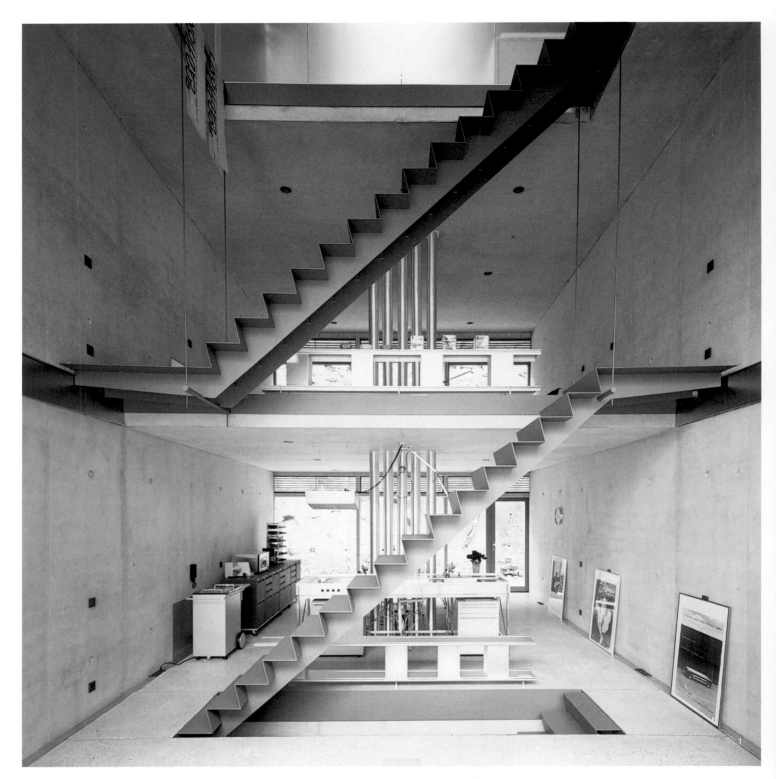

△ In a space devoid of partitions, the staircase can be used as an element to separate and distribute the space. In this case, the design plays with the symmetry created by the staircase, which emerges from the floor like a hanging bridge.

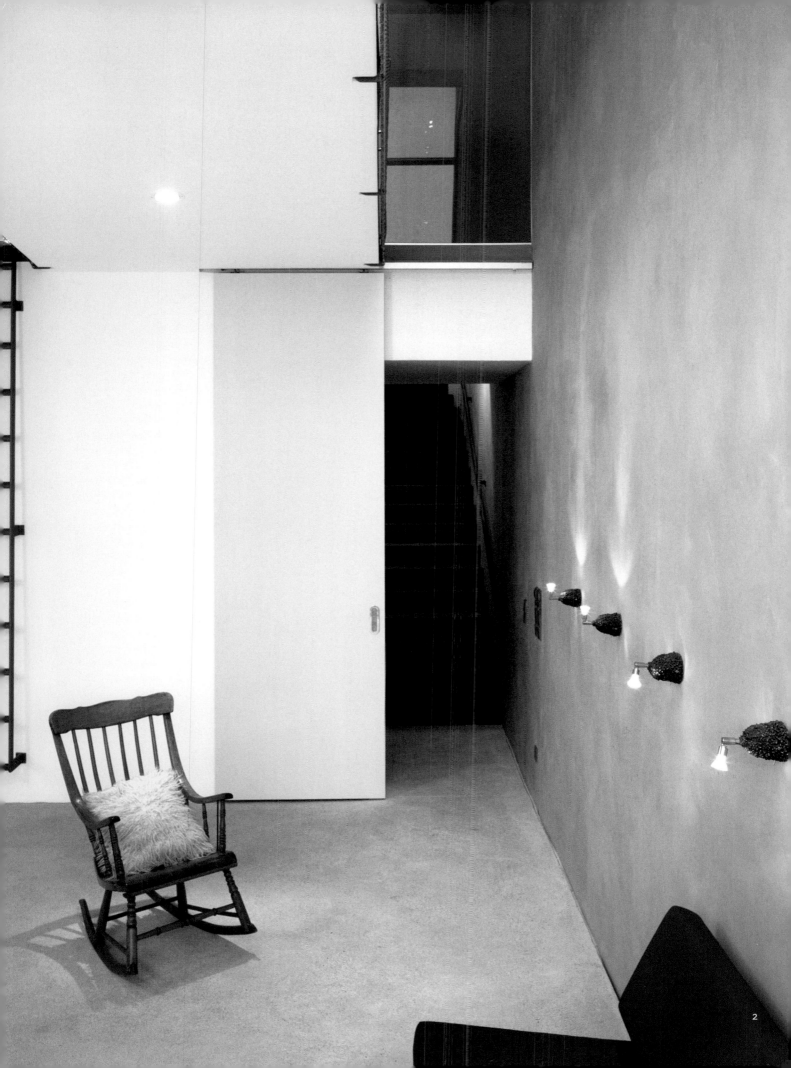

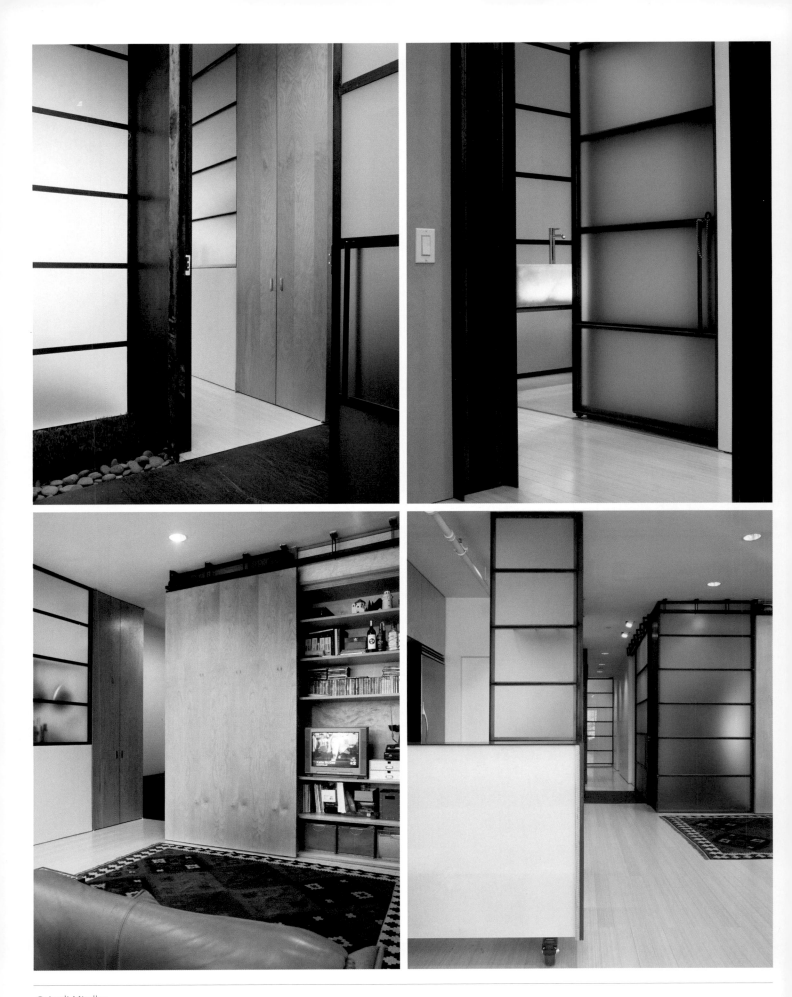

© Jordi Miralles

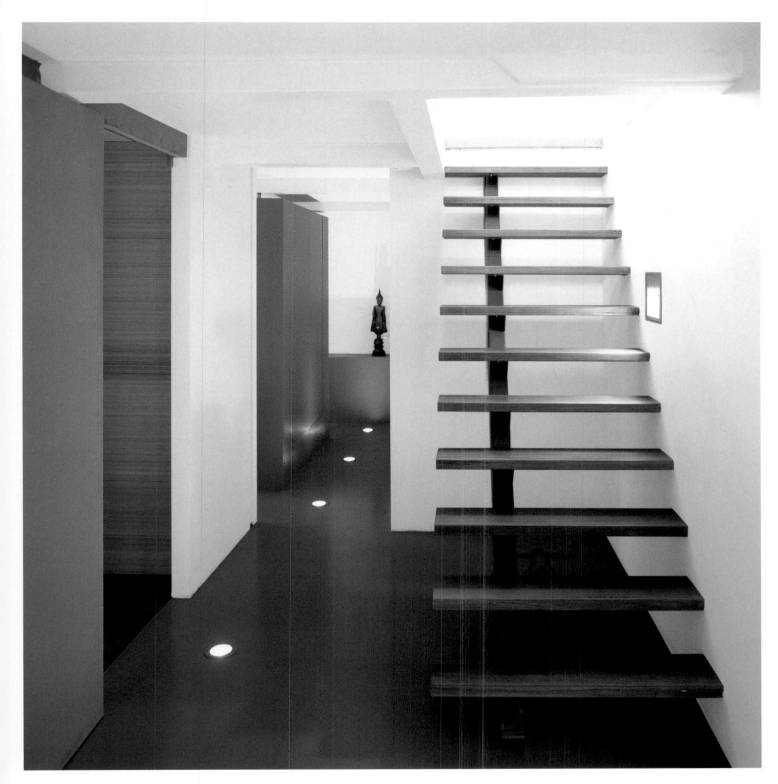

◁ Translucent panels help achieve a homogenous atmosphere by unifying the lighting. Movable panels are often used to save space.

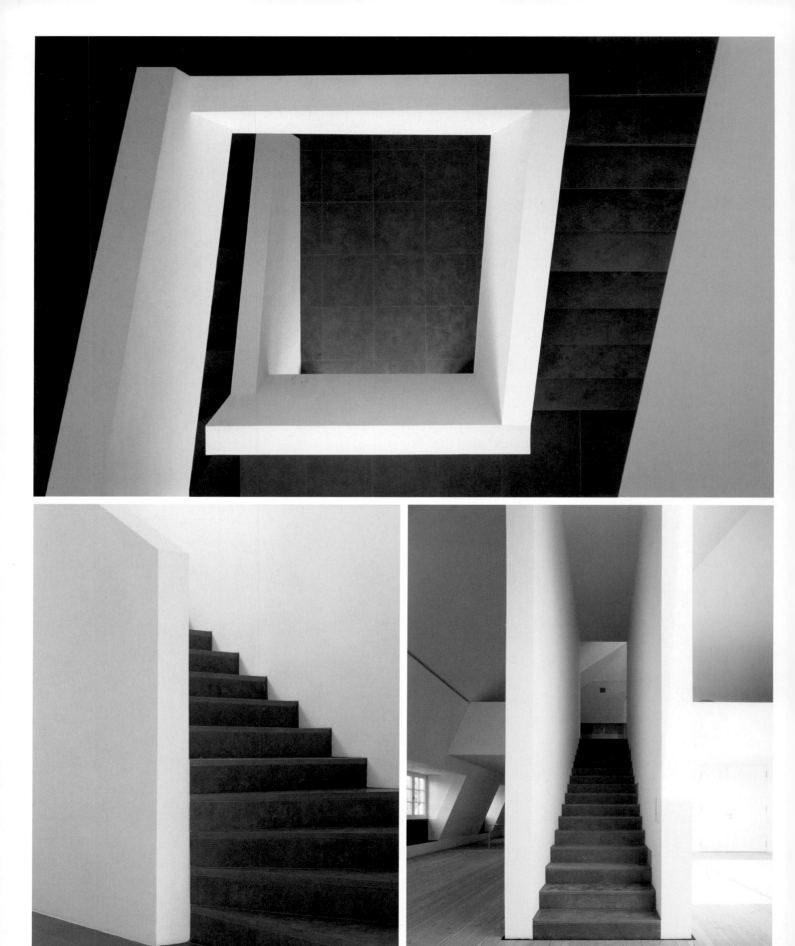

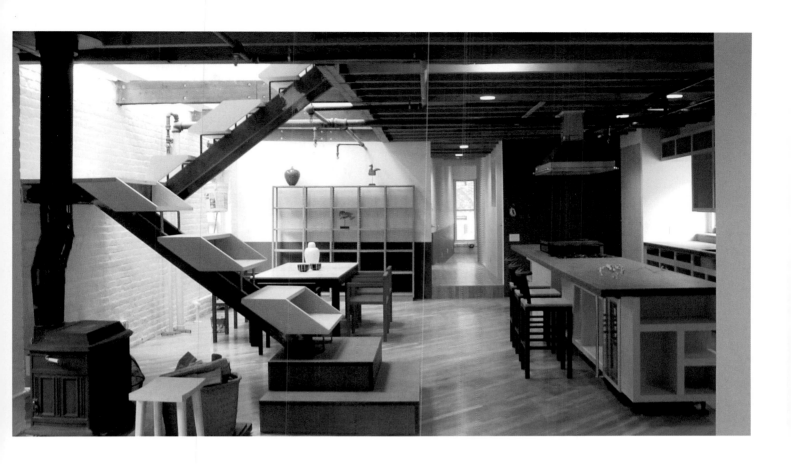

The architects Cha and Innerhofer play with timeless forms and integrate exposed structural elements into the interior design.

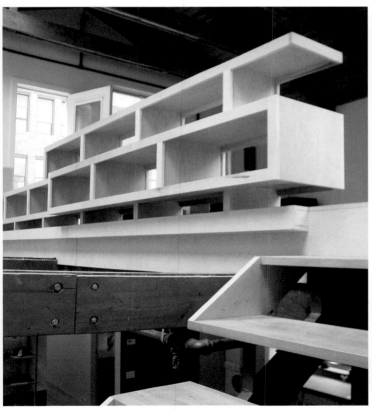

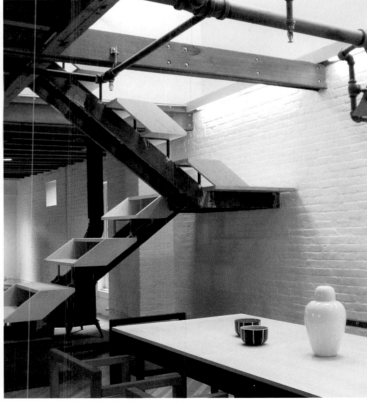

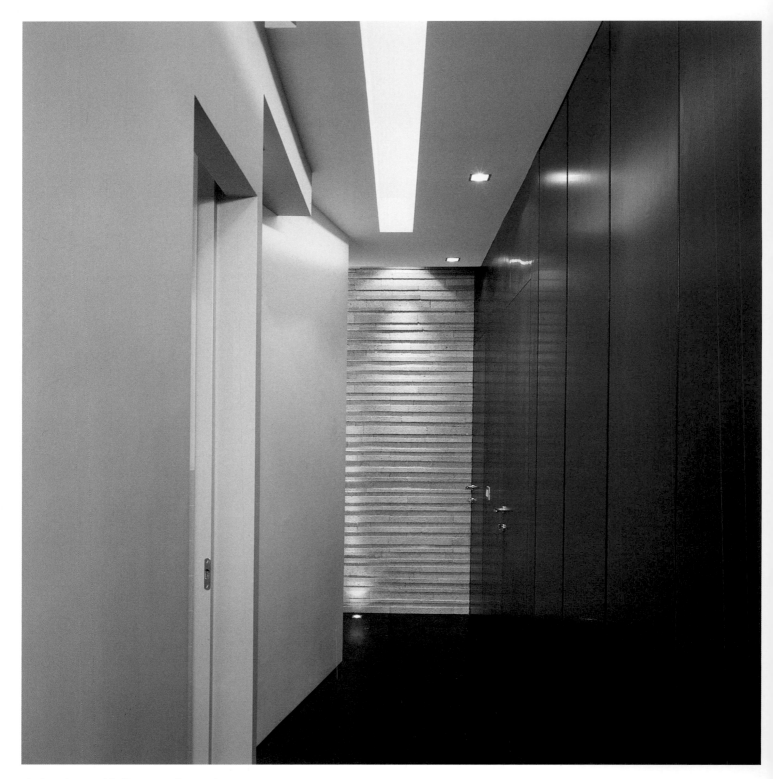

△ Corridors and hallways can be used as storage space.

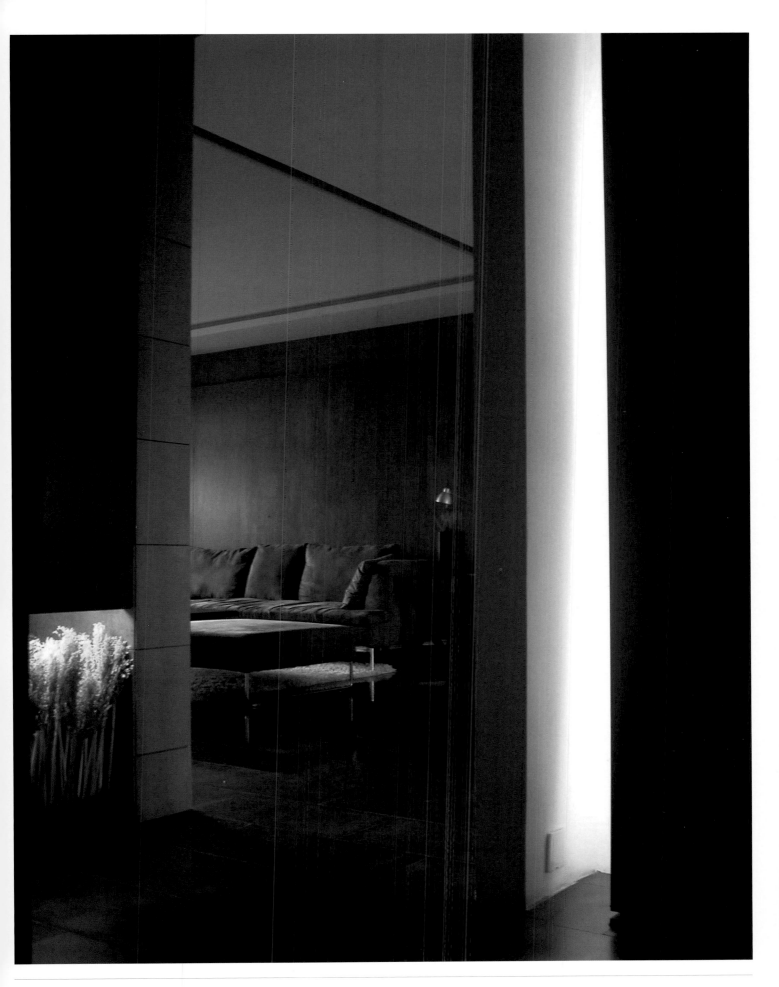

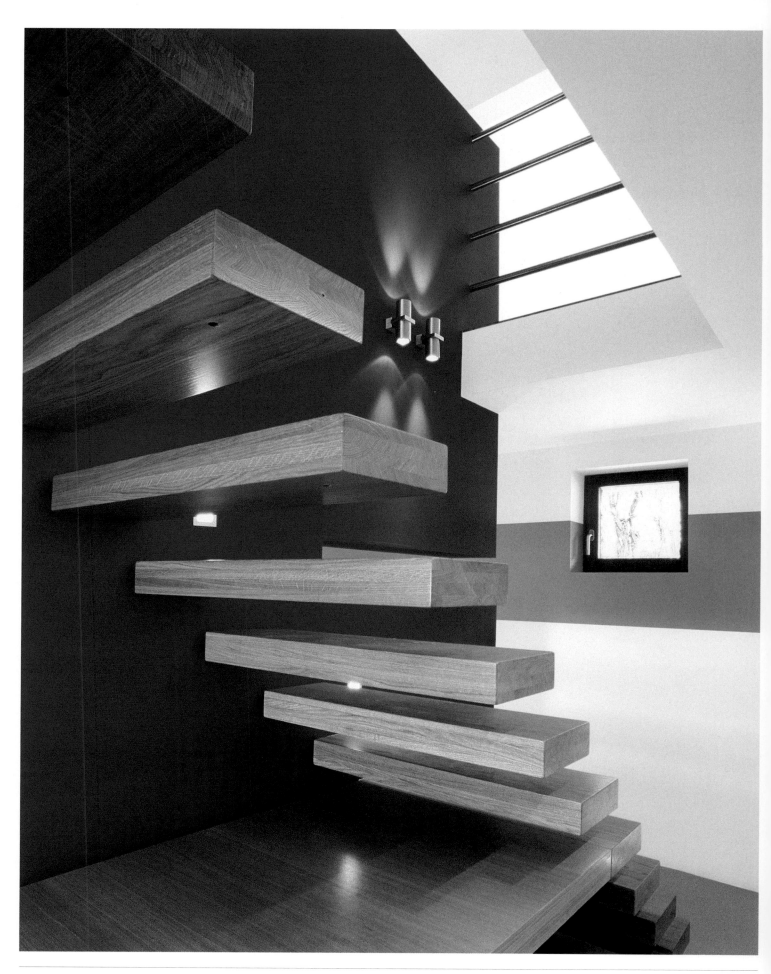

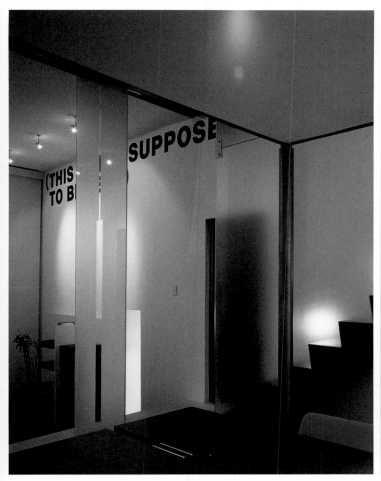

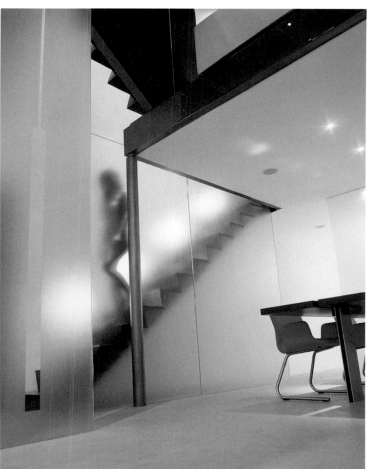

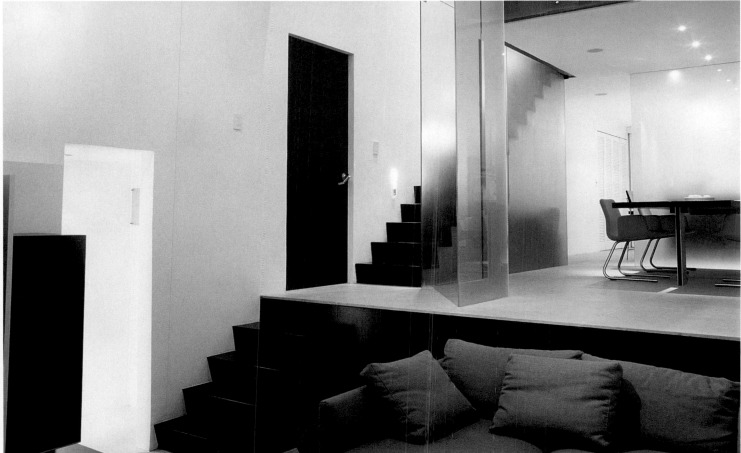

© Jaime Navarro

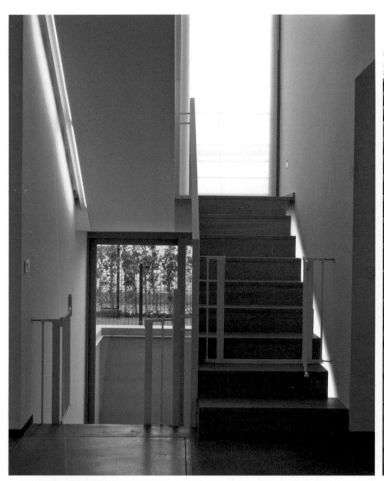
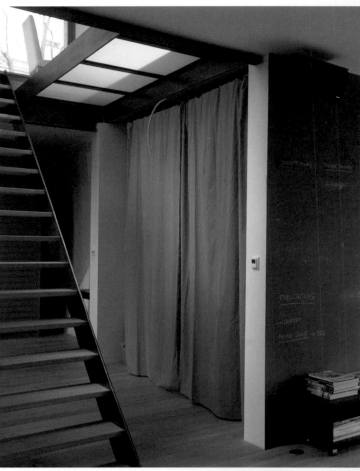
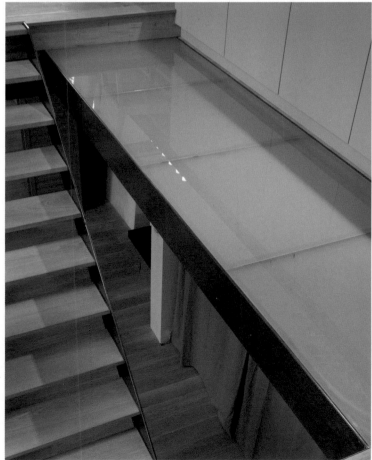
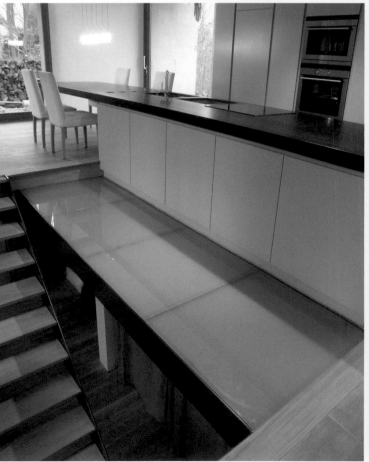

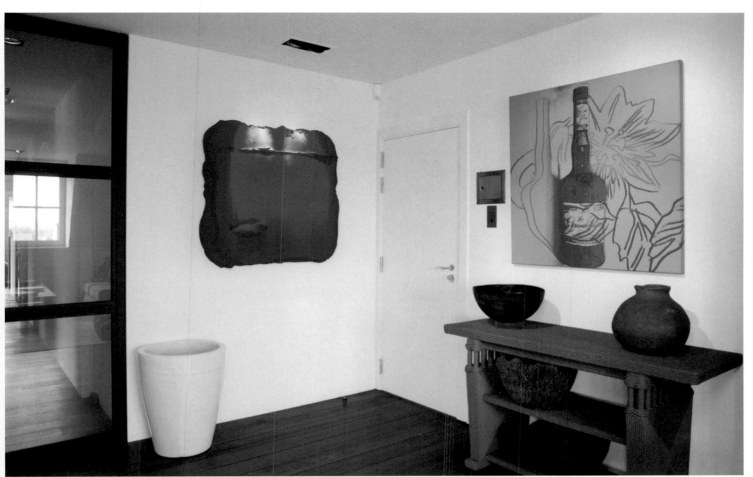

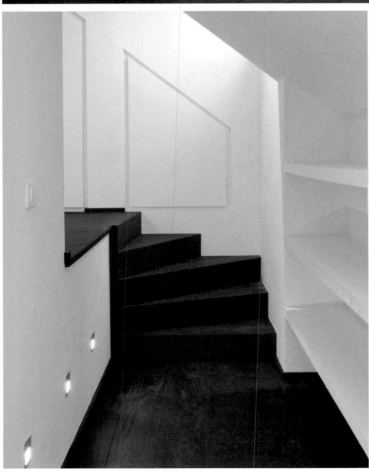

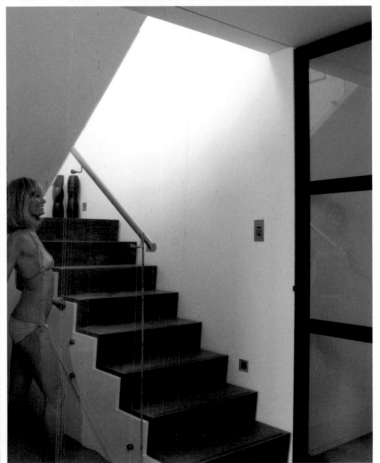

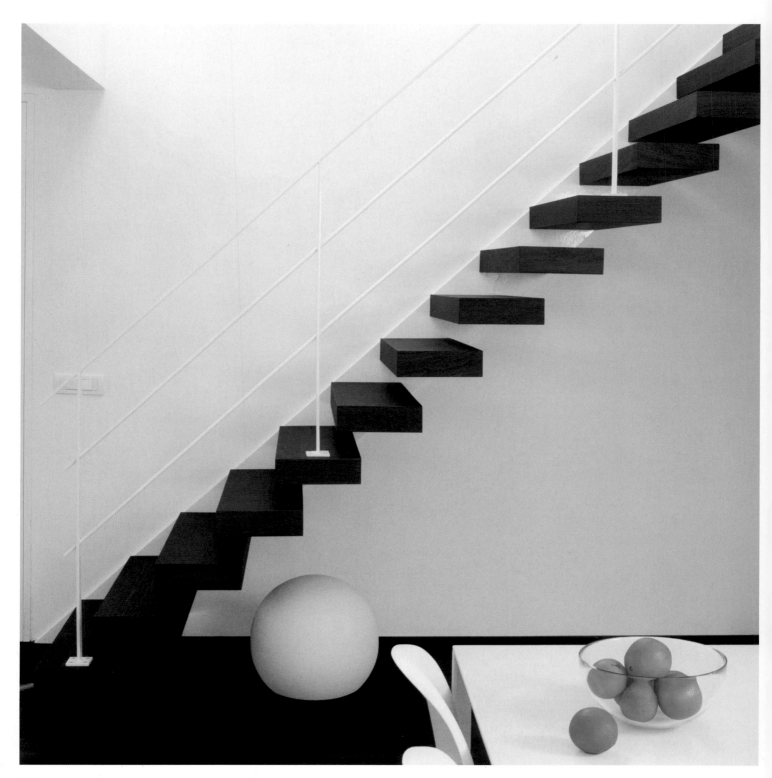

☐ Staircases can create a geometrical dialogue with other elements.

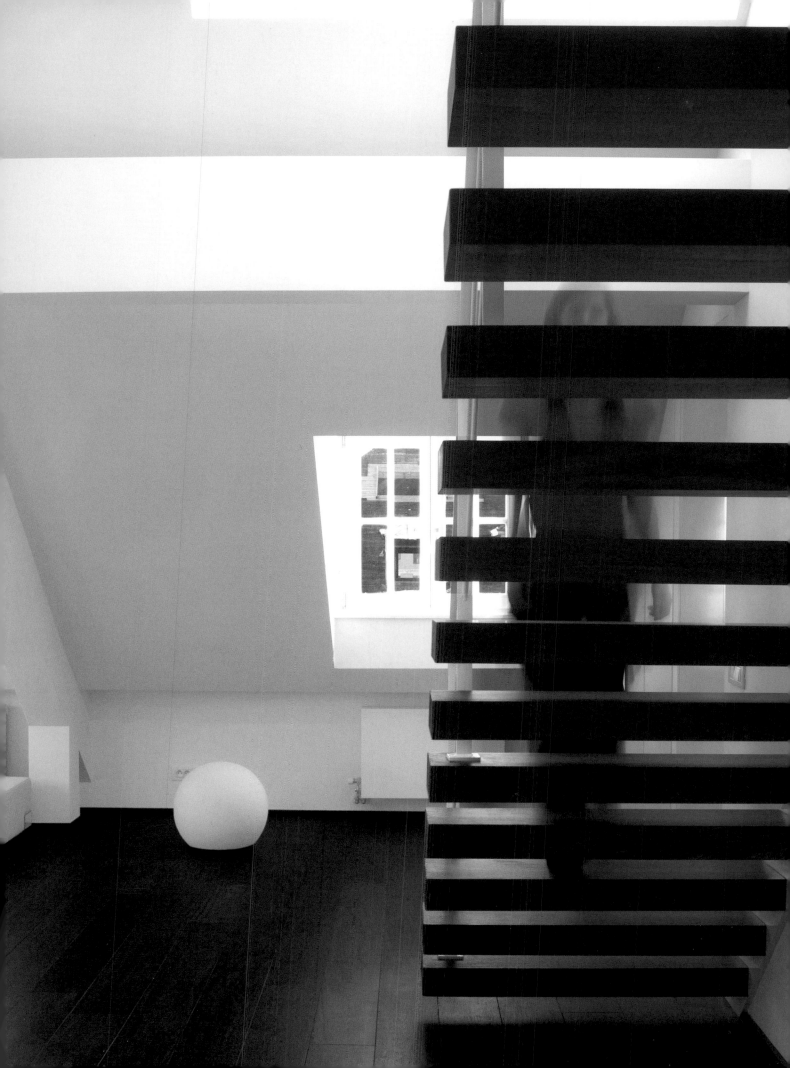

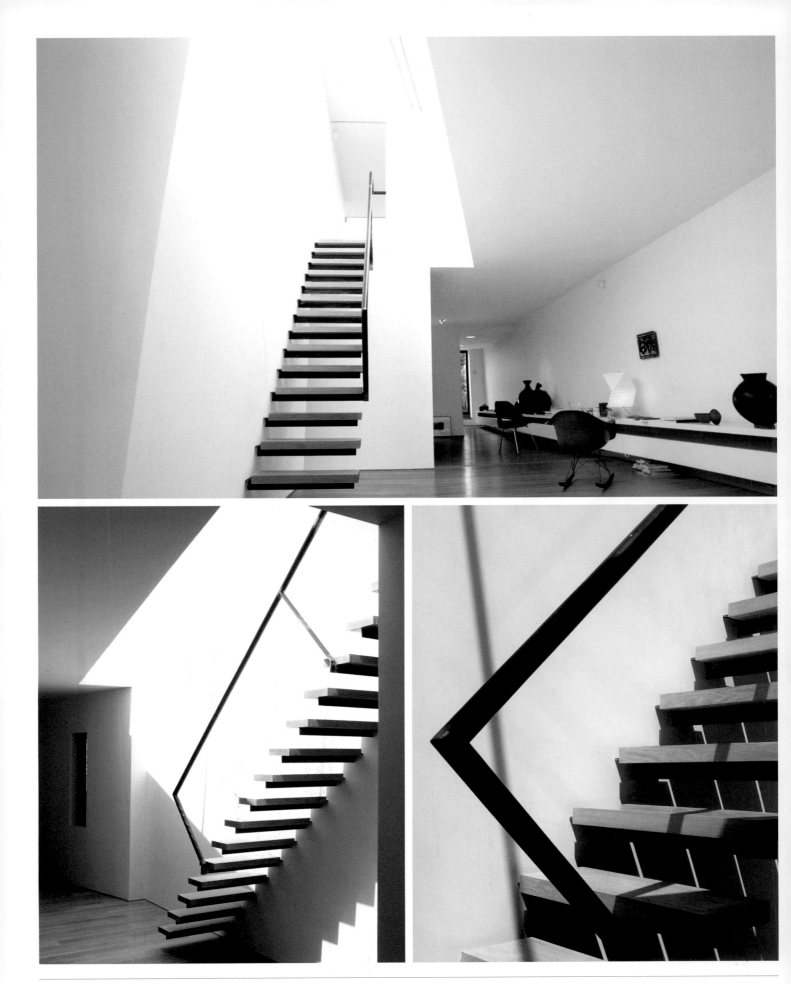

© Laurent Brandajs

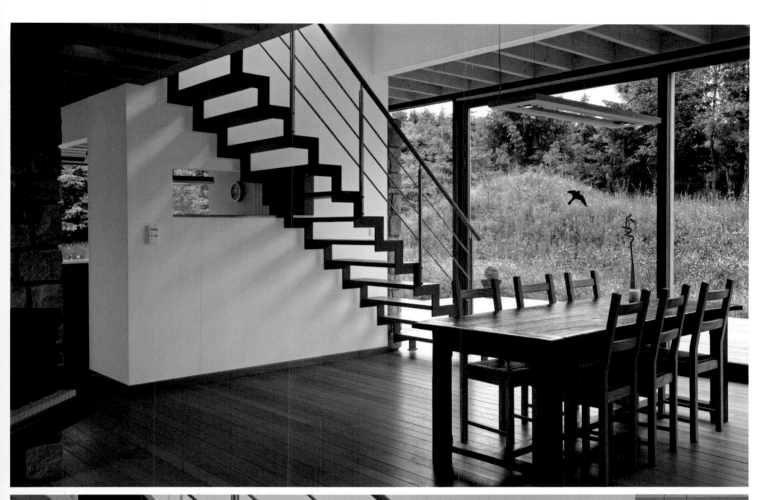

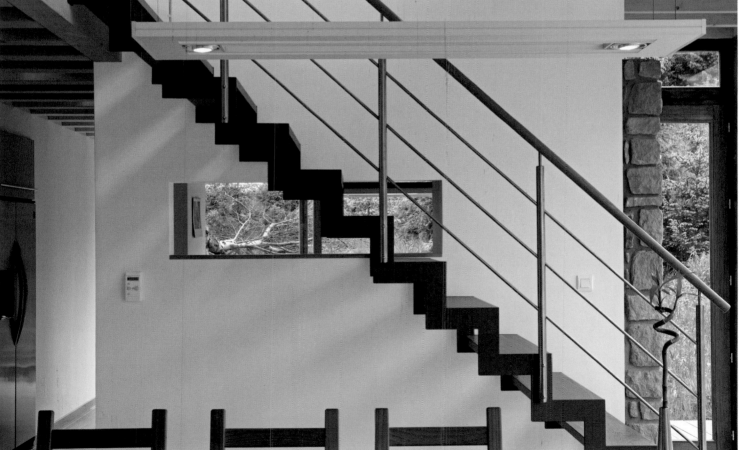

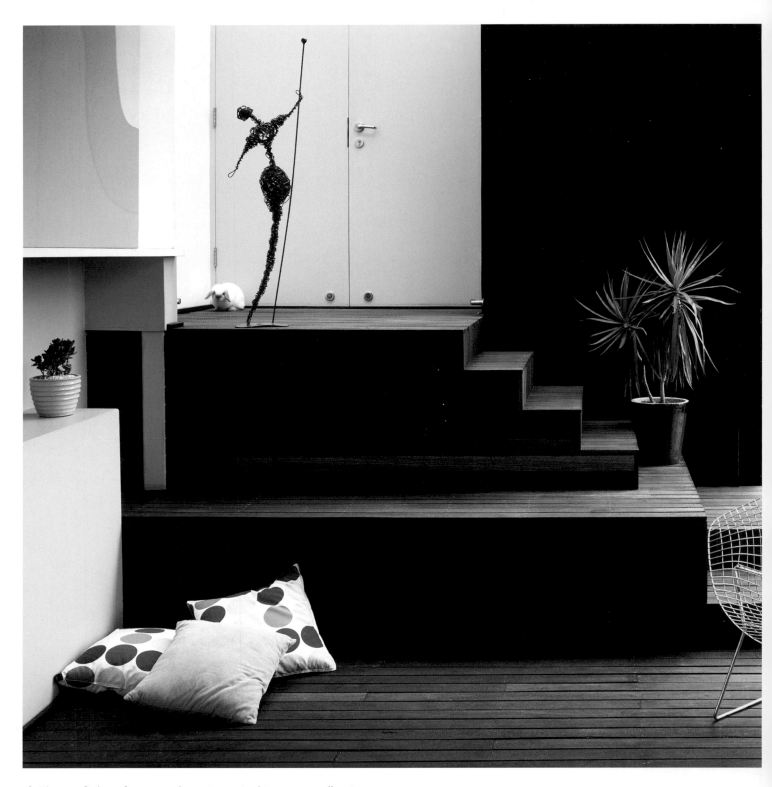

△ The two flights of steps on the staircase in this entrance allow it to serve several functions: as shelves, storage space and even somewhere to sit.

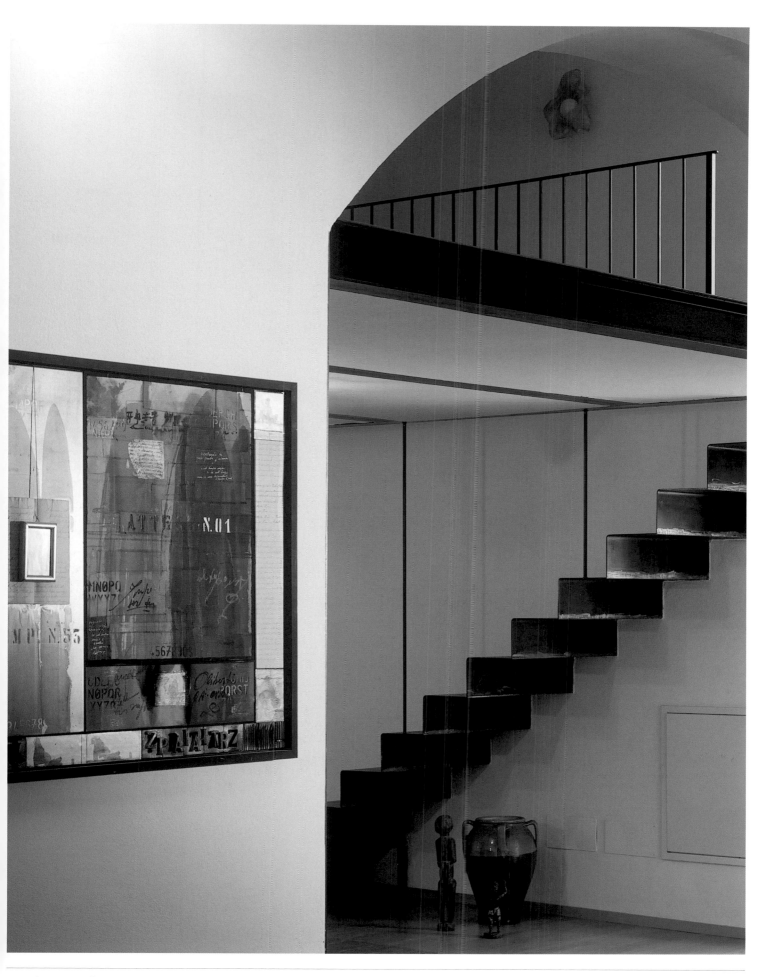

Kitchens

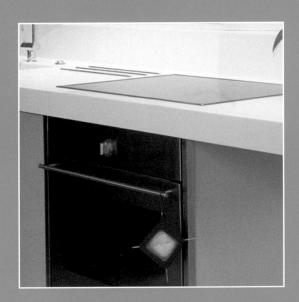

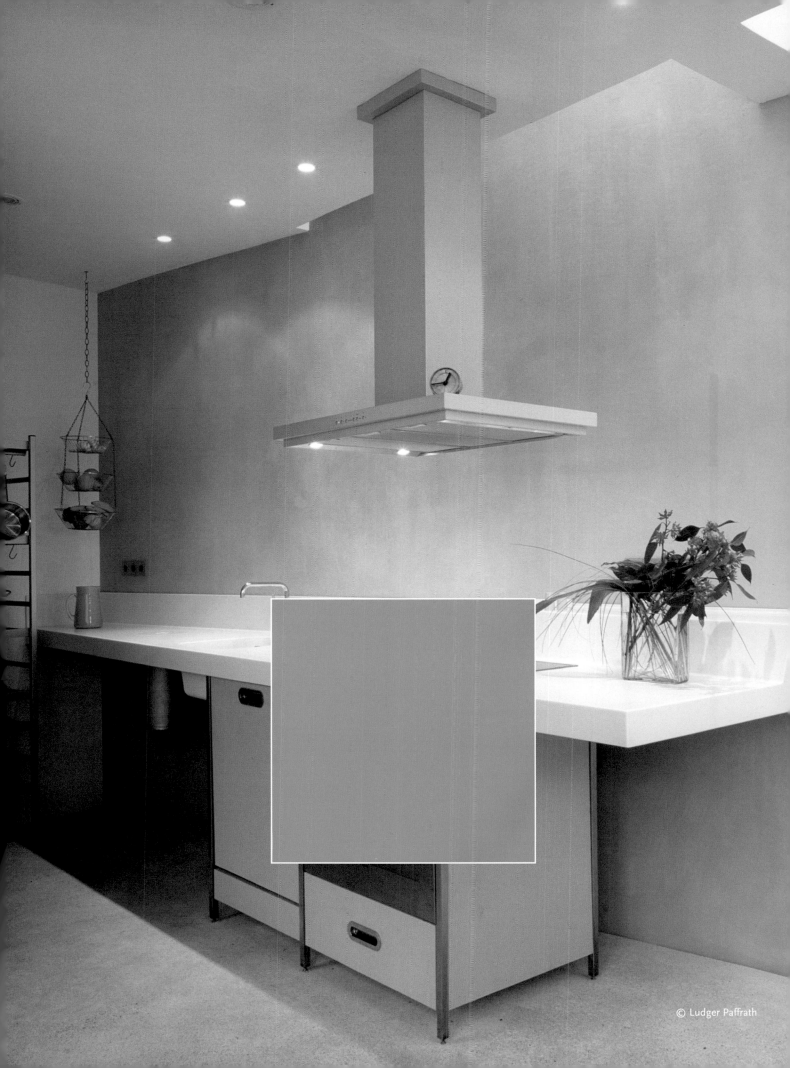

Kitchens

Social development and sophisticated cuisine go hand in hand

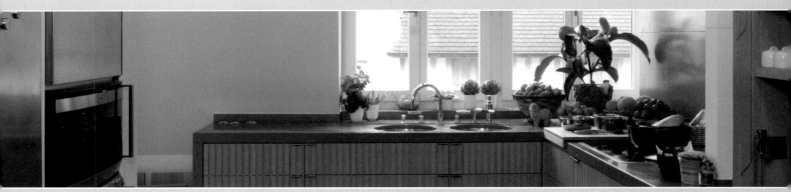

© Laurent Brandajs

Social development encroaches on every aspect of life, including food. In fact, the development of a culture, whether extinct or current, can be assessed on the basis of its culinary traditions. Social development and sophisticated culinary customs go hand in hand.

The artistic expression of a culture reflects one of the most important aspects of a society, amounting to a heritage of great historical and anthropological value. Classical culture often provided scenes of war and eating; it is no accident that the famous bacchanal comprised one of the social highpoints of Roman life. Bacchus, the Roman god of wine who inspired the word bacchanal, is one of the most well-known Roman deities today. For the Romans, a banquet was one of the most popular means of giving pleasure to friends, relatives, and colleagues. They were veritable food orgies in which the participants spent hours eating until no food was left, or until alcohol prevented them from eating any more.

Although we don't intend to invite the readers of this book to follow the example of the Romans, we do offer a vision of how to enjoy your kitchen to the maximum, turning it into a space as practical, comfortable, and visually attractive as possible. As the expression goes, "we are what we eat"—so eating properly is not just a manner of providing energy for our body. Sophisticated food offers many additional sensations and has other functions beyond the merely nutritional. Cooking is a way of appreciating ourselves and appreciating those around us, and the kitchen is the laboratory in which this process is developed. Therefore, a good kitchen can exert a direct influence on our quality of life and on that of our immediate circle.

This chapter is not, however, aimed exclusively at lovers of luxury or skilled cooks; it also provides solutions for those who want to give more space to other rooms in the house, or who for whatever reason do not have much room available for a kitchen. In either case, they are not standardized solutions.

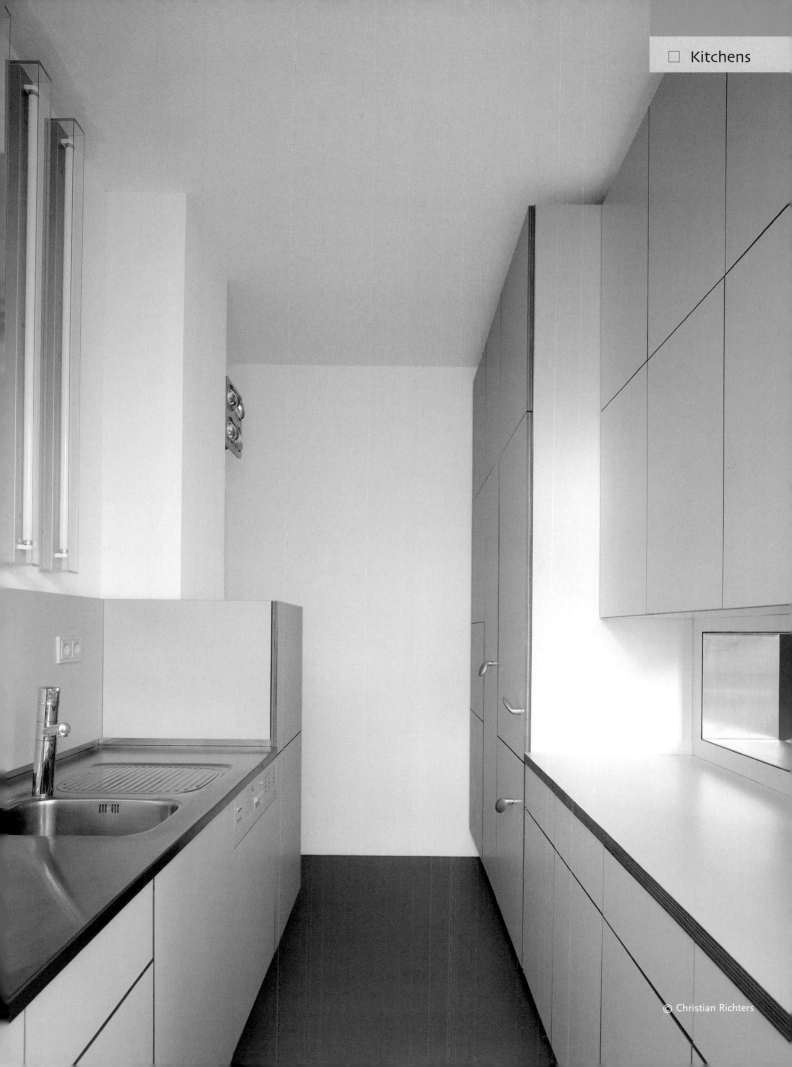

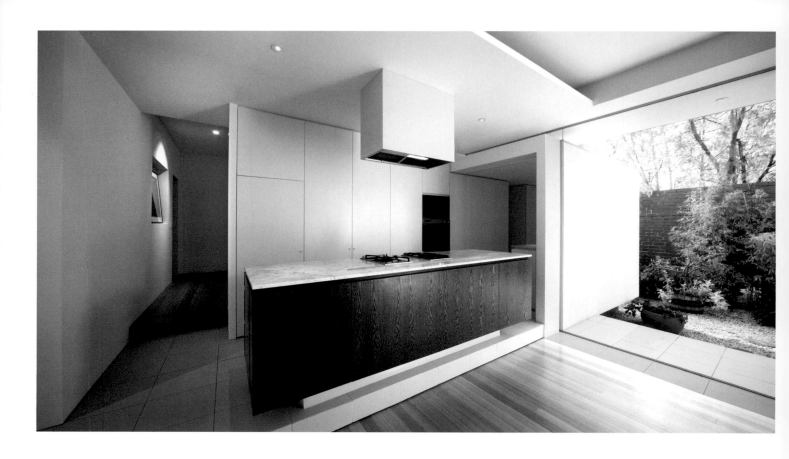

"The historical context has been accentuated with the introduction of new industrial materials for domestic application," Greg Gong, Australian architect.

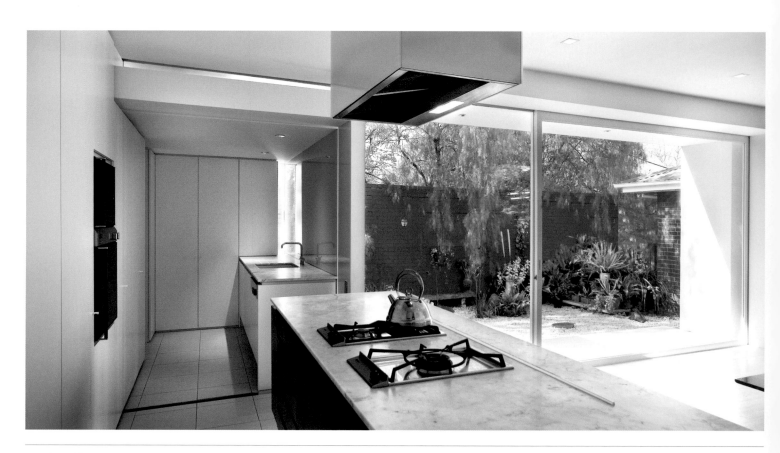

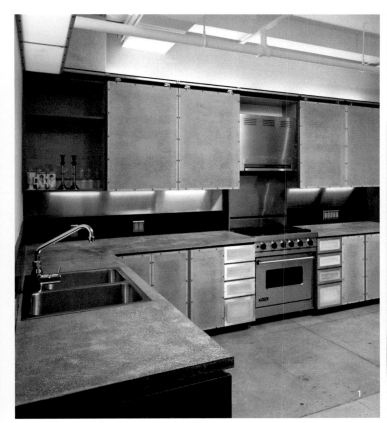

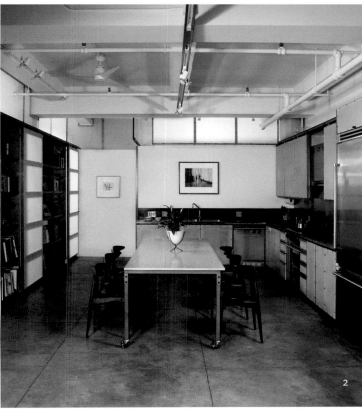

The reinforced concrete worktop and translucent panels permit the passage of light in an old clothes factory-turned-home in New York, refurbished by Bone/Levine Architects. Below, an industrial building refurbished by Tom McCallum and Shania Shegedyn.

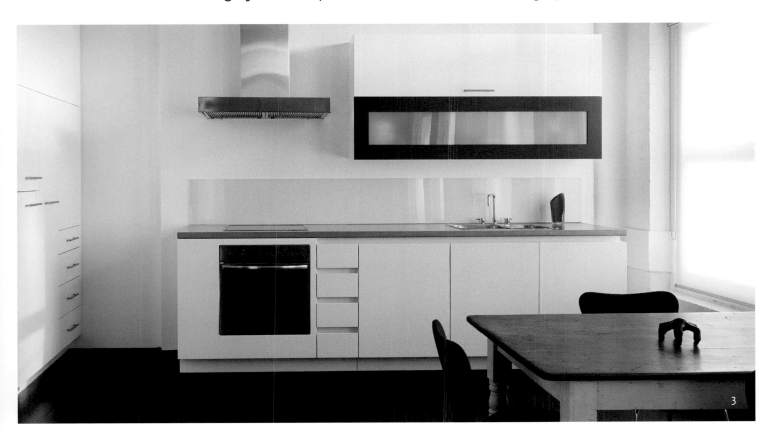

1, 2 © Jack Kucy   3 © Shania Shegedyn

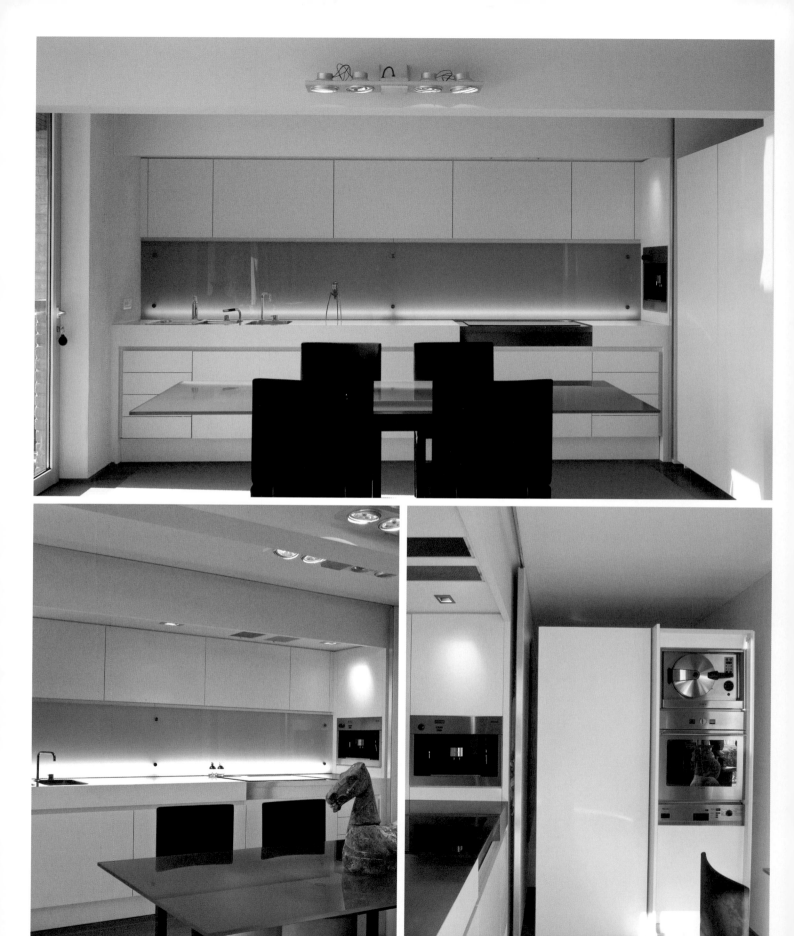

© Laurent Brandajs

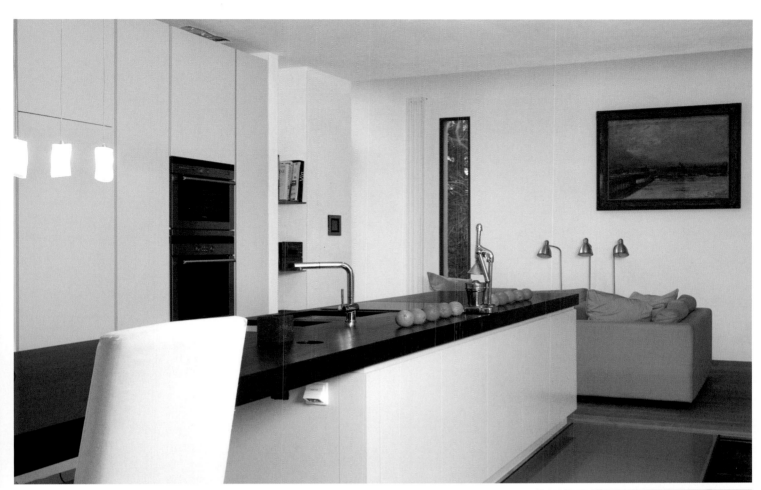

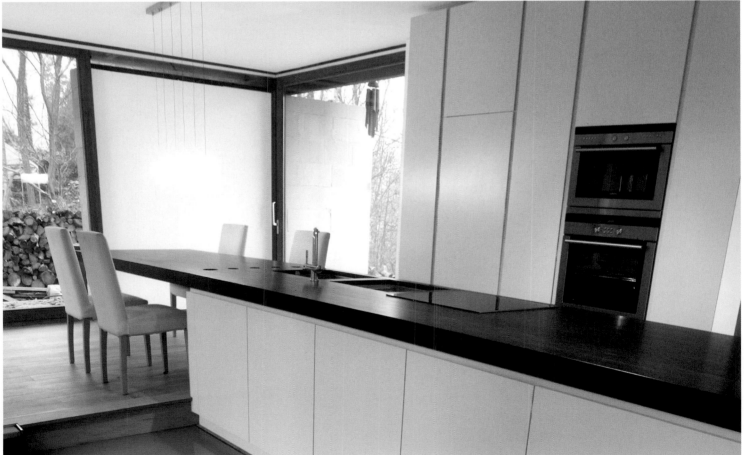

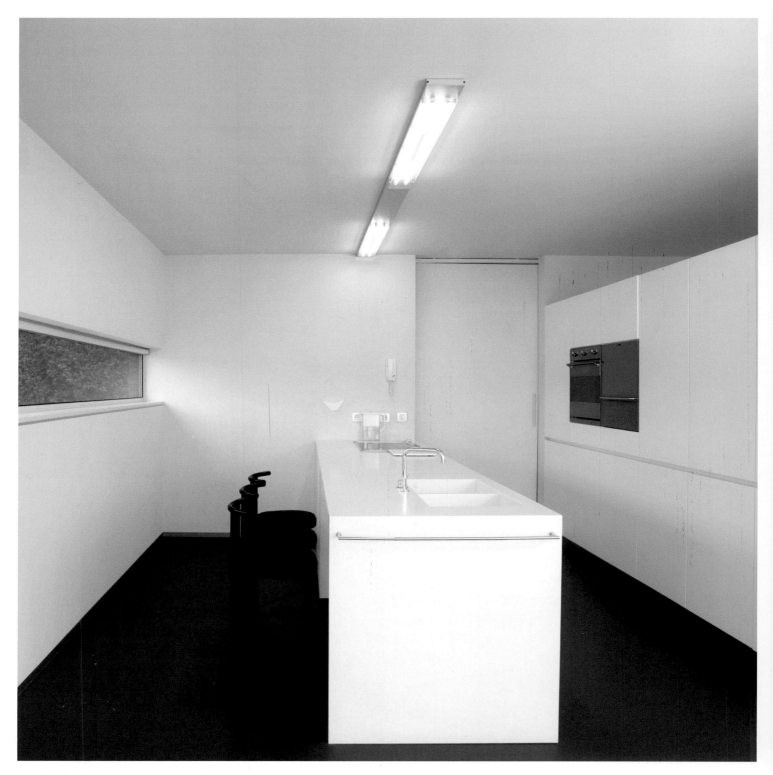

☐ This kitchen is integrated into the rest of the space by means of neutral lighting and an identical color scheme. On the next page, a loft in Belgium, where the structural elements have been exploited to design the kitchen.

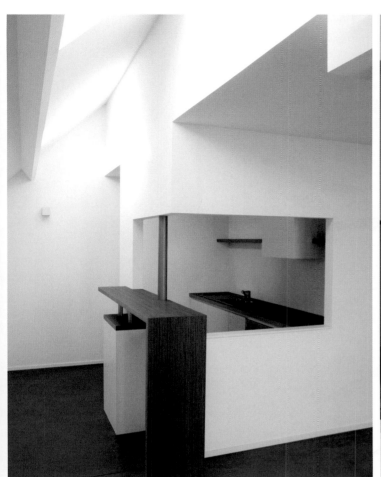
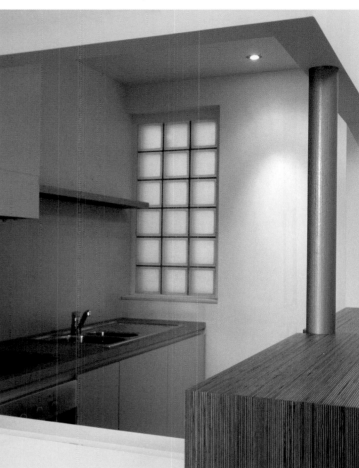
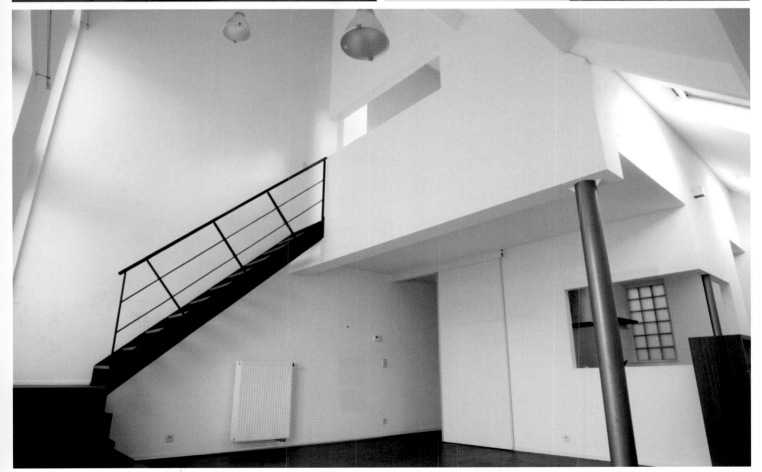

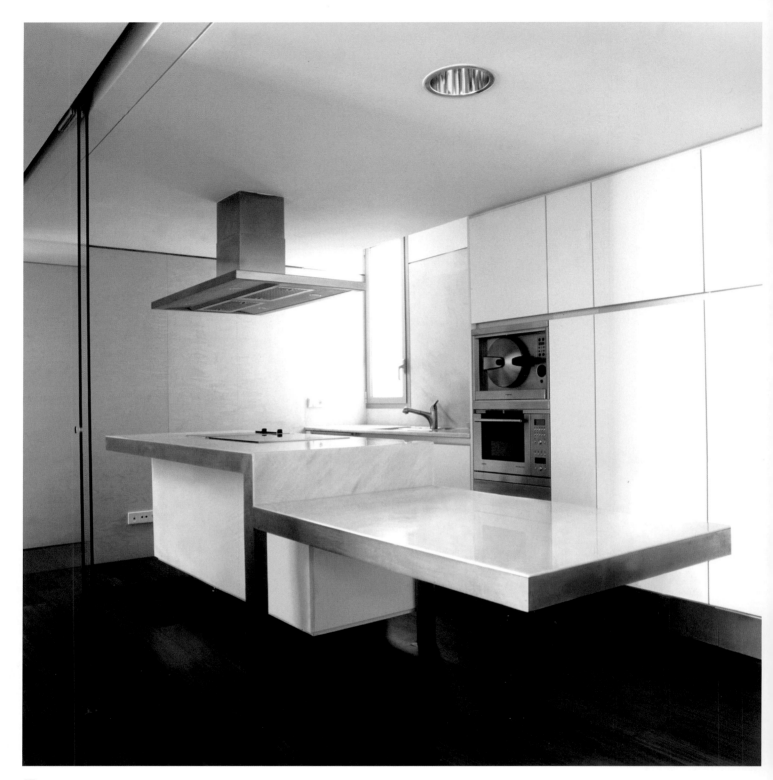

☐ Sliding glass panels isolate the kitchen if necessary, but they do not block the passage of light. Both in this kitchen and the one opposite, the worktop has been extended to add a surface for eating.

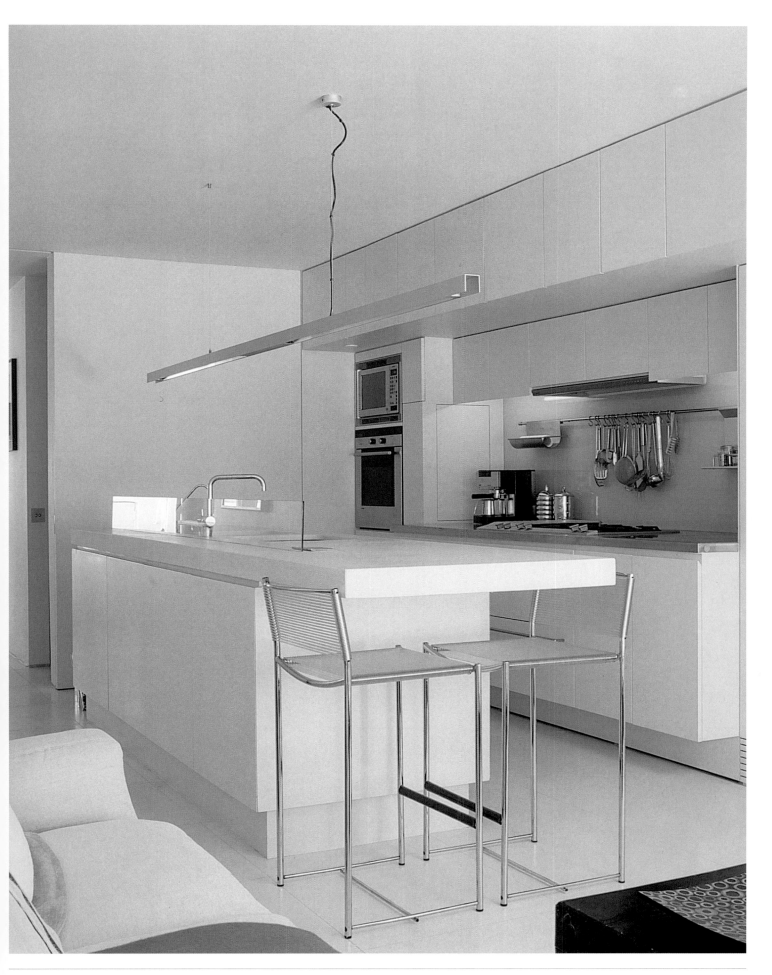

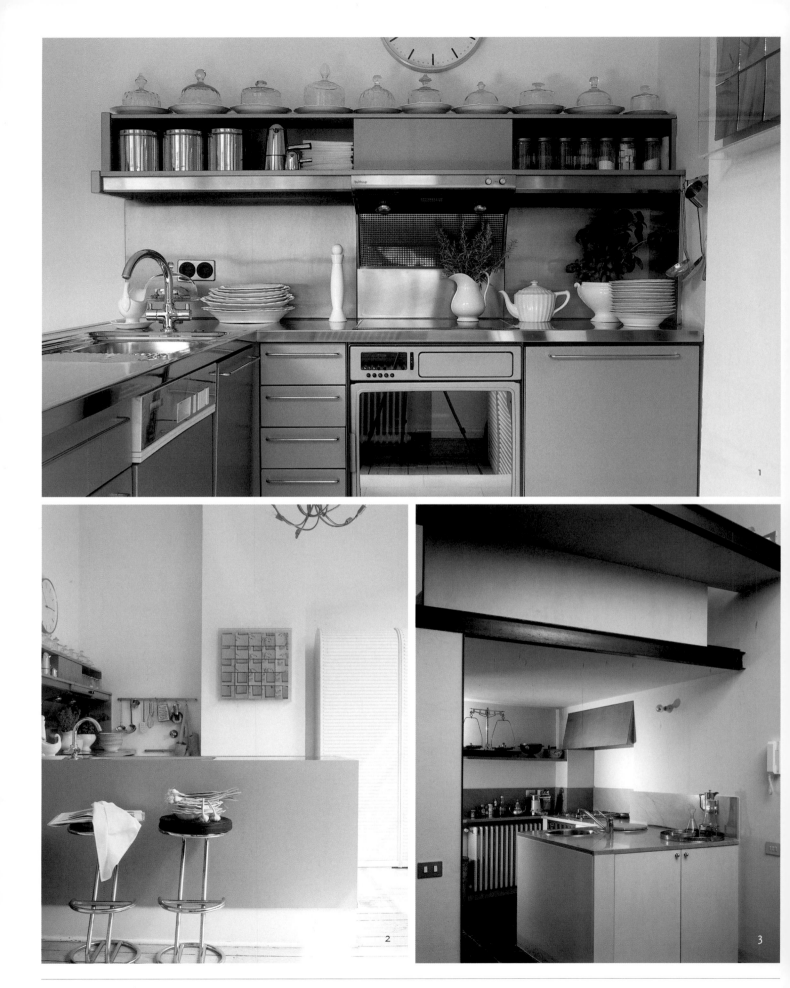

1, 2 © Giulio Oriani/Vega MG   3 © Andrea Martiradonna

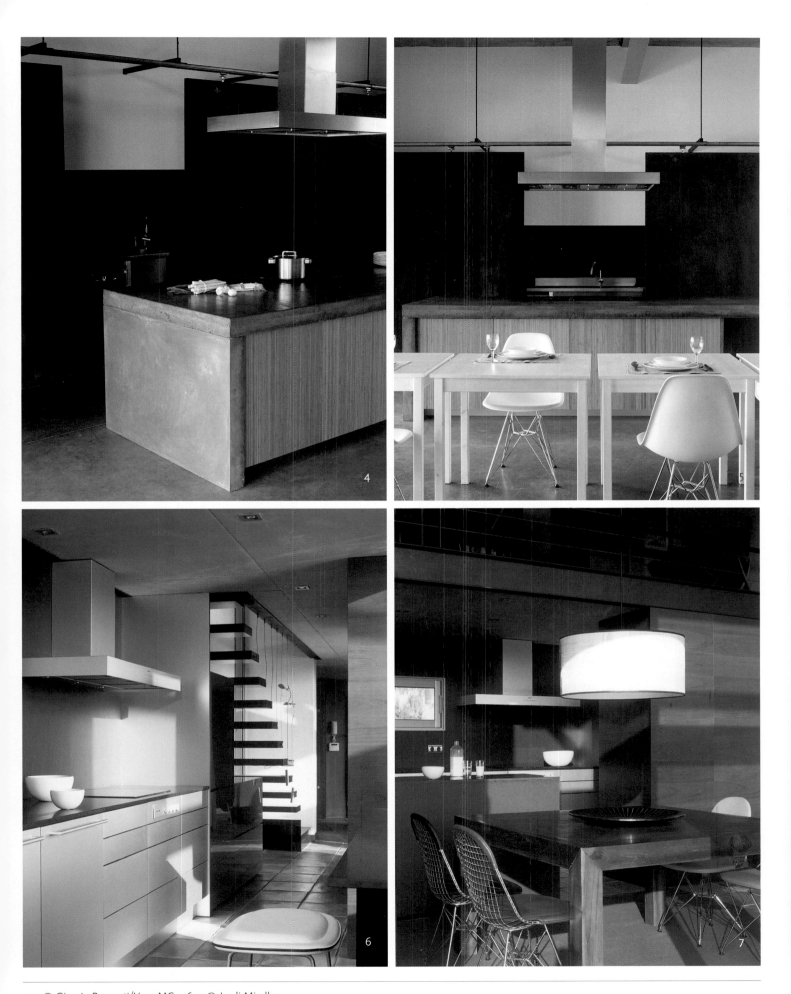

4, 5 © Giorgio Possenti/Vega MG   6, 7 © Jordi Miralles

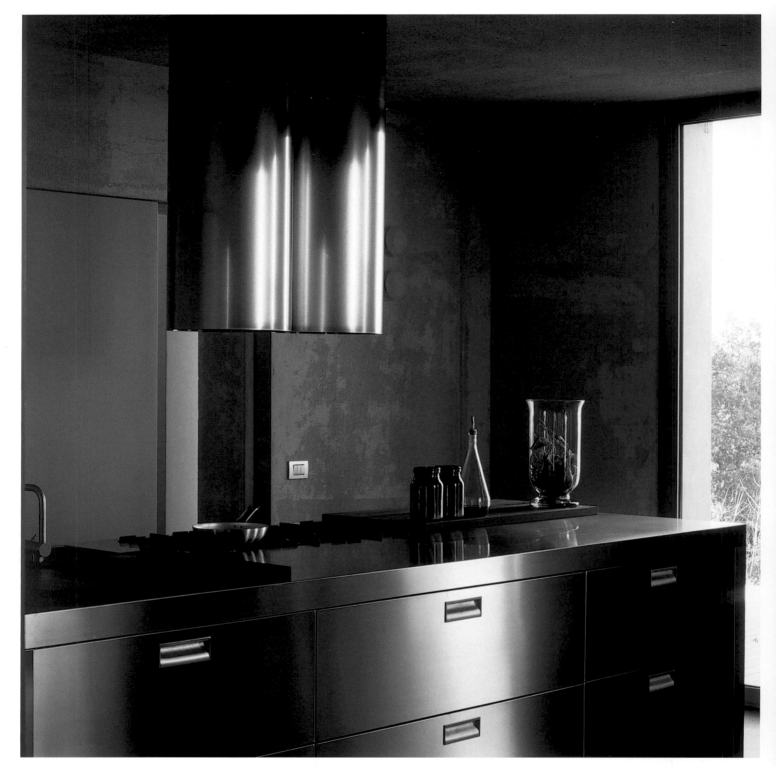

△ The lack of a wall endows a kitchen with more space, thus making it possible to insert central elements that serve different functions: rings for cooking, a surface for food preparation, and a place to eat. This approach is also the result of the adaptation of industrial aesthetics and techniques to domestic uses.

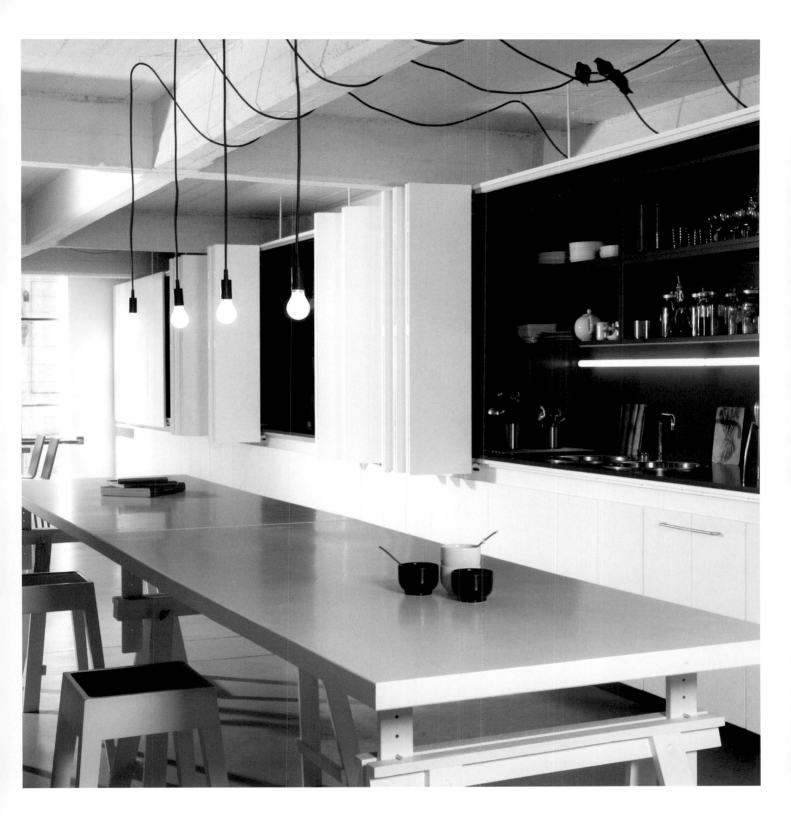

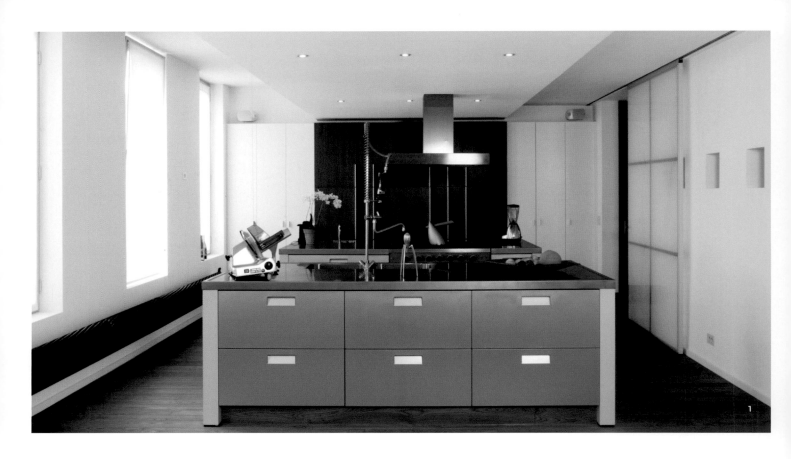

Metal offers aesthetic and functional advantages that have turned it into the prime material for contemporary designs of kitchens and their furnishings.

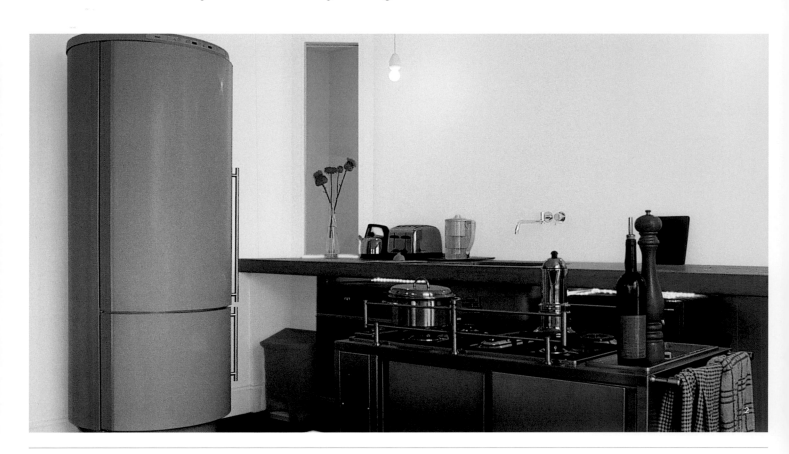

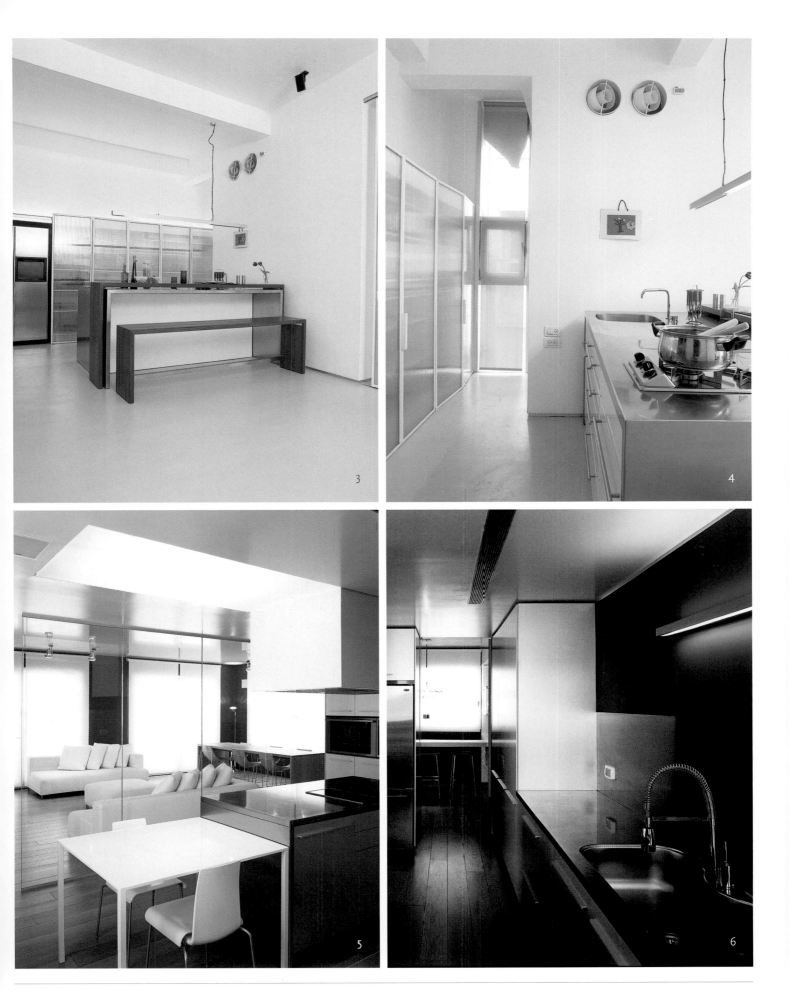

3, 4 © Yael Pincus   5, 6 © Amit Geron

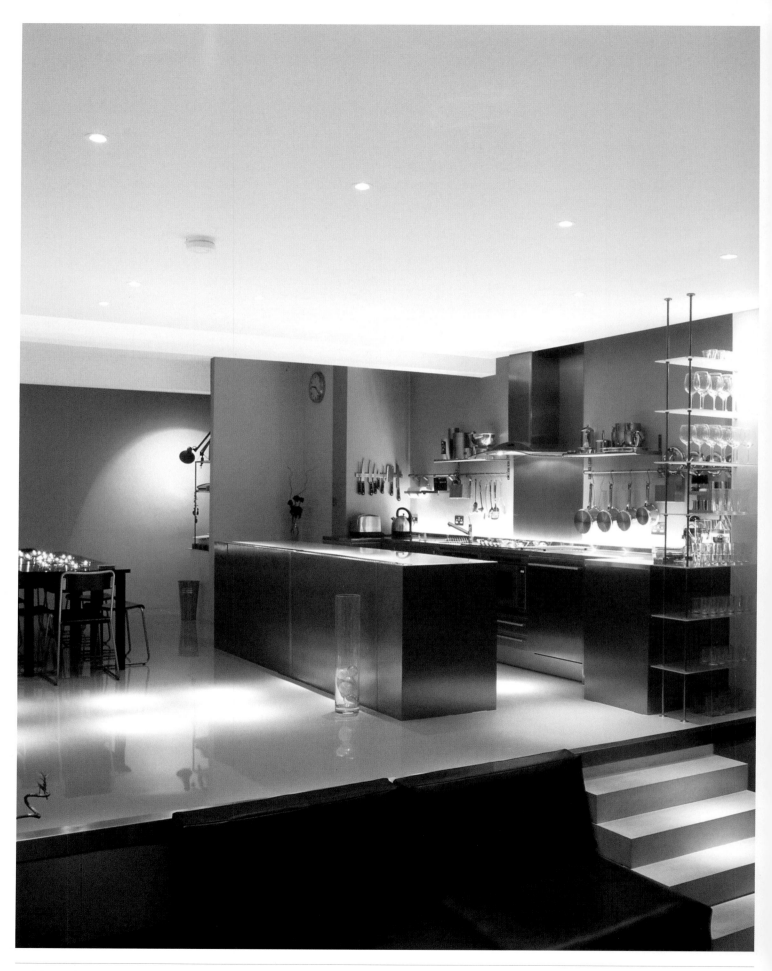

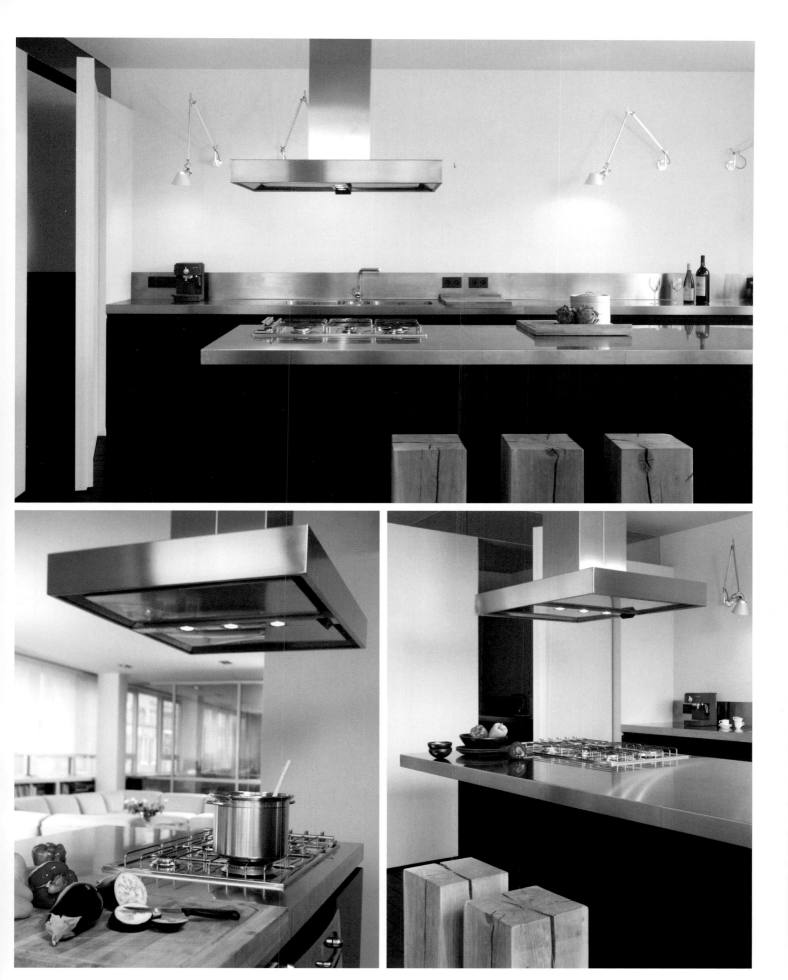

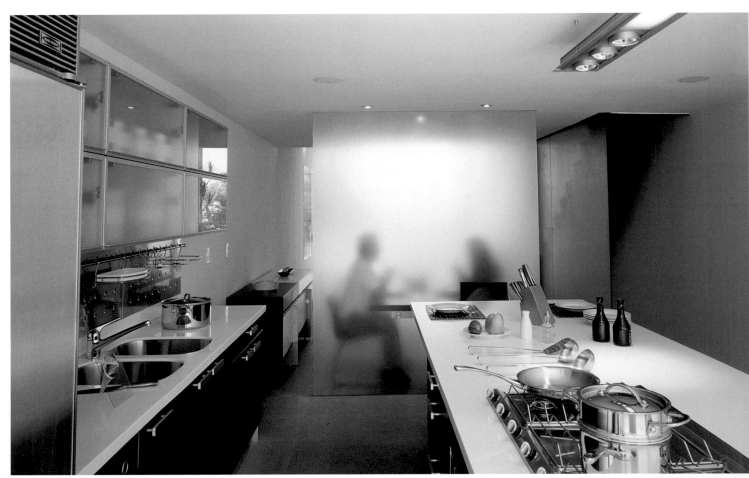

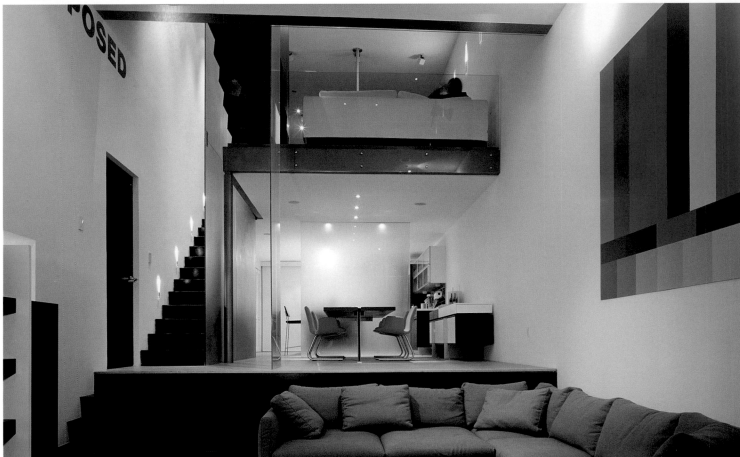

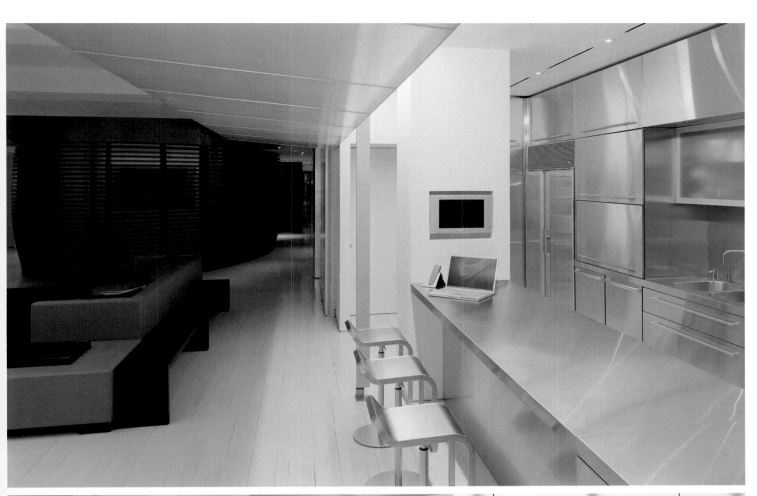

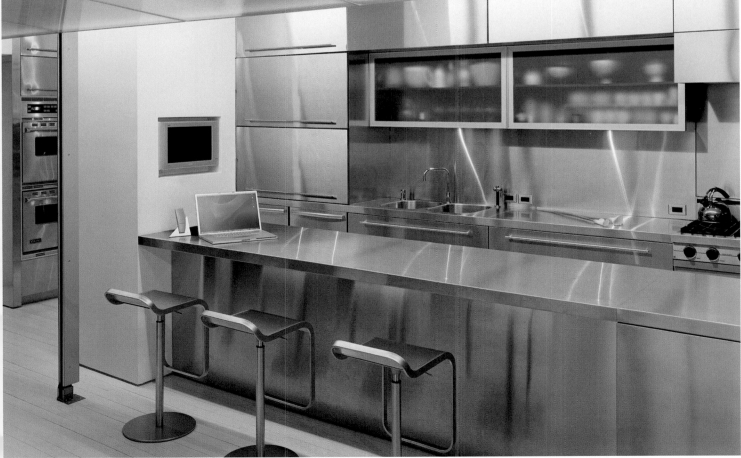

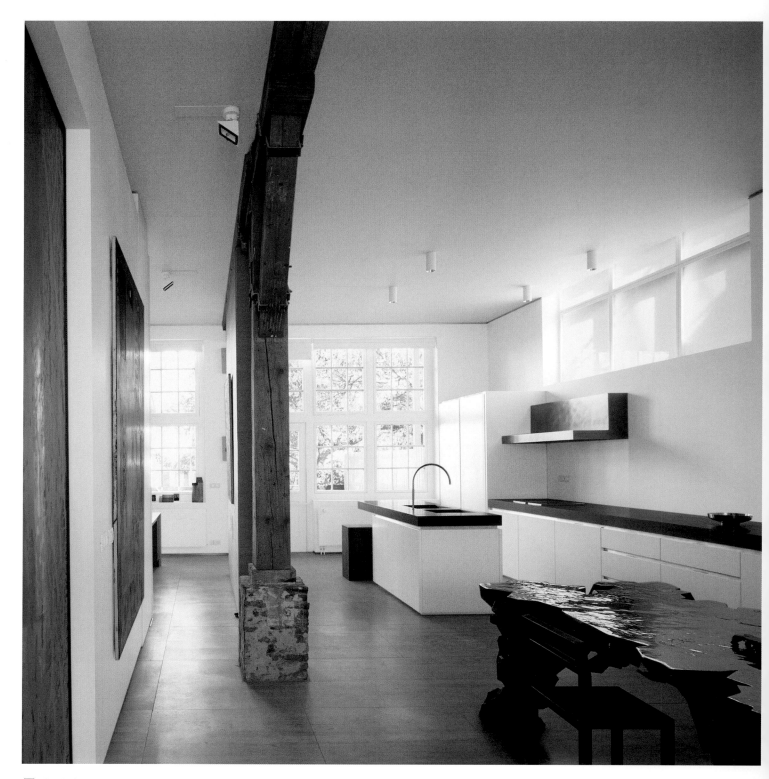

☐ This loft in a utilitarian 19th-century building in Amsterdam is the work of Marc Prosman. The traditional materials used in this home—wood, stone, and glass—take on a new contemporary feeling.

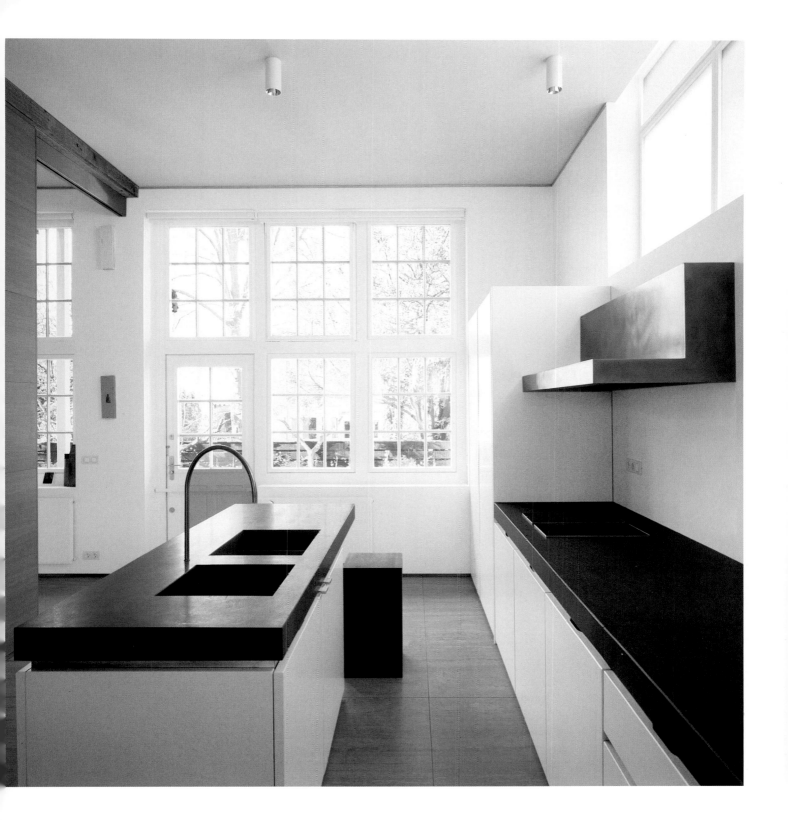

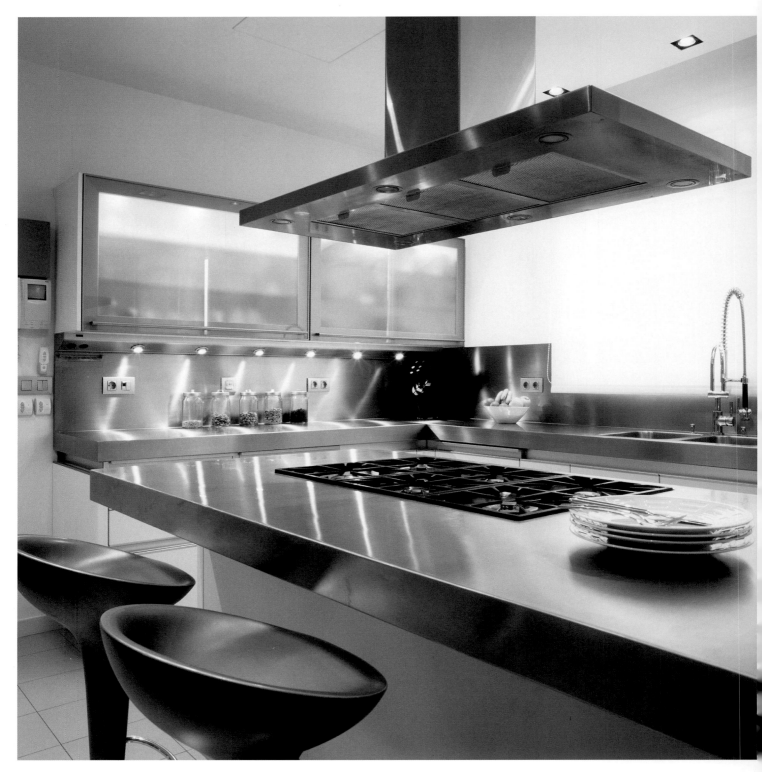

☐ A layout typical of areas devoted to the preparation of food: a large central work table that can also be used for eating and around it areas for storage and cleaning equipment. Flexibility is becoming increasingly important in the design world.

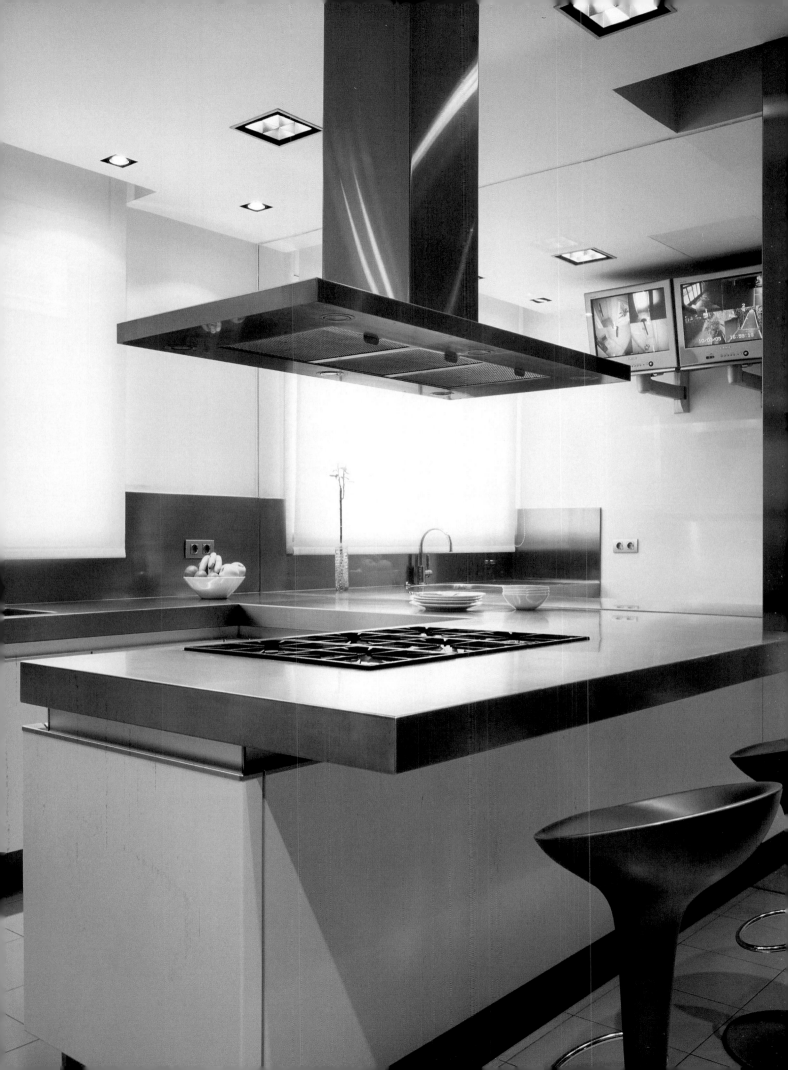

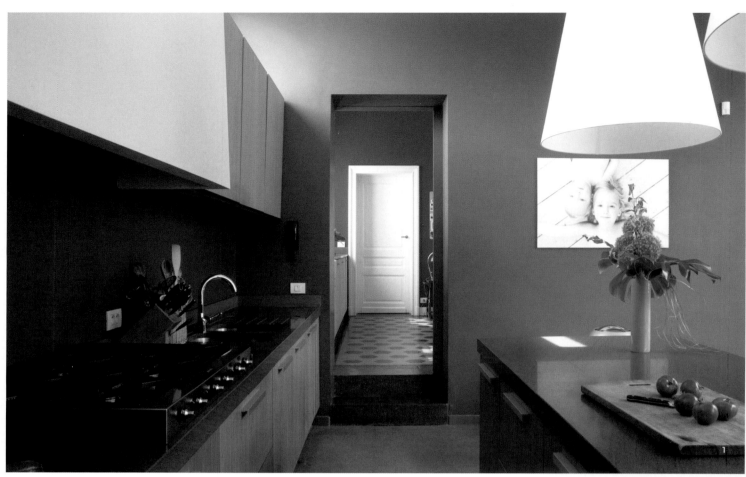

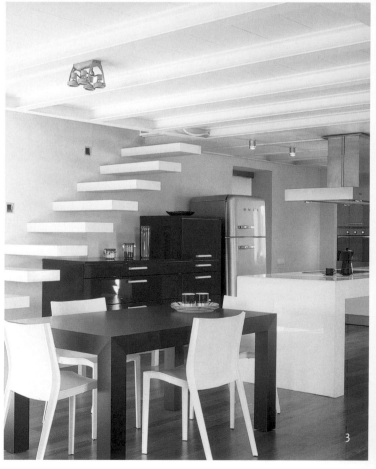

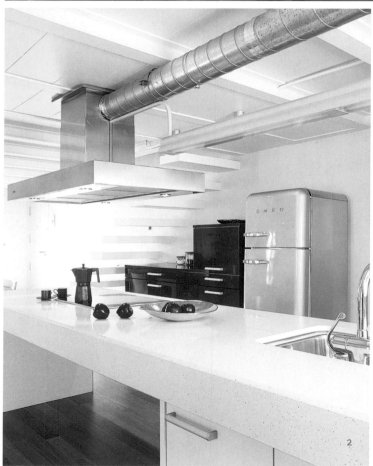

1 © Laurent Brandajs 2, 3 © Jordi Miralles

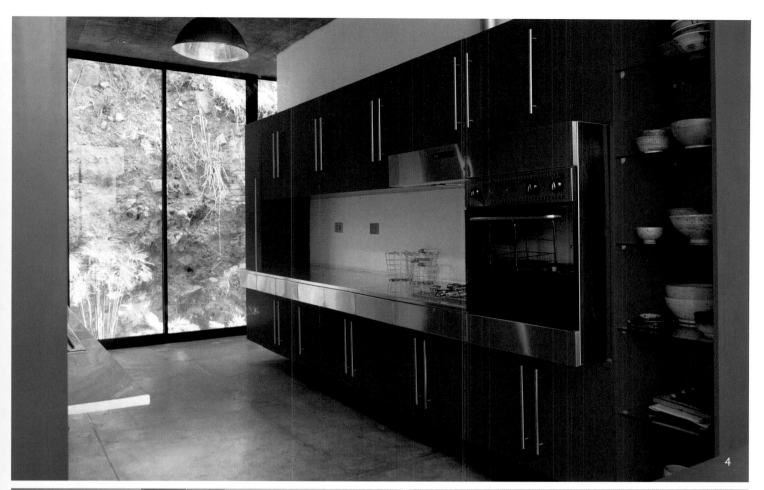

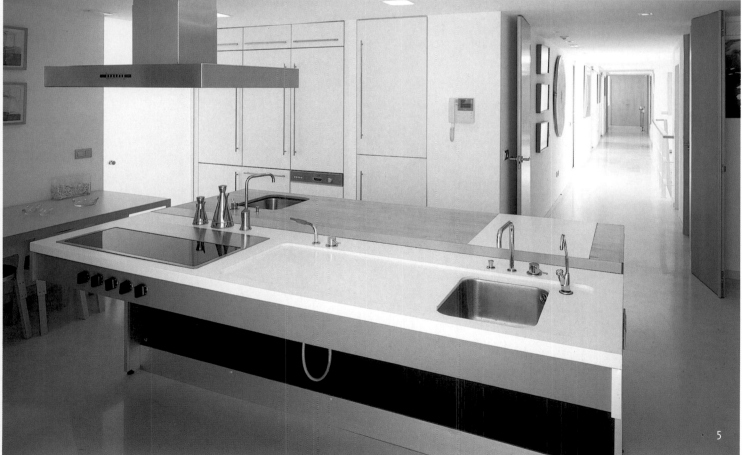

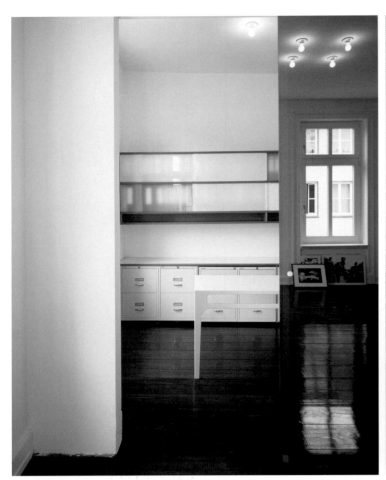
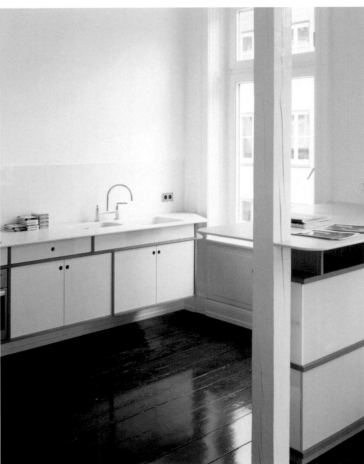
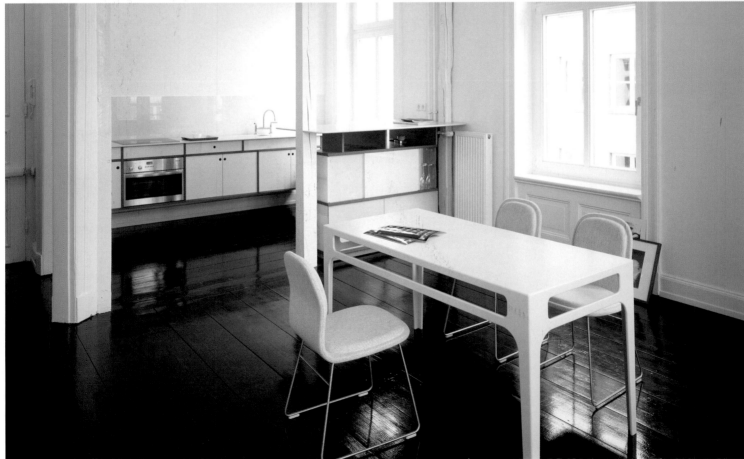

© Thomas Meyer/Ostkreuz | González & Haase/Atelier Architecture & Scenography

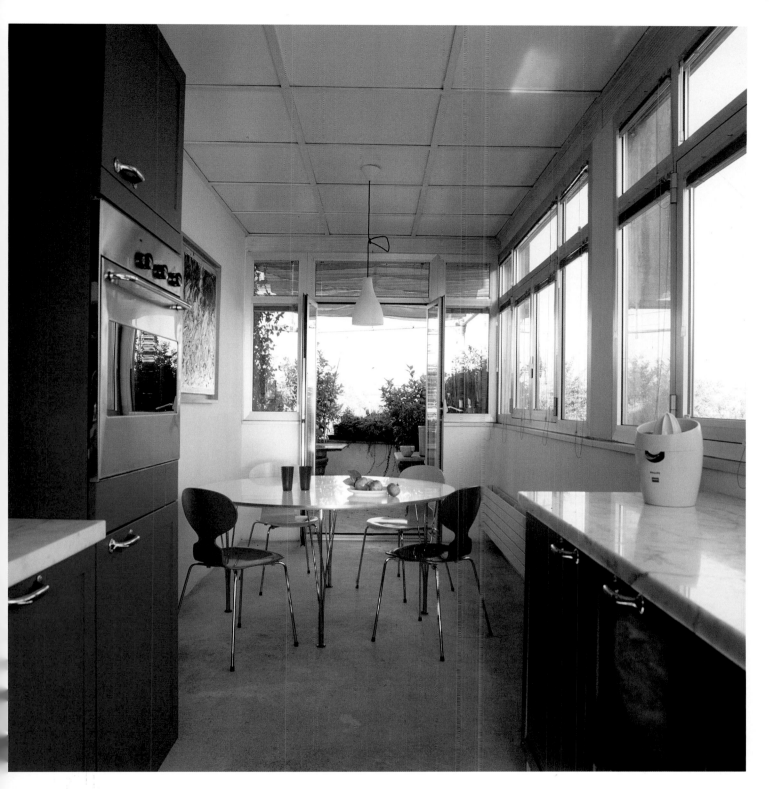

△ Well-lit spaces make it possible to use dark colors in the furniture, as in the case of this kitchen in the house of the Italian architect Maximiliano Fuksas.

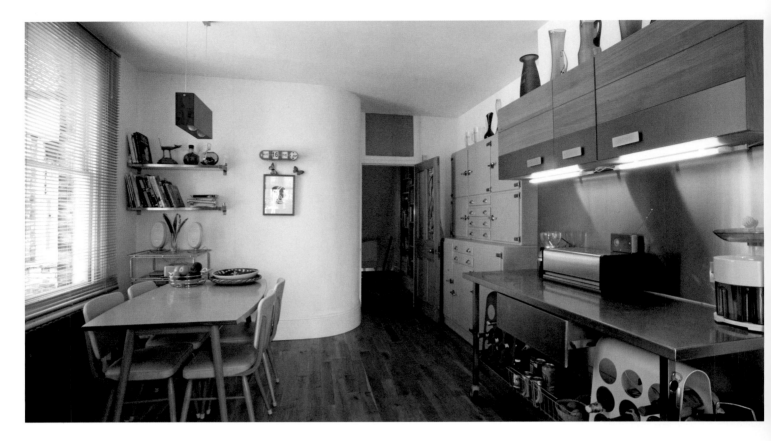

"When I bought this 100-year-old house, I decided to give it a more modern look, using materials like metal and maintaining the welcoming atmosphere by using wood on the floor and warm colors on the furniture." Carlos Domínguez, photographer and designer.

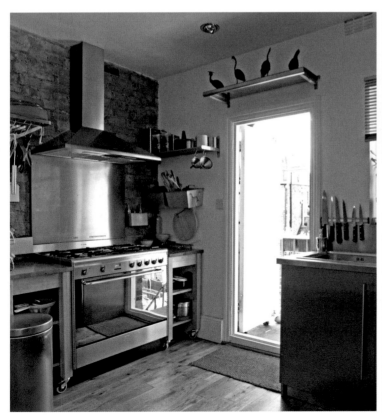

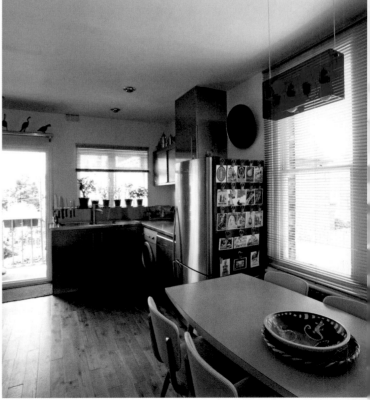

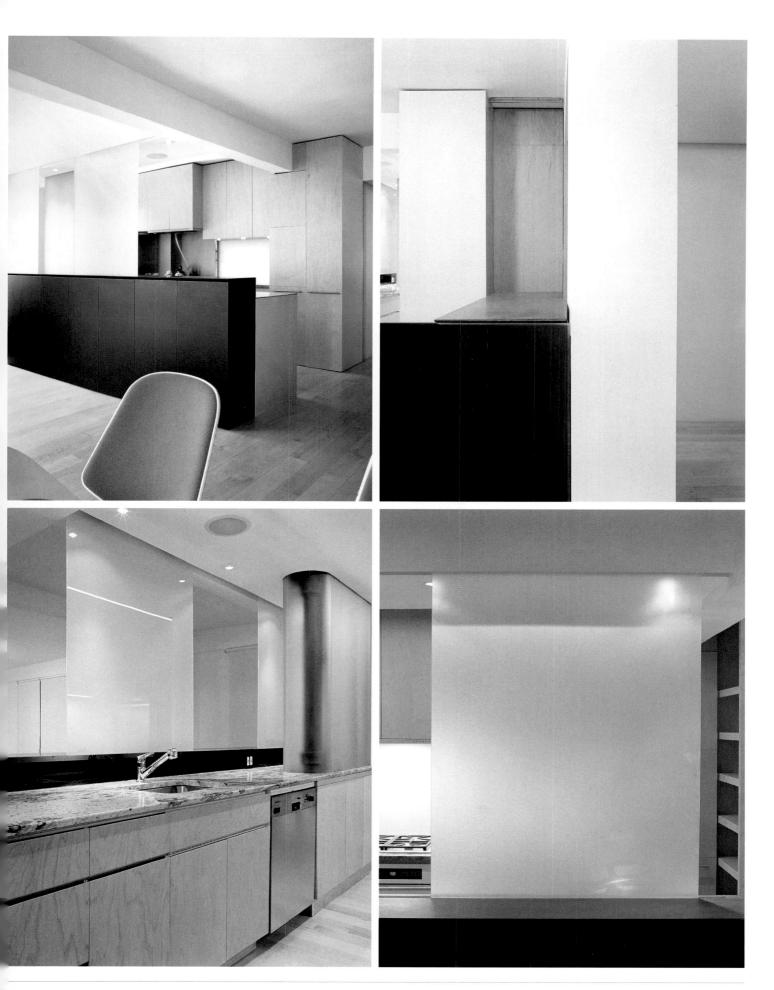

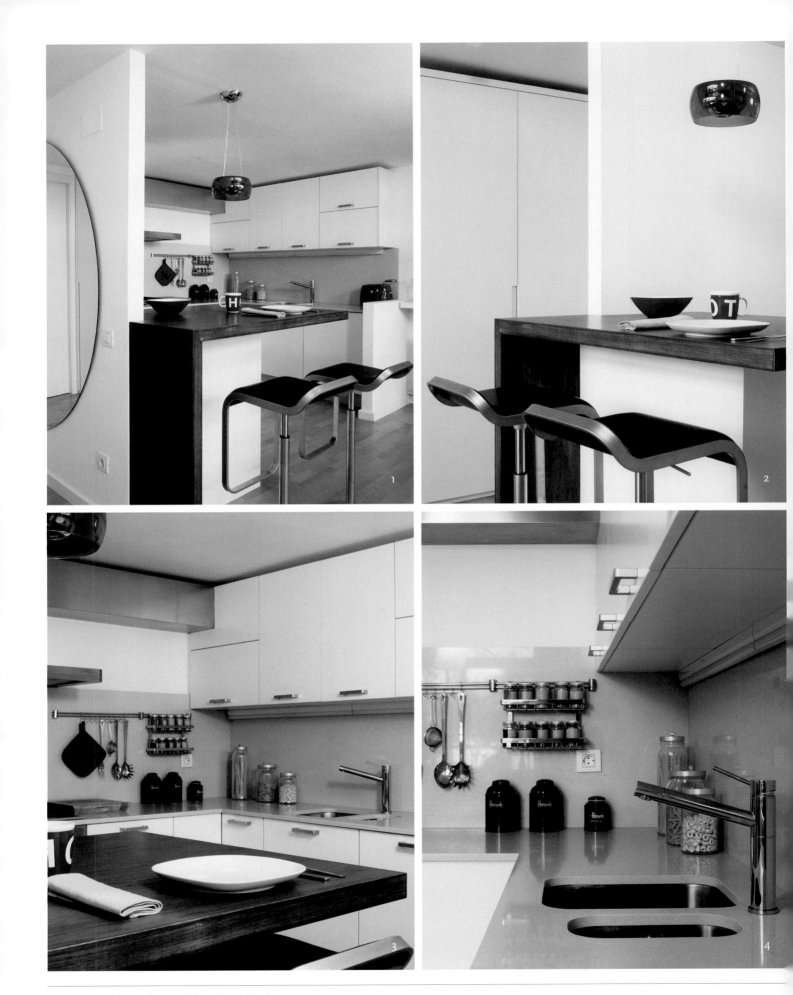

1, 2, 3, 4 © Jordi Miralles   5 © Dominique Vorillon

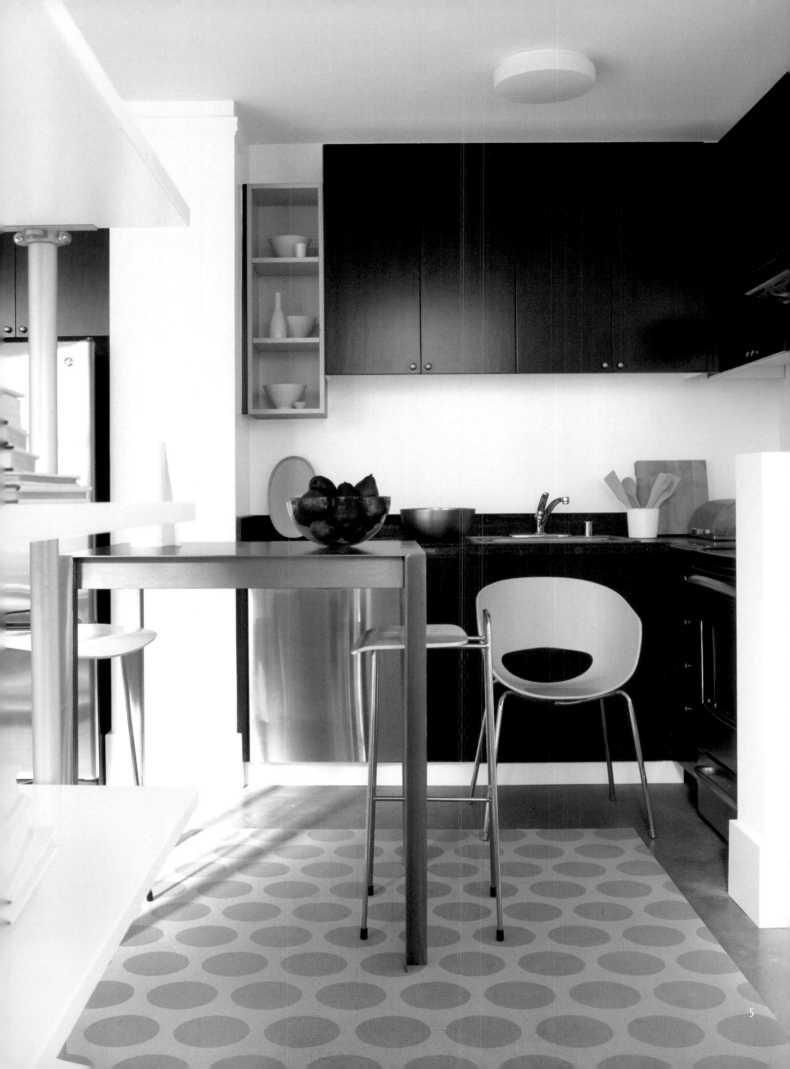

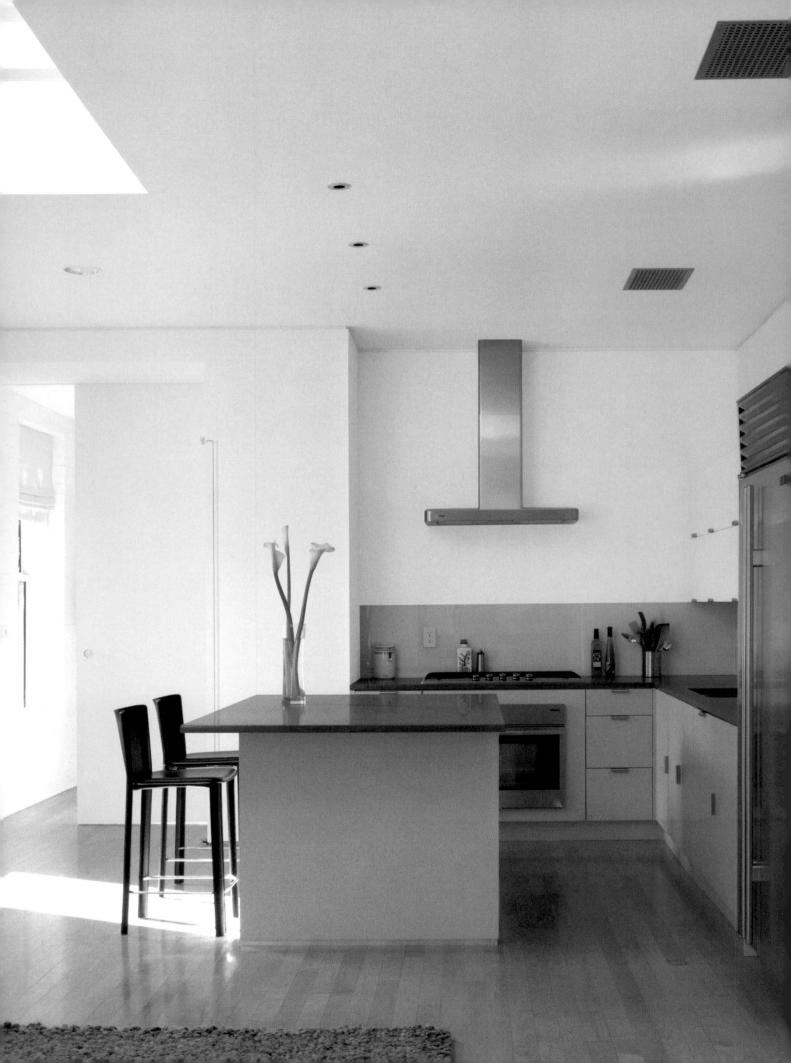

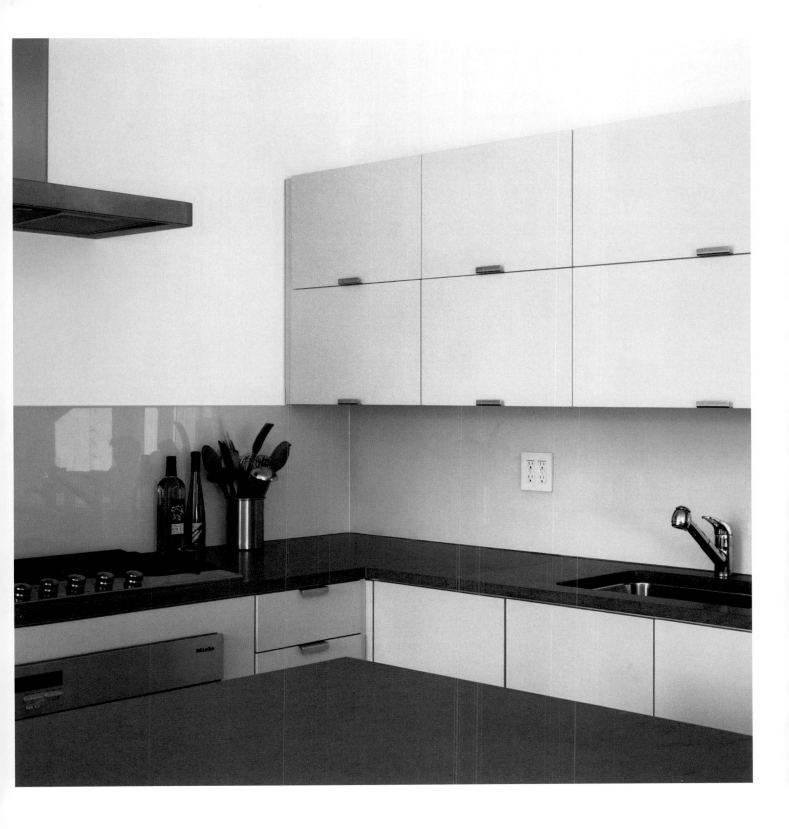

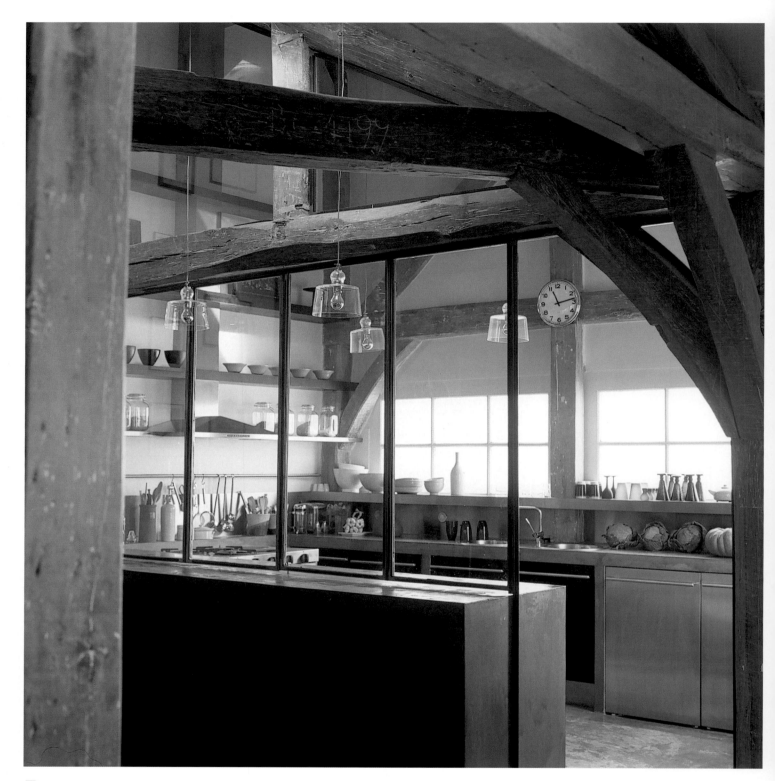

☐ This kitchen, the work of the French designers Guita Maleki and Pascal Cheikh Djavadi, has dispensed with partitions and exposed the structural beams, which distribute the space and serve as a frame for the basic kitchen, where the outstanding features are not the furnishings but the utensils. The result: the beauty of pure simplicity and functionality.

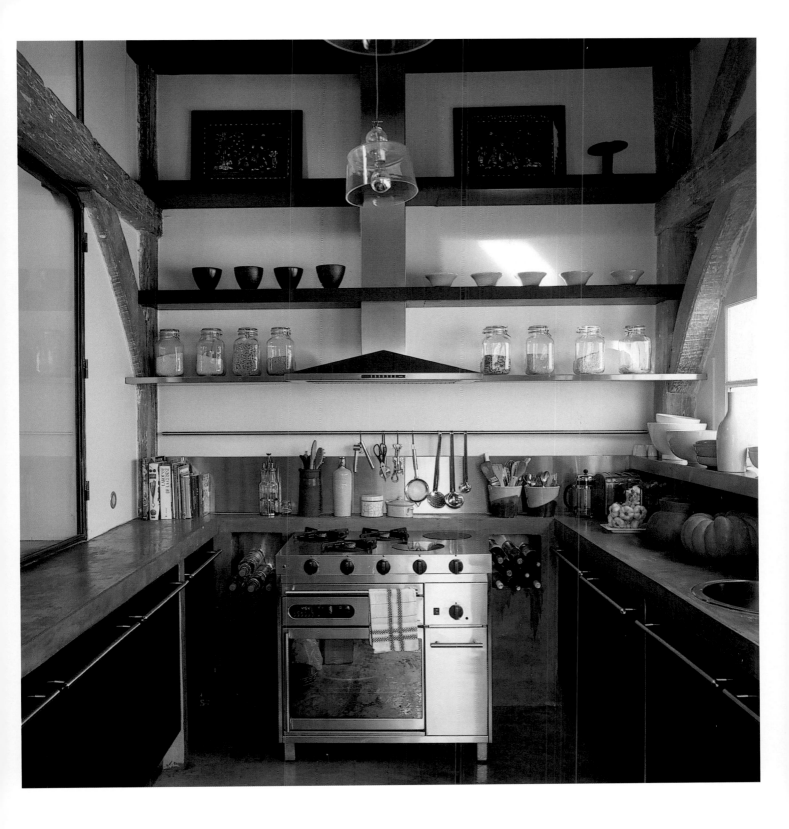

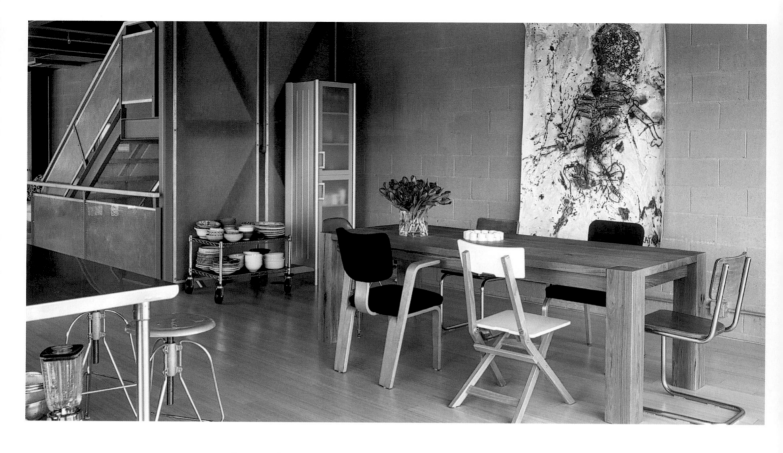

"Wood, metal, brick, and glass are predominant and left exposed
to view to give the interior of the space an industrial character."
Mark Mack Architects.

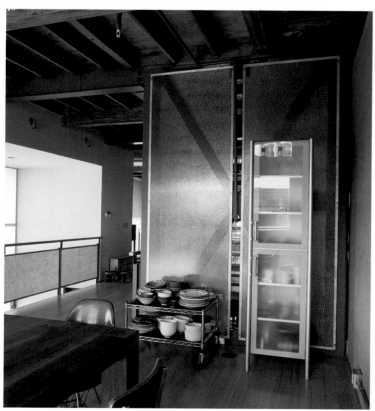

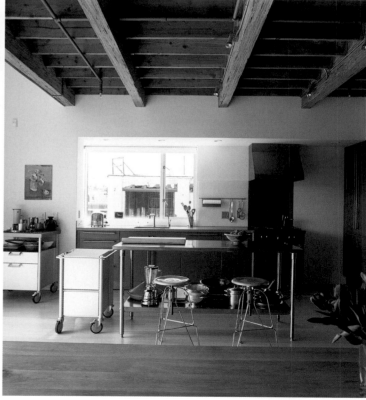

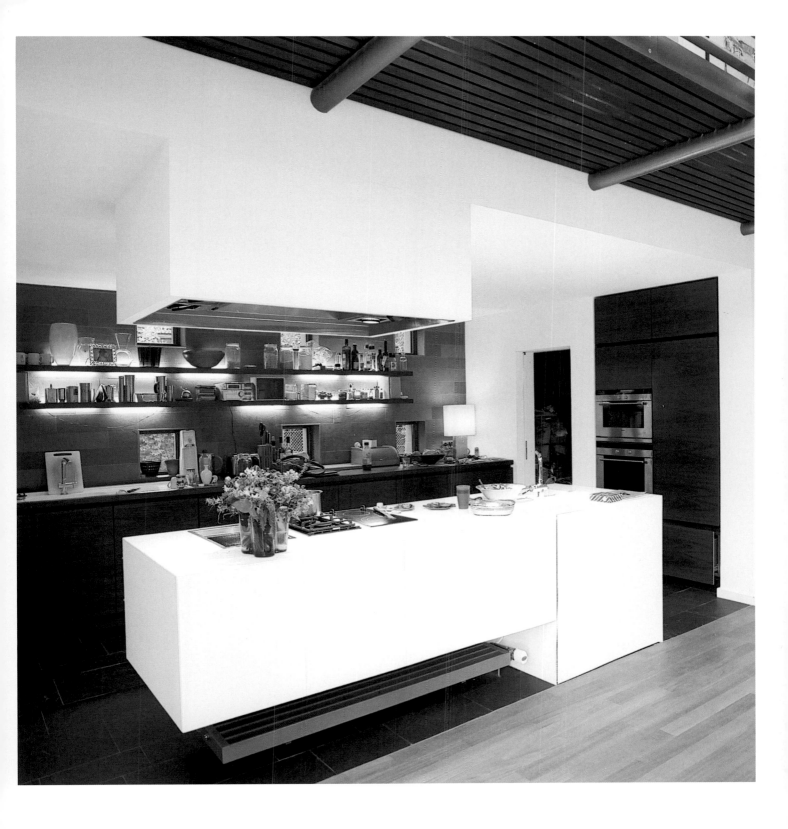

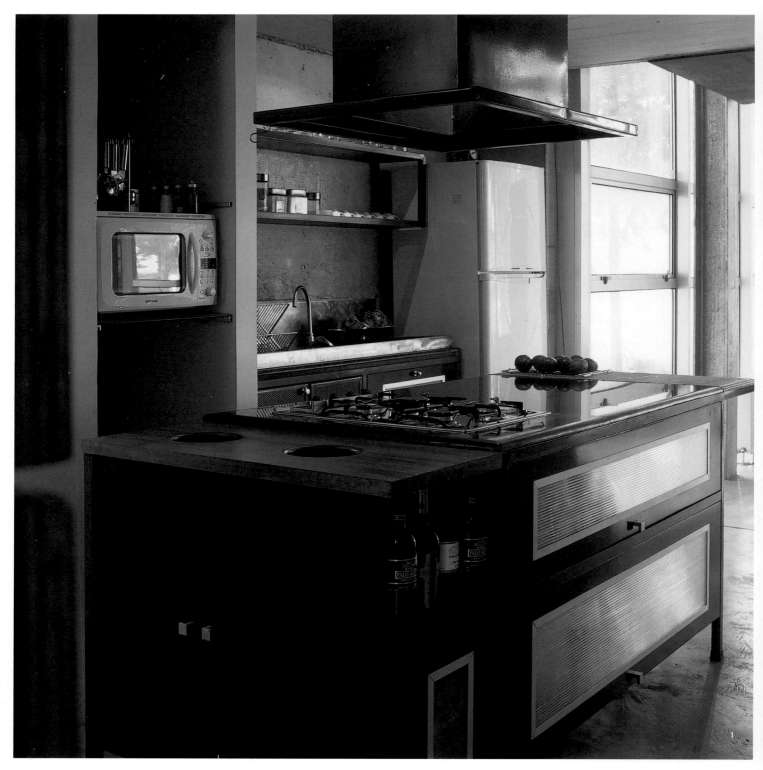

△ The concrete walls set off the colors used for the shelves and
the partitions.

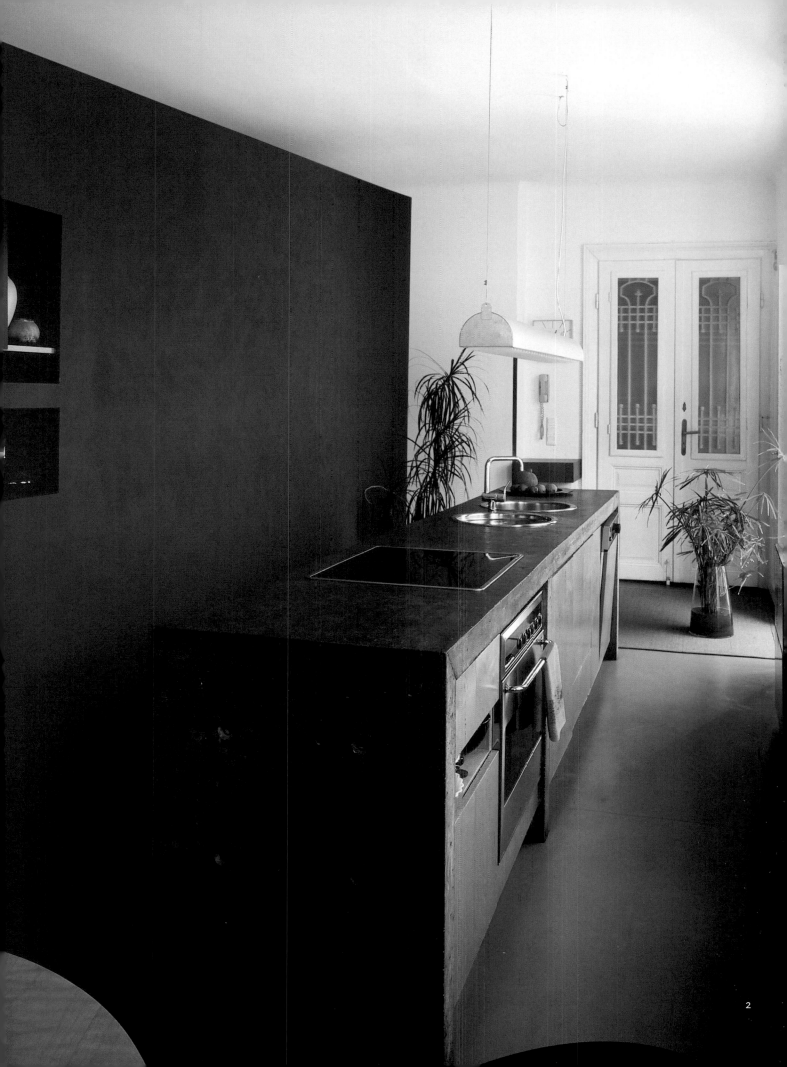

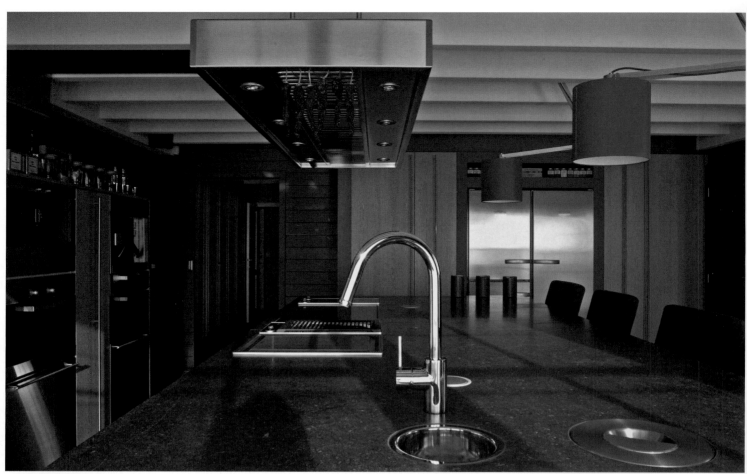

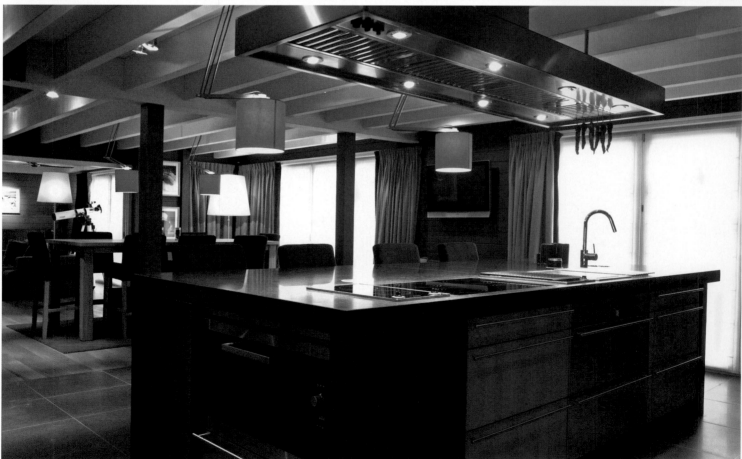

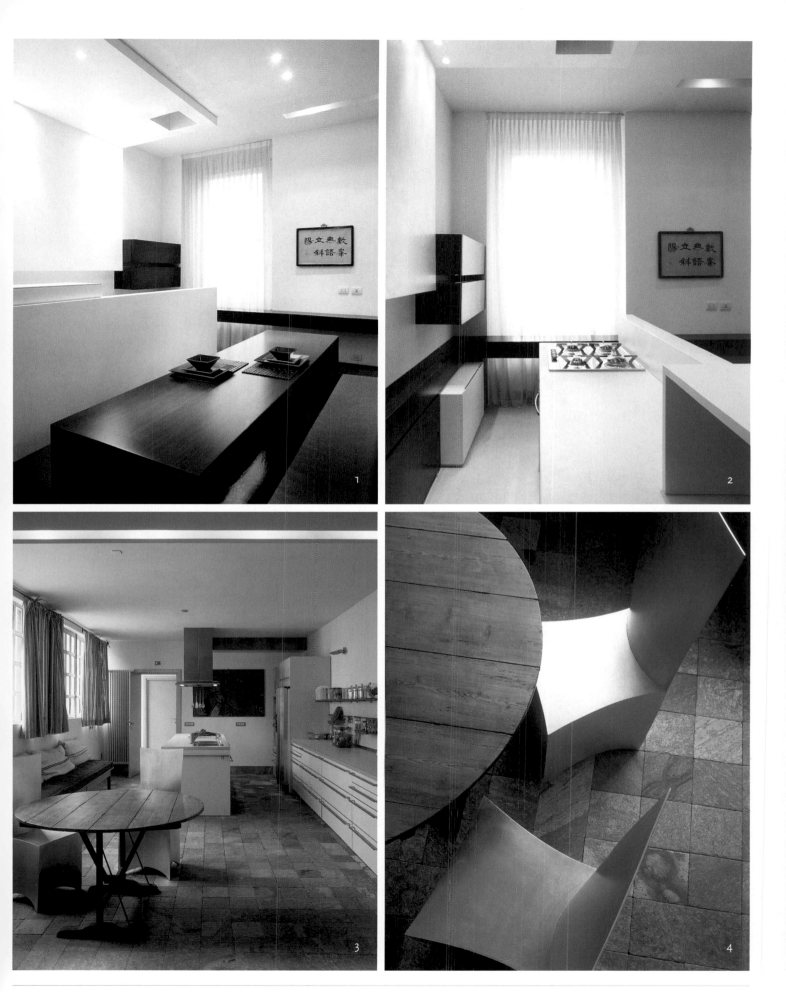

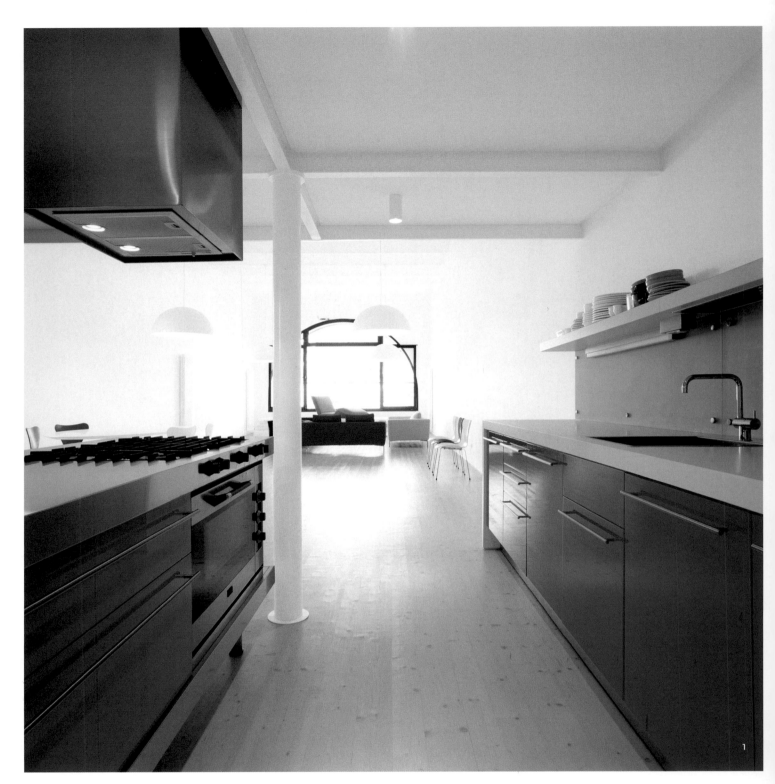

☐ Geometrical forms—rectangles and circles—reveal the retro inspiration of this kitchen. On the following page, the height of the ceilings makes it possible to use elements that take on an almost sculptural dimension: the fireplace, for example, acts as an axis around which the rest of the kitchen and the sitting room are articulated.

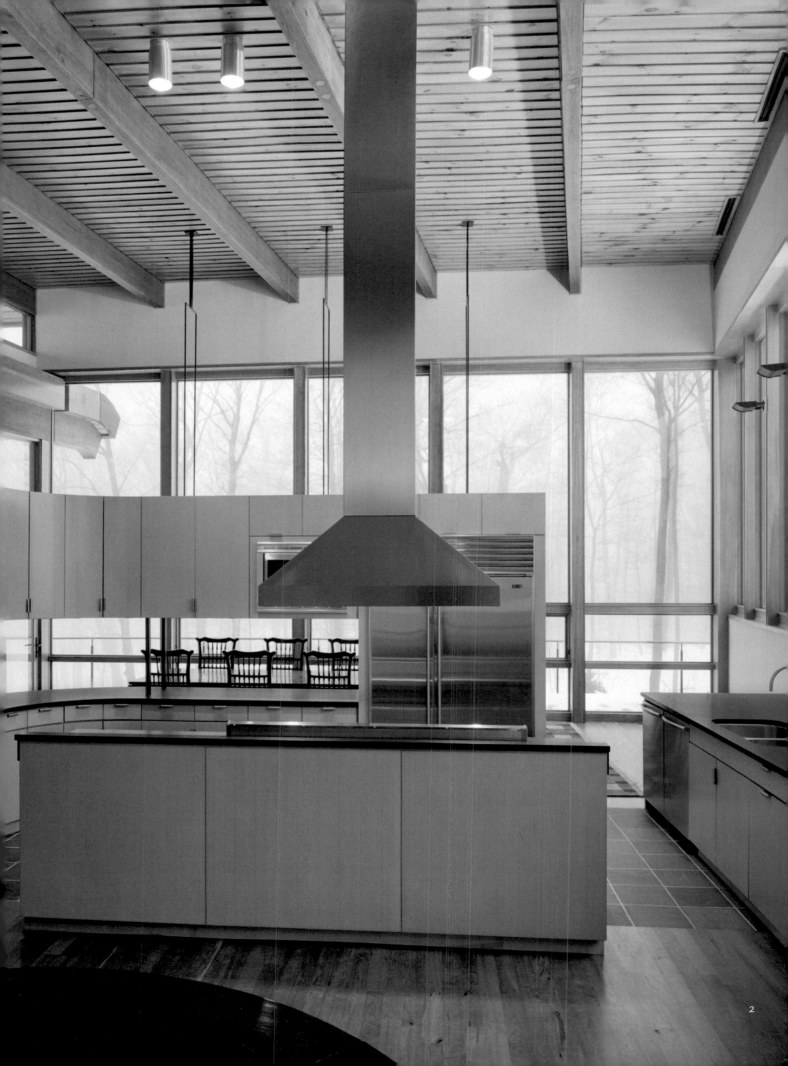

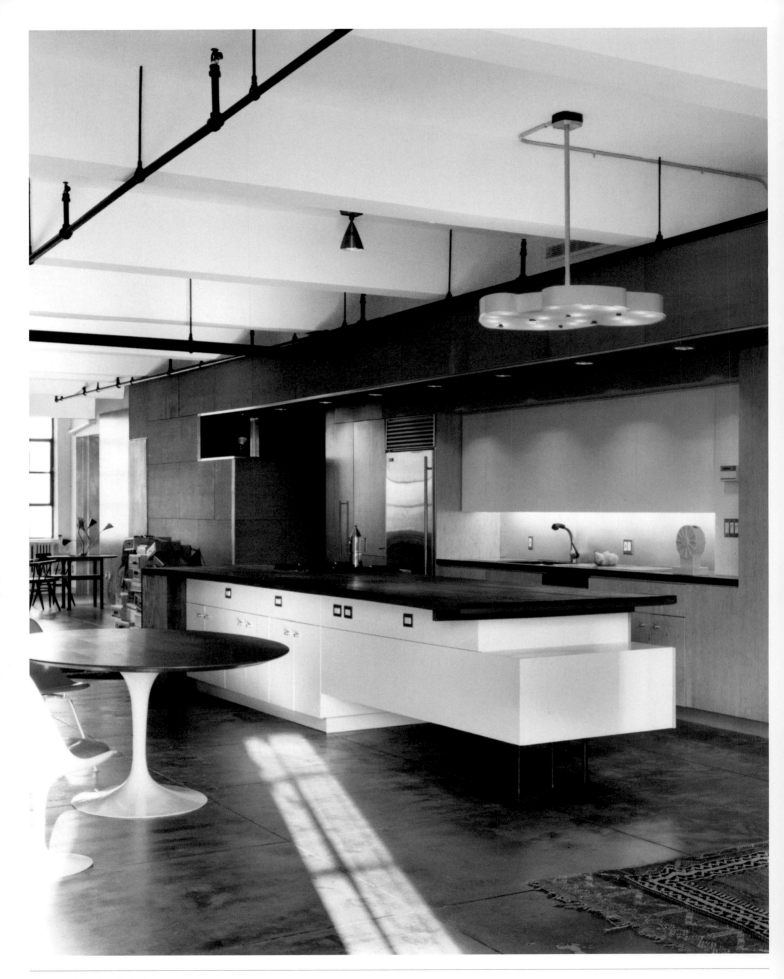

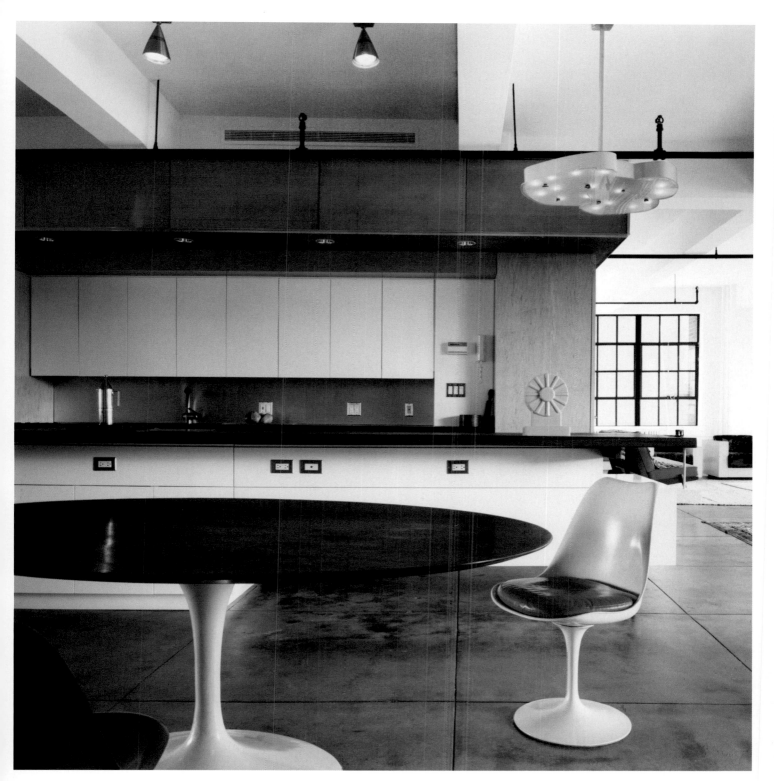

☐ The furniture, lamps, and strong colors used in the kitchen were inspired by the 1970s aesthetic. The industrial style makes it possible to leave the water system exposed to view as well as the ceiling beams.

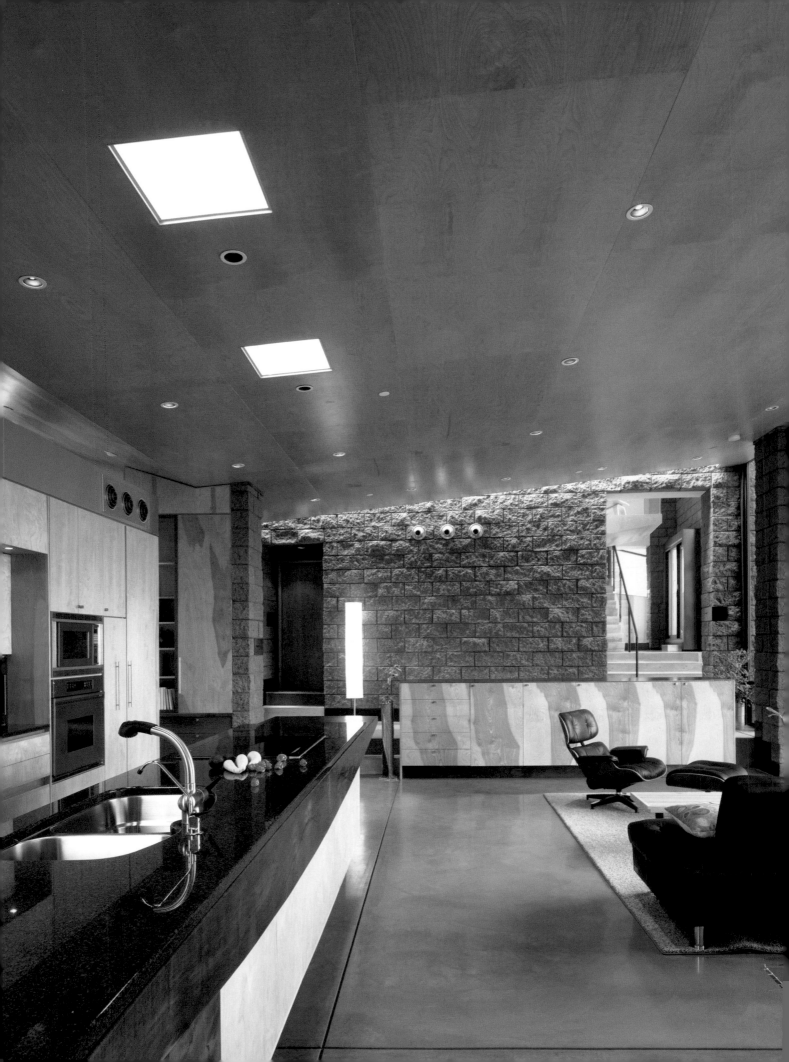

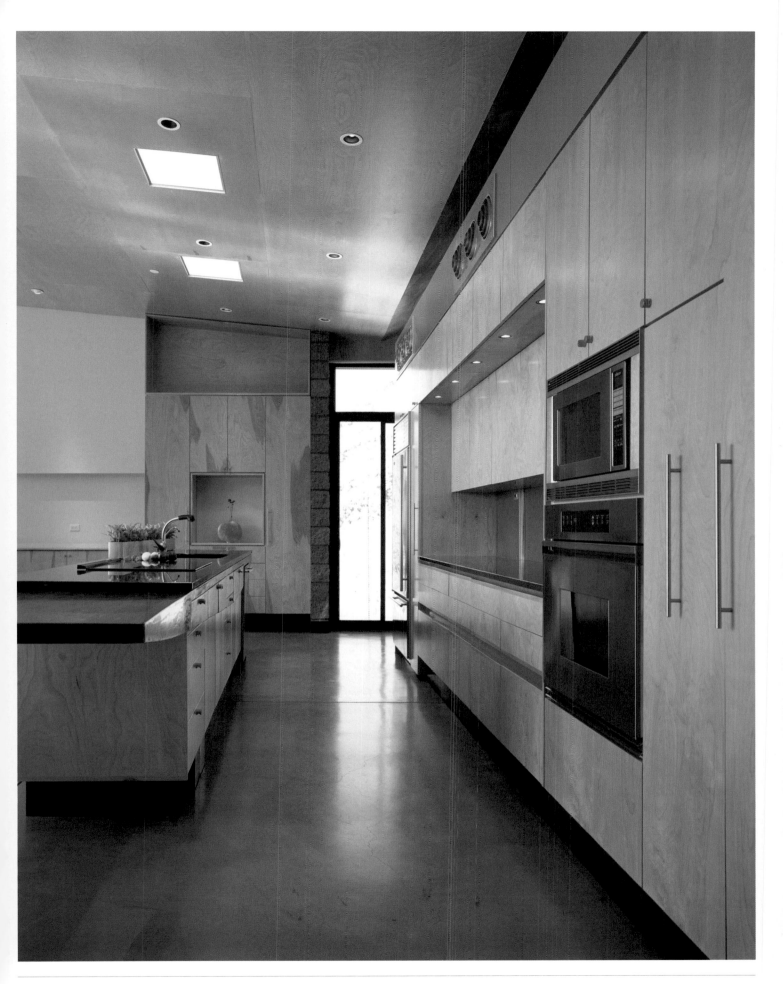

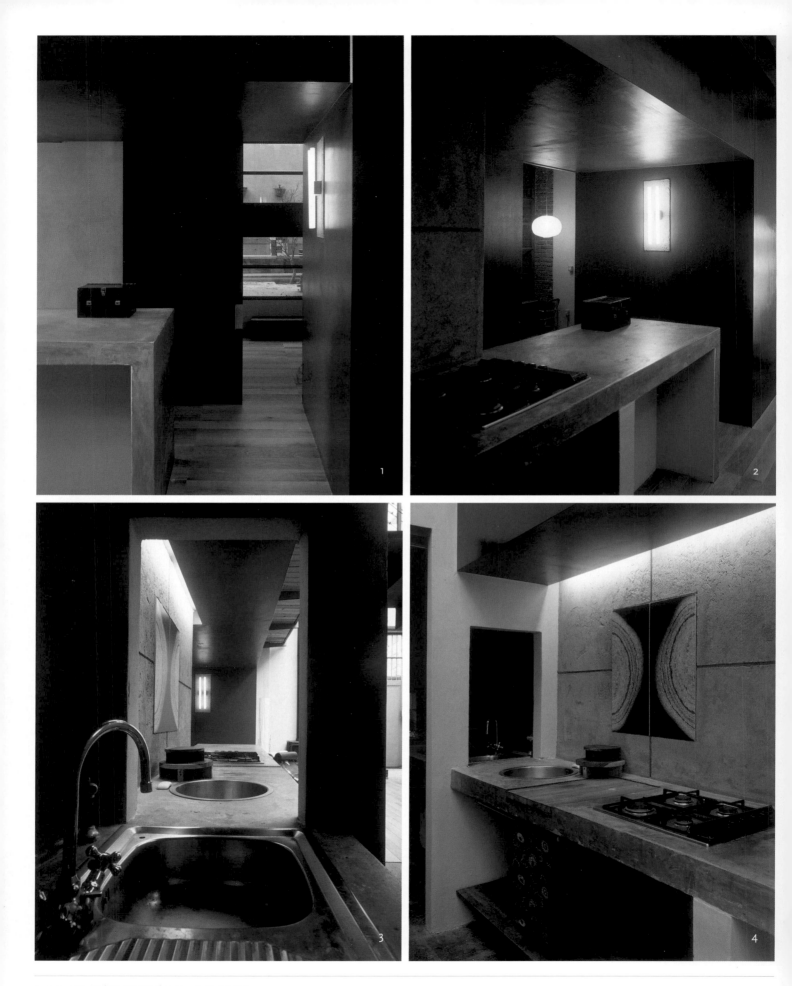

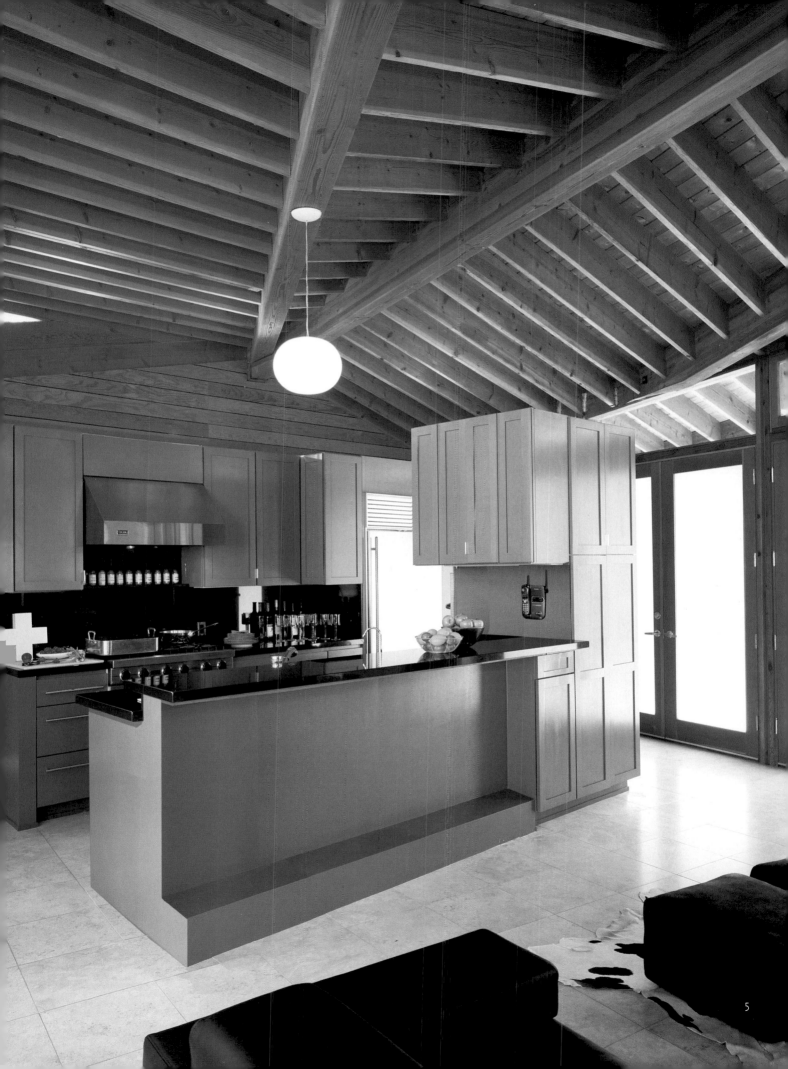

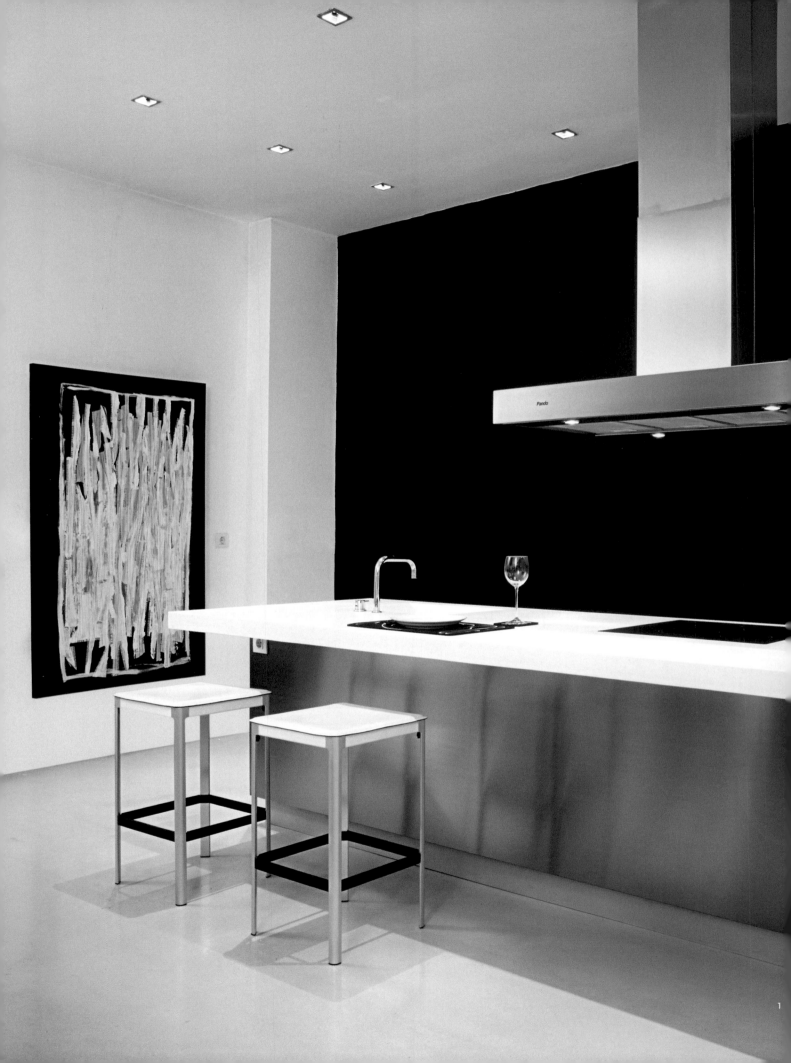

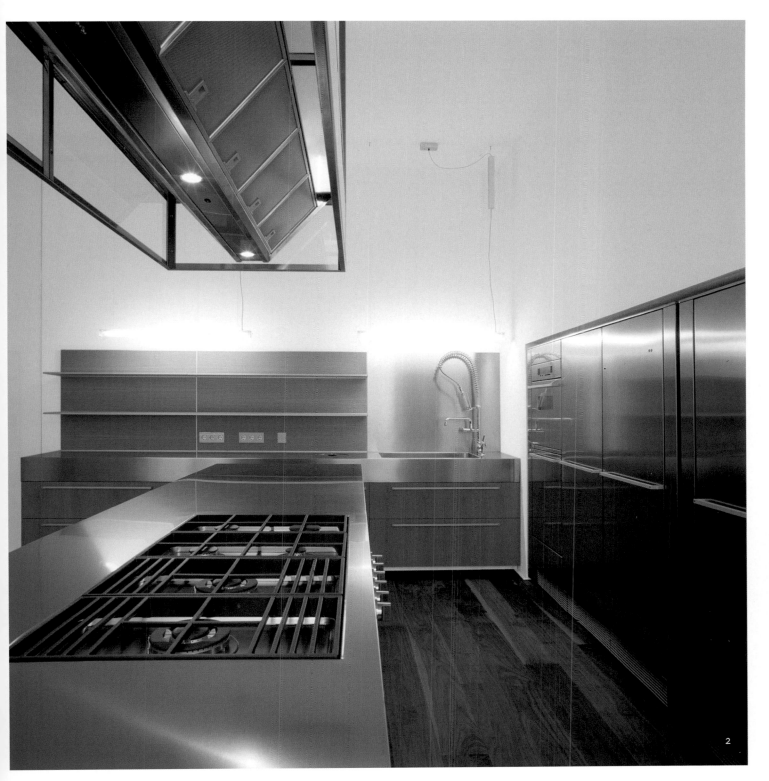

△ This refurbishment by the architect Johannes Will of a building dating from 1900 is an example of what we could call industrial minimalism: the less-is-more philosophy of minimalism joins forces with the functionalism of industrial materials.

◁ On the previous page, simple lines and large unbroken surfaces, an imaginative and subtle use of color generate a glamorous kitchen.

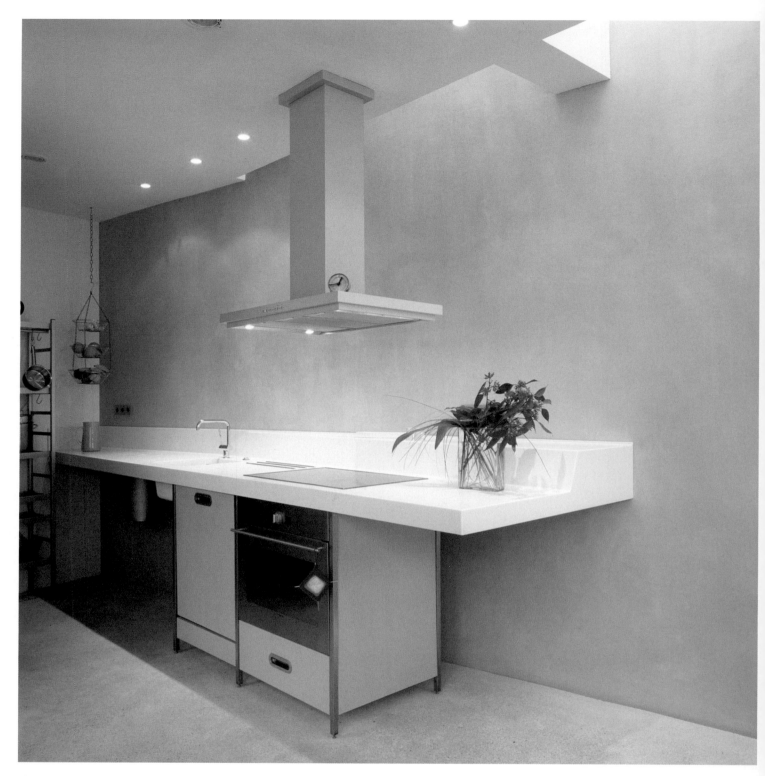

△ "The cooking area is situated between the entrance and the dining room. The worktop is made of white Corian and its geometry impregnates the rest of the room." Deadline Architects, Berlin.

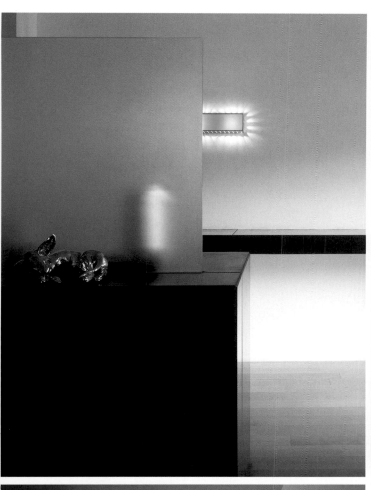
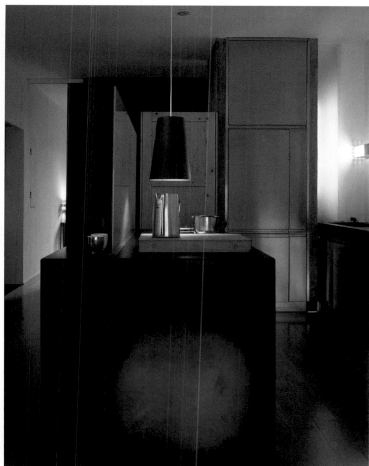
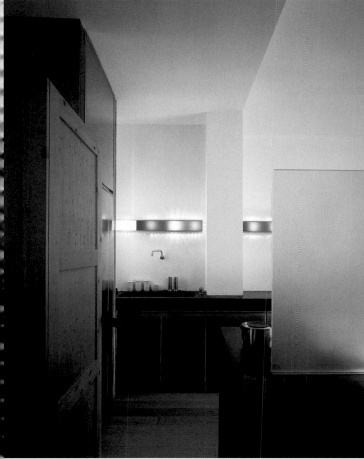
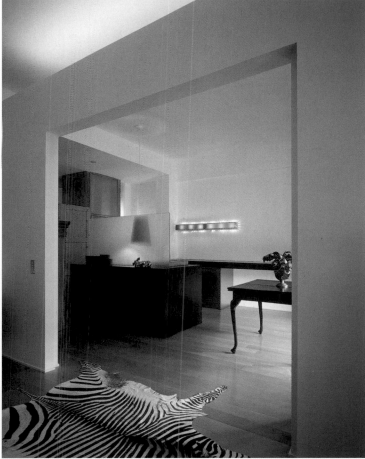

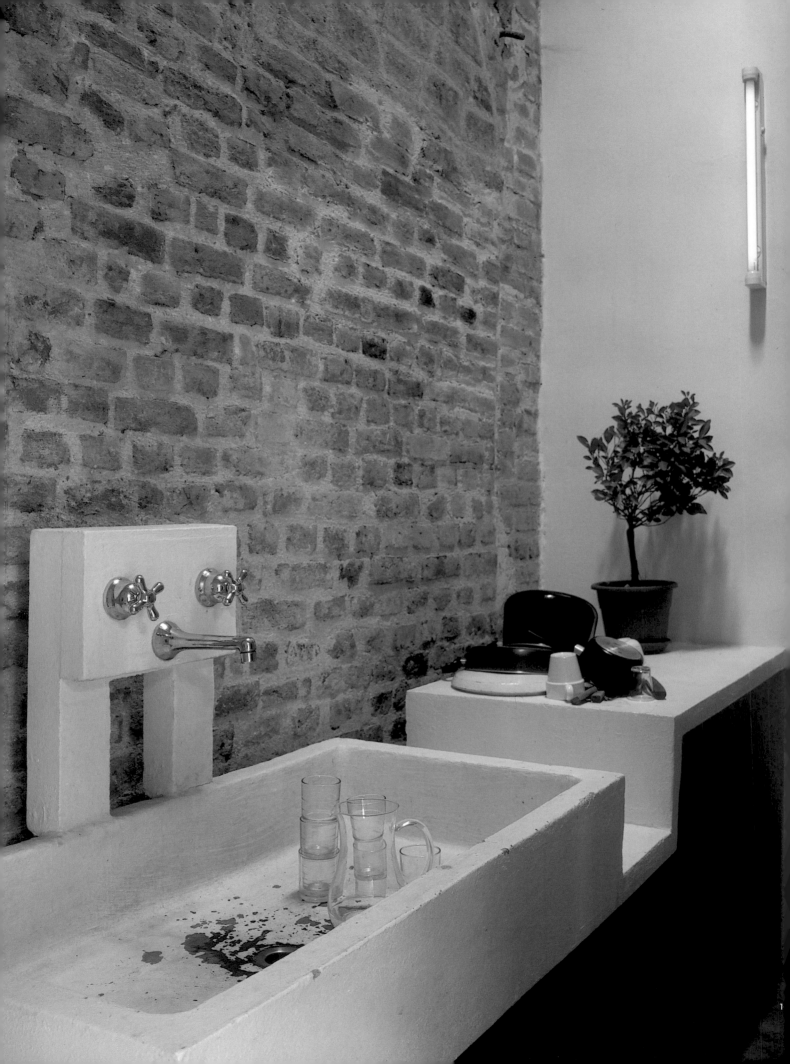

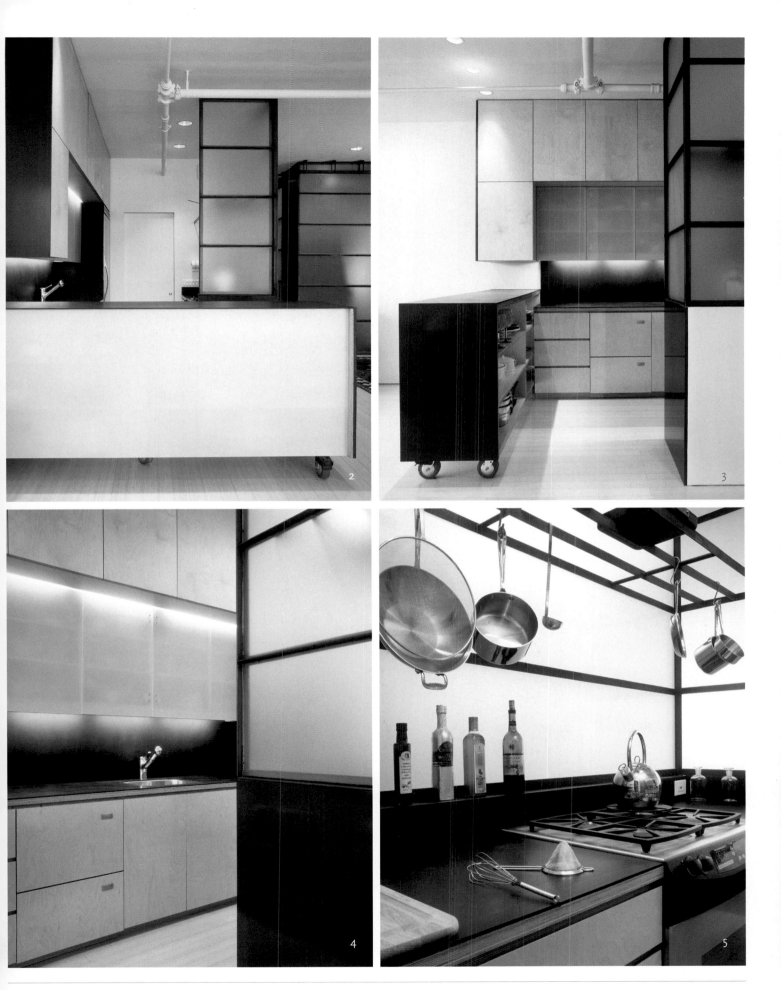

1 © Andrea Martiradonna   2, 3, 4, 5 © Jordi Miralles

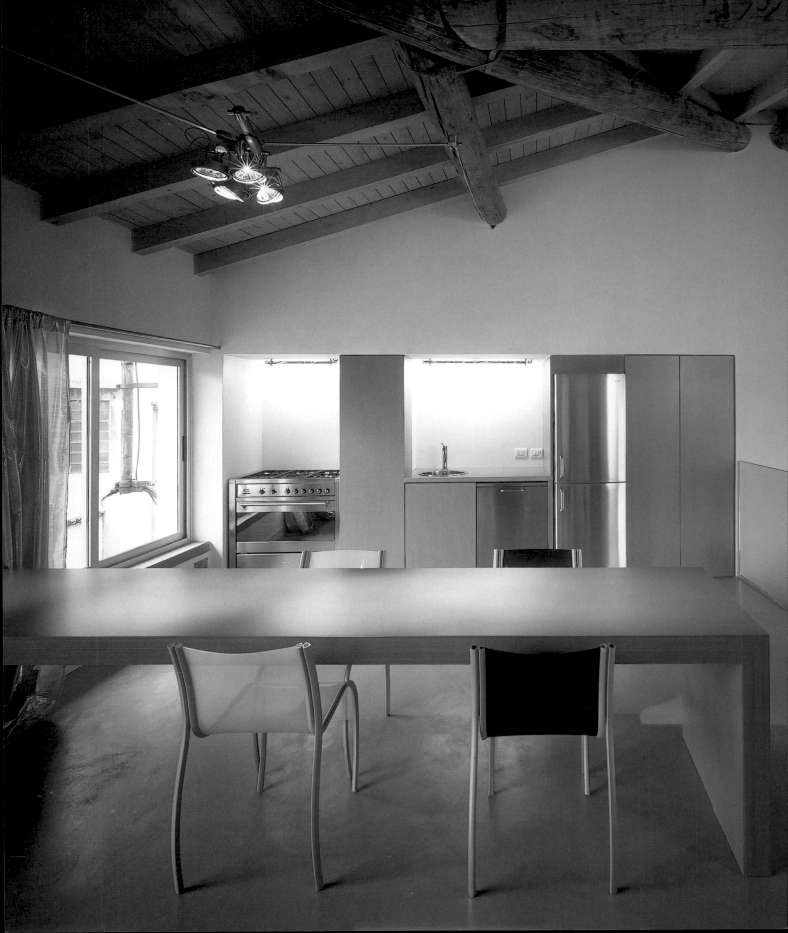

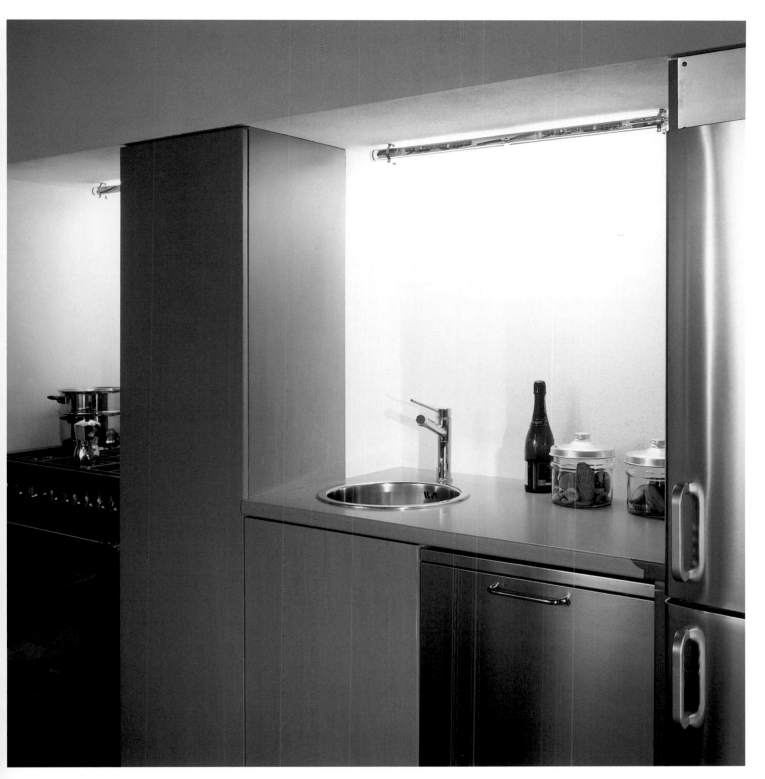

☐ In this Italian home, the work of the local architect Bettinelli, the pale
colors of the furniture set off the original wooden-beamed ceiling.

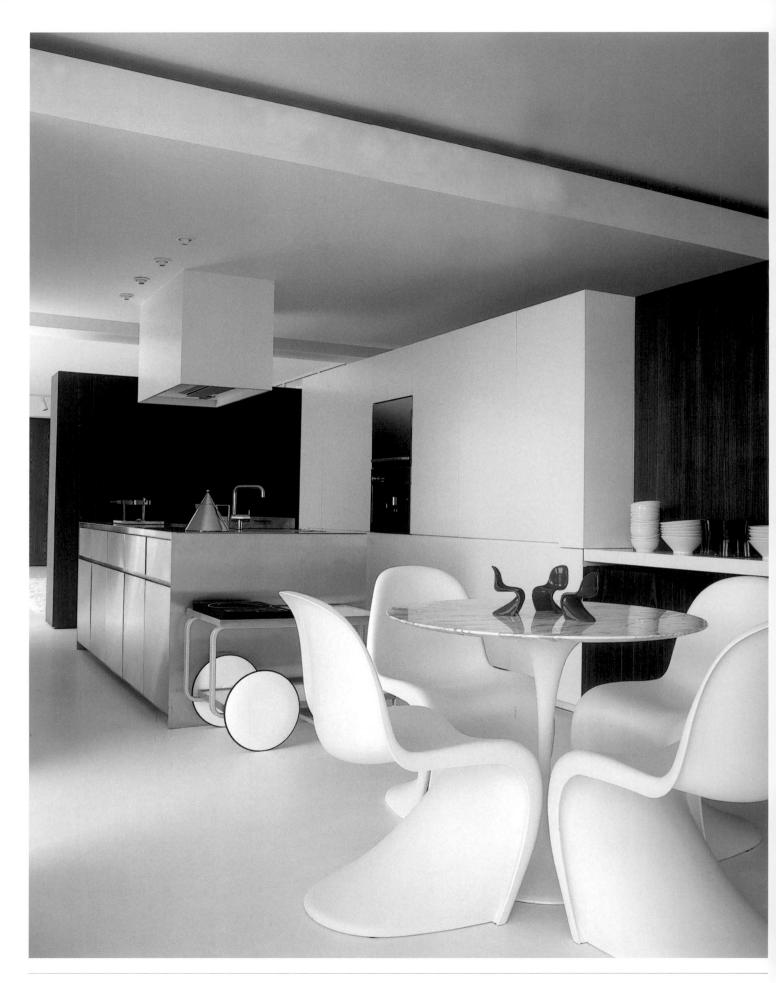

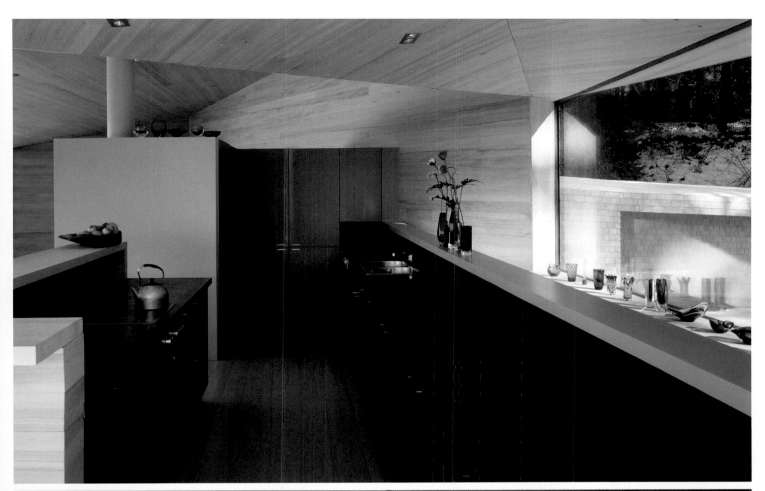

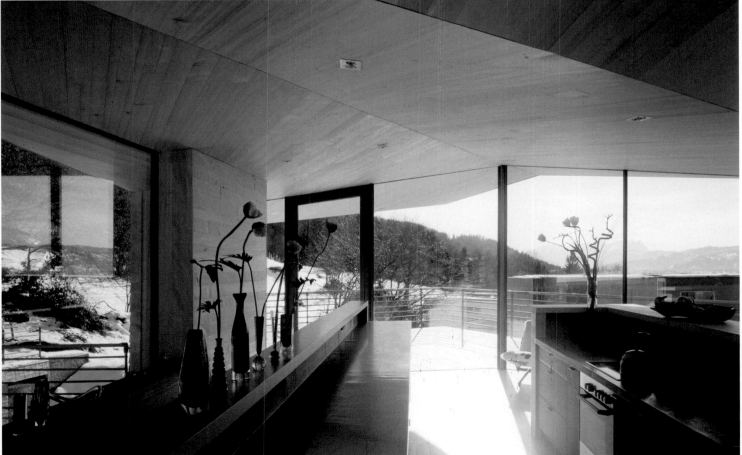

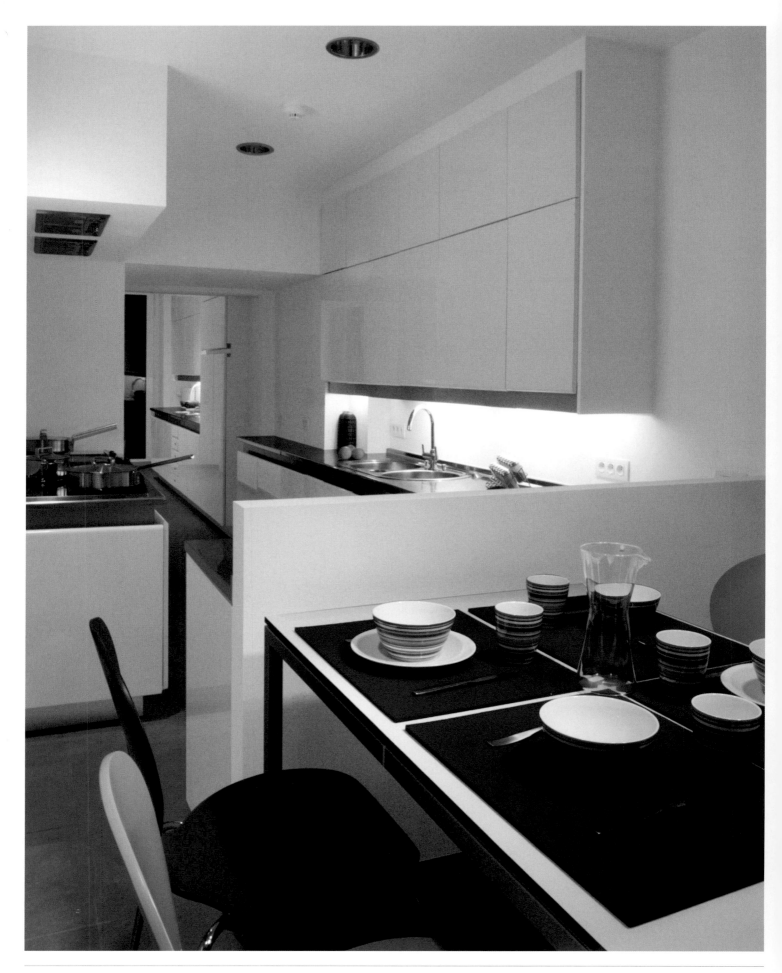

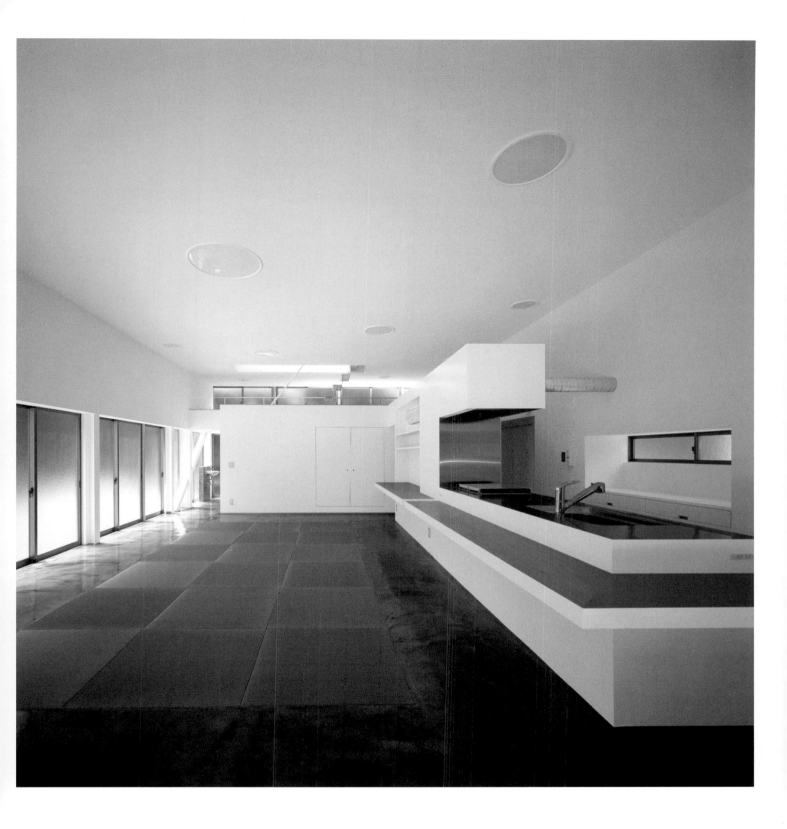

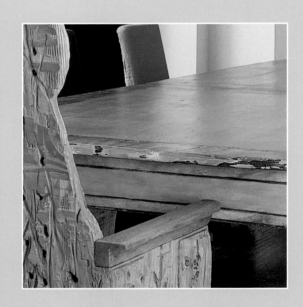

Dining Rooms

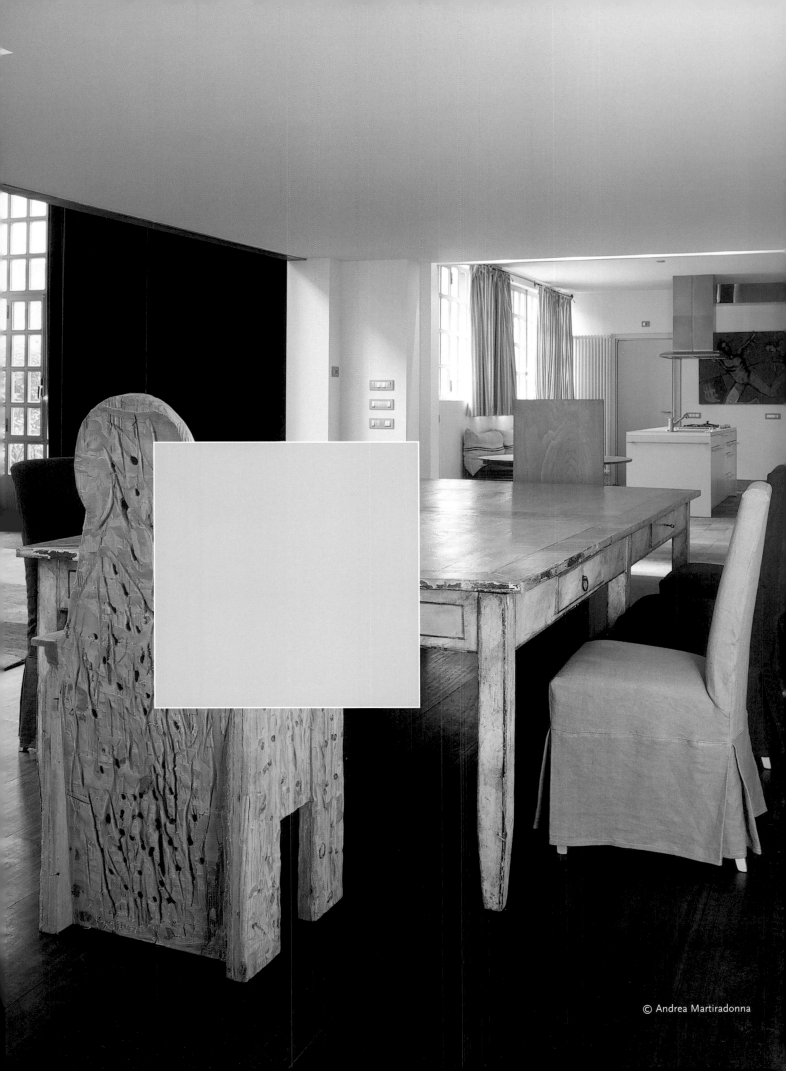

© Andrea Martiradonna

Dining Rooms

The dining room has become a stage where people can express themselves and entertain their guests

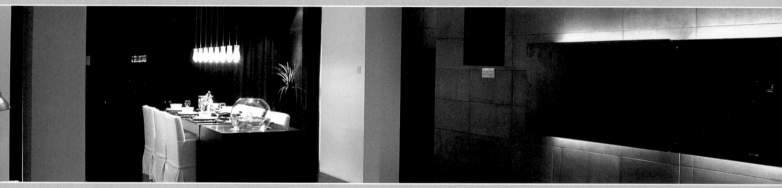

© Maoder Chou

There is no love more sincere than the love of food," wrote George Bernard Shaw in *Man and Superman* (1903). What better place than a dining room for this relationship to prosper and grow.

As the quality of life has improved, our needs have become more hedonistic. What was once considered basic has now acquired a social, pleasurable, and even artistic dimension. One characteristic of life today is the capacity to choose what, how, and where to eat, elevating eating into an act that expresses personal taste. We no longer eat just what's there, but instead decide how we are going to eat. It has become an activity in which we identify ourselves and find enjoyment.

As interest in the culinary arts increase, the dining room has become a stage where people can express themselves and entertain their guests. This results in kitchens that are more than just places for

cooking and dining rooms that aren't simply places for eating. Both have become screens on which we can project our personalities.

Dining rooms have also felt the influence of other cultures—factors like climate, social customs, and even religion help determine the layout of our houses, the shape of our furniture, and the placement of kitchen tools. Today some of these factors have disappeared as technology has reduced the effects of climate. The interchange of culture, information, and images has also made us more tolerant of and receptive to new forms and aesthetics. Consequently, a custom such as eating on the floor without chairs, typical of hot countries, no longer surprises us when we see it in other cultures, or even in local restaurants.

This chapter presents examples of the variations possible in rooms devoted to eating, helping us see how to fill them with personality.

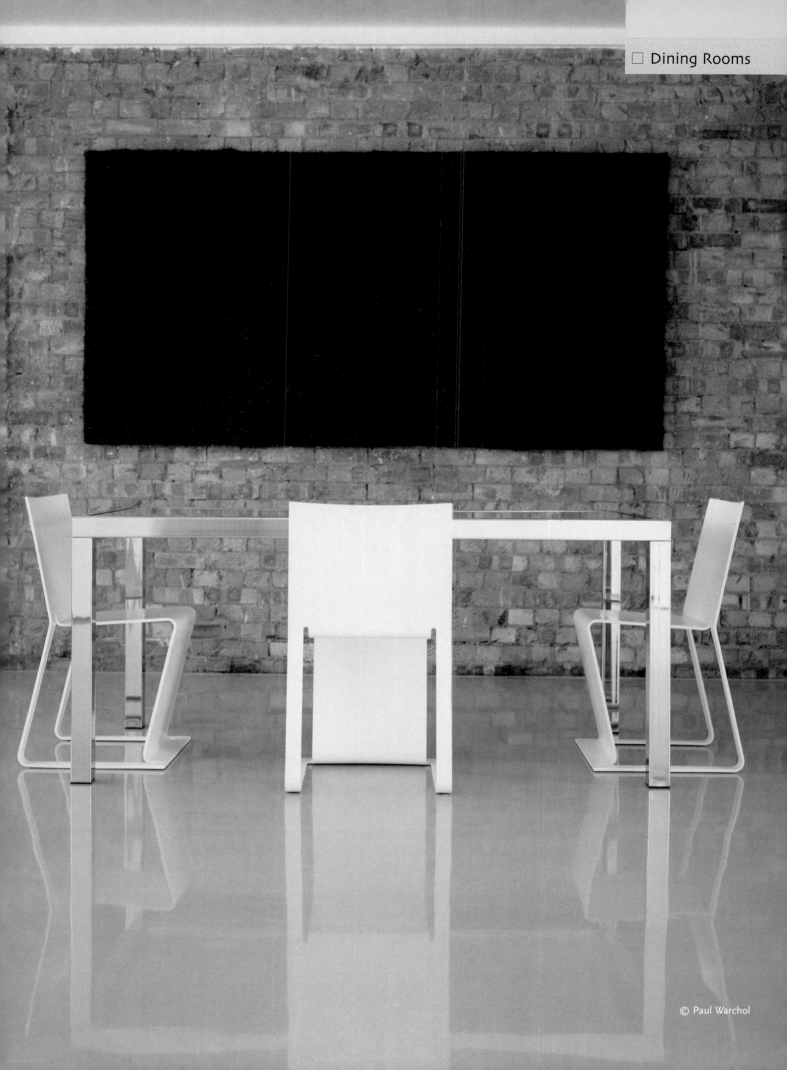

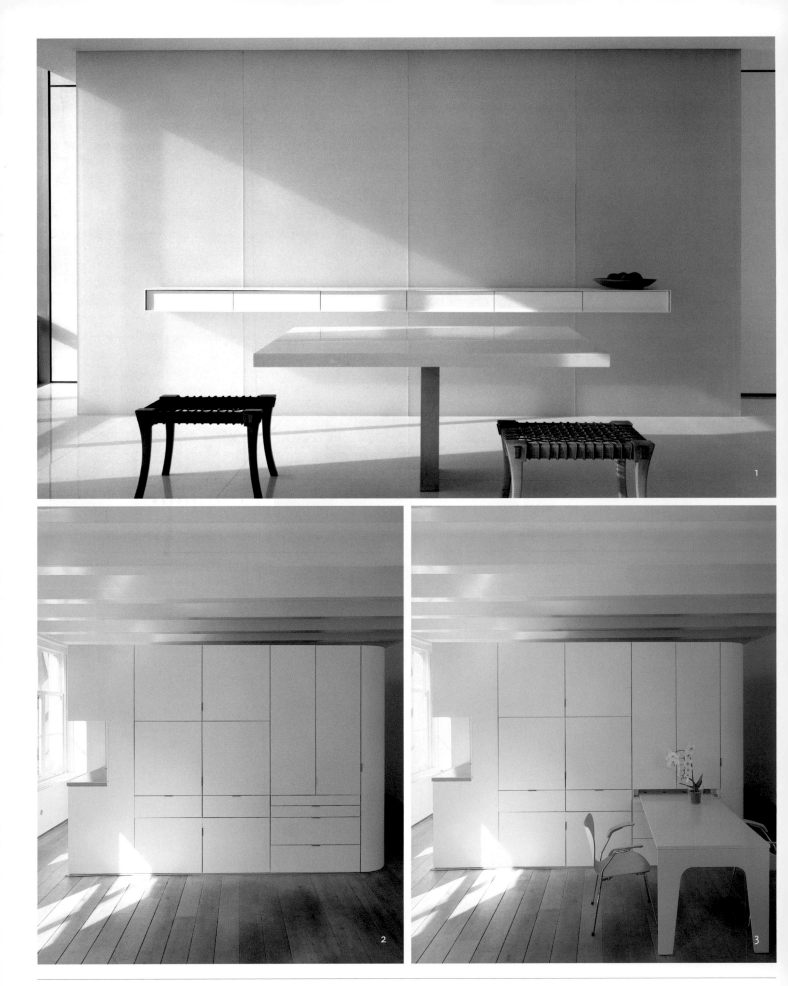

1 © Paul Warchol   2, 3 © Christian Richters

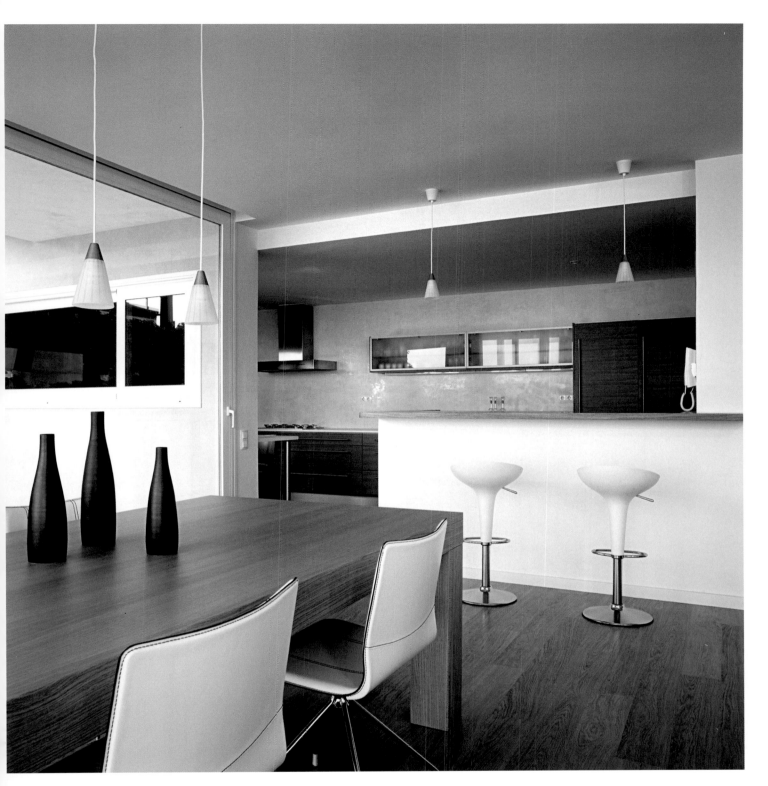

□ Three proposals for dining rooms, all in a minimal style. One is set apart from the kitchen, the second can be put away after each meal, and the third provides a view of the cooking process.

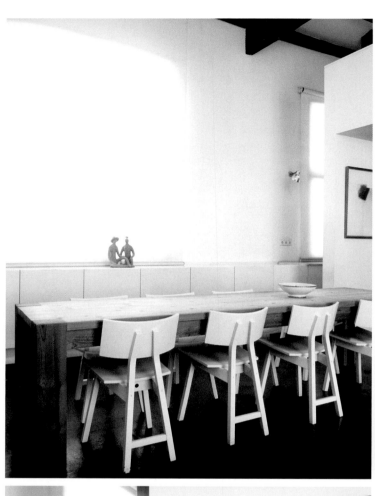
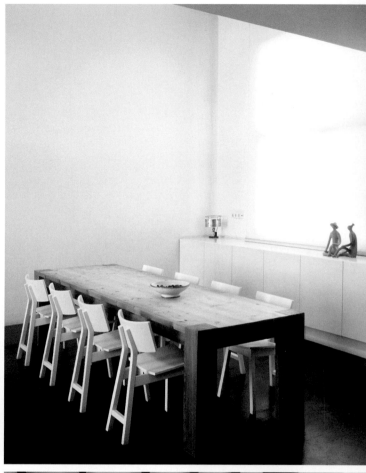
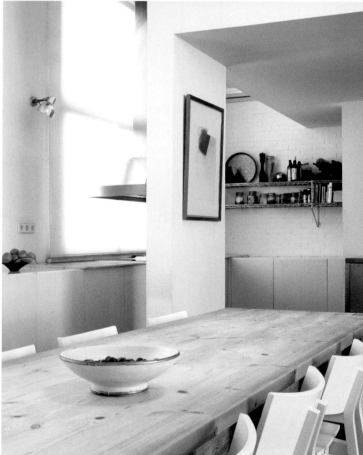
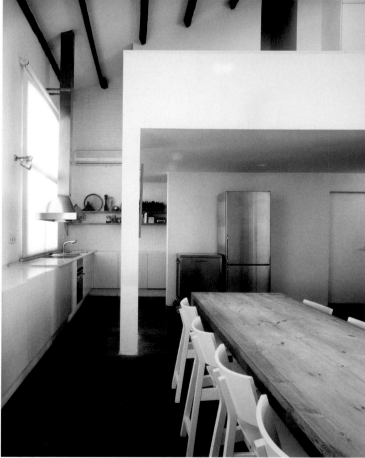

© Jordi Miralles

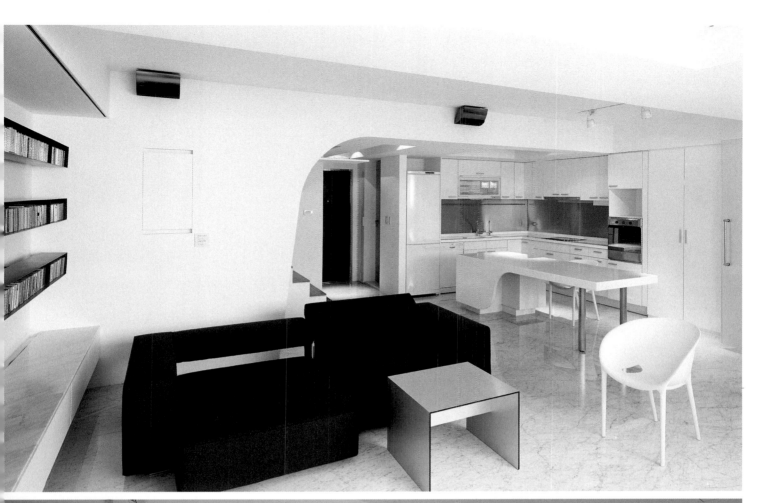

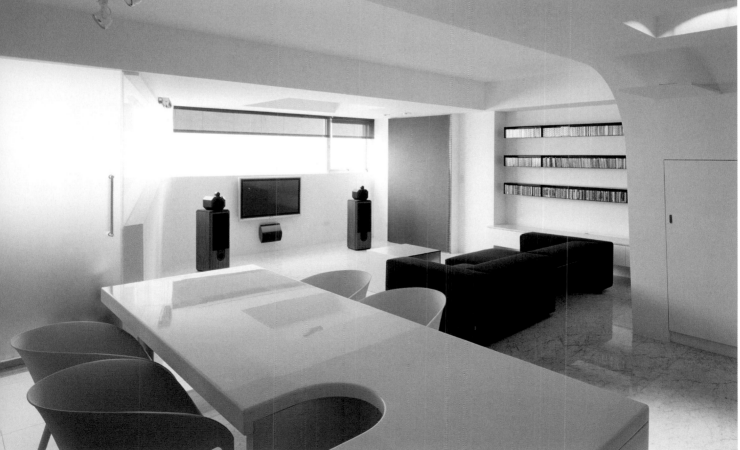

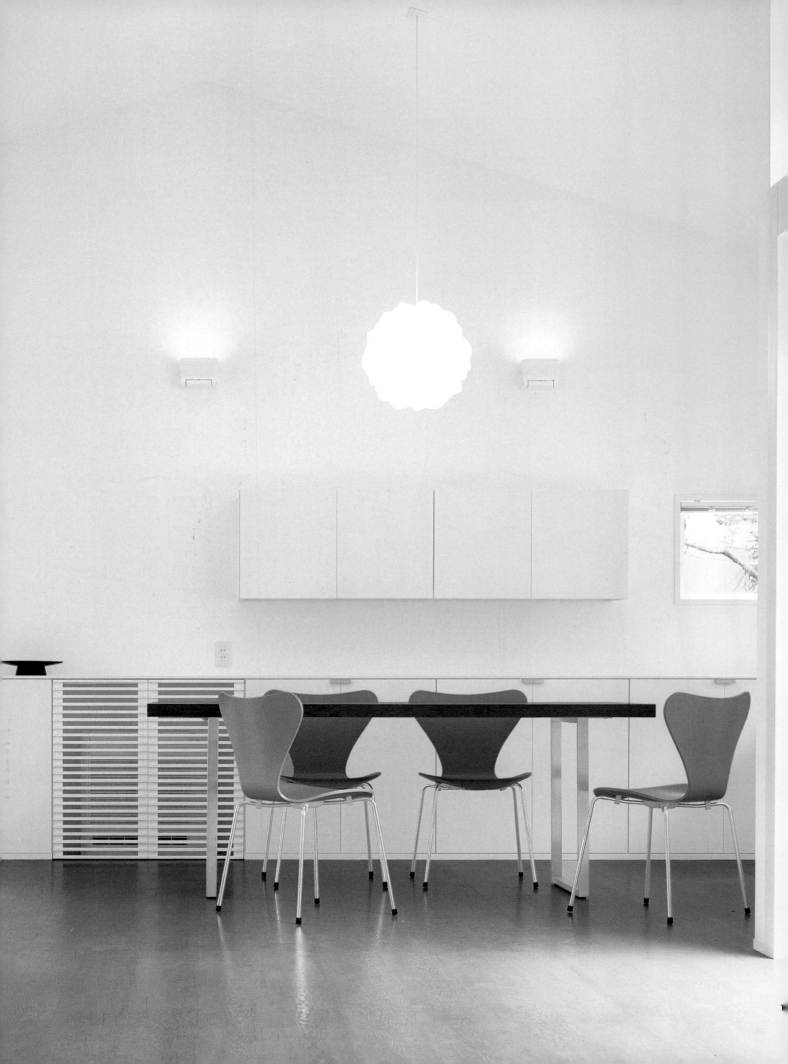

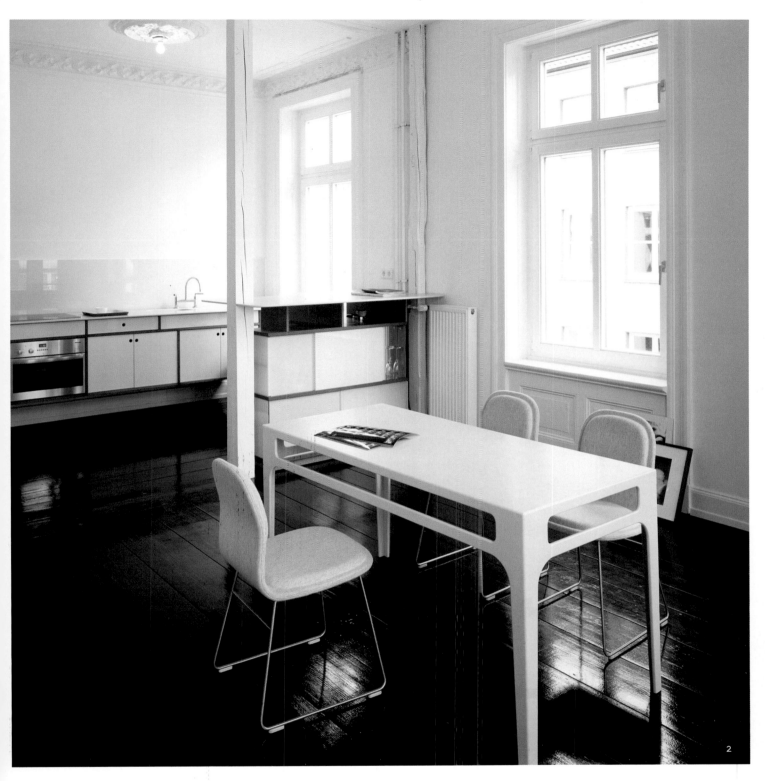

△ Above, a design by González and Haase, marked by the interplay between the kitchen furniture and the window frames.

◁ Opposite, Moriko Kira Architects provide clear solutions for every design problem, often in a minimalist vein.

1 © Satoshi Asakawa   2 © Thomas Meyer/Ostkreuz | González & Haase/Atelier Architecture & Scenography

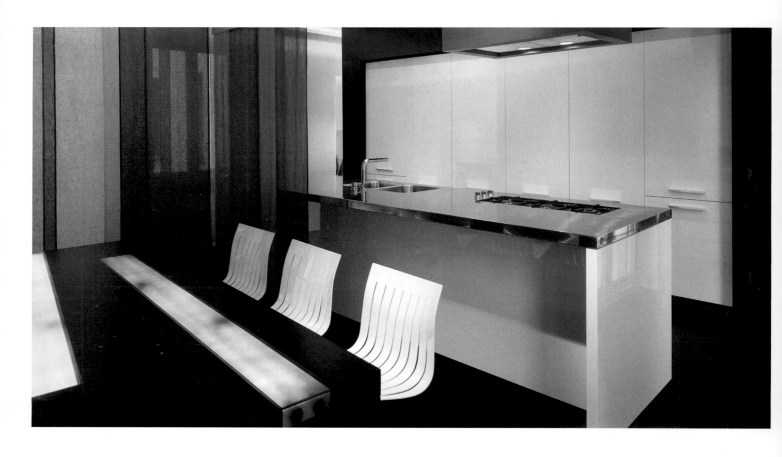

The work of Filippo Bombace is characterized by a meticulous analysis of the expressive possibilities of materials and the evocative and compositional qualities of light.

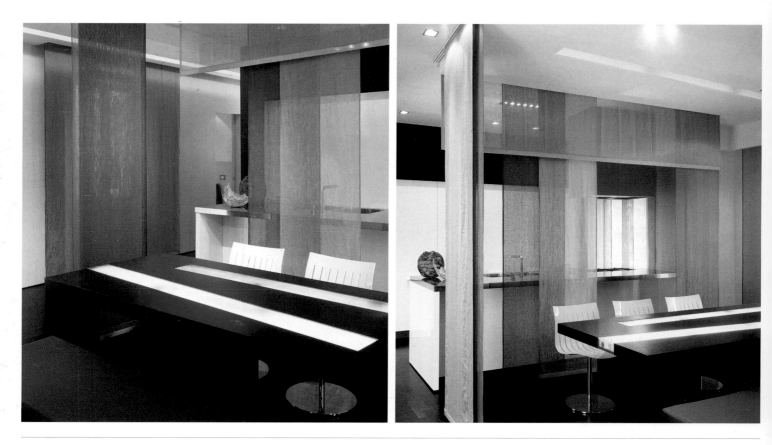

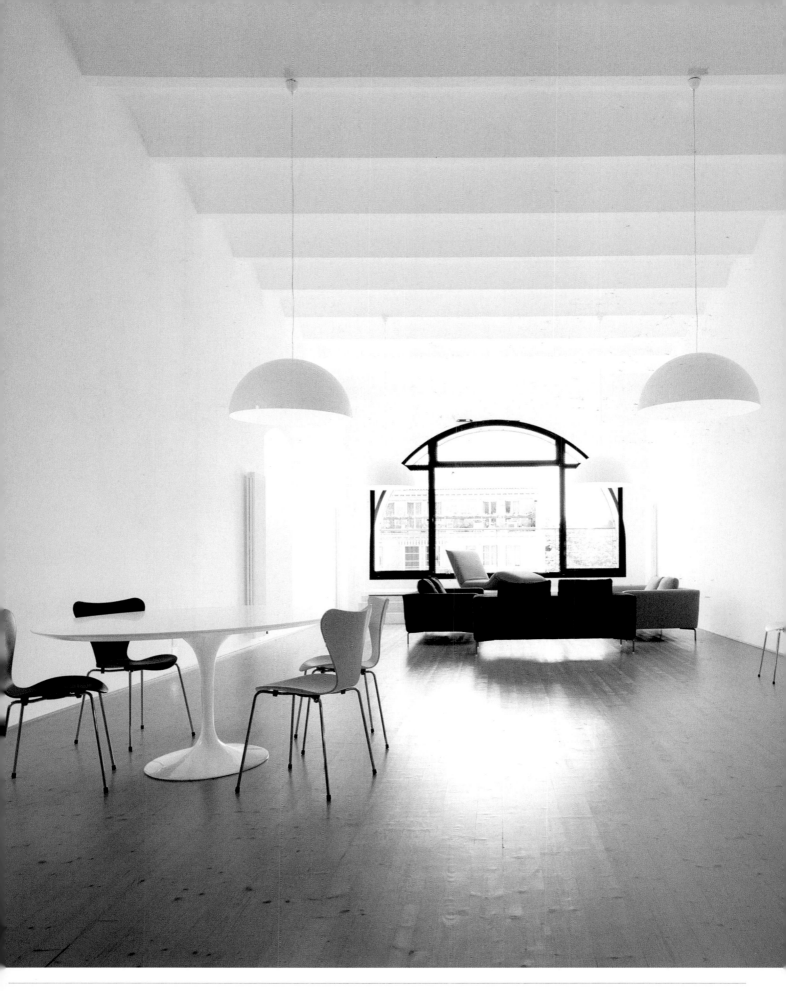

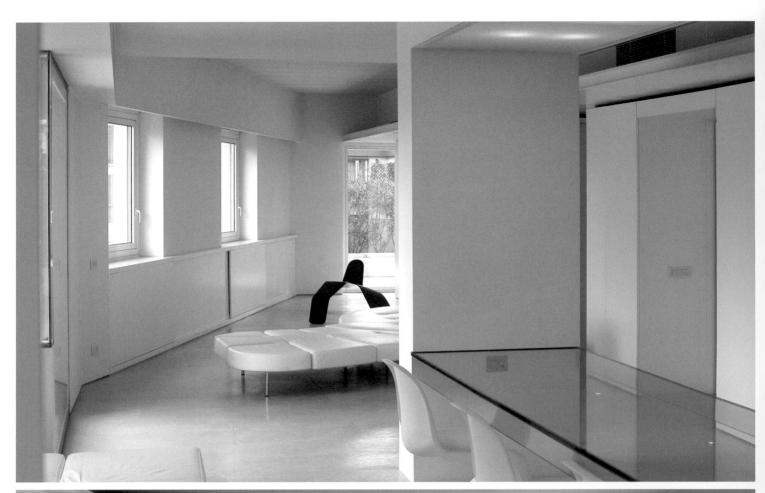

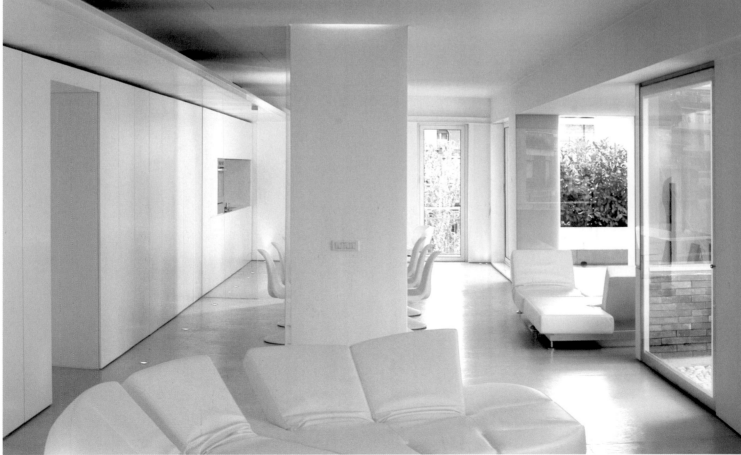

© Davide Marchetti

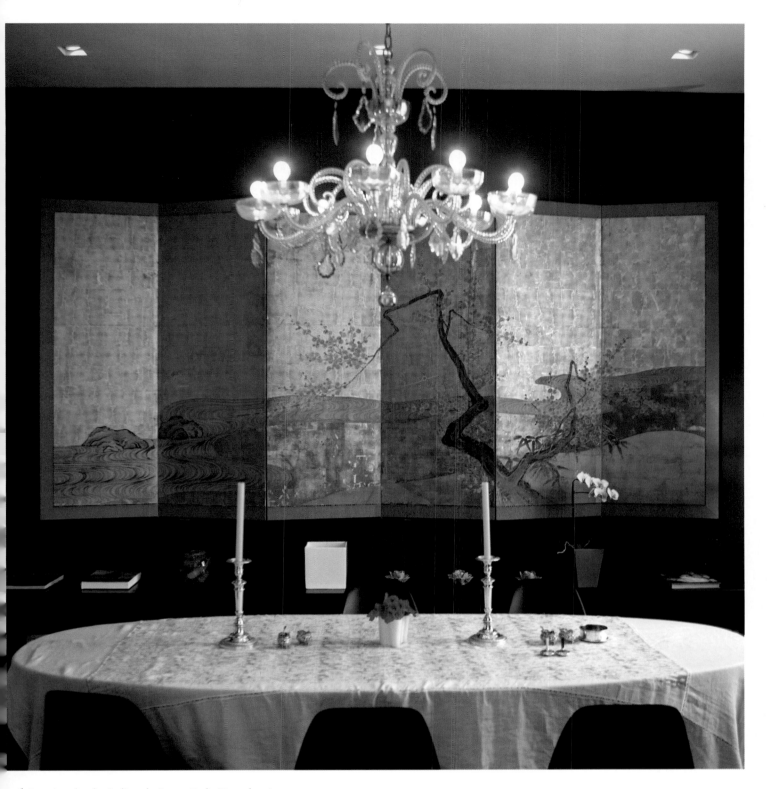

◁ A project by the Italian designer Carlo Berarducci.

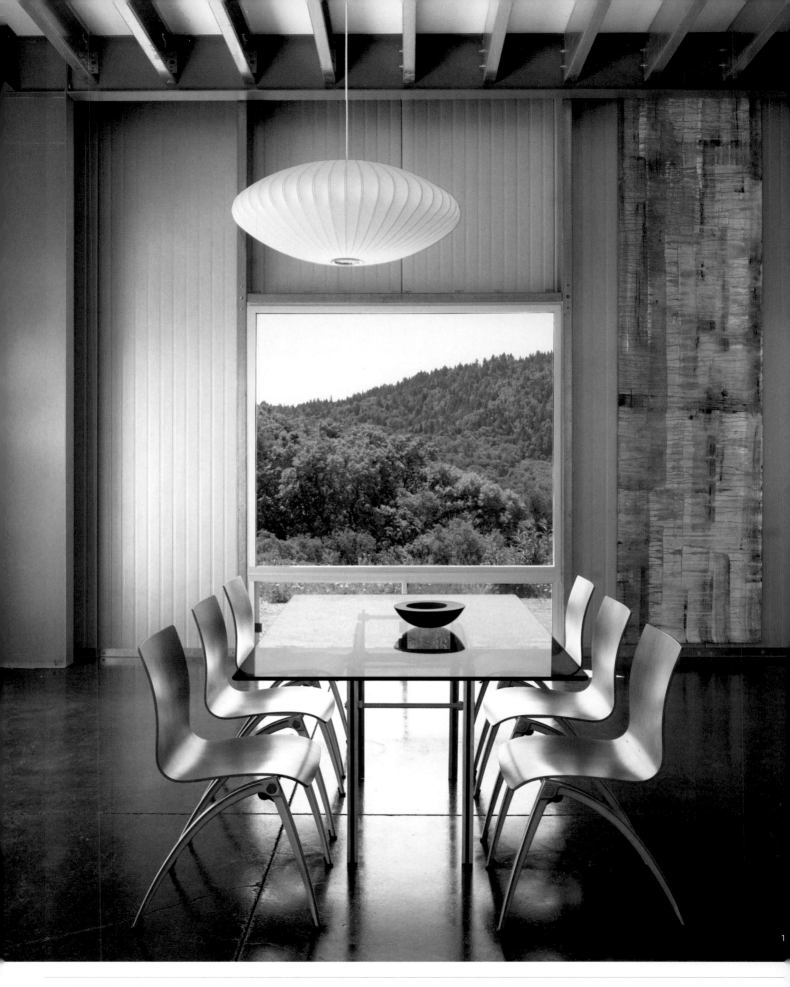

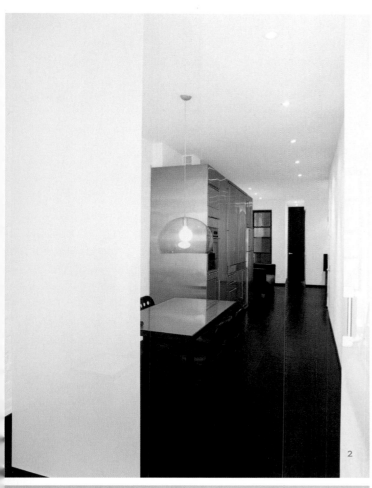

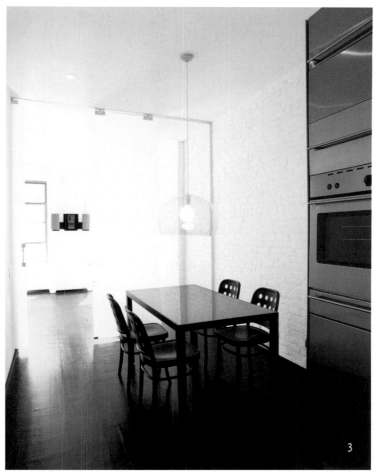

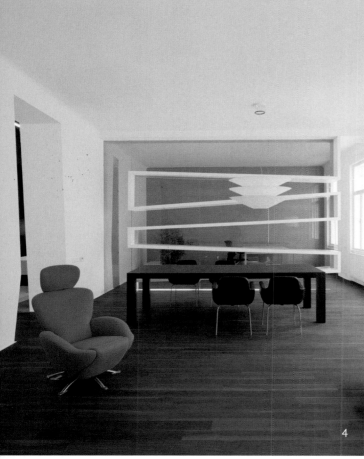

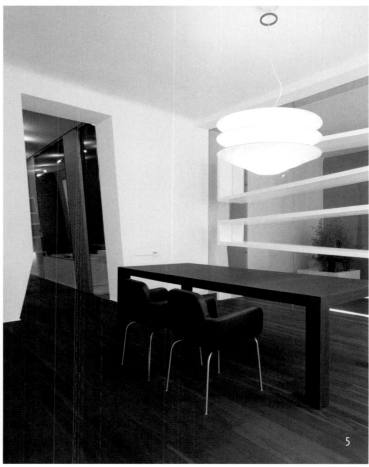

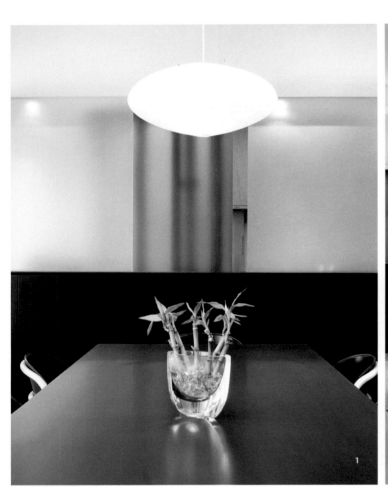

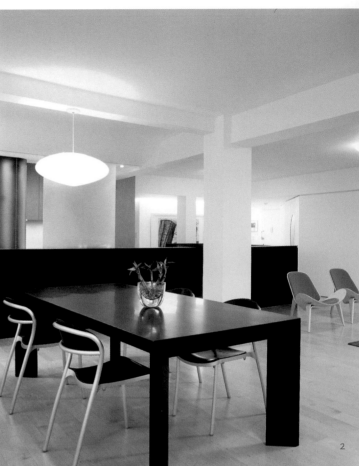

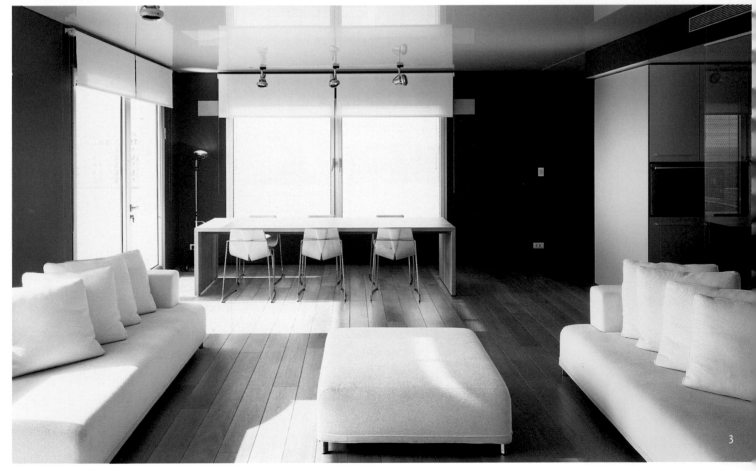

1, 2 © Jordi Miralles   3 © Amit Geron

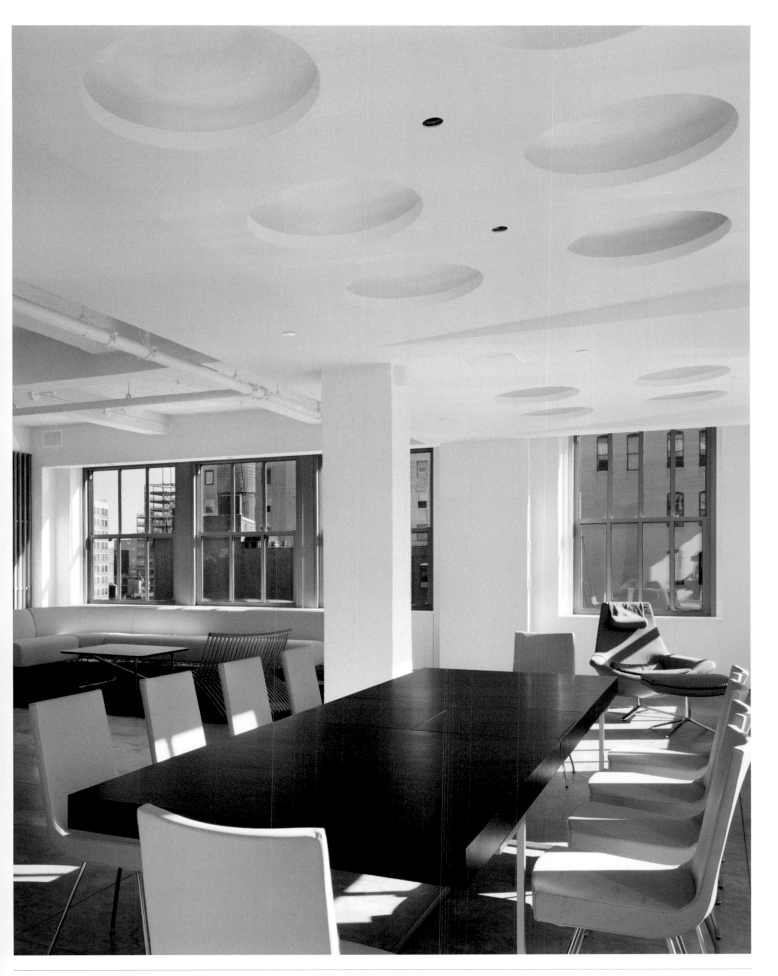

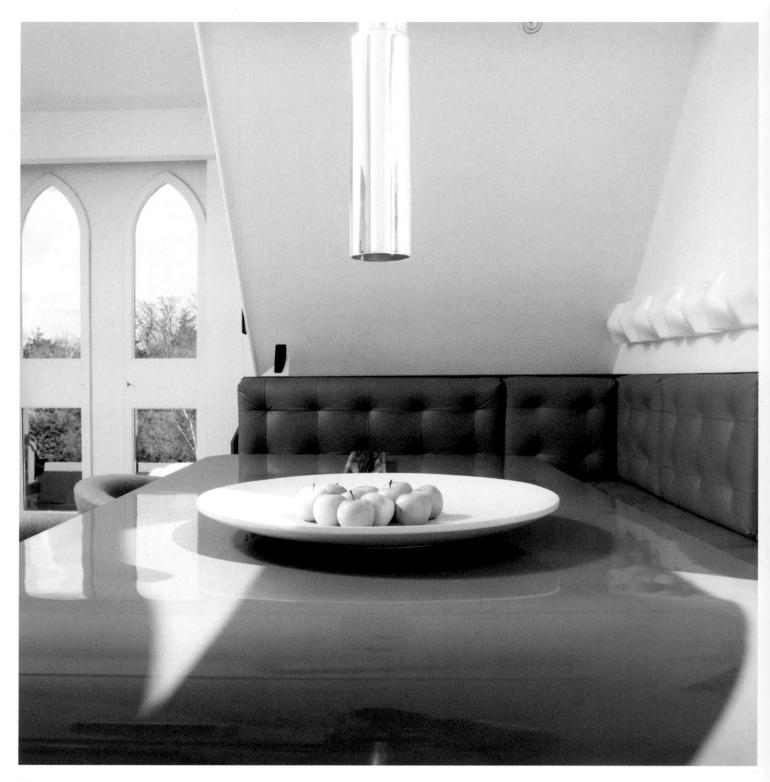

☐ Jo Warman separated this dining area from the rest of the living room by setting it on a raised level.

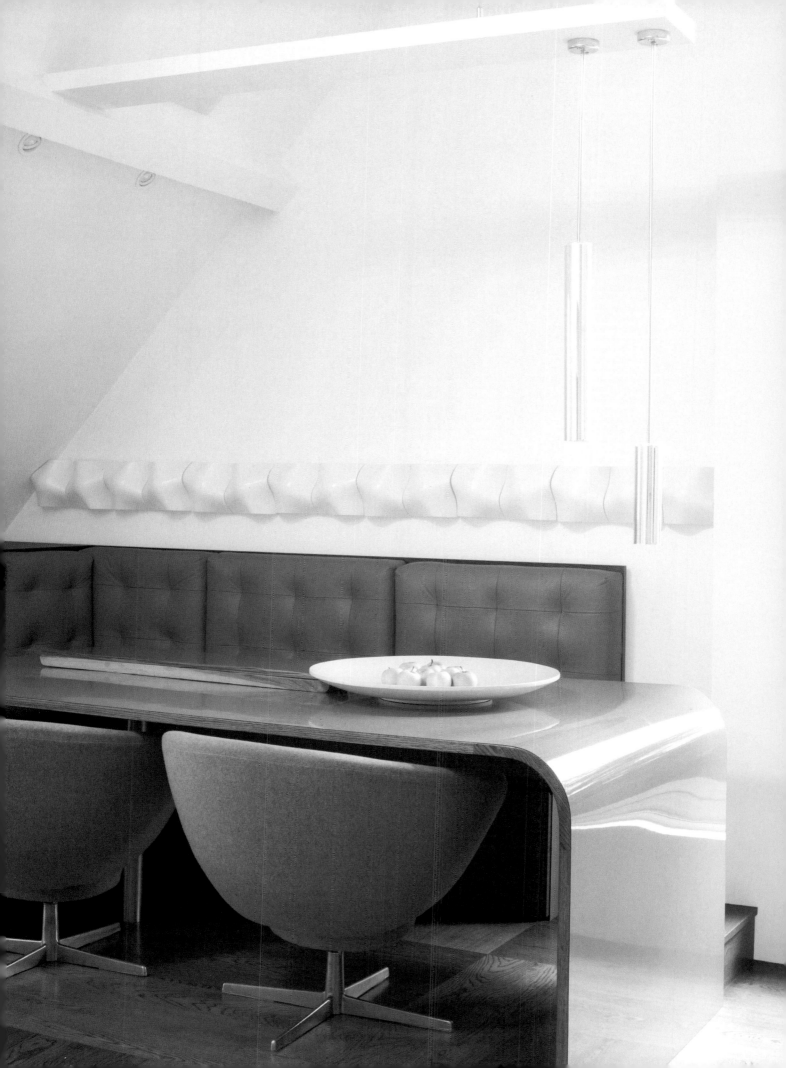

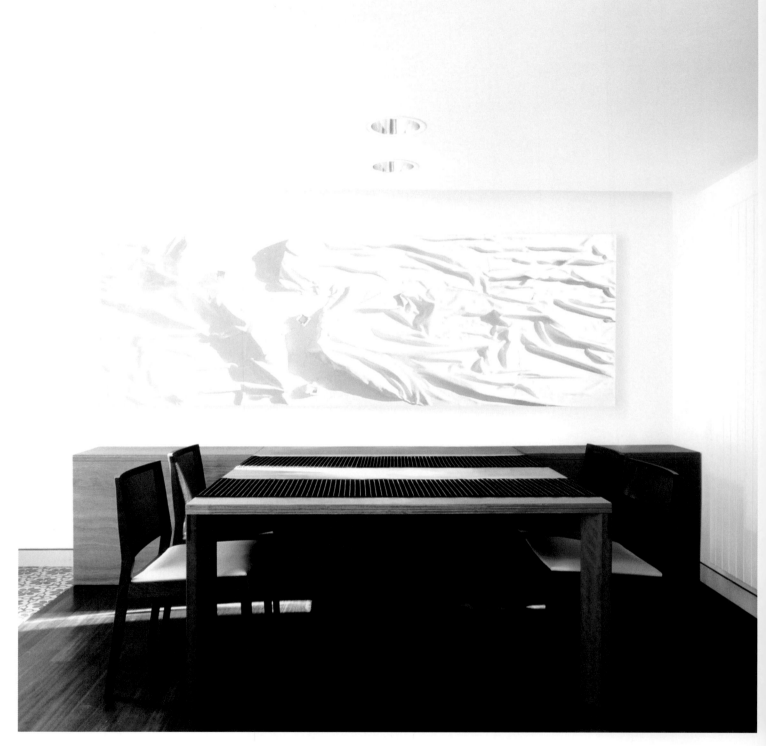

☐ This apartment, in a retro style, plays with the symmetry between the false ceiling and the parquet floor. The floor marks off the dining-room area and separates it visually from the rest of the house.

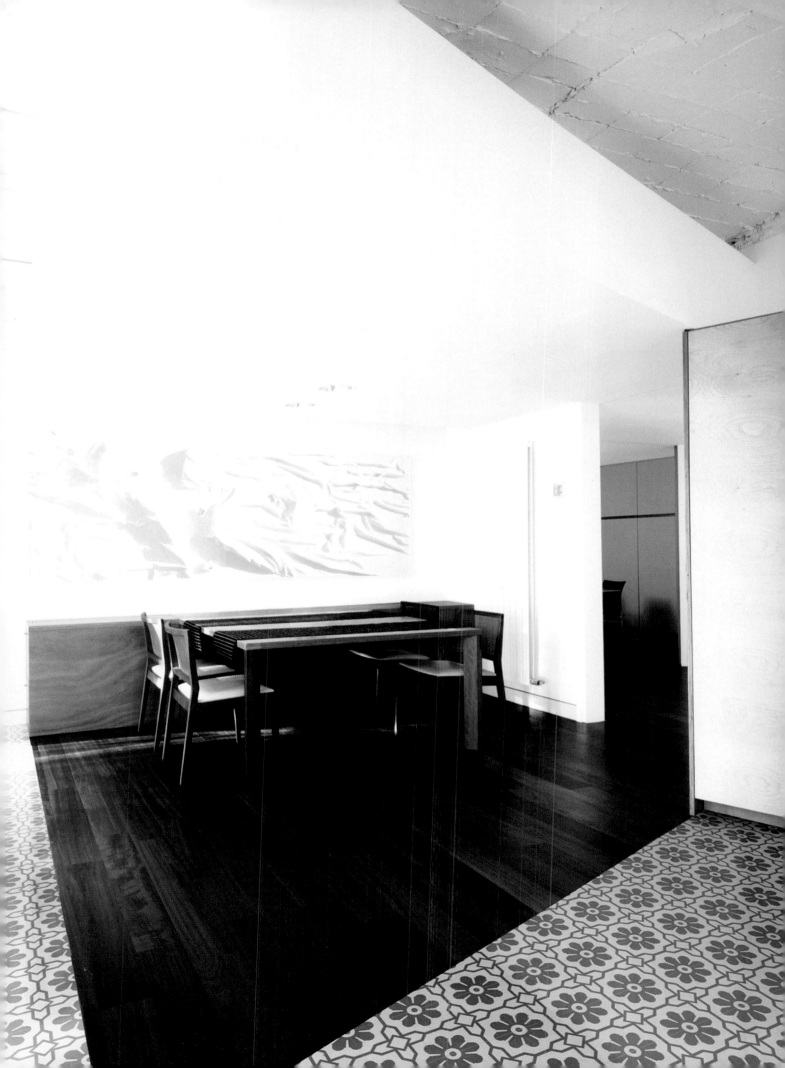

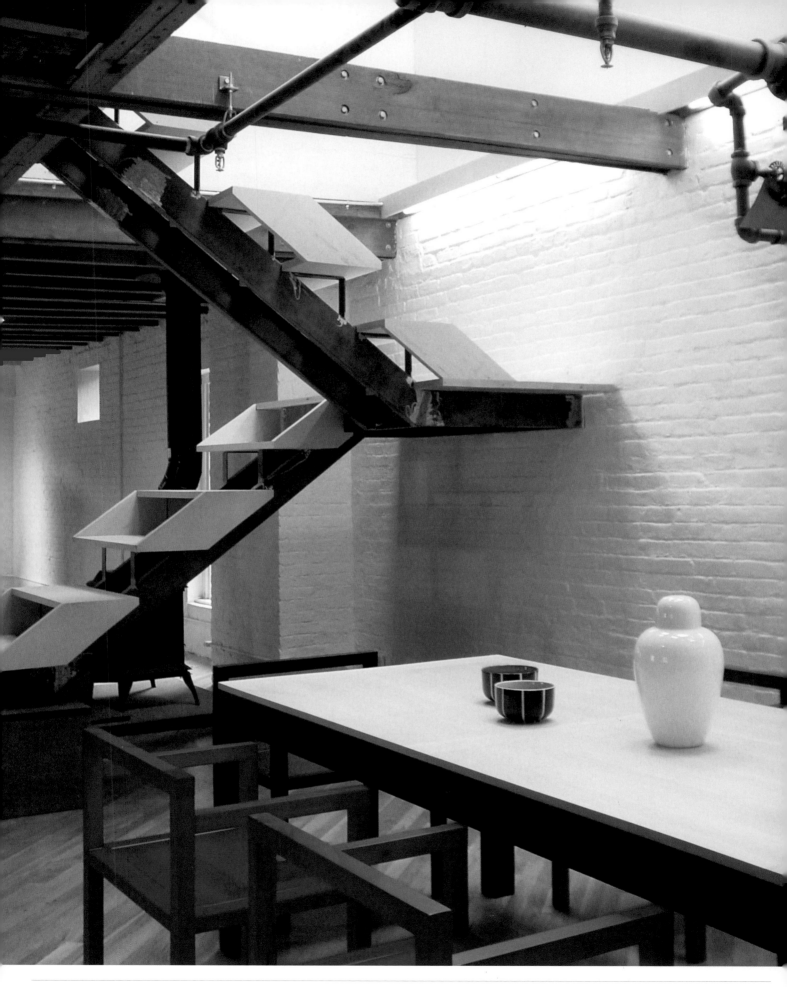

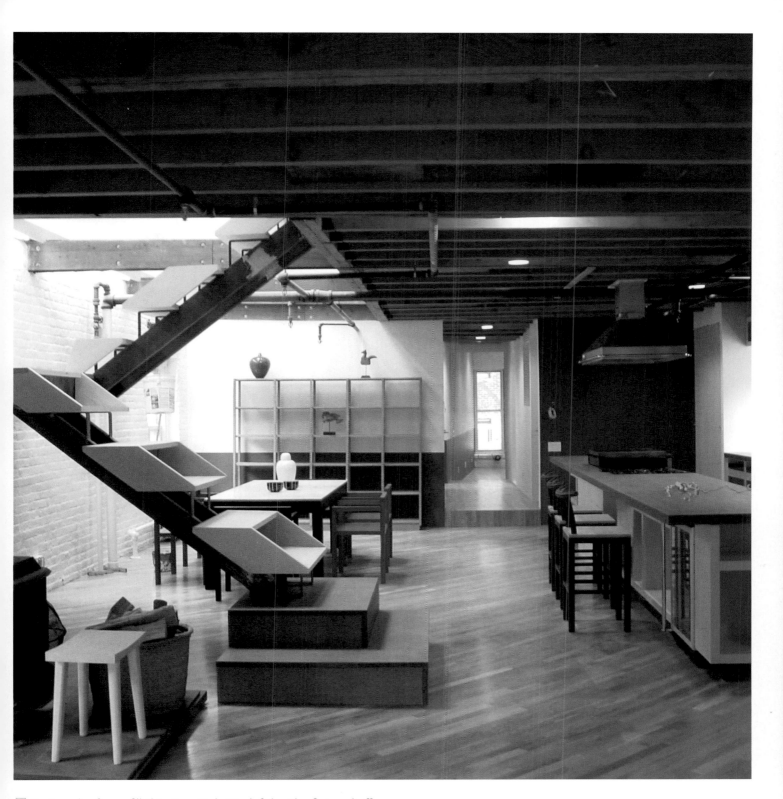

☐ Rectangular forms fill this New York City loft by Cha & Innerhoffer
Design, evoking its former function as a warehouse; even the steps of the
staircases are designed as if they were boxes.

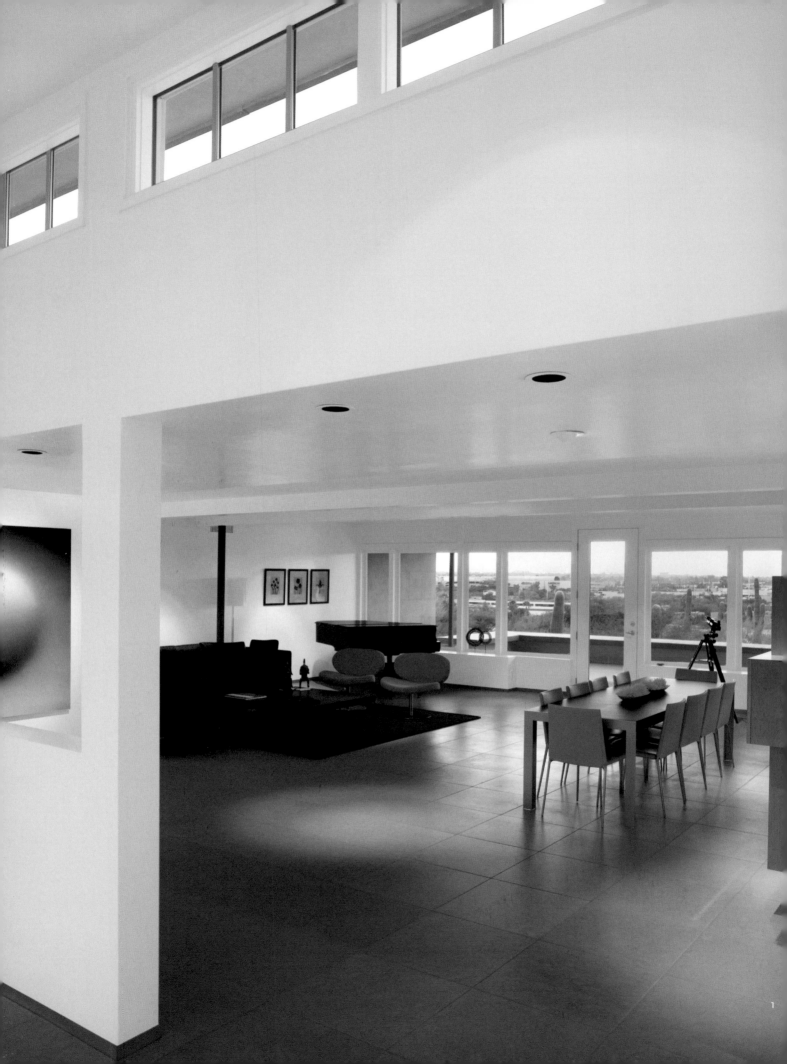

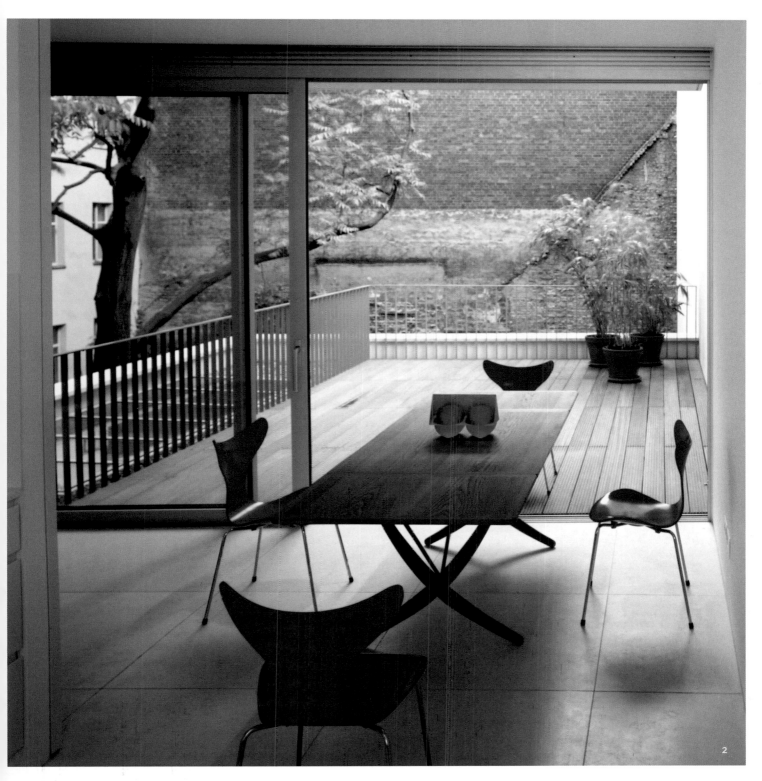

△ Jean Marc Abcarius and Christopher Burns—architects residing in Berlin but originally from Lebanon and the United States, respectively— have opted to set the dining room in the most luminous part of the house.

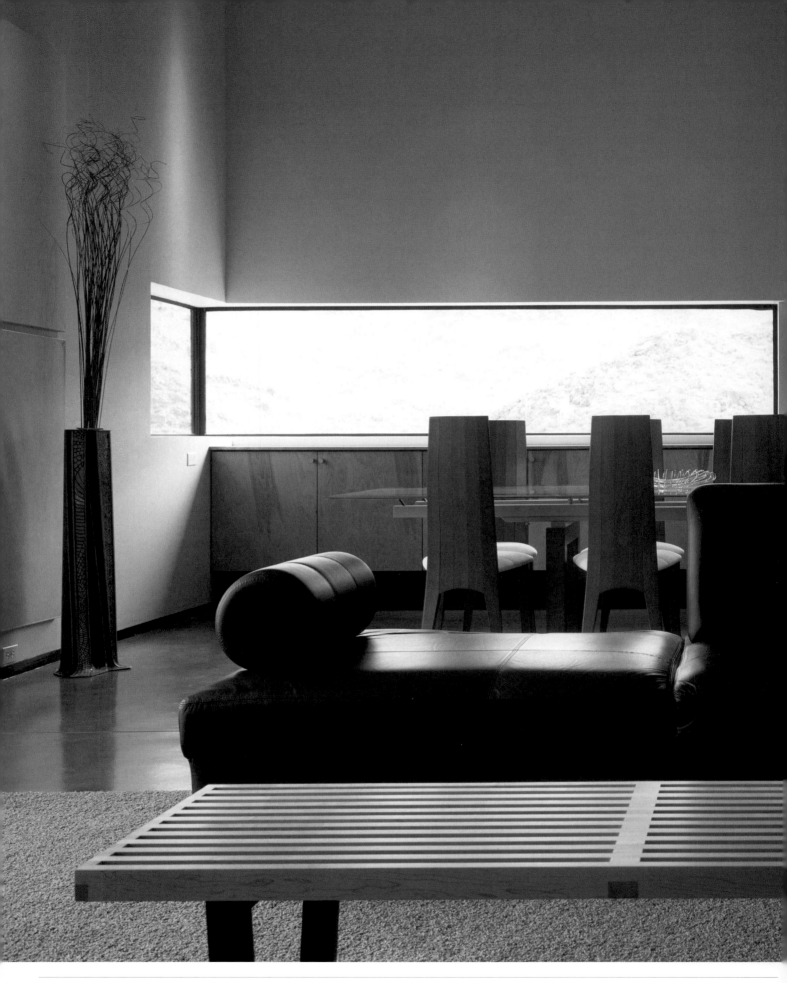

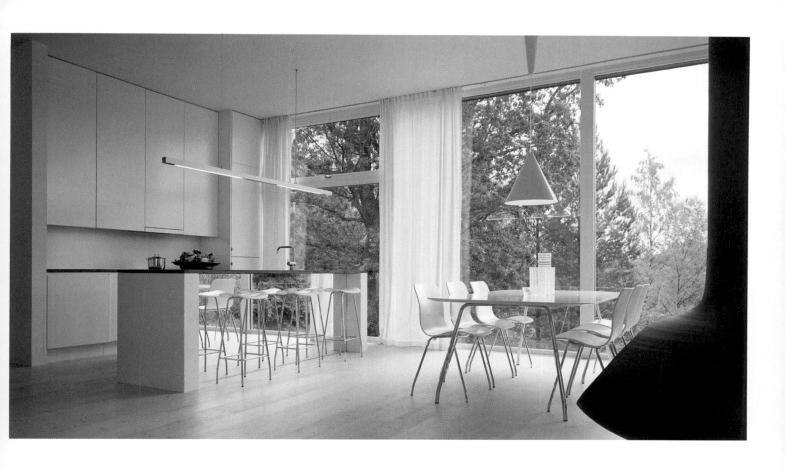

"Think rationally and, at the same time, cultivate an artistic sensibility." Henry van de Velde, 1903.

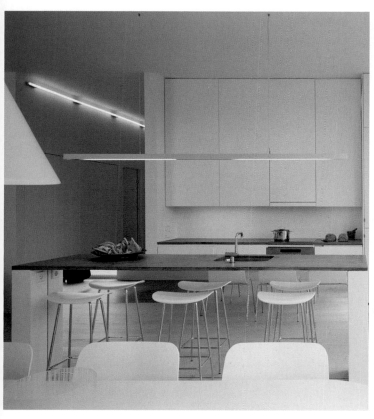

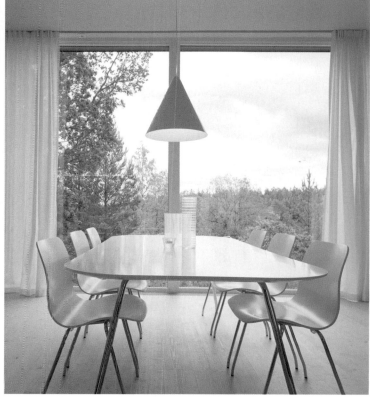

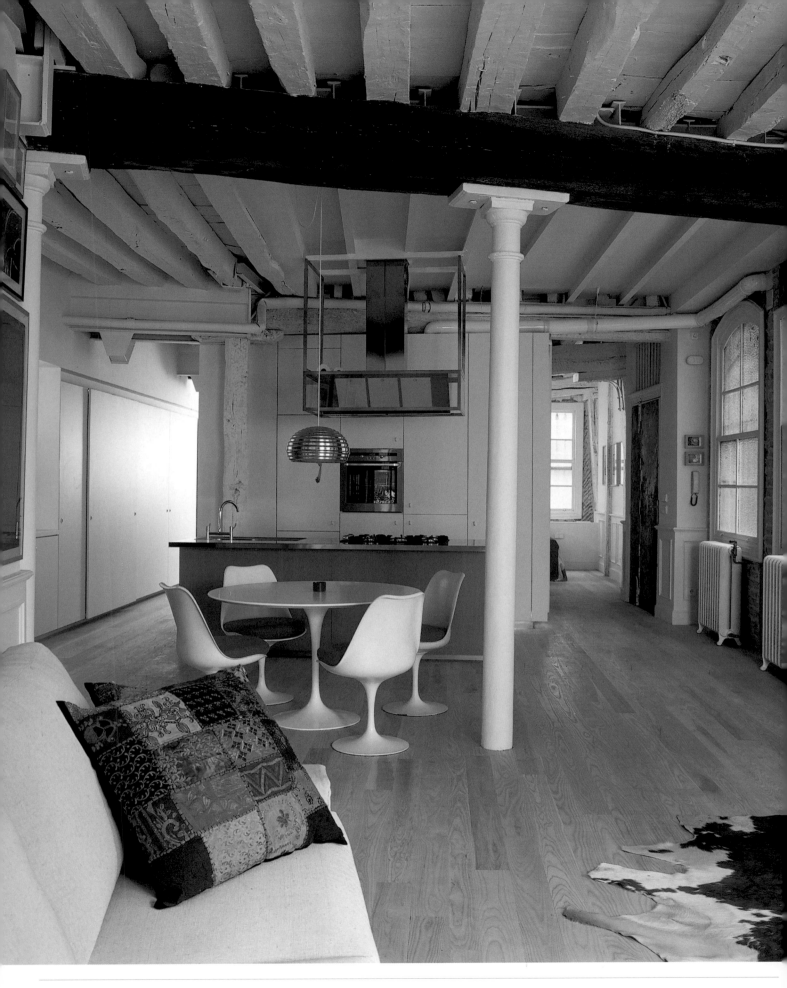

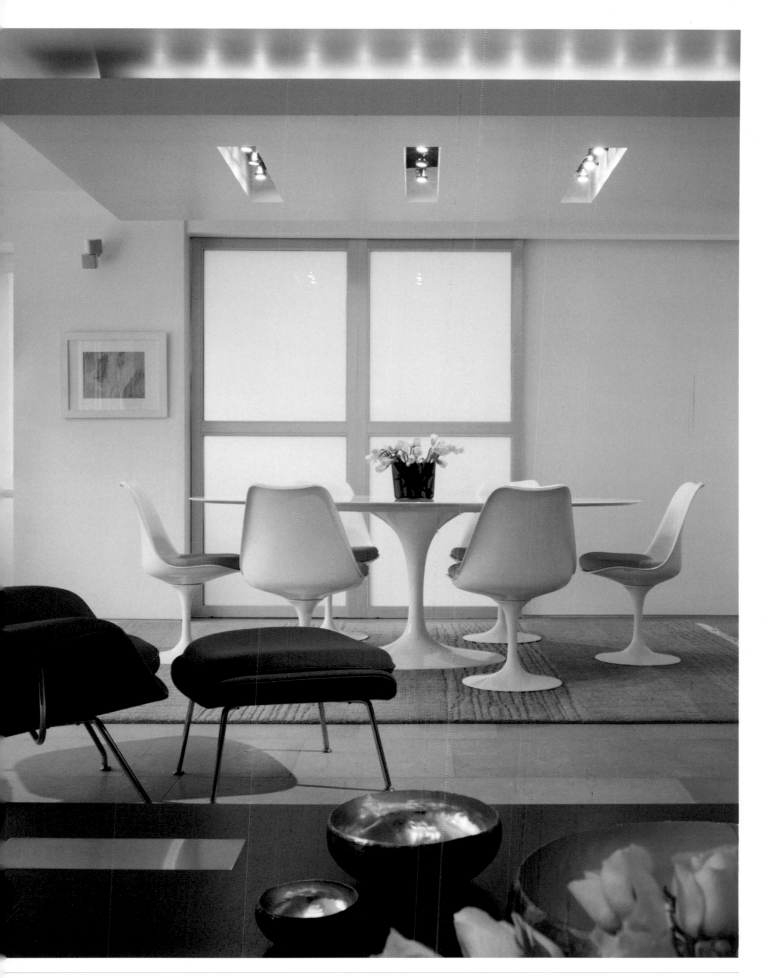

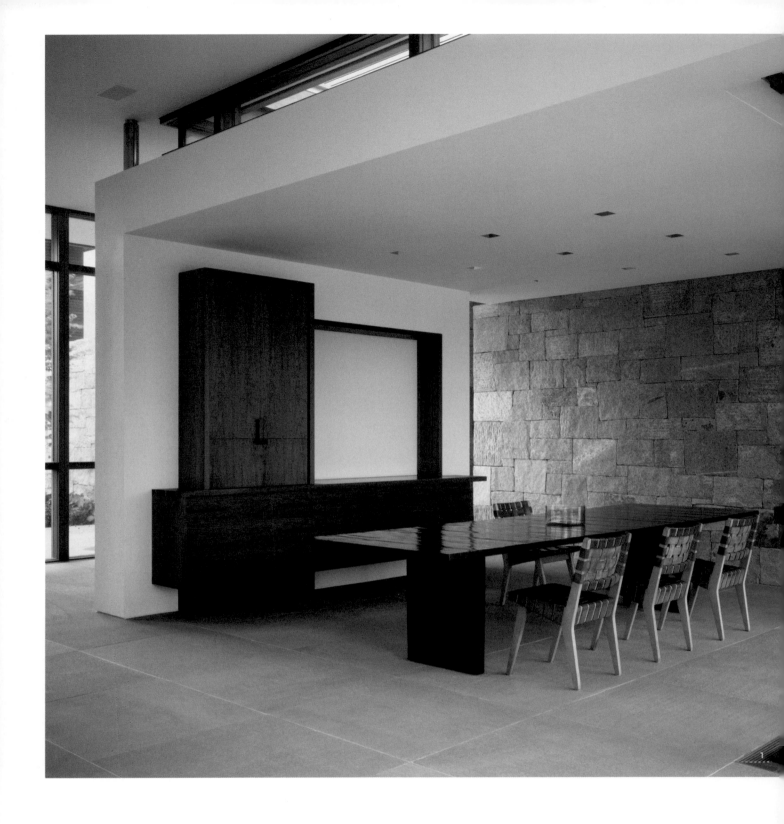

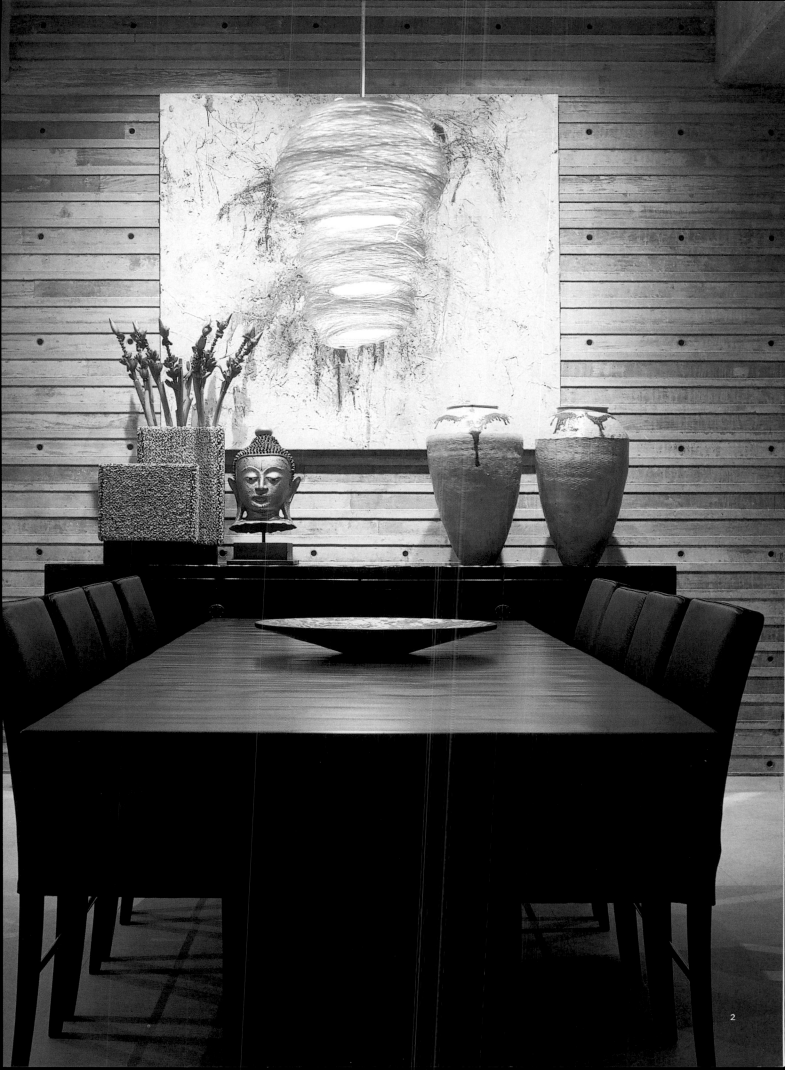

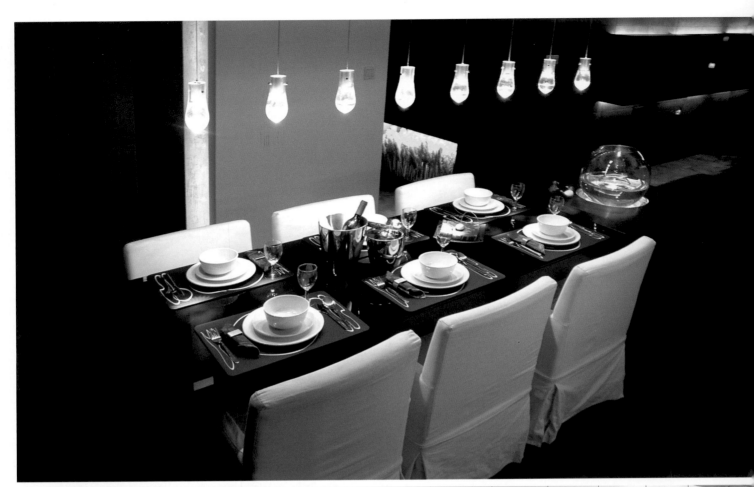

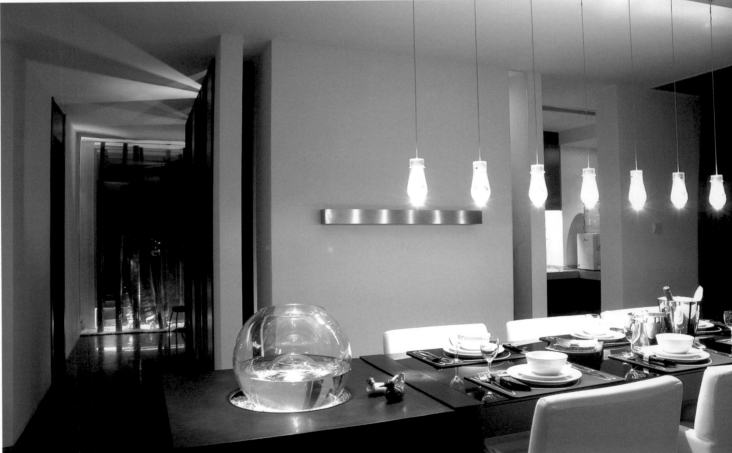

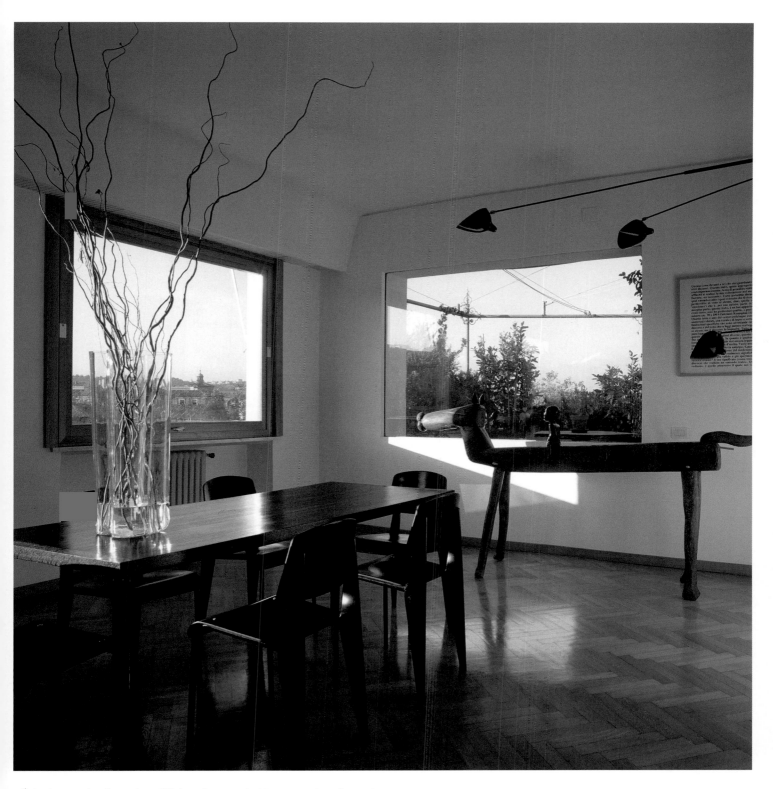

◁ An interesting interplay of light, glass, and chiaroscuro in a home in
Shanghai, the work of Milda Internacional.

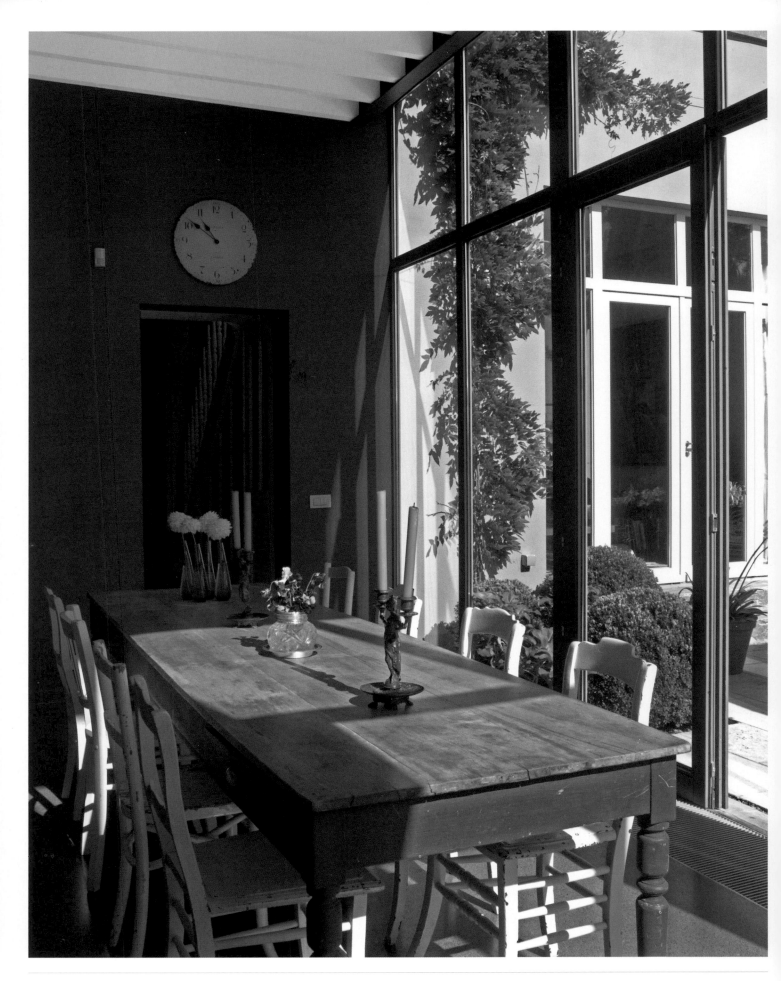

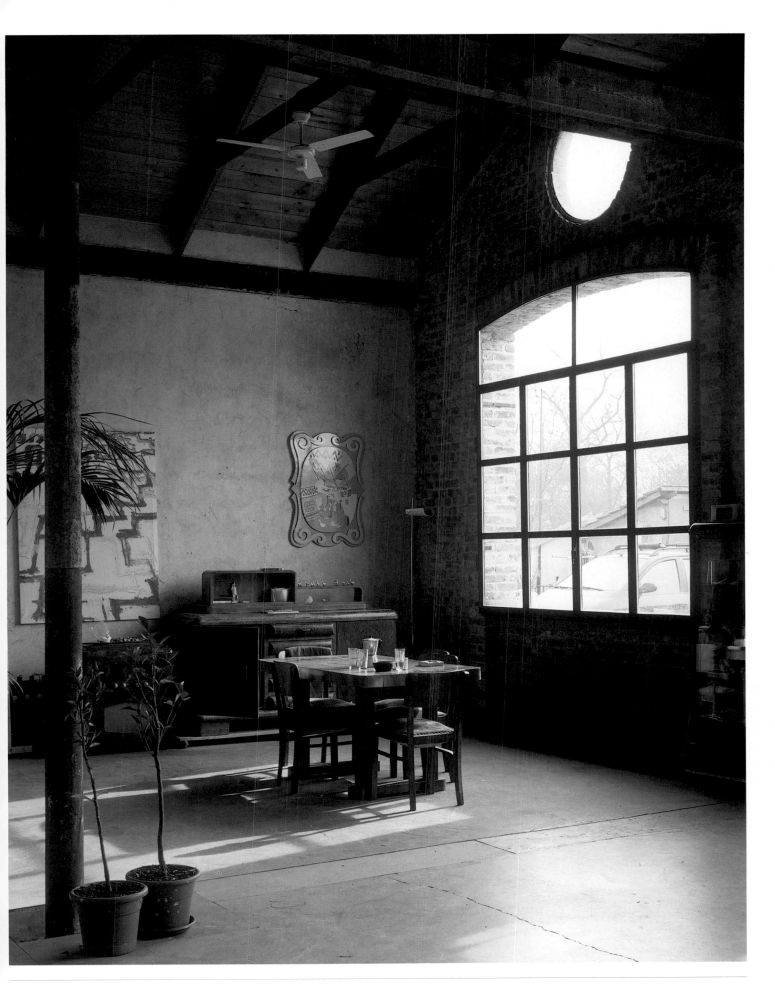

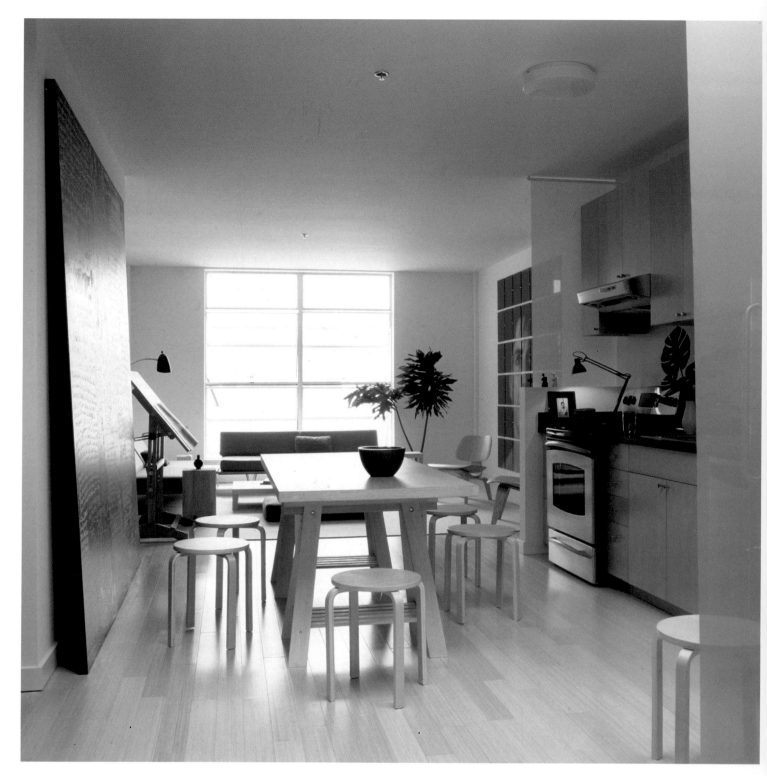

△ "I disregard fashions and trends. Creating a timeless and enduring interior is very important to me." Kerry Joyce, Los Angeles, USA.

© Dominique Vorillon

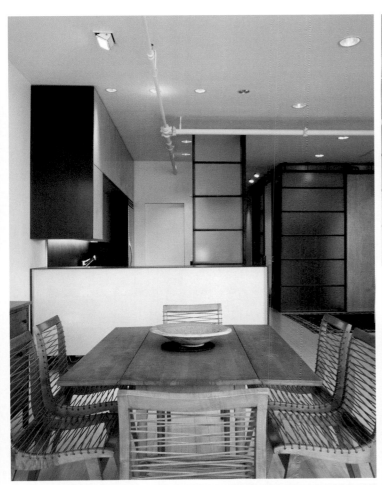
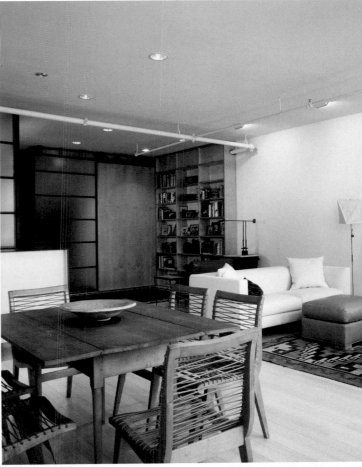
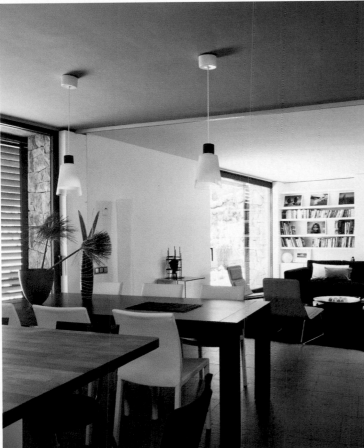
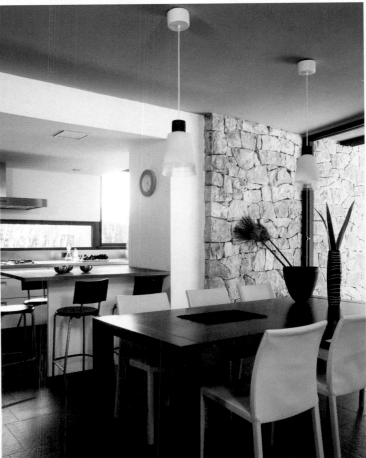

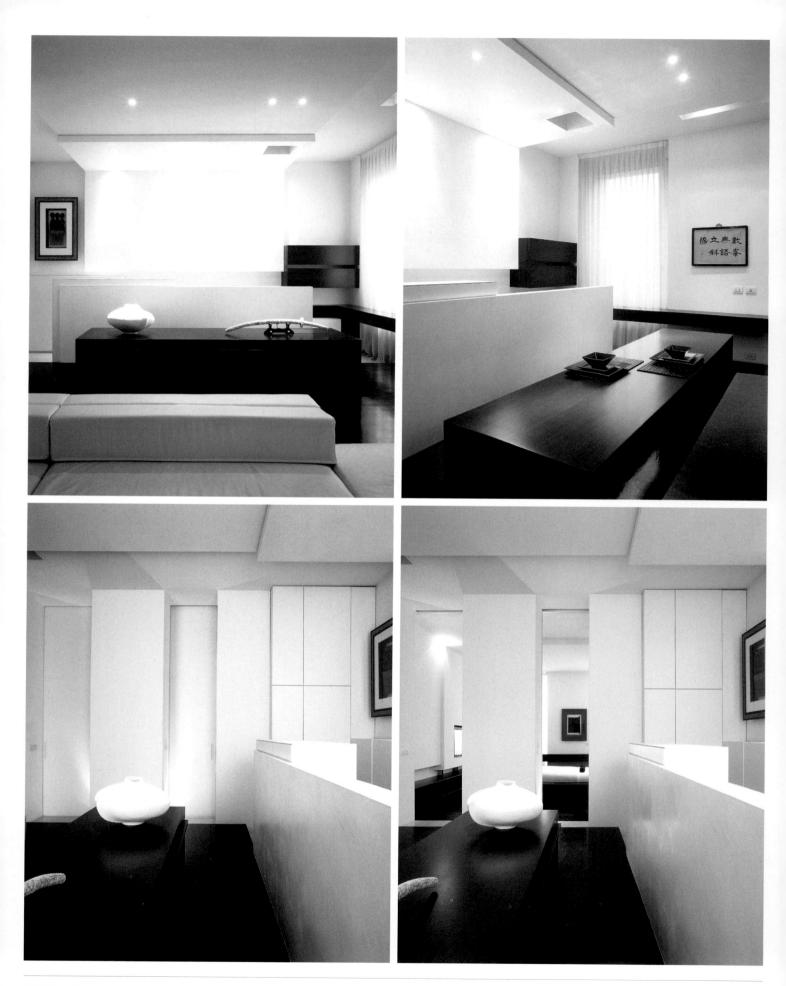

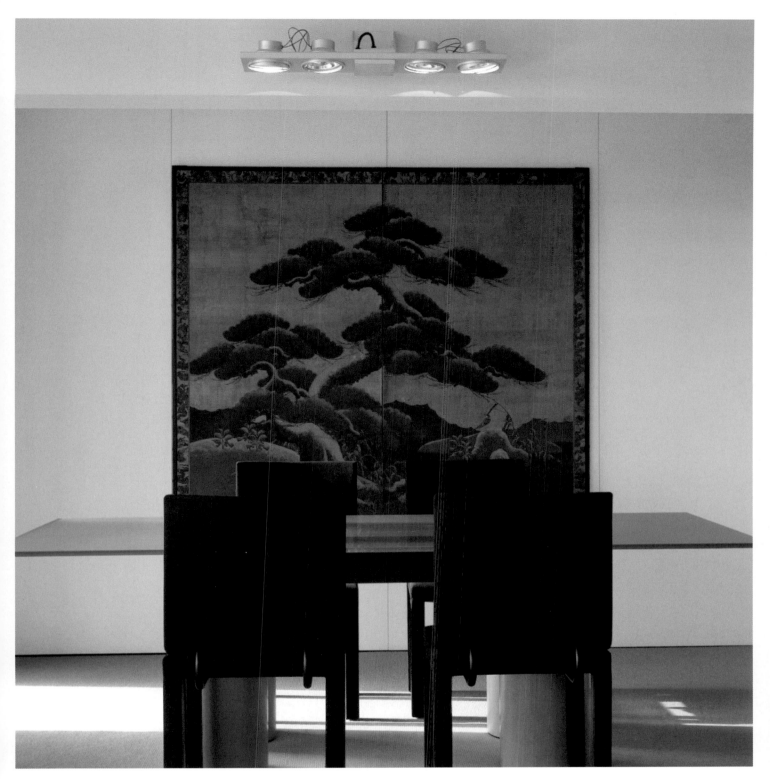

△ The Zen style in architecture goes back to the 13th century, when it spread from the monasteries to upper-class houses, before permeating other strata of society. The principles of Zen architecture have influenced 20th-century architects like Bruno Taut, Mies van der Rohe, and Frank Lloyd Wright, and they are apparent nowadays in the work of Tadao Ando and John Pawson. This is due to the timelessness of Zen's constructional premises: simple materials, an intense relationship with nature and the suppression of any superfluous and unnecessary elements.

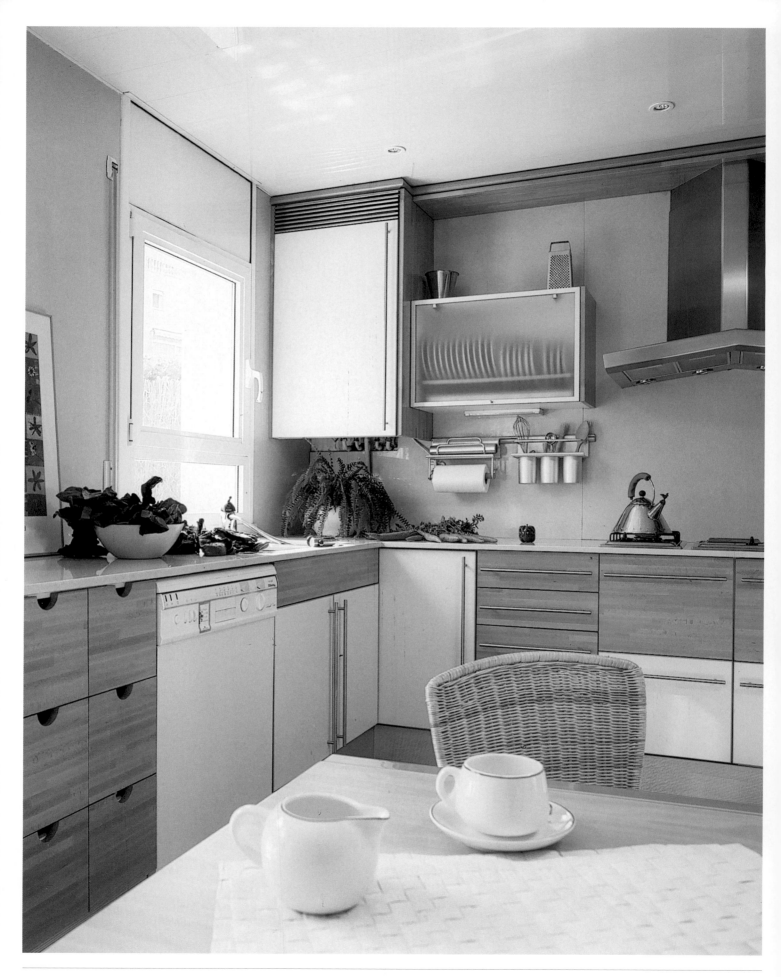

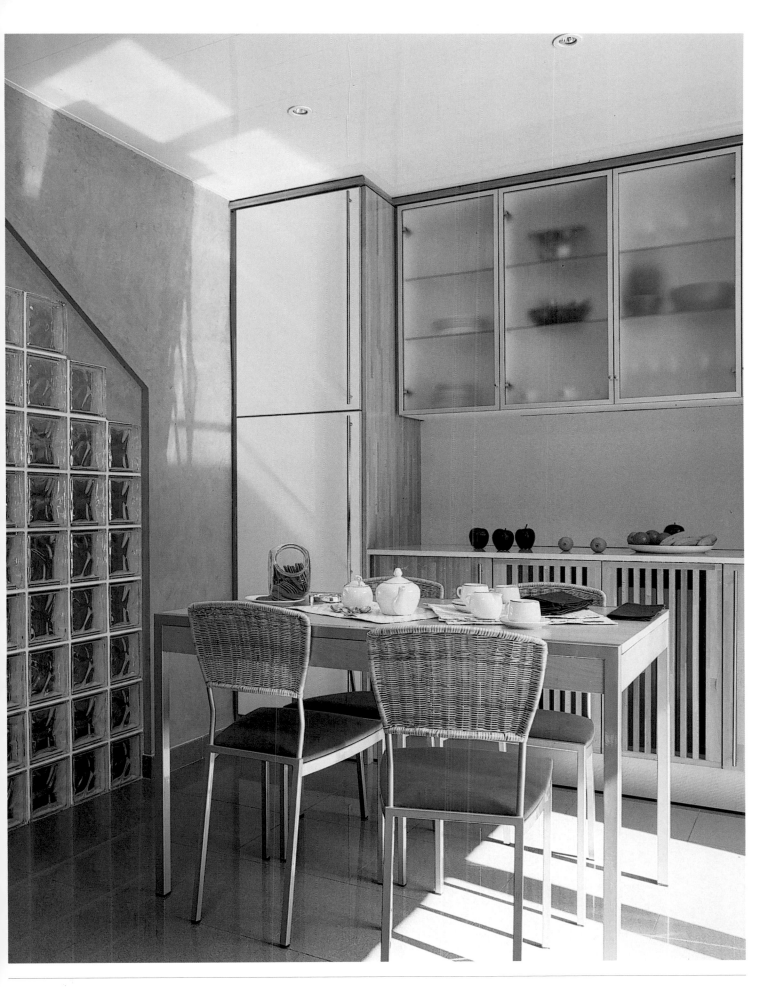

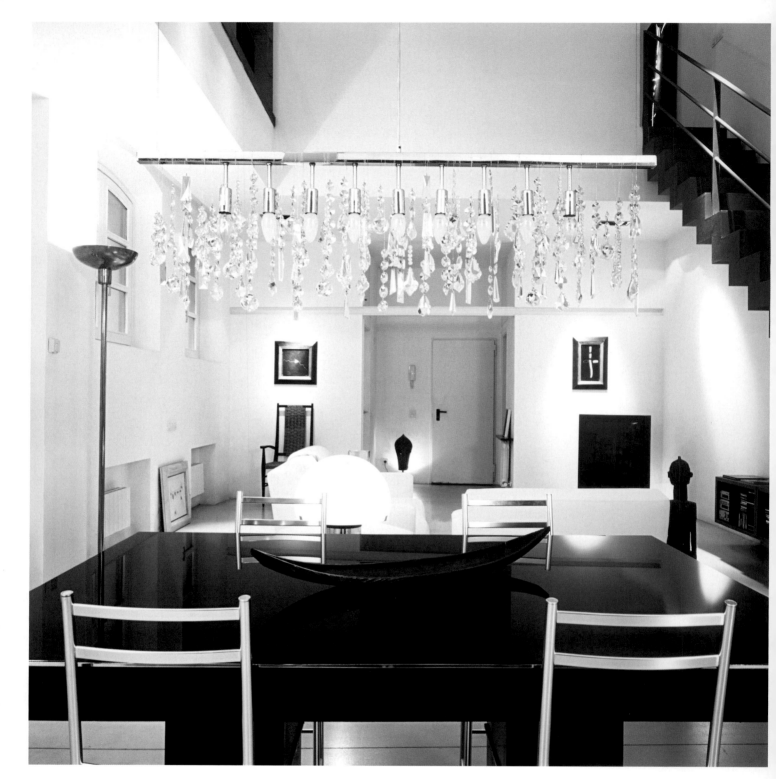

Elegance and sobriety are not a contradiction in terms. In this duplex in Barcelona, a kitchen designed according to clearly minimalist and industrial precepts is given an almost rococo twist by a reinterpretation of the chandelier. An interesting, almost theatrical effect is achieved by making the lamp the same length as the table, so that it hangs over the table like a stage curtain.

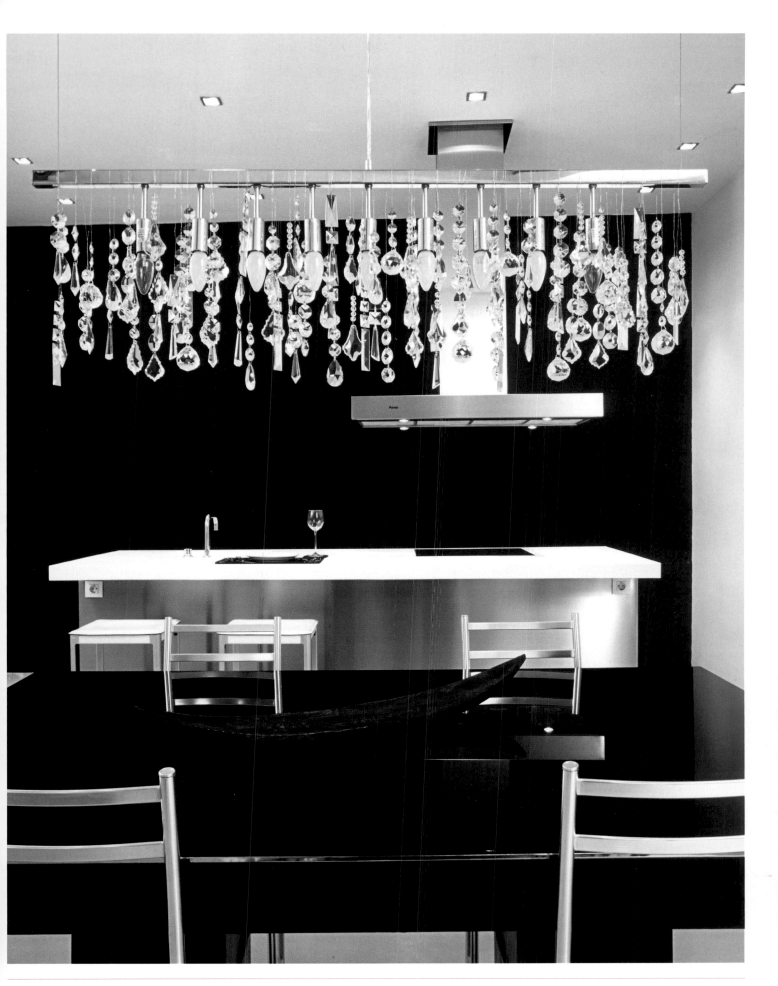

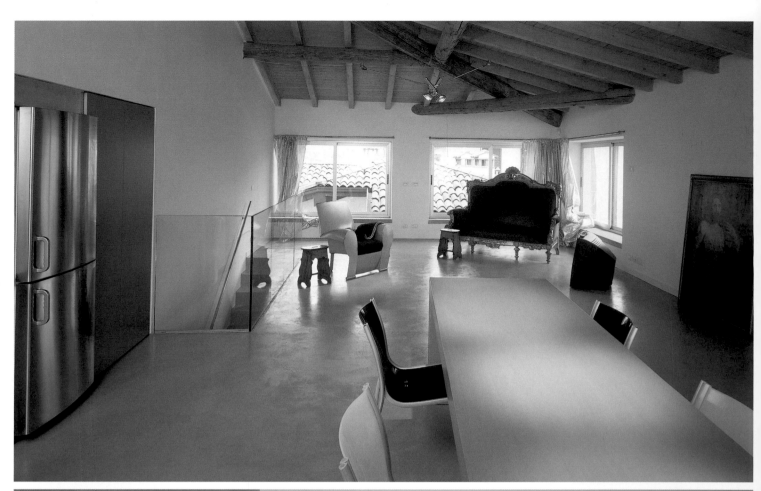

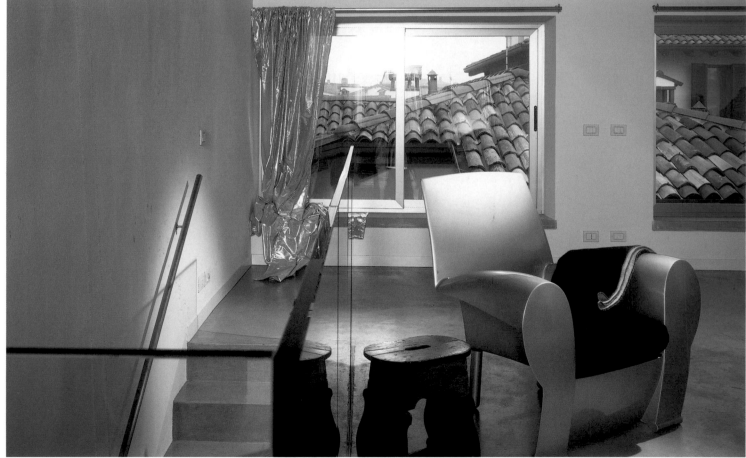

© Andrea Martiradonna

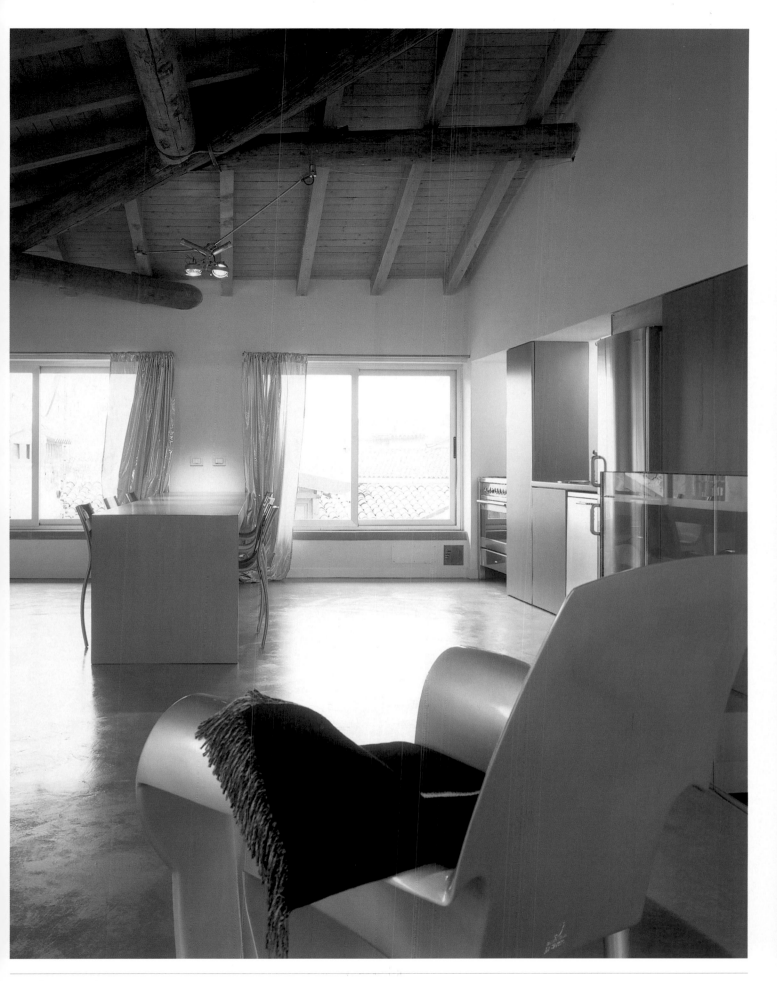

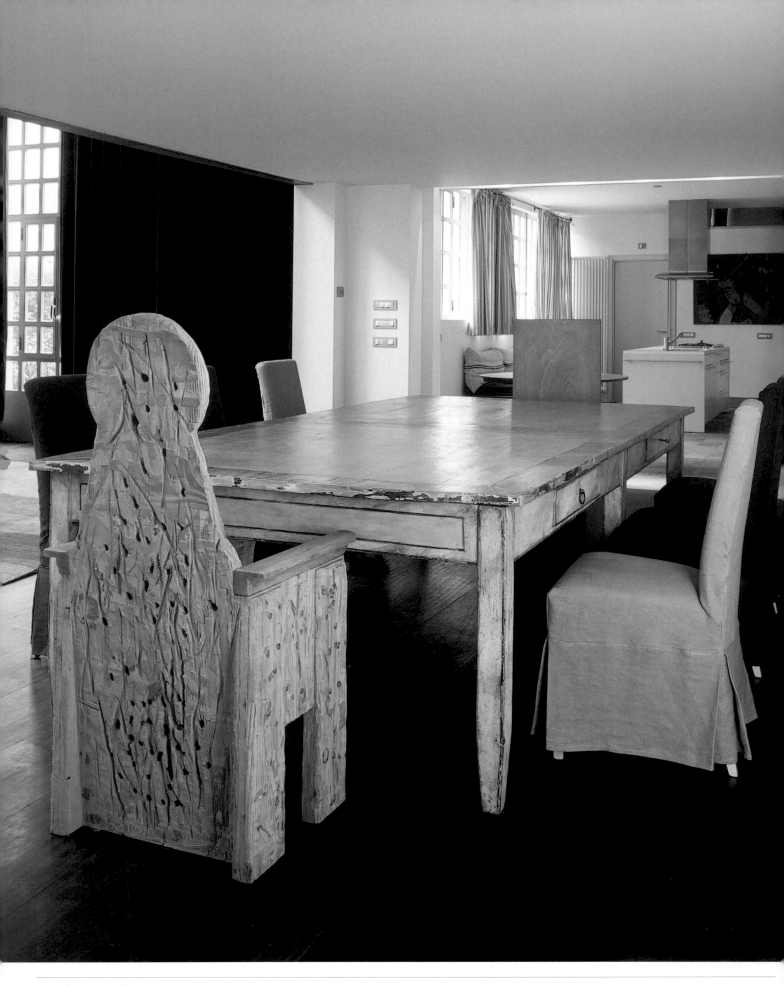

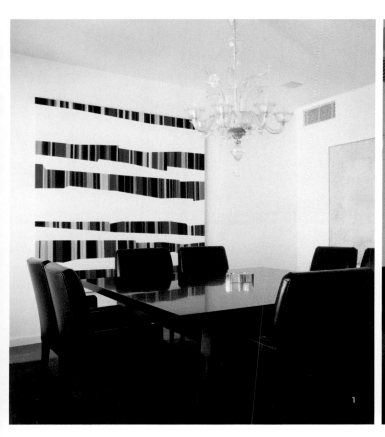

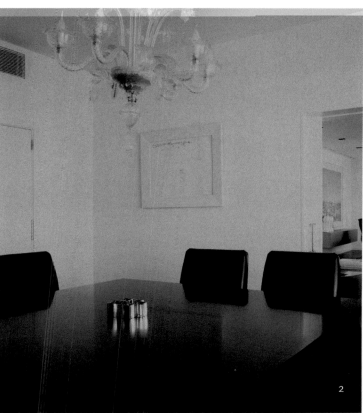

Space permitting, the introduction of a table and chairs with personality can prove an effective stratagem.

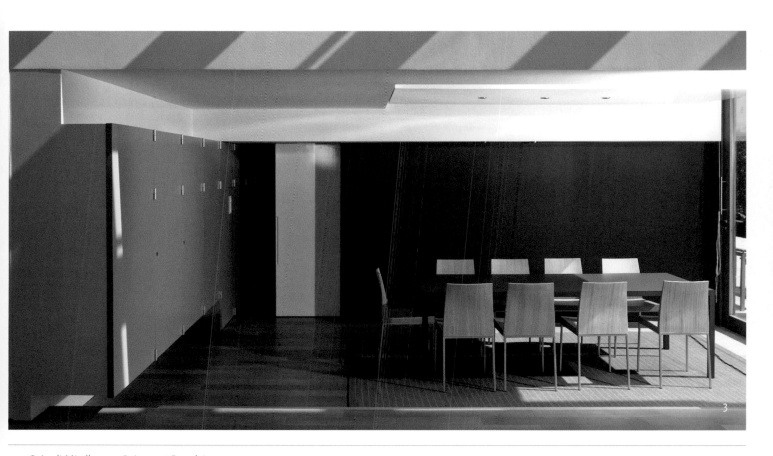

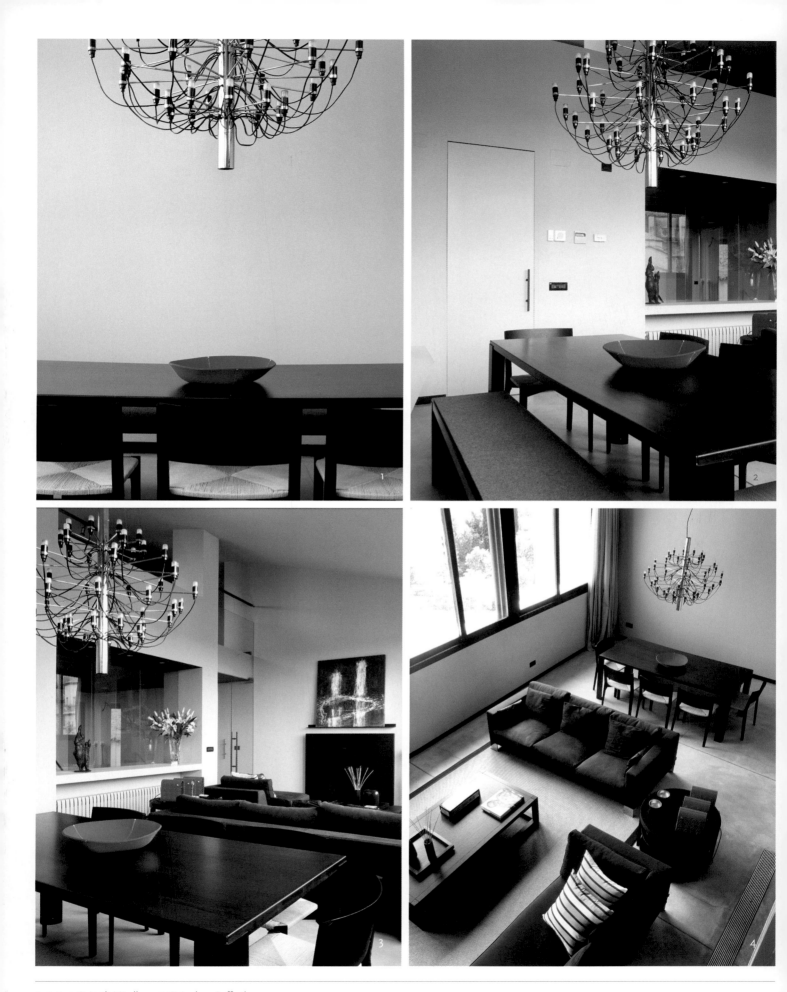

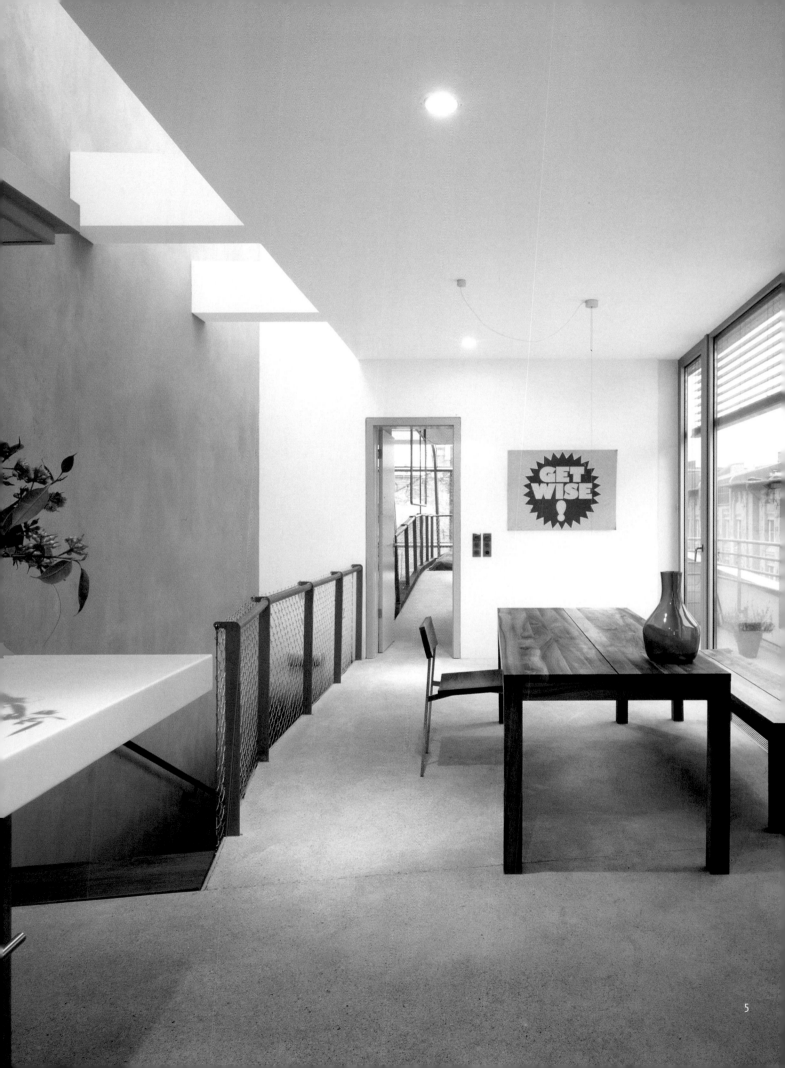

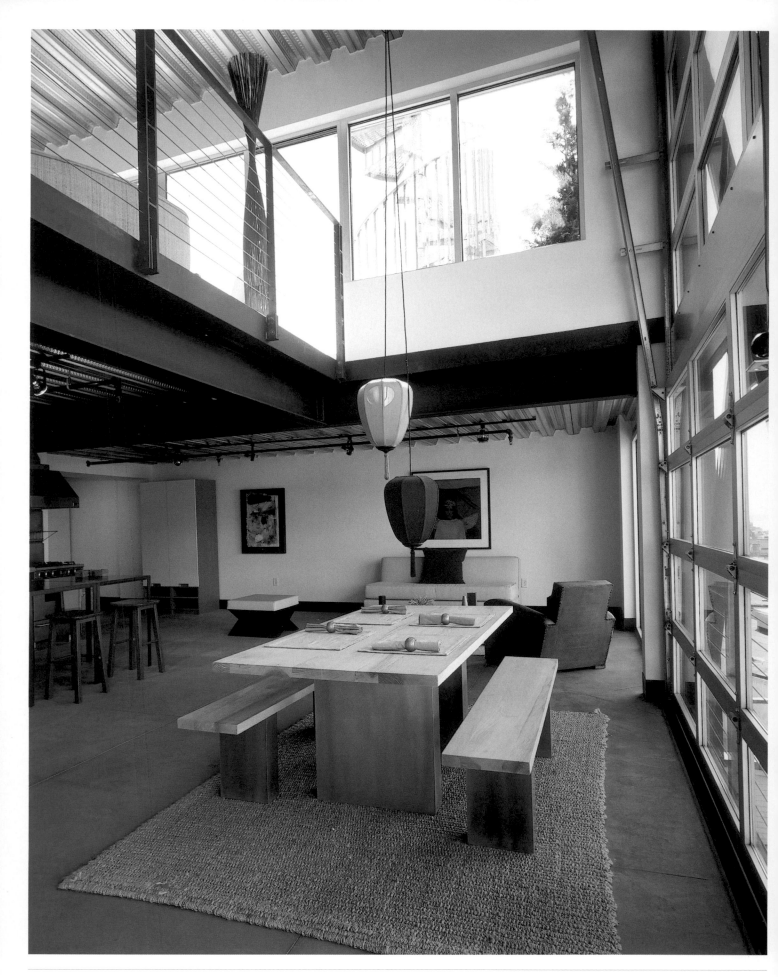

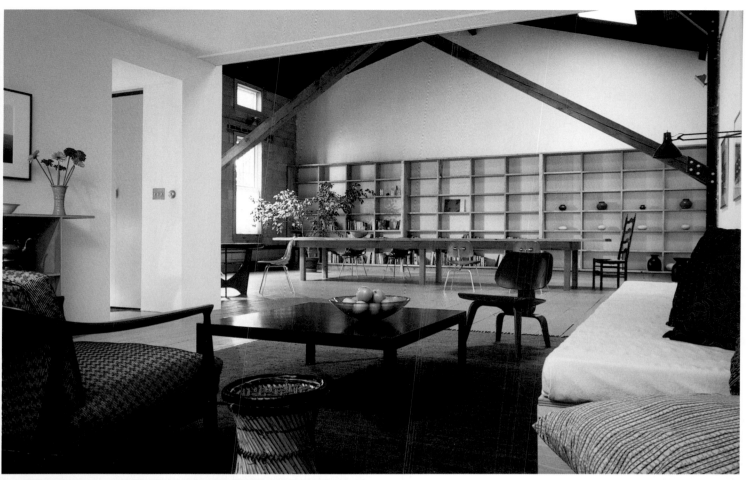

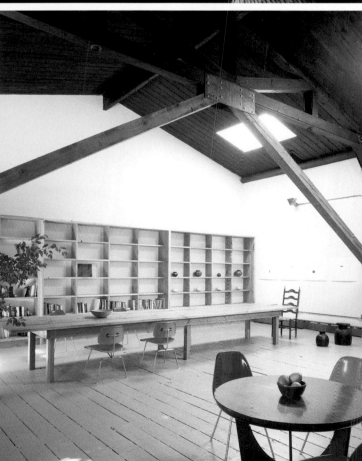

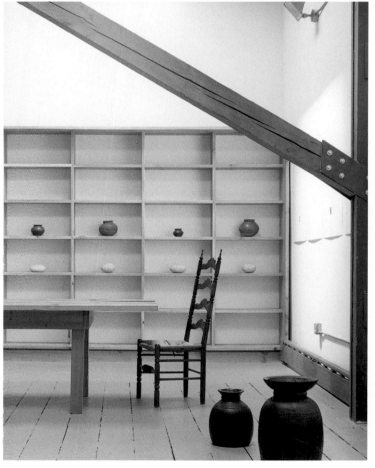

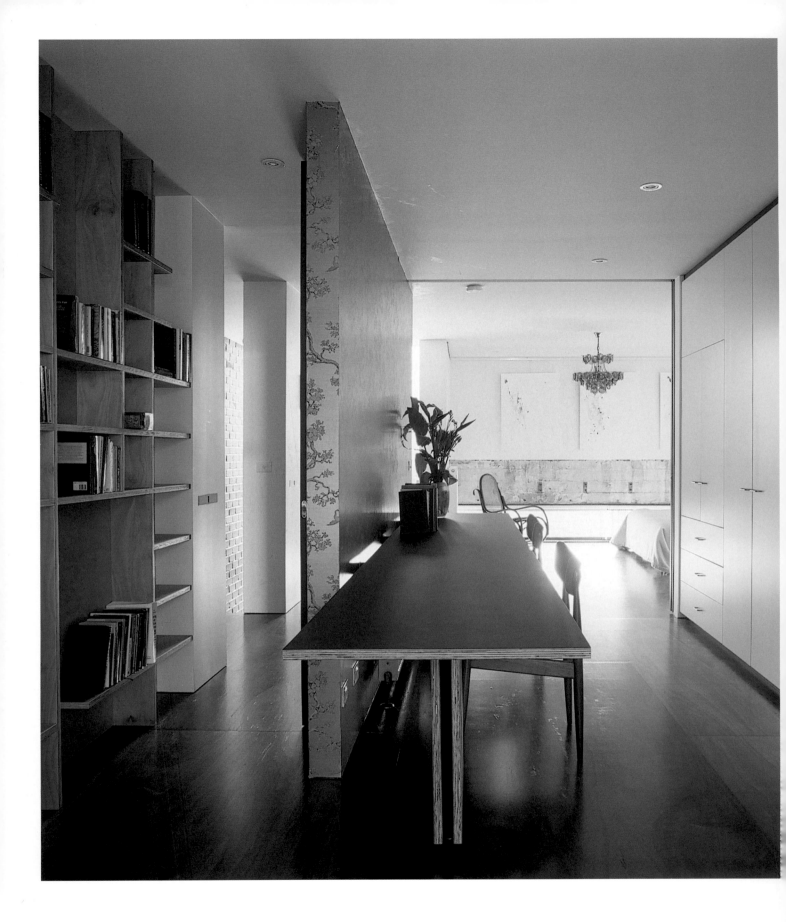

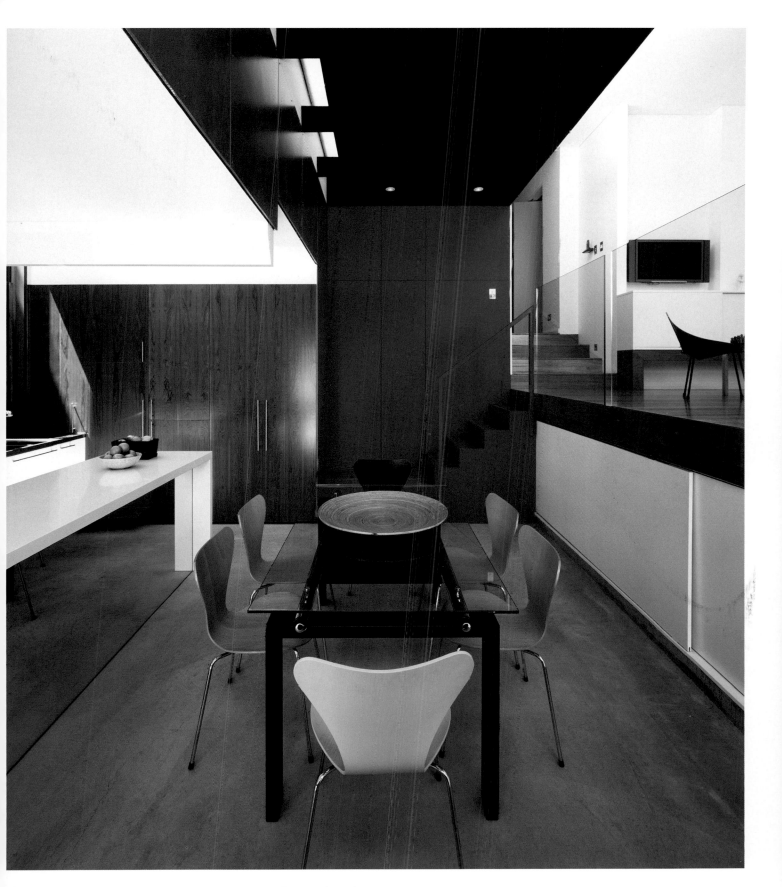

△ Cubist interior design: asymmetry and a mixture of materials, colors, lighting, furniture, and visual textures.

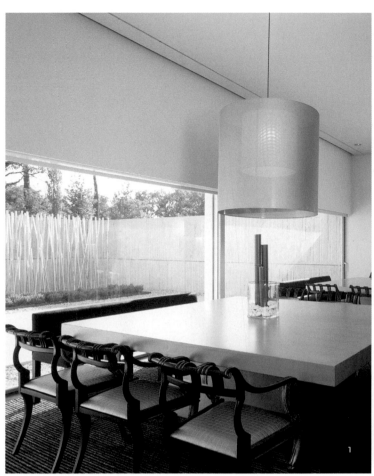

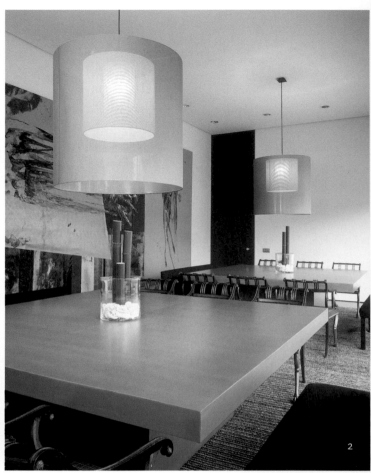

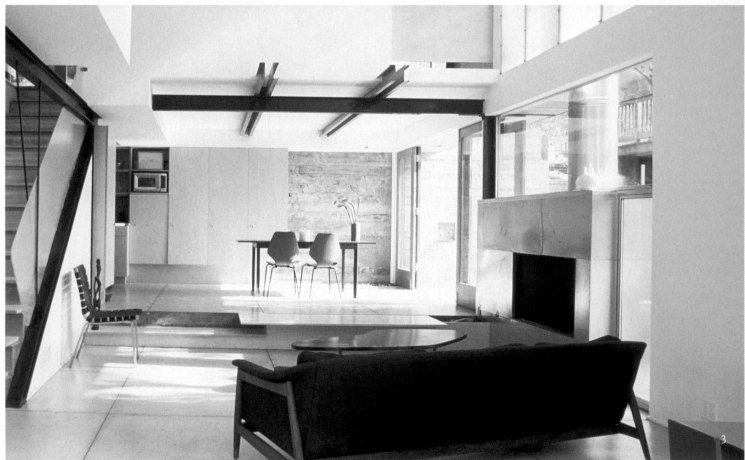

1,2 © Eugeni Pons   3 © Deborah Bird

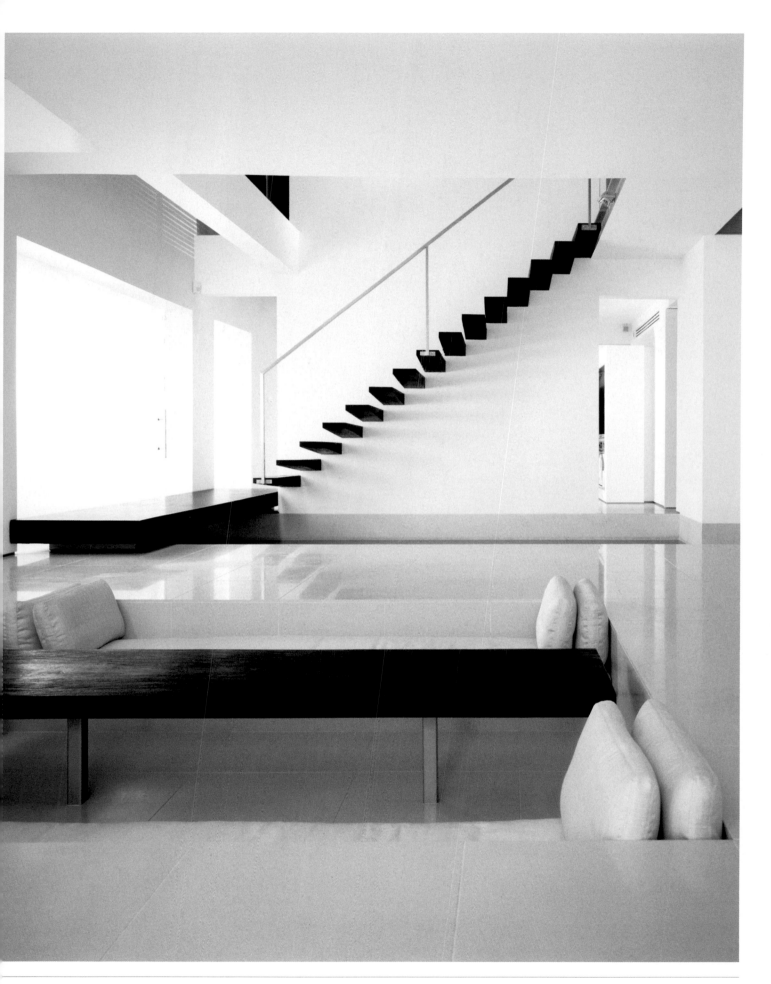

173

Living Rooms

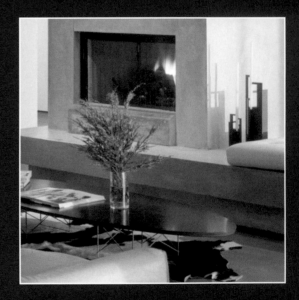

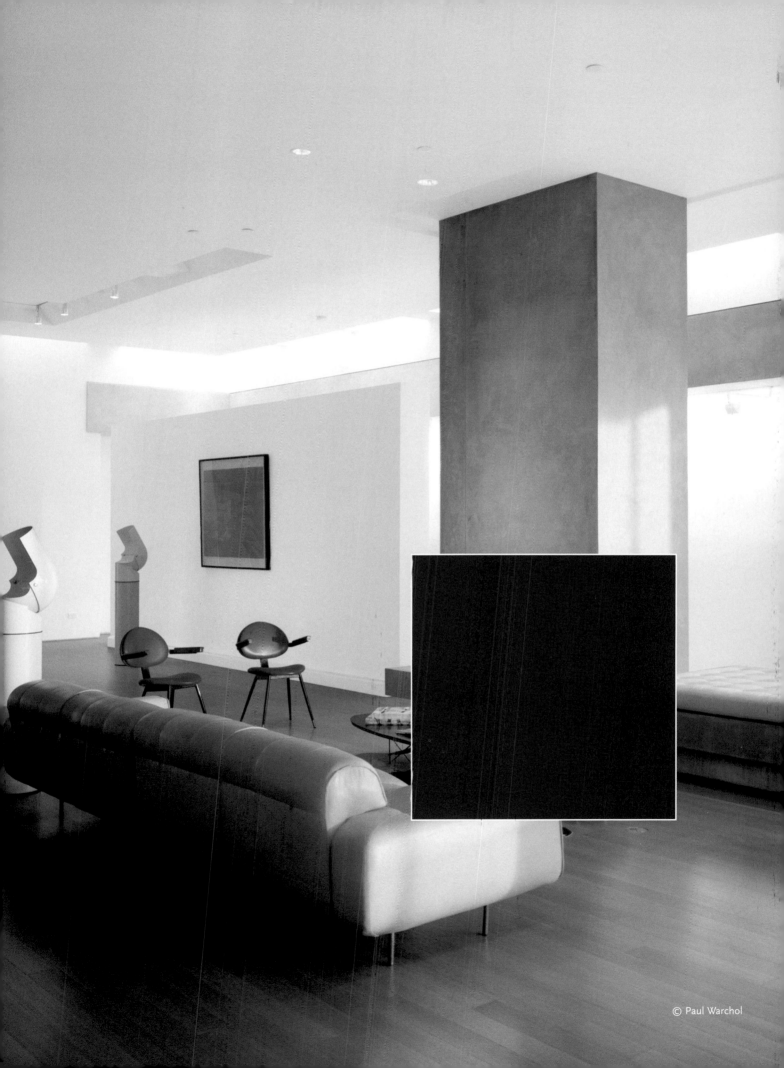

Living Rooms

A soothing retreat after every day's frenzy

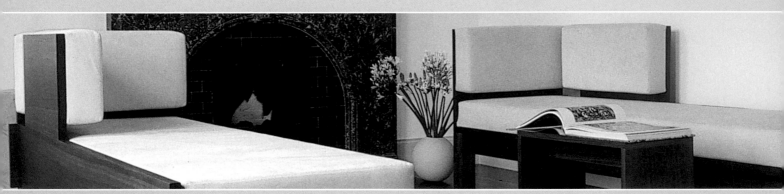

© Christoph Kicherer

Worldwide, homes have always reserved a place for gathering, sharing, and relaxing; in other words, they have a living room. Today these rooms are changing. Communications have taken cultures far beyond their former limits, and so it is with architecture and design, which often try to join aesthetic and practical values. They are no longer based on traditional patterns, but rather on the mixture, fusion, and exchange of cultural references.

The evolution of the home has reached a stage where the distribution of its spaces is similar around the world, varying only slightly from place to place. Nevertheless, diversity and innovation can be achieved by adding new elements designed to improve our quality of life.

New trends in living room design may echo Asian influences in furnishings such as stools and tables, as well as the materials used. Other trends include the revival of designs from earlier designers, such as Mies van der Rohe, Alvar Aalto, and Nana Ditzel. All these trends reflect a growing awareness and pursuit of spiritual well-being and a rejection of materialism.

Contemporary forms tend to favor comfort and the use of natural materials. Elements that were previously considered essential have tended to disappear. The concepts of "old-fashioned" and "brand new" are no longer absolute, nor are styles exclusively eastern or western. In general, new design trends aim at improving the quality of life. Among the styles shown in this book are new rococo, post-industrialism, retro, and neo-rural. They display the relationship between people and their environment, and they illustrate how living rooms are conceived as the places in which to unwind after a hard day's work. They have less furniture than before, more space, and prove an ideal setting for calming both body and mind.

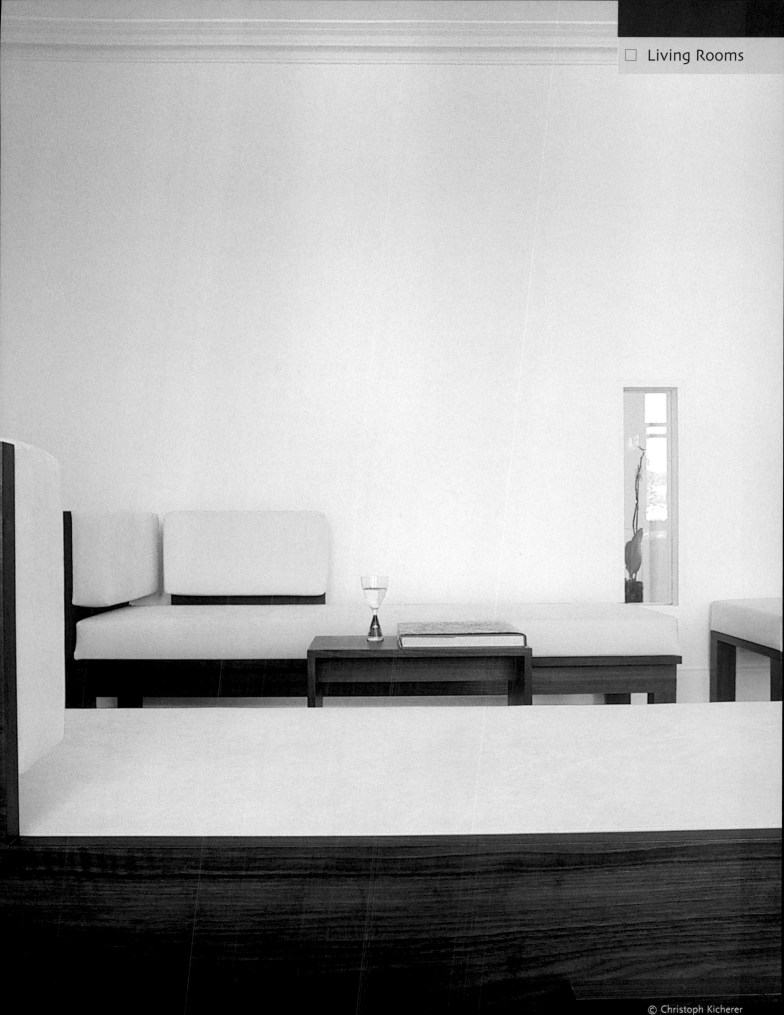

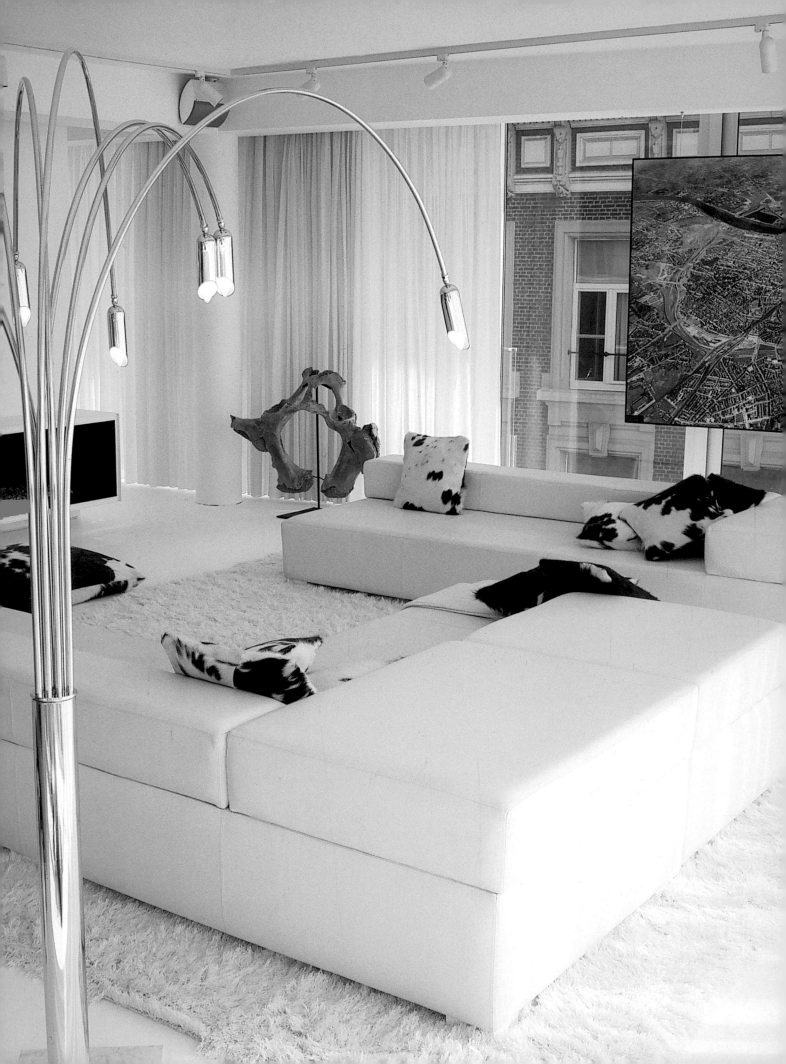

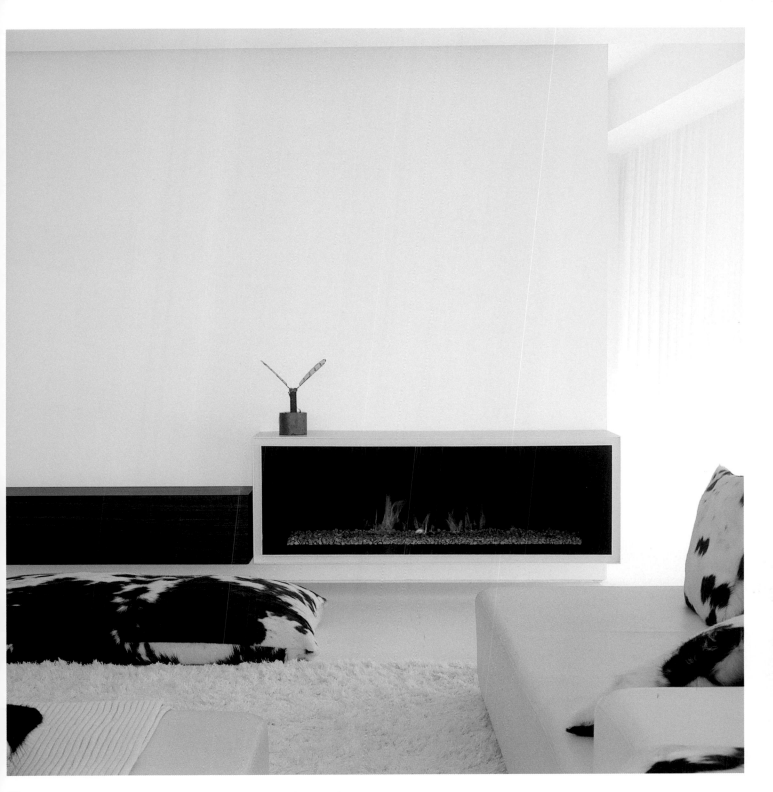

☐ This house in an Italian town reflects a development of minimalism, as ethnic elements and warm materials have been added to provide a warmer feel. The use of white and the classic straight lines of minimalism are combined with forms that evoke the natural world, such as the lamp whose outline recalls a tree or a jet of water.

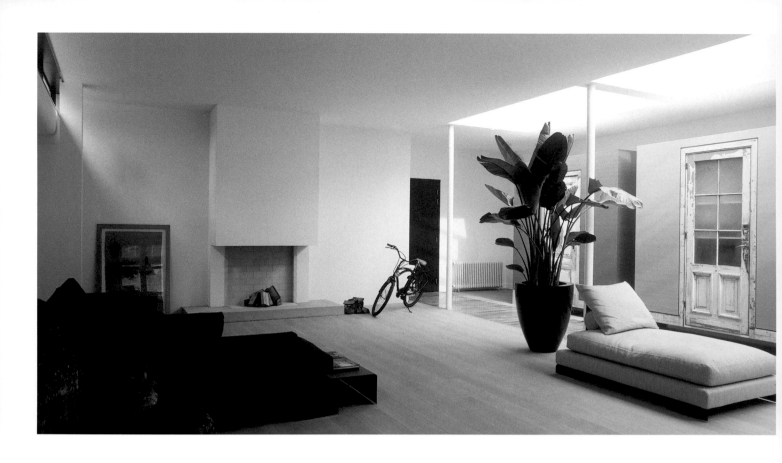

The refurbishment of spaces is a reinterpretation of something that already exists. Here the design disrupts the symmetry and uniformity with small details like the paint on the doors.

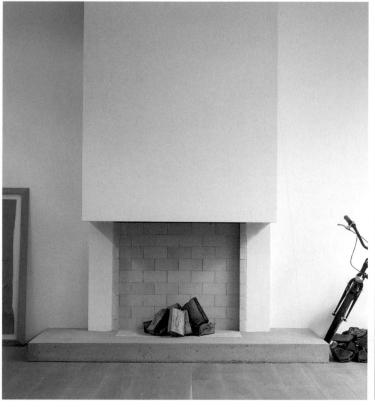

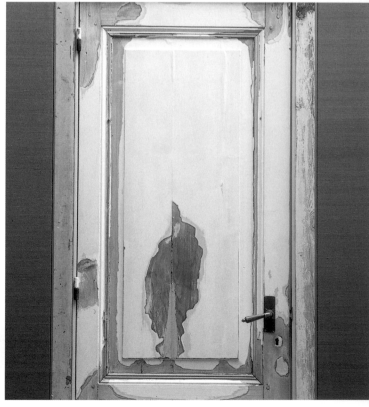

© Giorgio Possenti/Vega MG

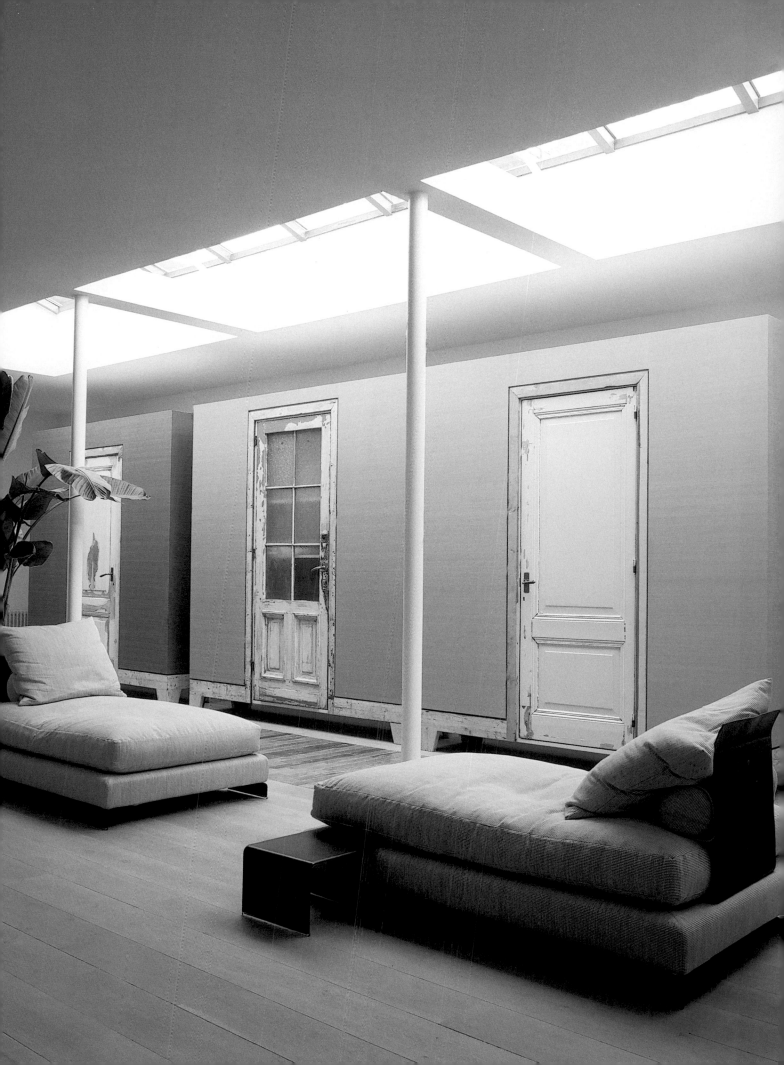

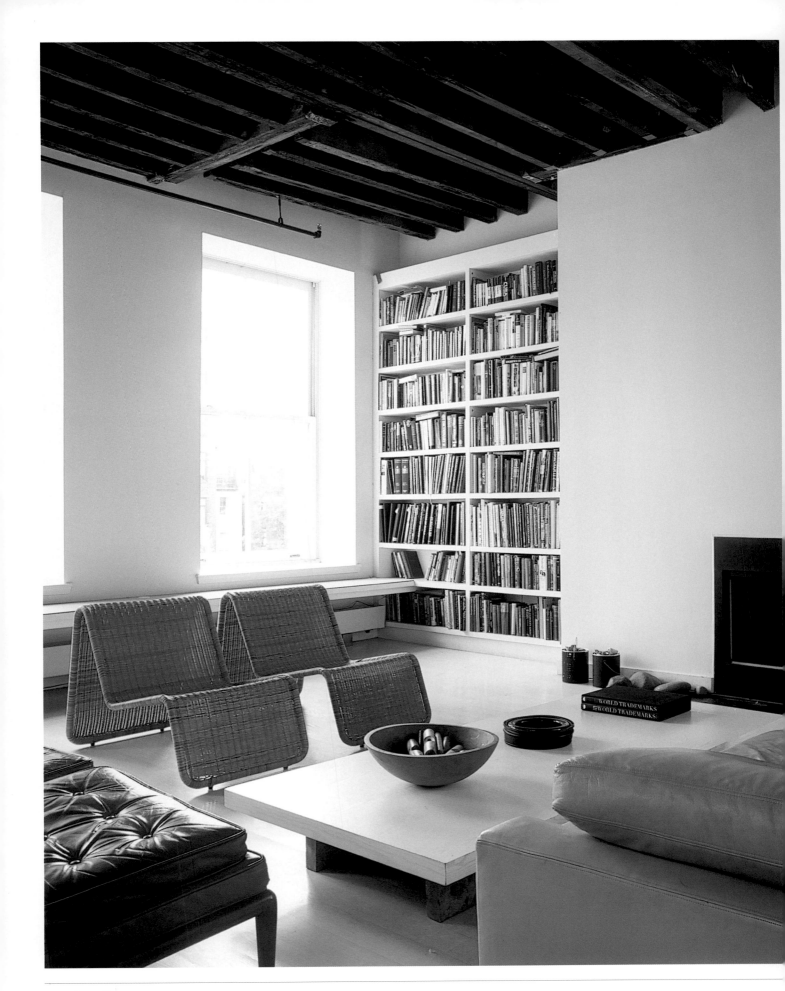

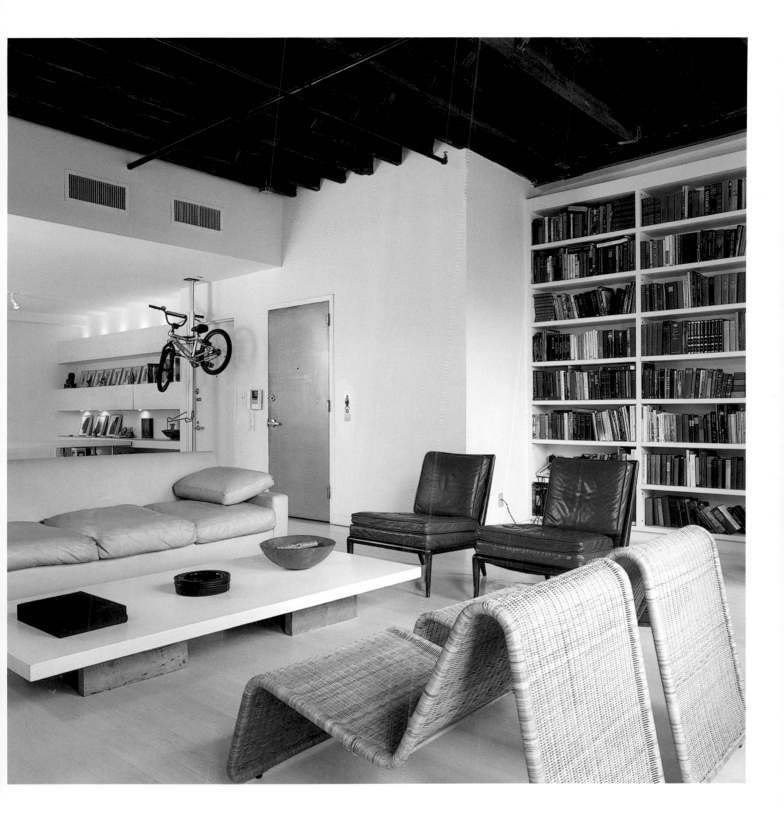

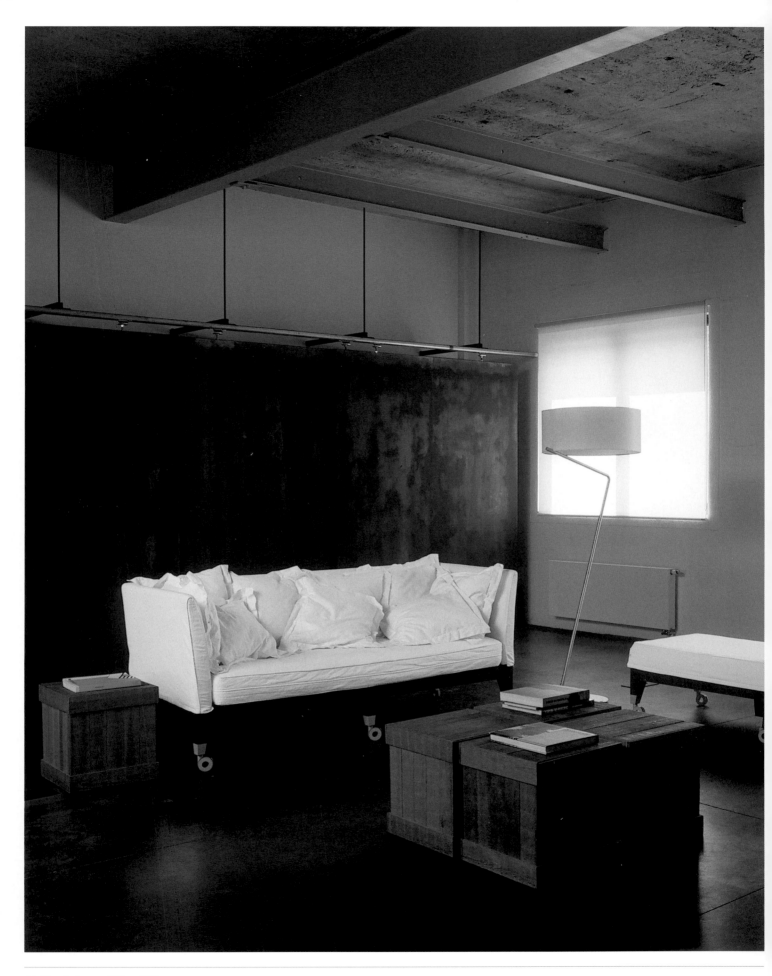

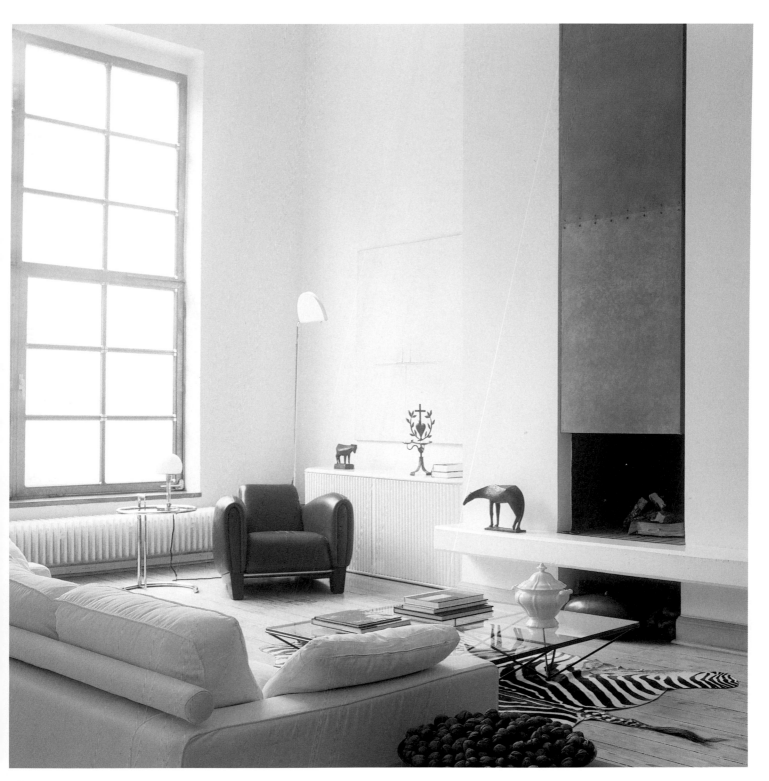

◁ Furniture is becoming personalized, and one-off pieces are no longer exclusive works of art available only to the rich: objects like wooden chests are used as side tables, in combination with retro-style furniture, to endow a space with an individual touch.

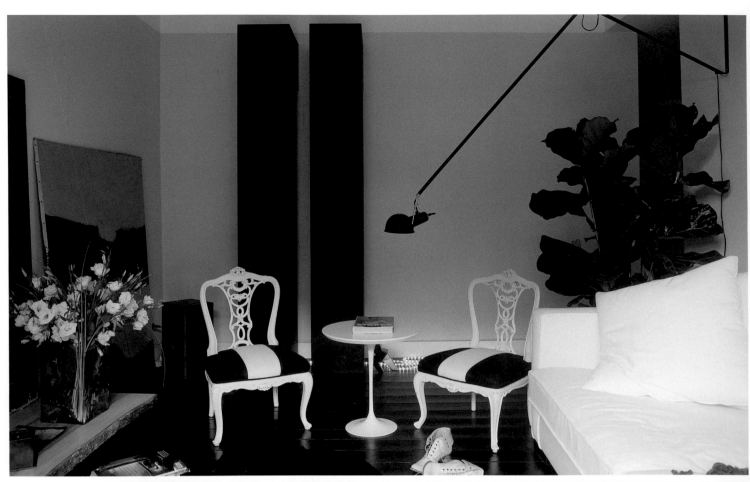

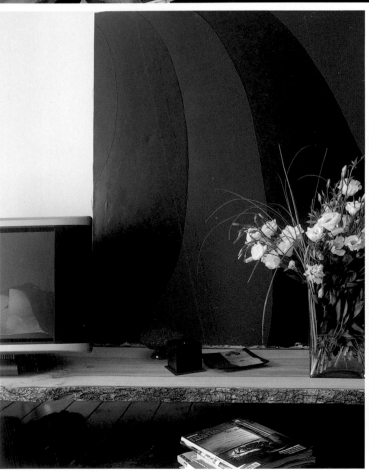

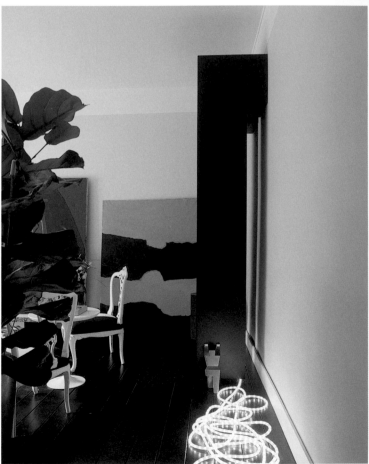

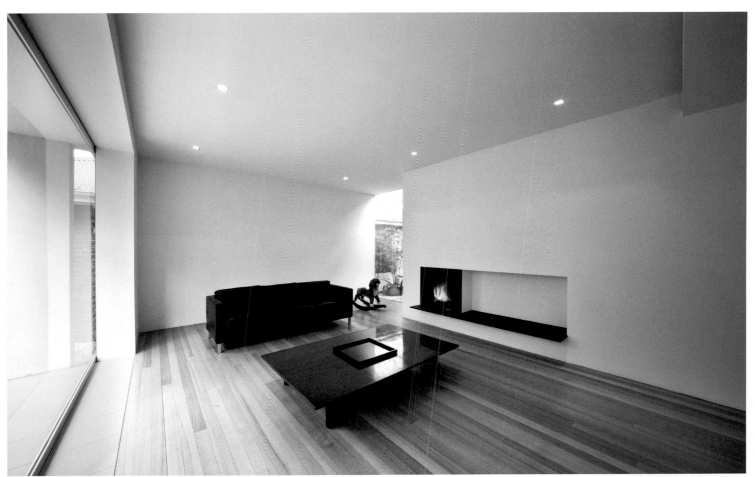

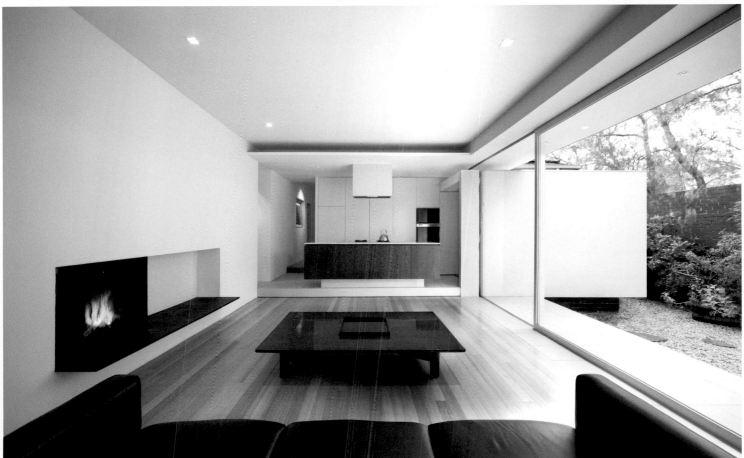

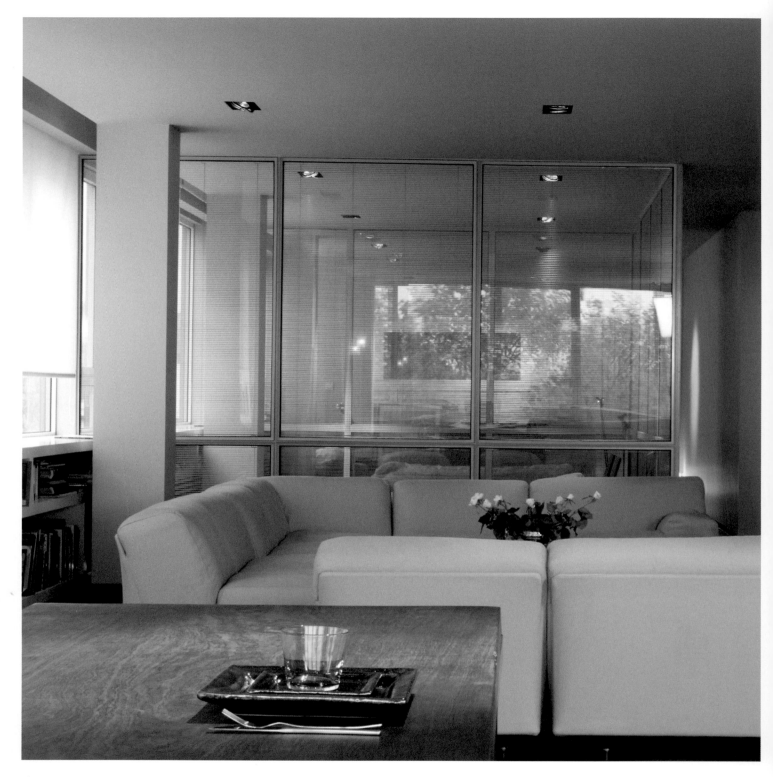

△ The glass panels that separate the living room from the bedroom allow
light to pass through.

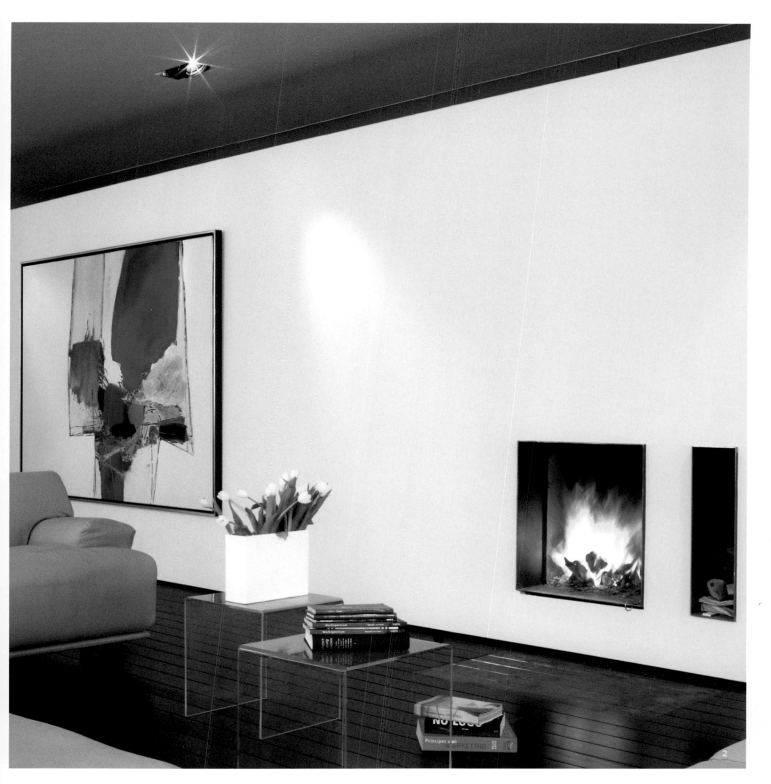

△ The false white partition acts as a backdrop on which elements such as a large painting and the fireplace are positioned to endow this area with personality.

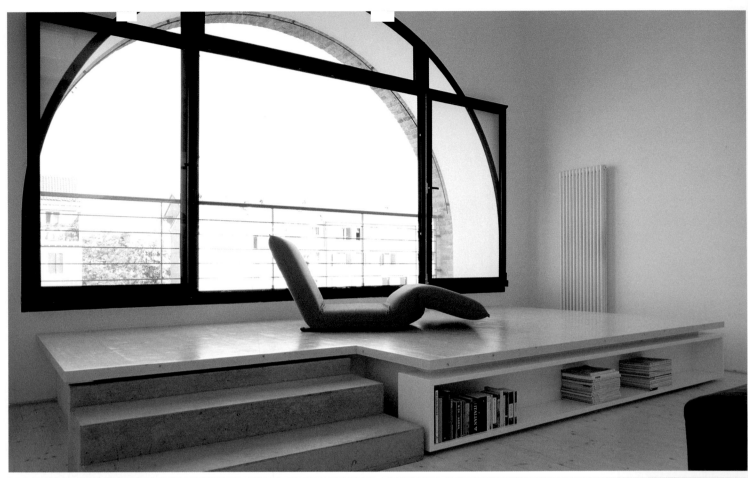

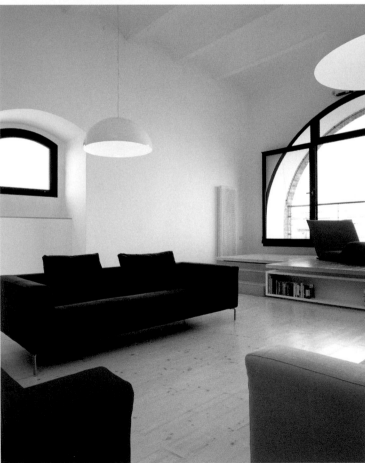
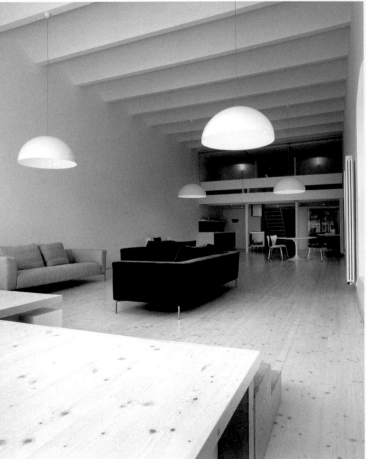

© Matteo Piazza

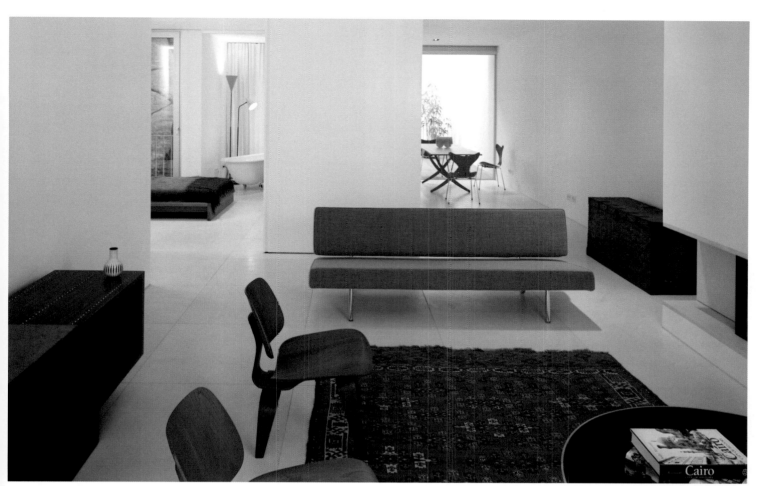

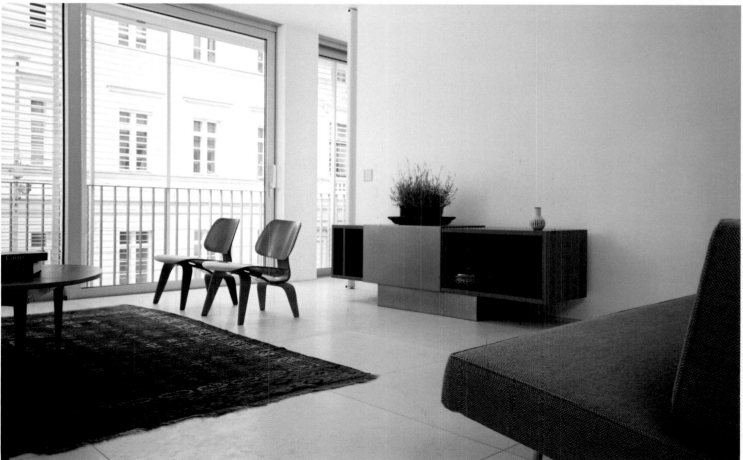

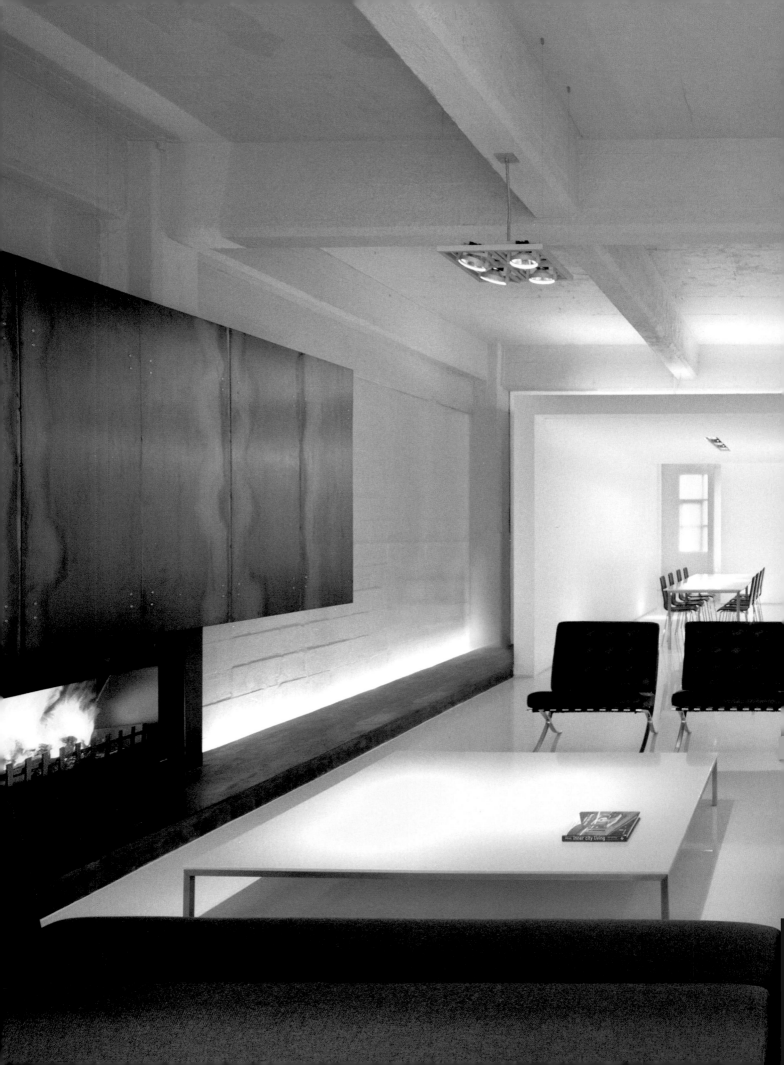

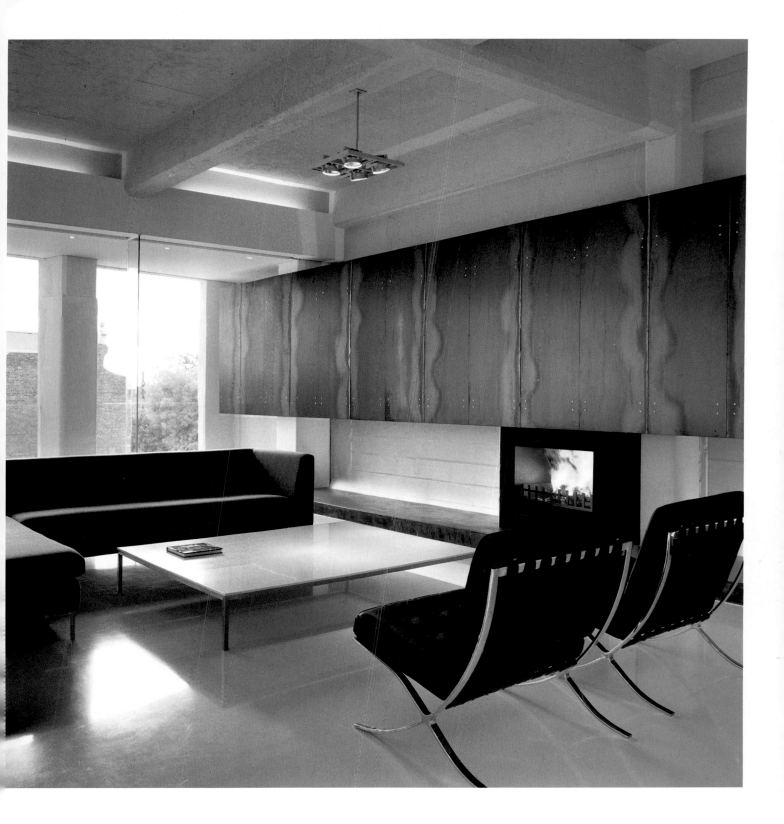

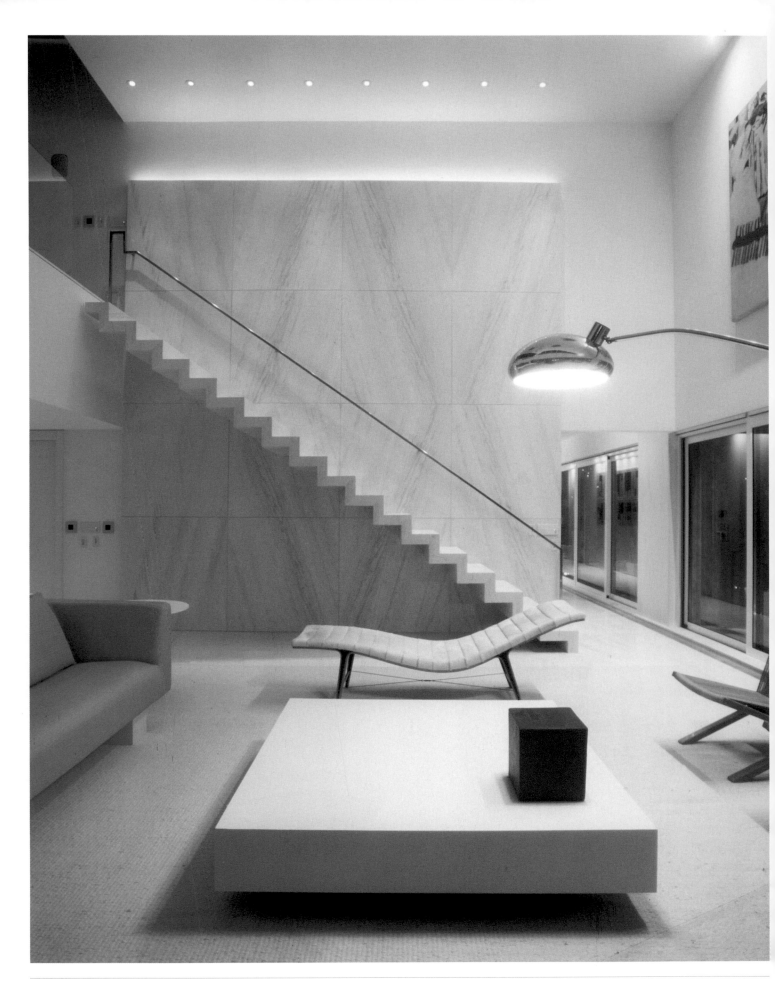

© Studio Arthur de Mattos Casas

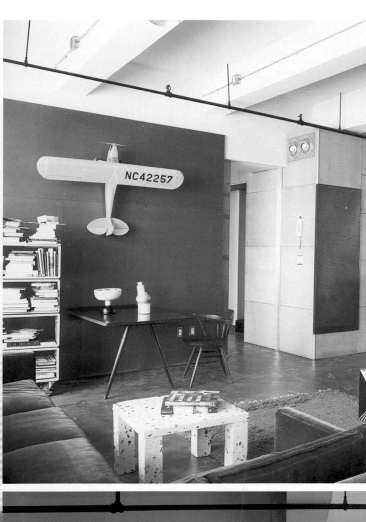

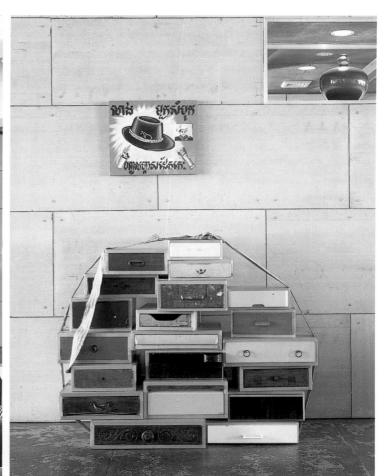

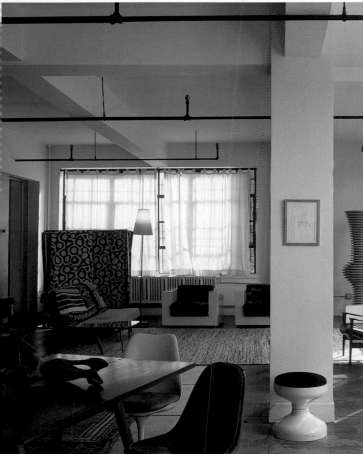

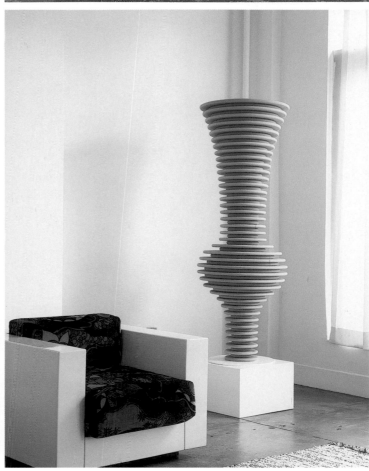

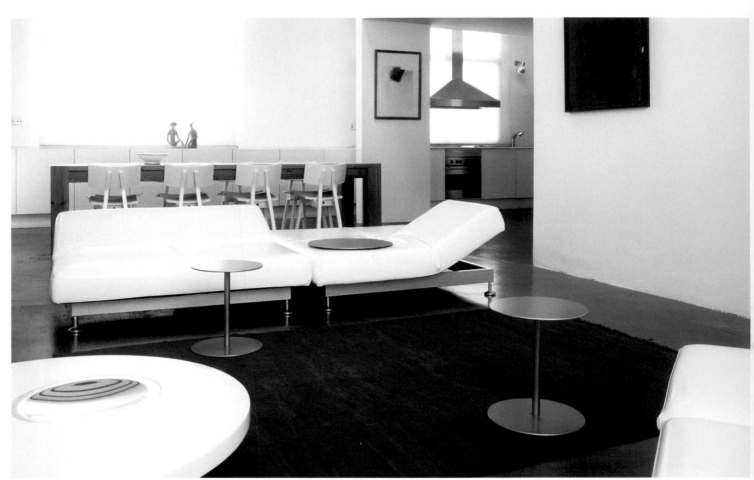

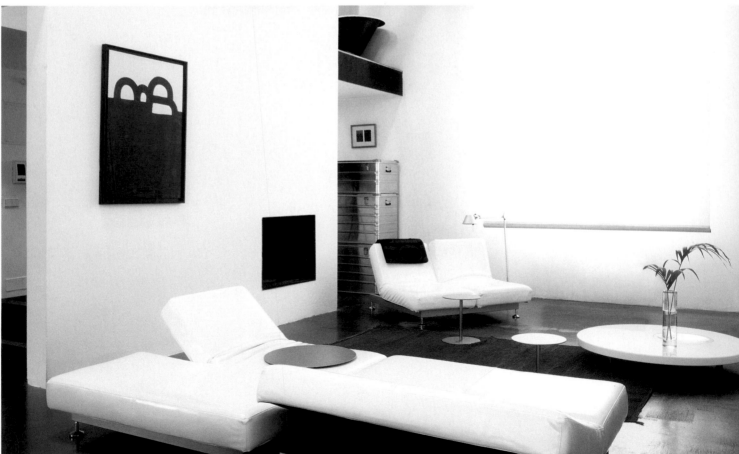

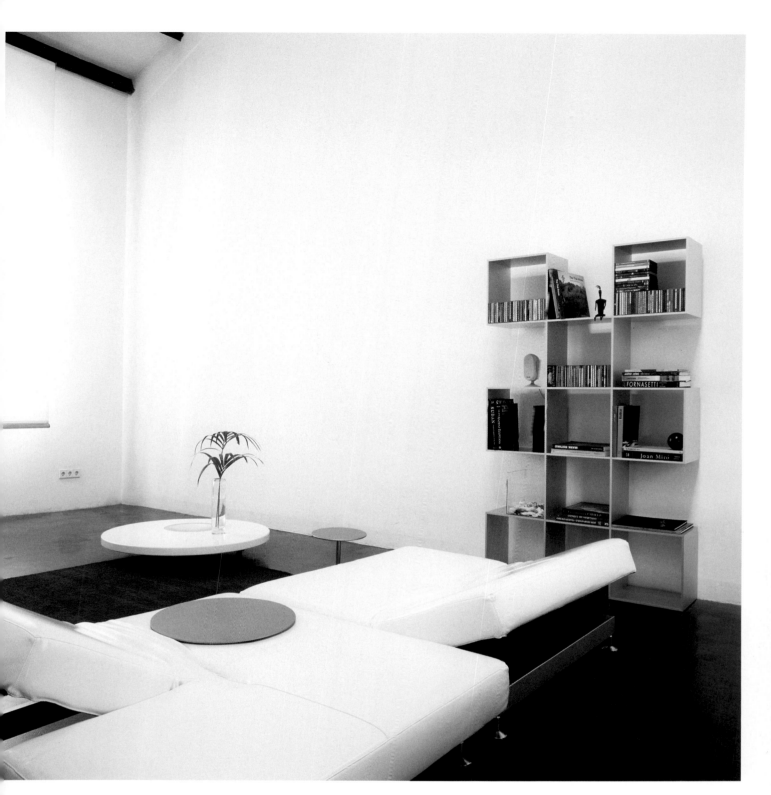

This highly minimalist loft plays with black and white as the main touches of personality. The two colors adorn the geometrical forms of the furniture and the three dominant materials: metal, wood, and plaster.

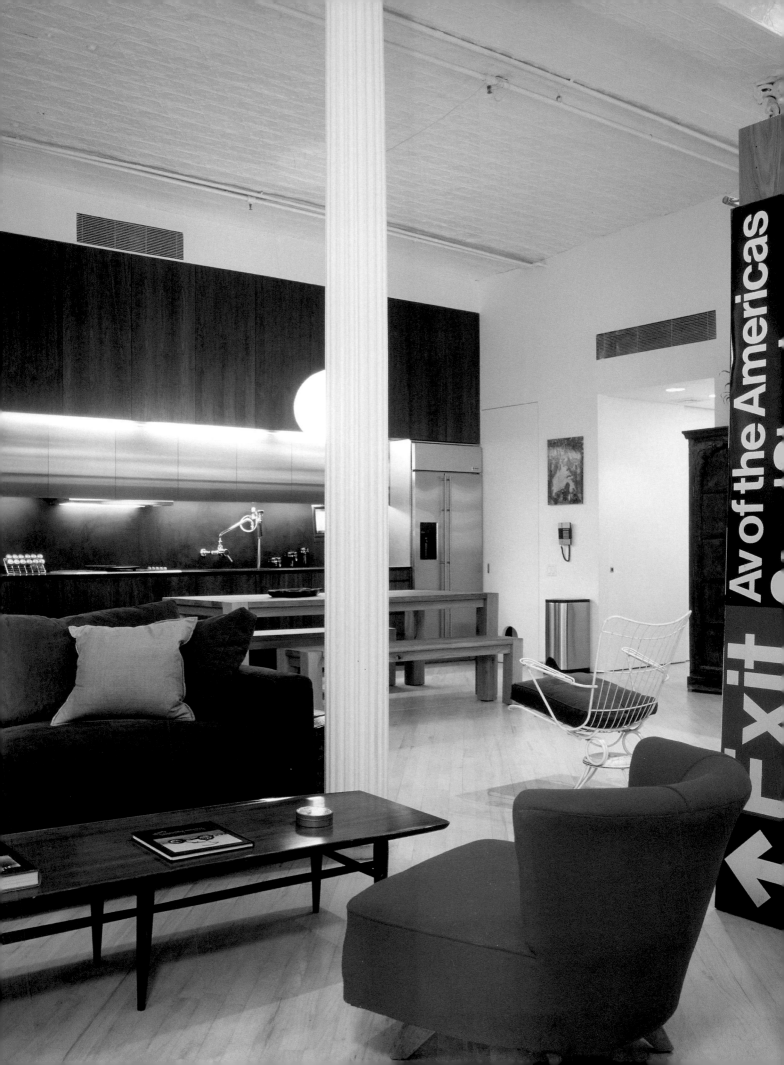

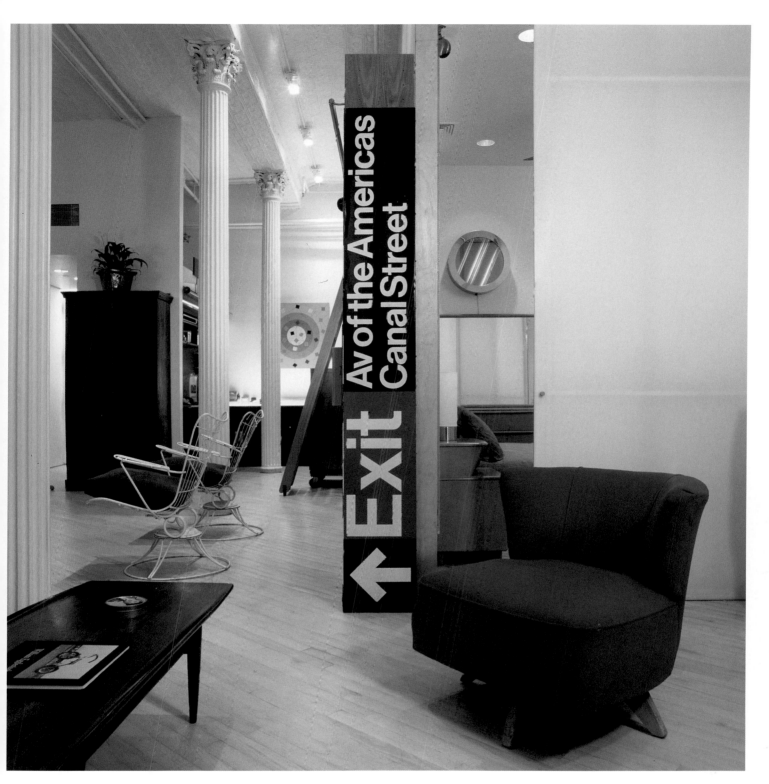

☐ This loft in New York creates an interesting contrast by respecting the original construction elements like the columns and combining them with retro-style furniture and urban decoration features to create a highly personal style.

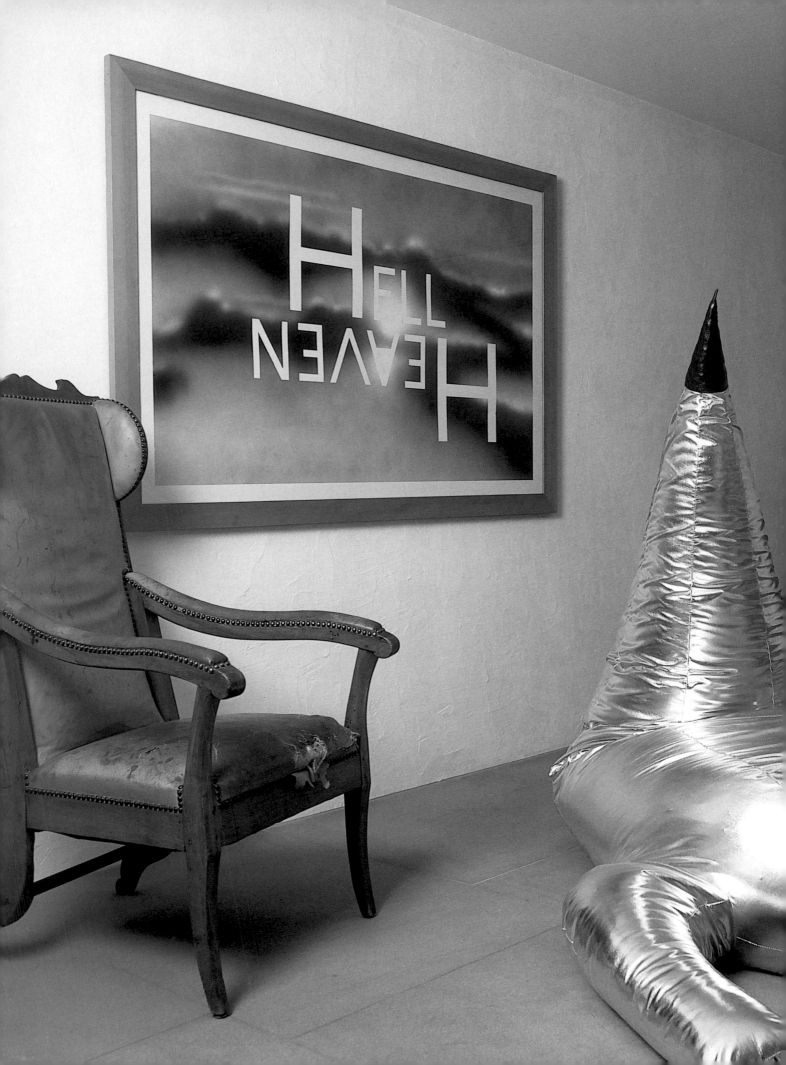

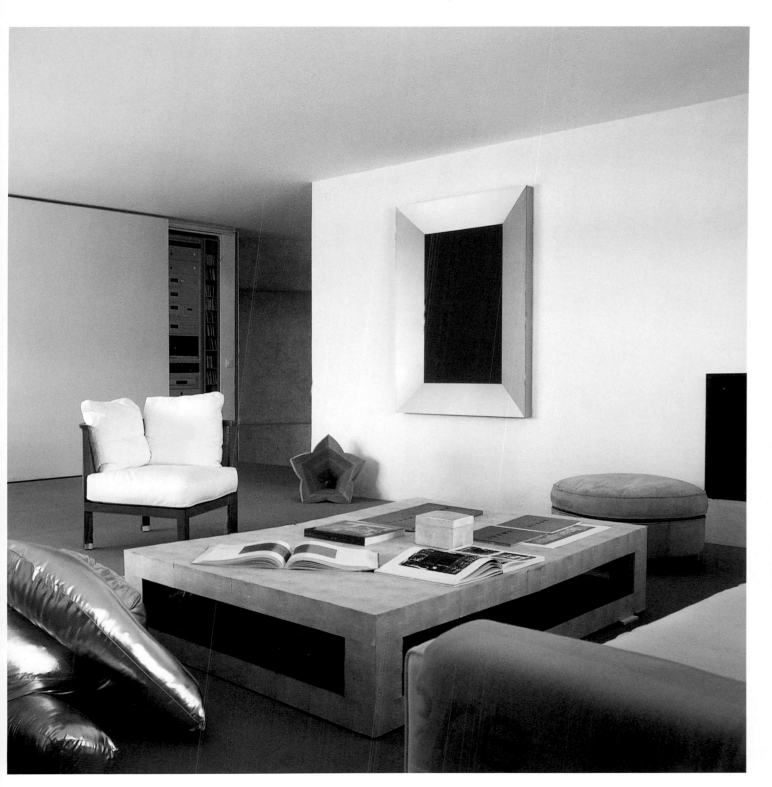

Taking elements out of their normal context is a good way of giving a living room a personal and original style, provided there is sufficient space and the overall atmosphere has a minimalist feel. In this case, a setting dominated by geometrical forms is punctuated by an inflatable sculpture.

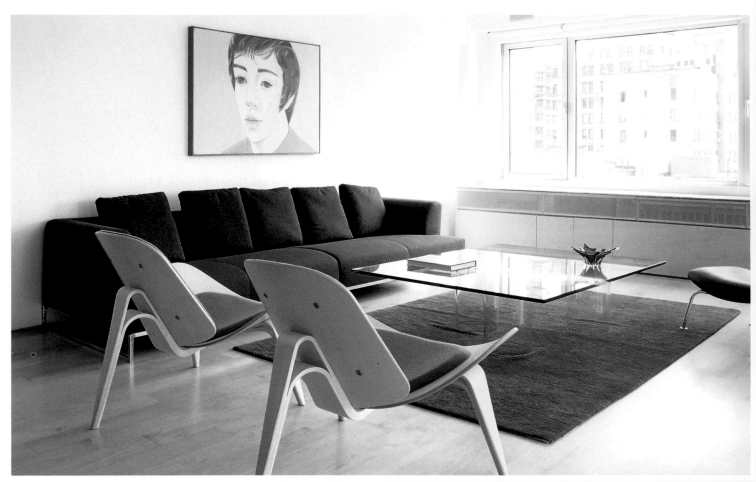

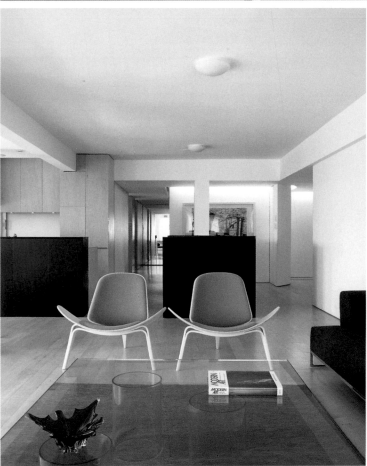

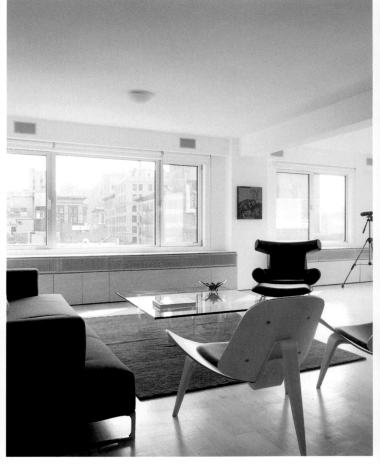

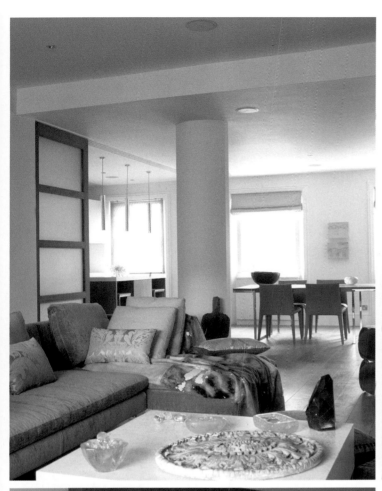
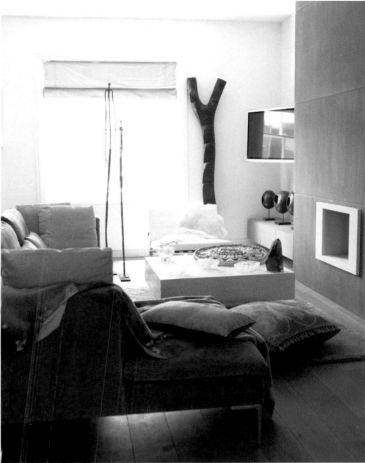
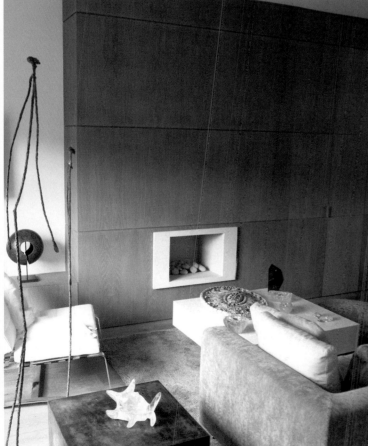
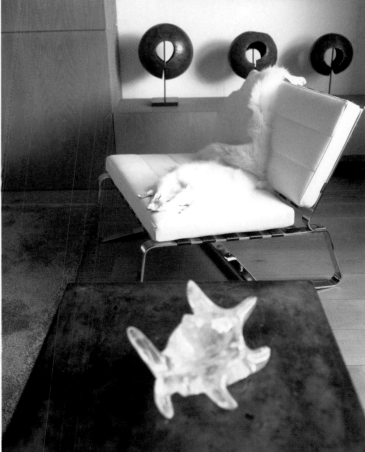

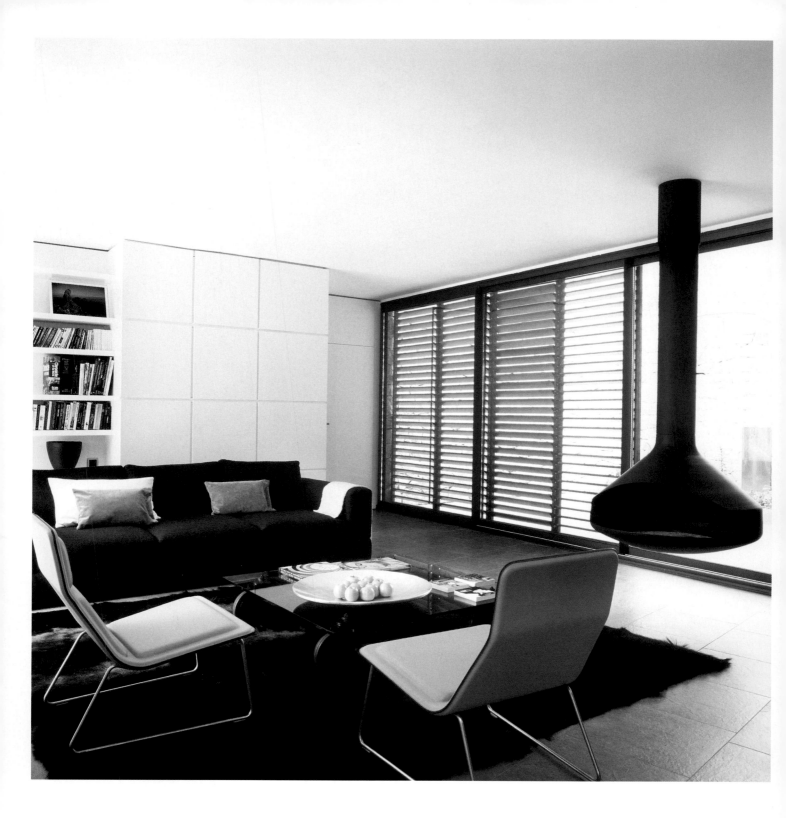

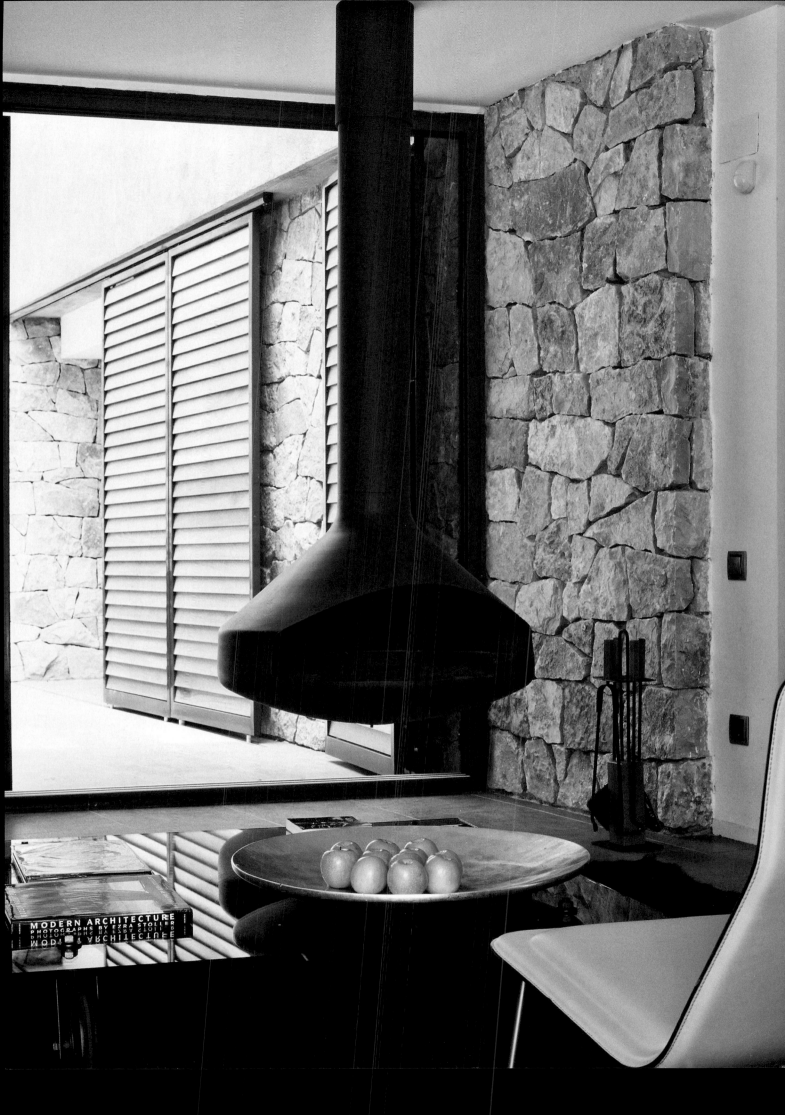

MODERN ARCHITECTURE
PHOTOGRAPHS BY EZRA STOLLER

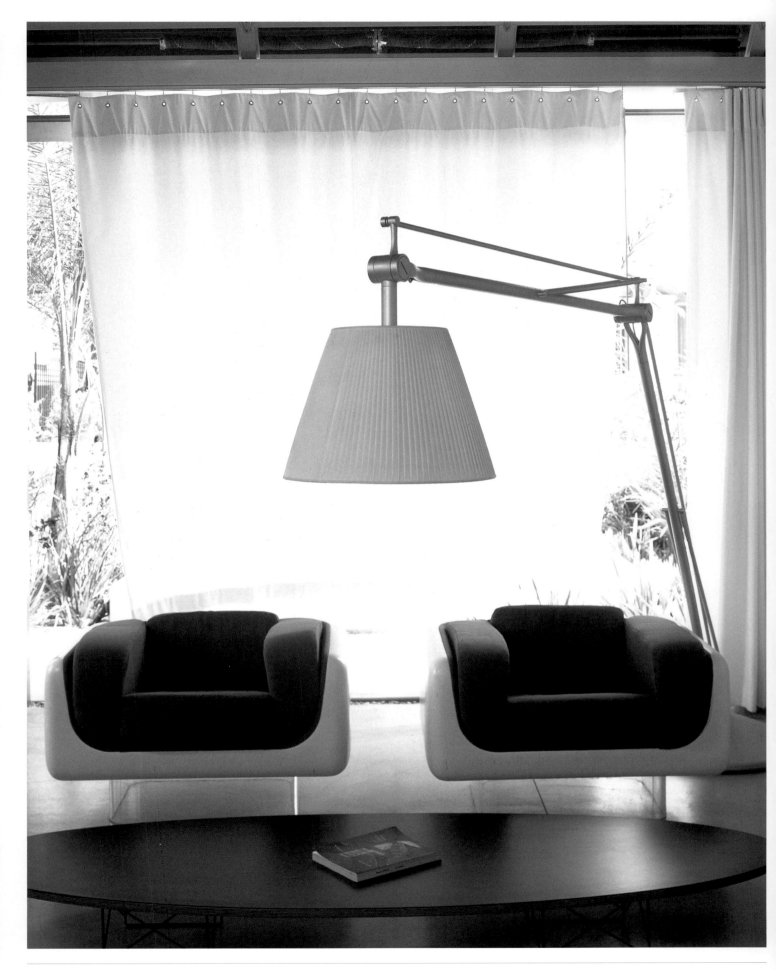

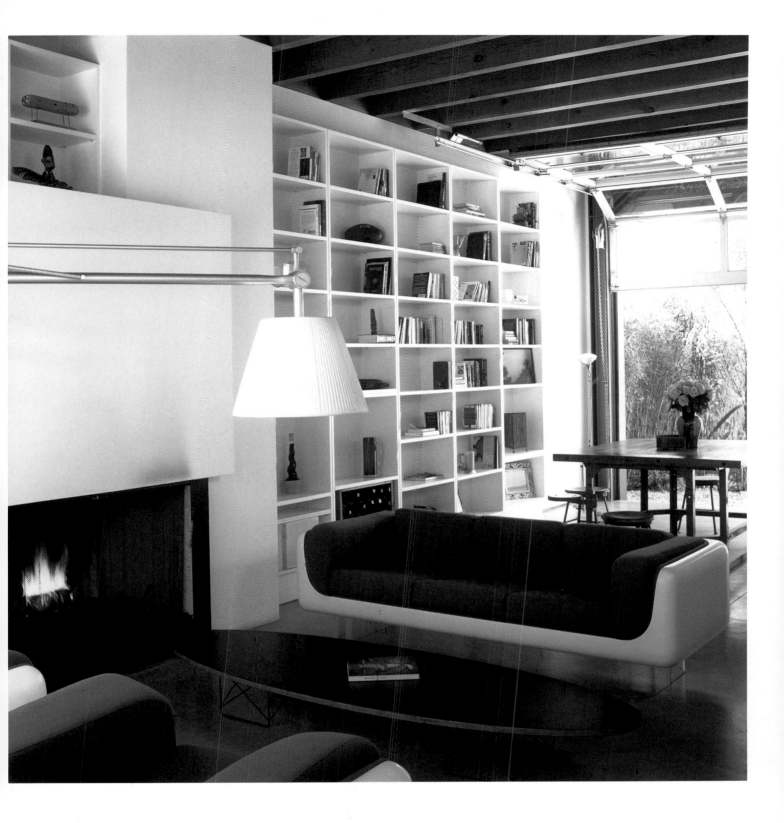

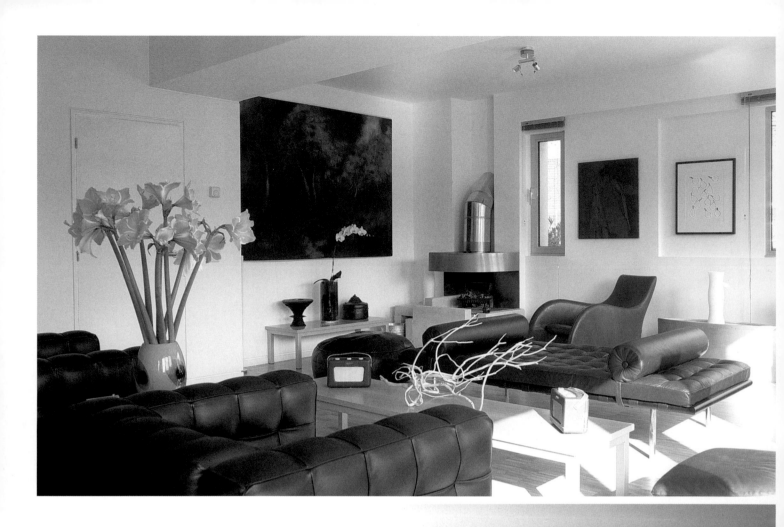

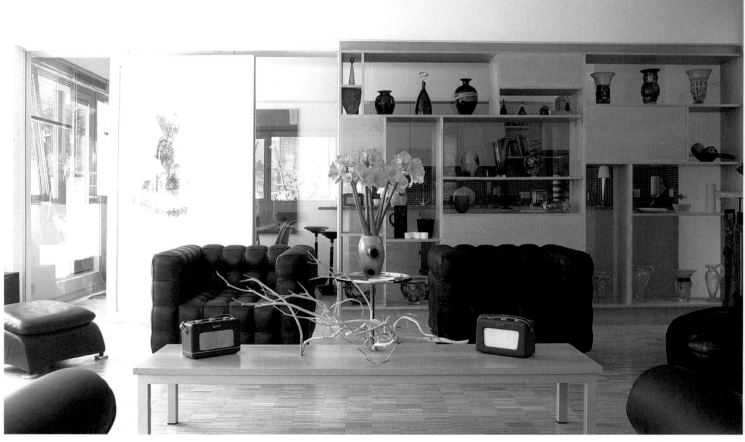

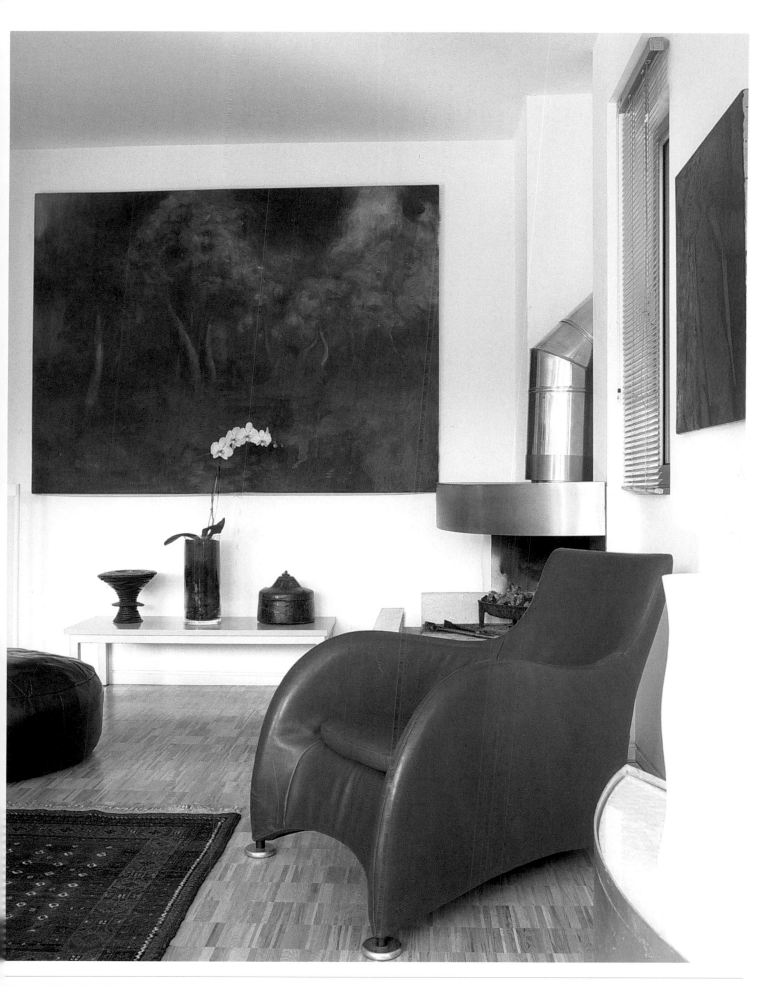

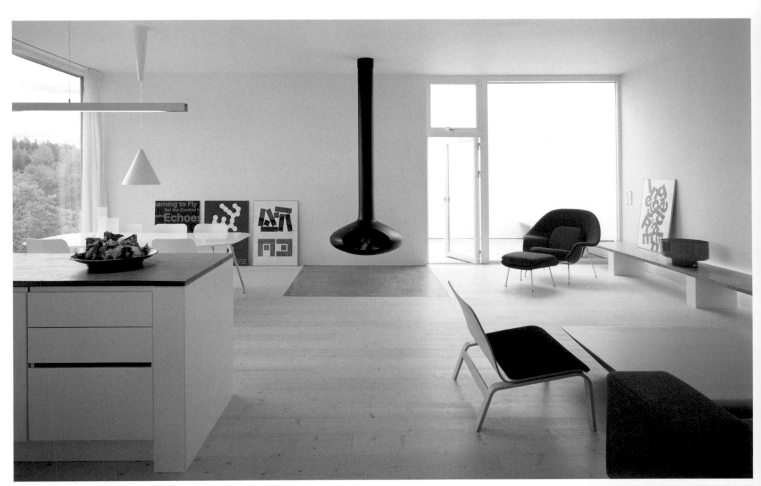

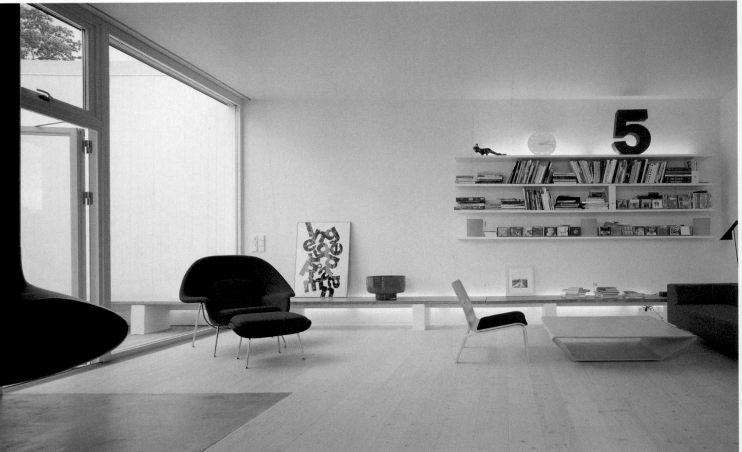

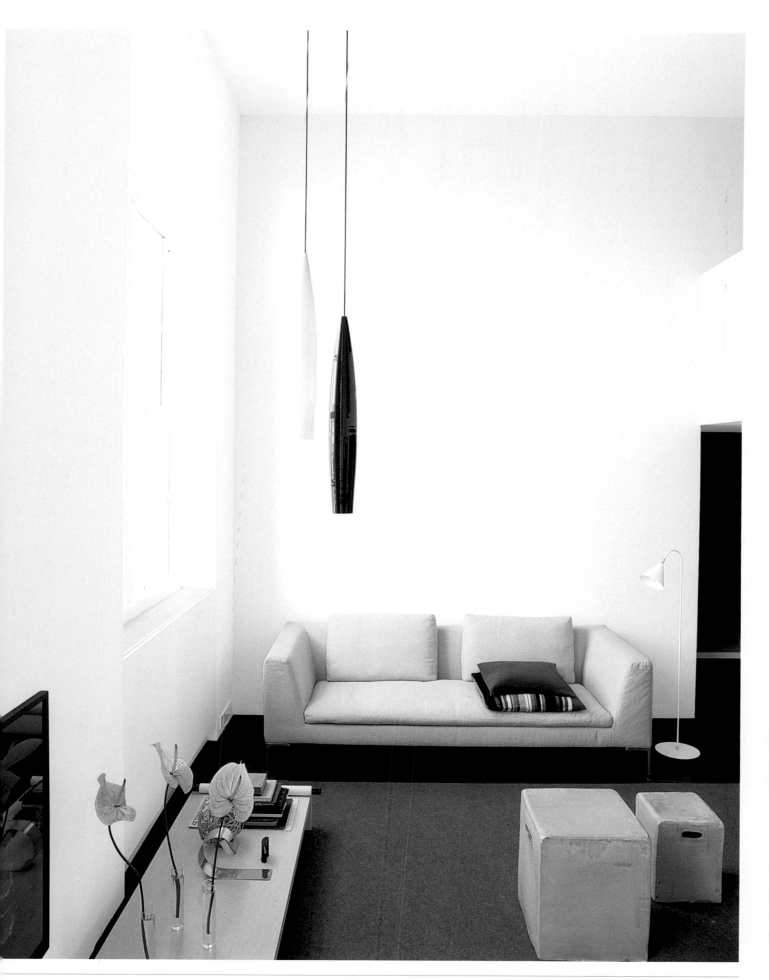

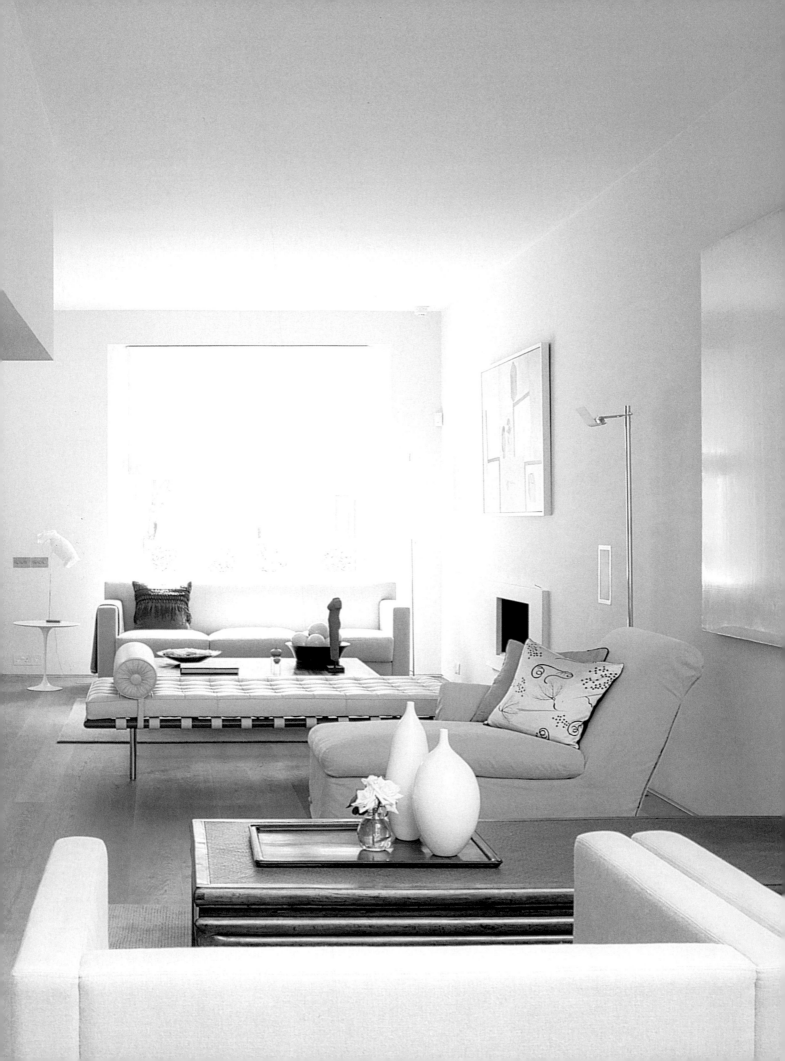

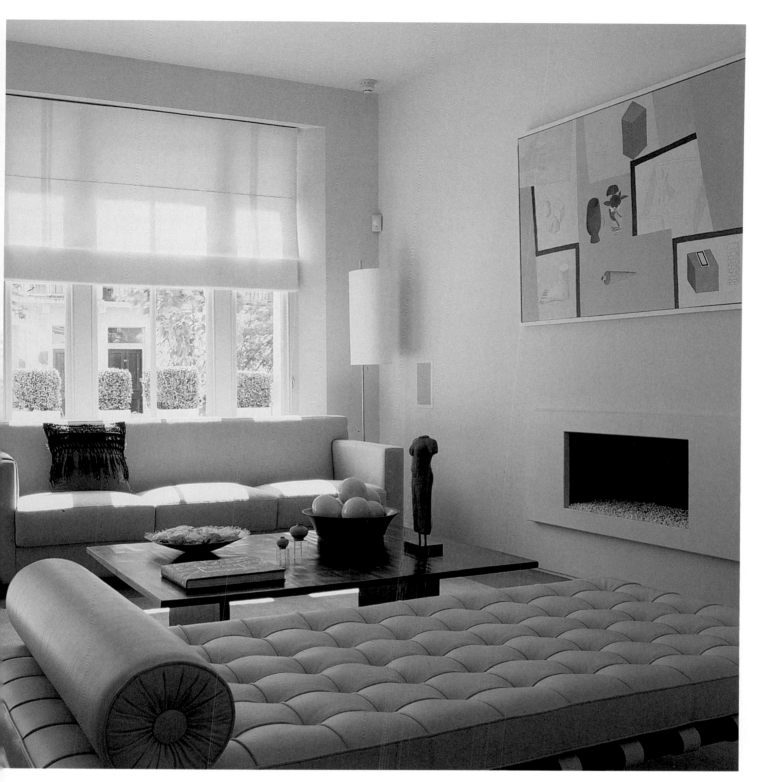

One way of gaining luminosity is the use of white, which also helps to gain space. In this case, the rectangular floor plan was exploited to create two distinct spaces that are set opposite each other, giving a sense of unity.

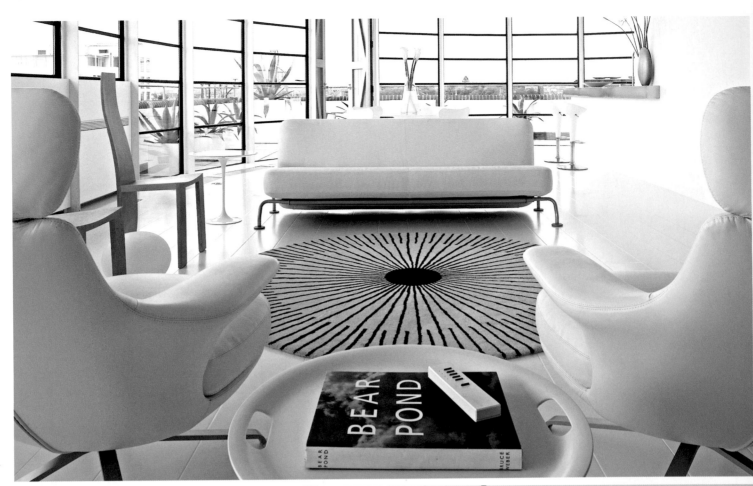

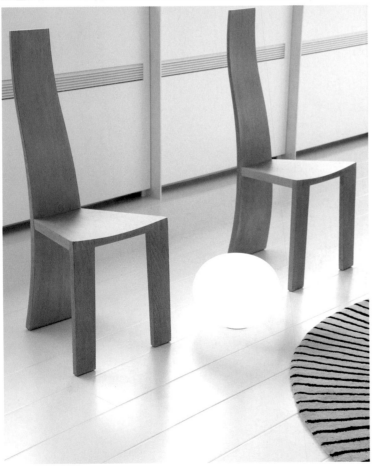

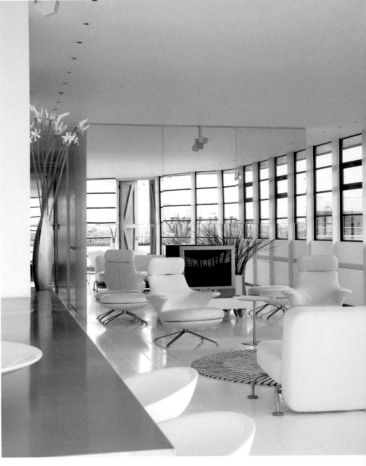

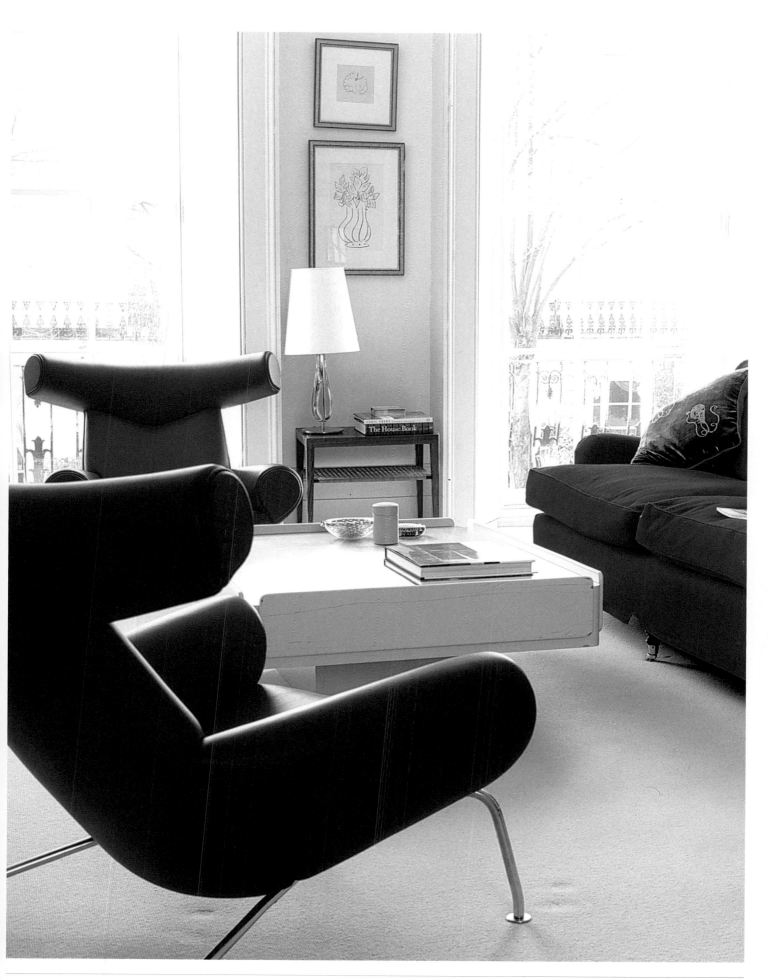

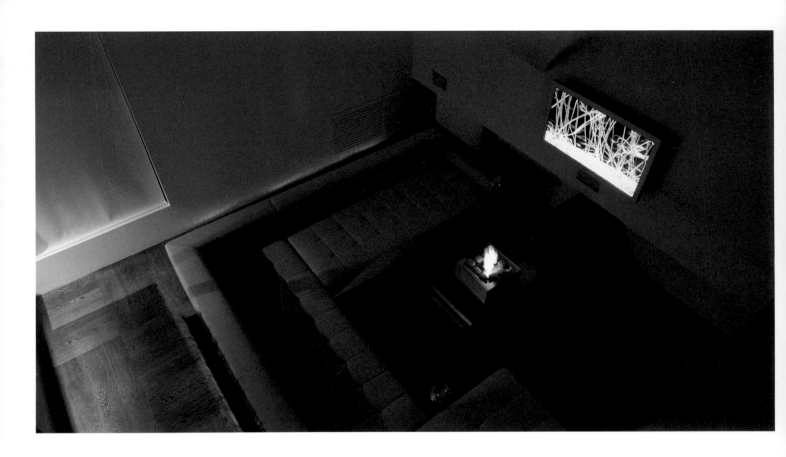

The large, olive-green windows and the predominance of white dotted with green reinforce the interplay of design, architecture, and nature in this apartment in a Victorian house.

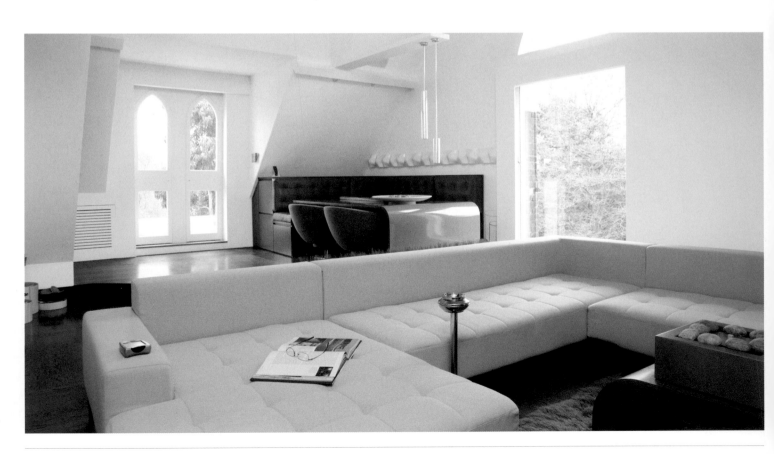

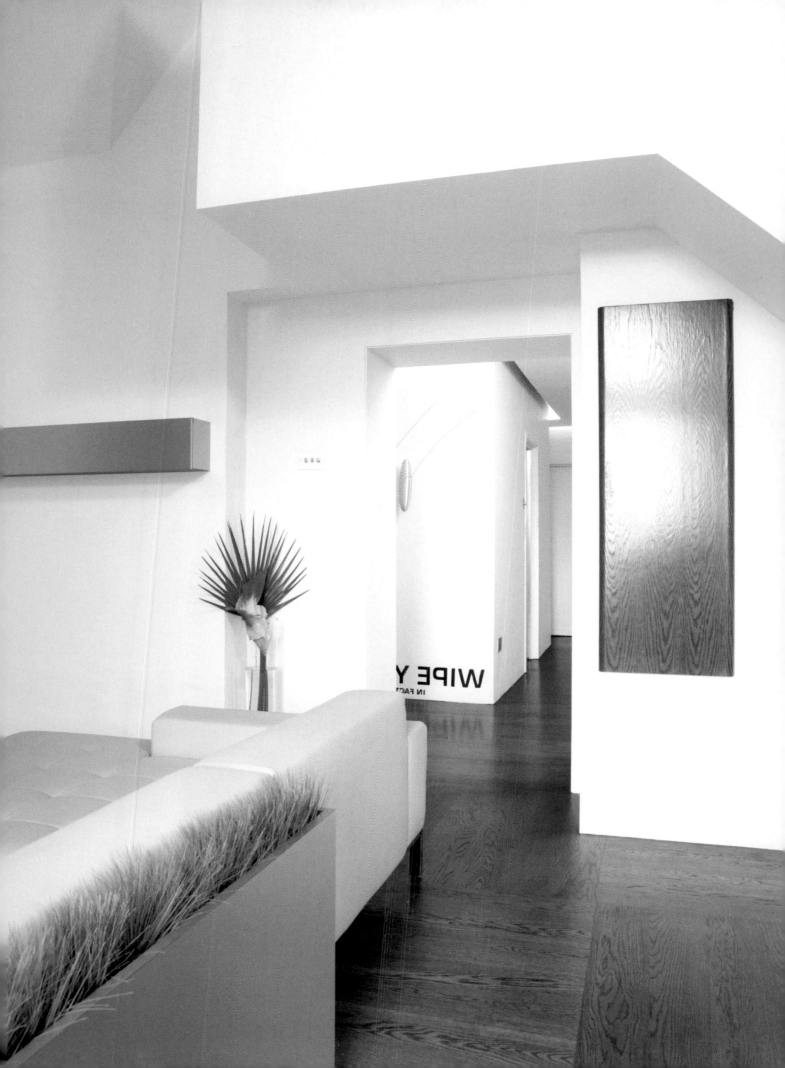

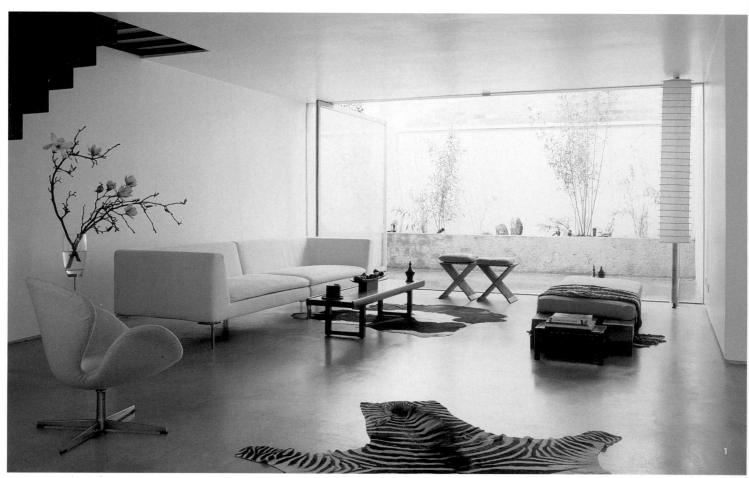

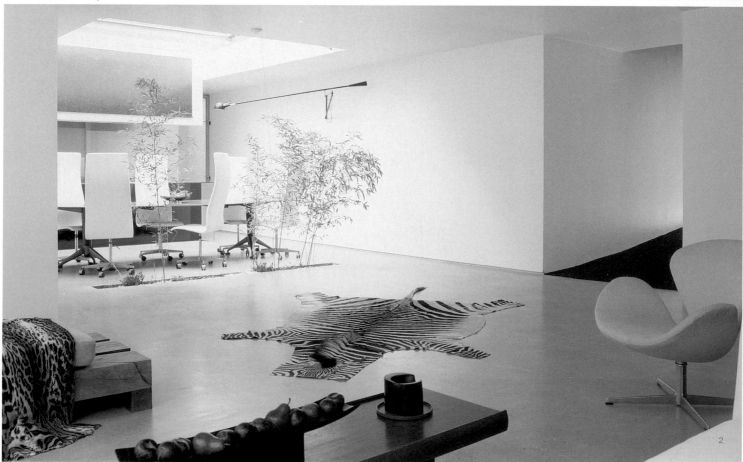

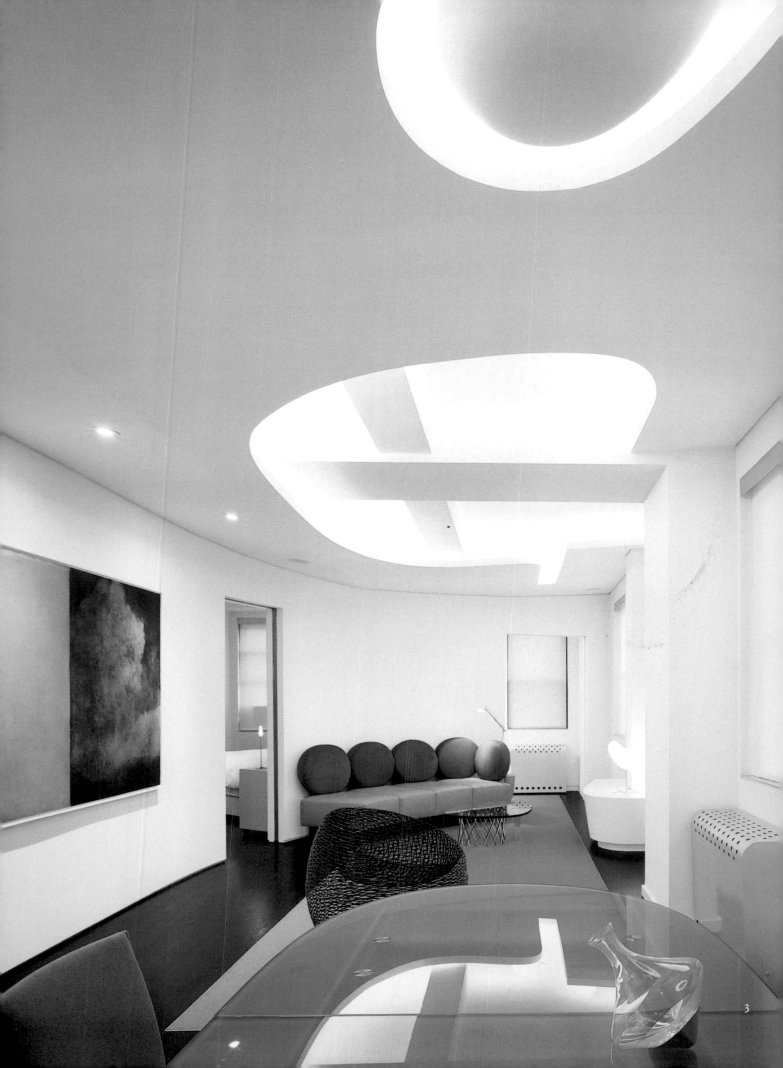

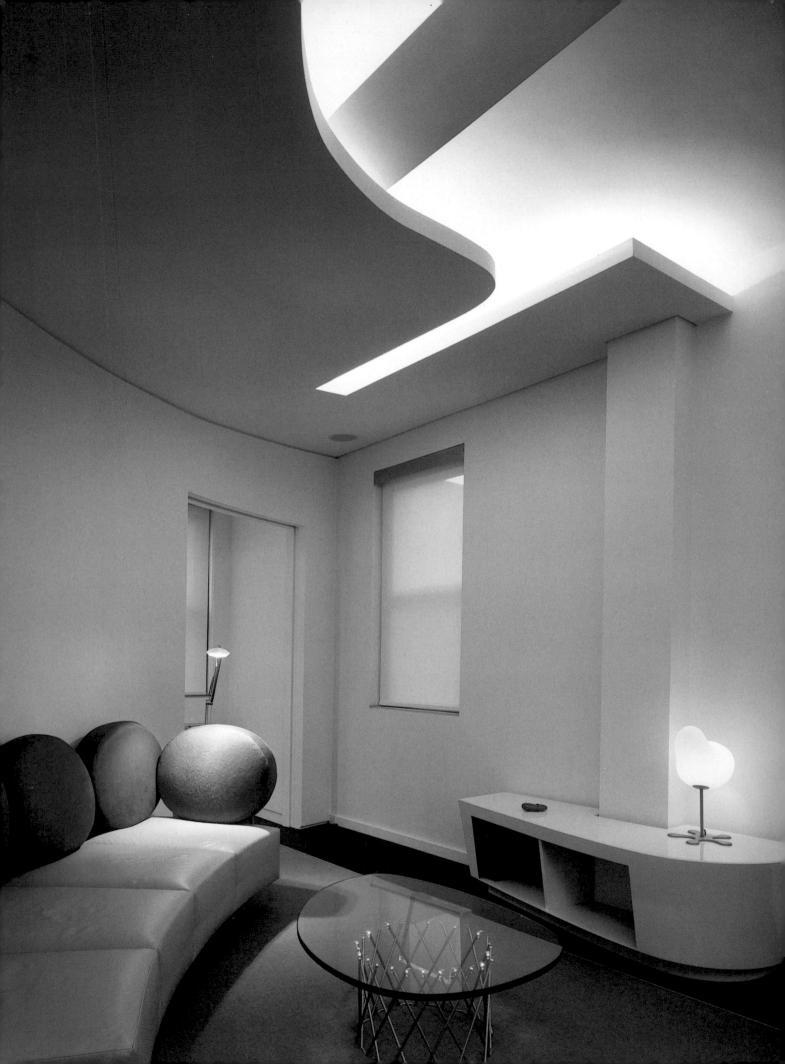

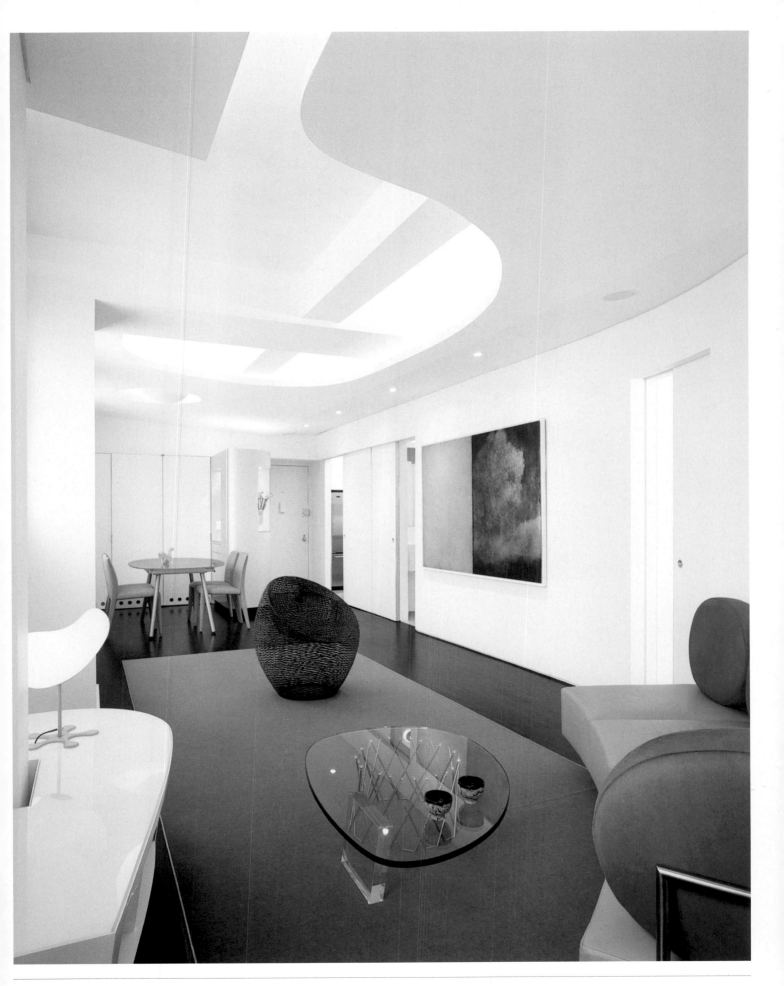

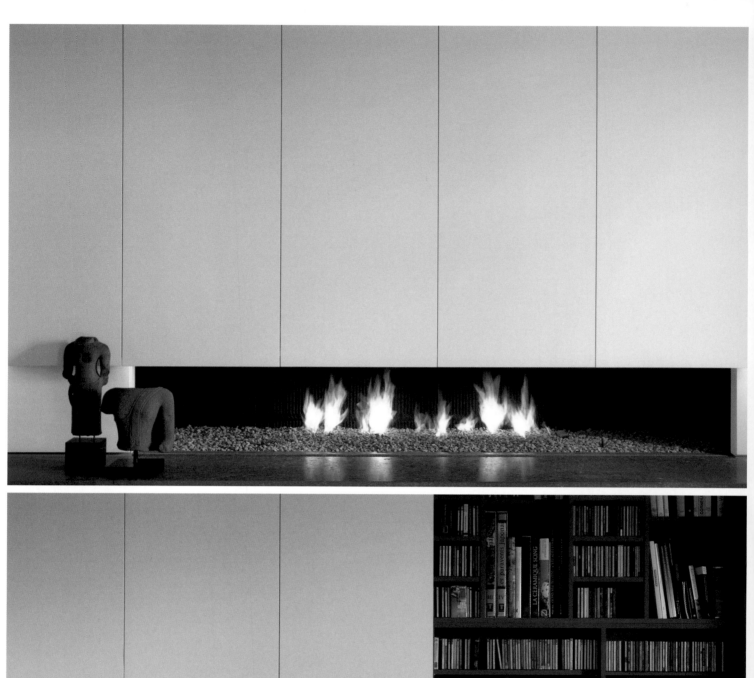

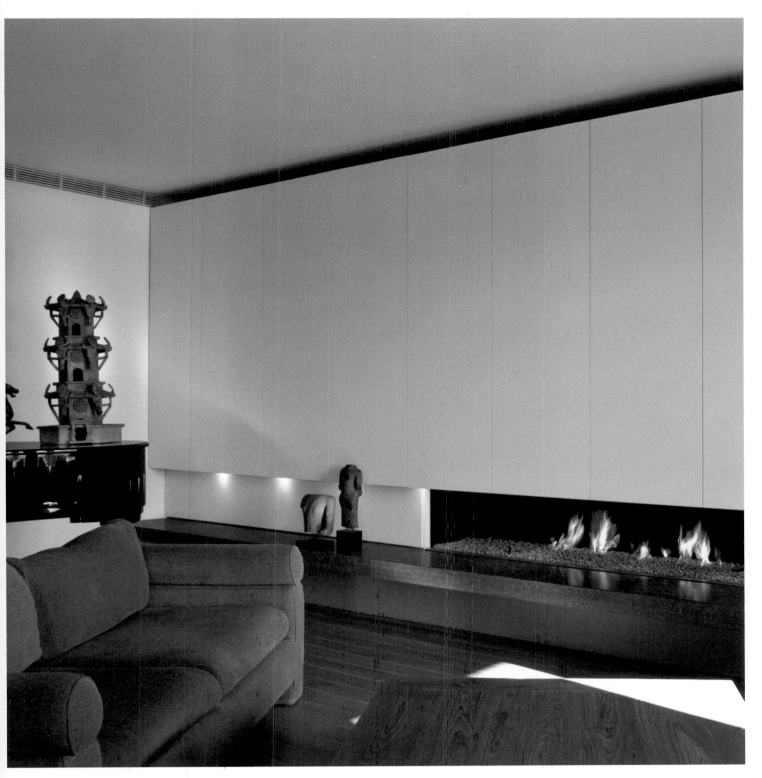

One way of achieving uniformity and balance in a space is by increasing the uses of furniture. In this case, a closet serves various functions in the living room: as the front of the fireplace, as a light source and as a closet in its own right. This avoids the need to add extra elements to a room that has opted for uniformity.

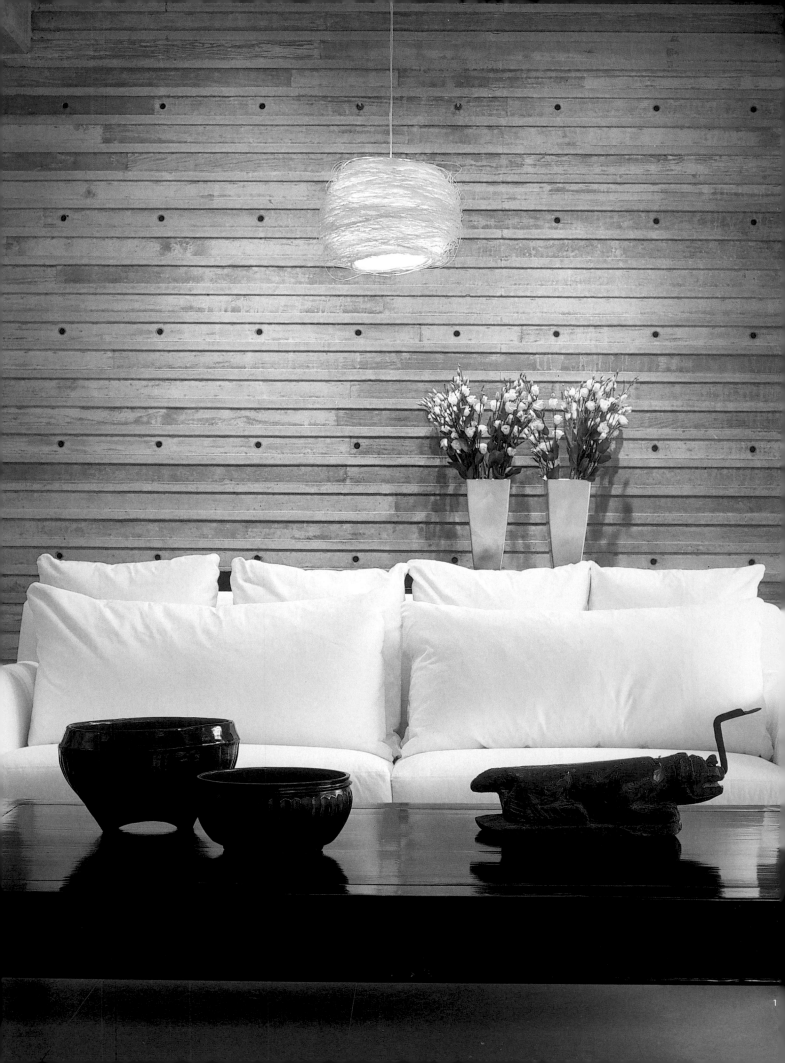

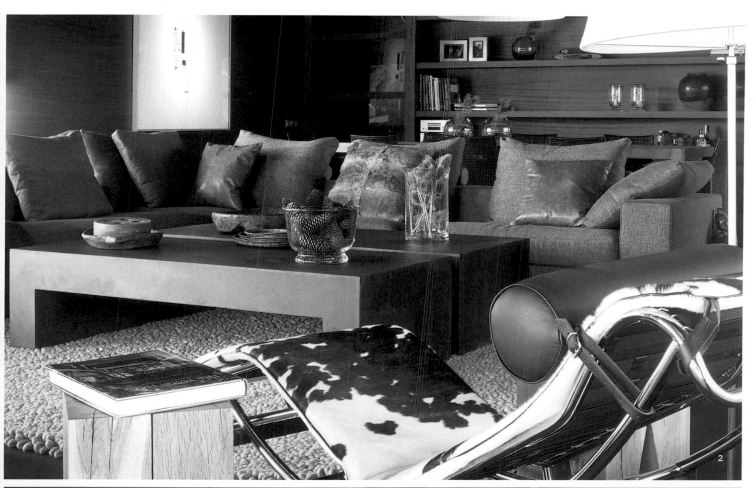

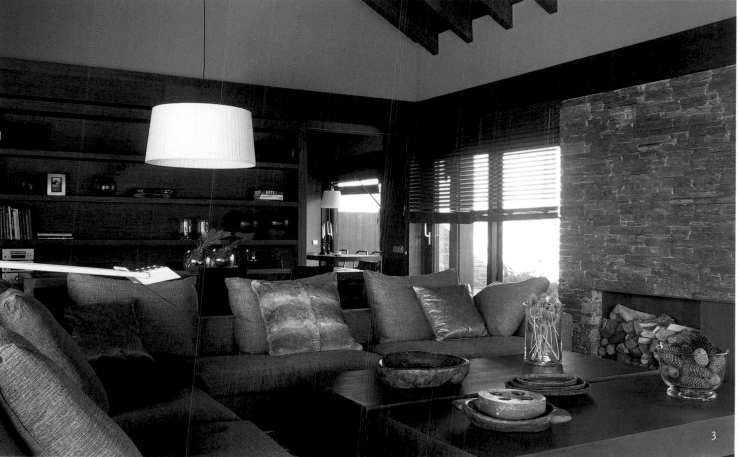

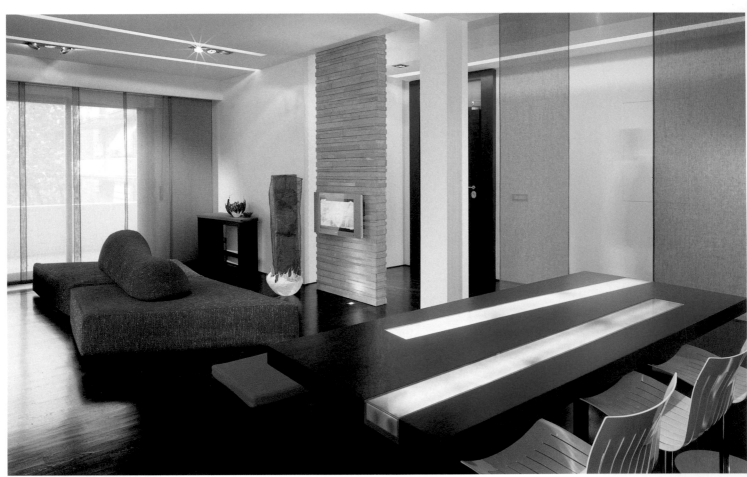

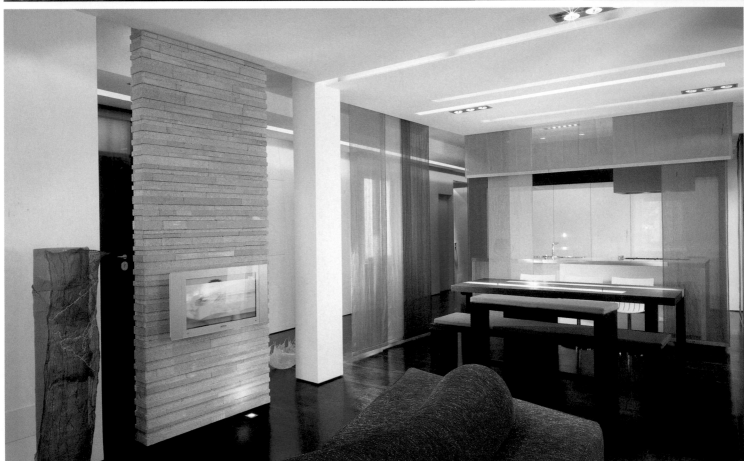

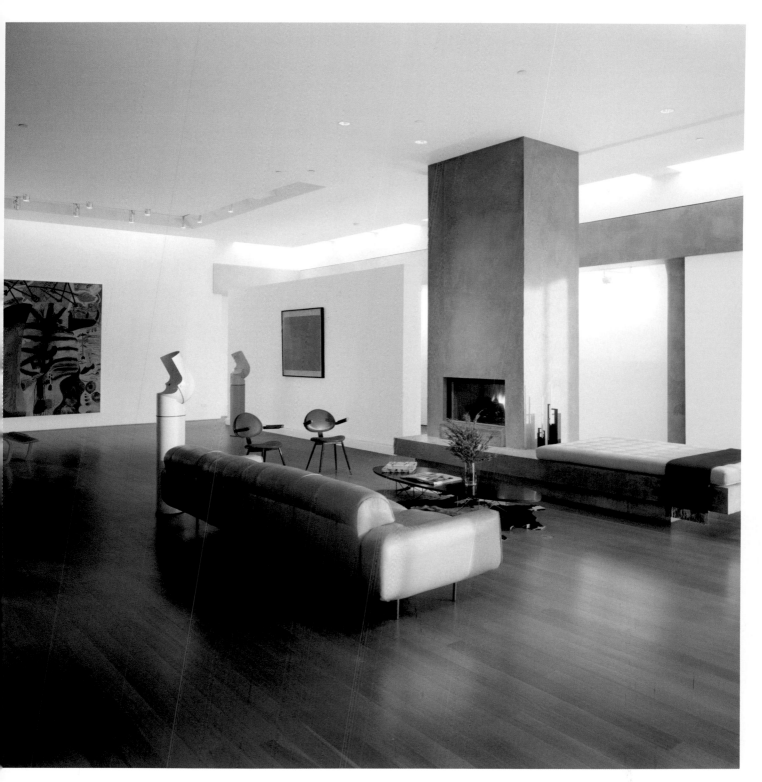

△ The initial structure of the partitions has been renounced to create an
area of light that "frames" the living room from the ceiling.

◁ "We have characterized this Roman house by the bold use of color and
by sliding 'sails' that follow the lines of the old walls," says Roman architect Fillipo Bombace.

© Paul Warchol

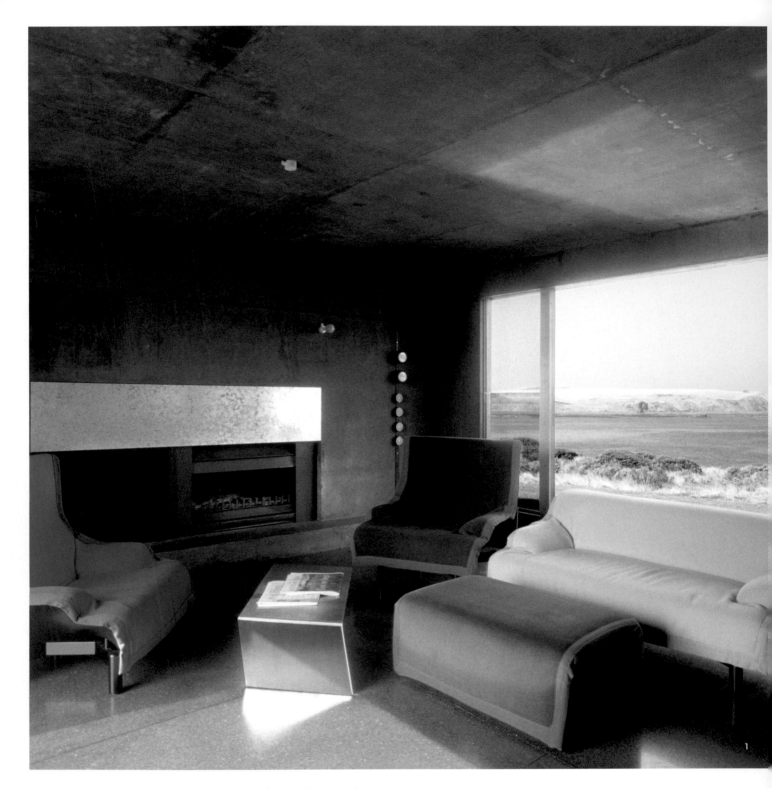

△ The windows in this living room function as frames that crop the views of the exterior. The walls and ceilings have been left without any cladding, with the concrete exposed and therefore highlighted.

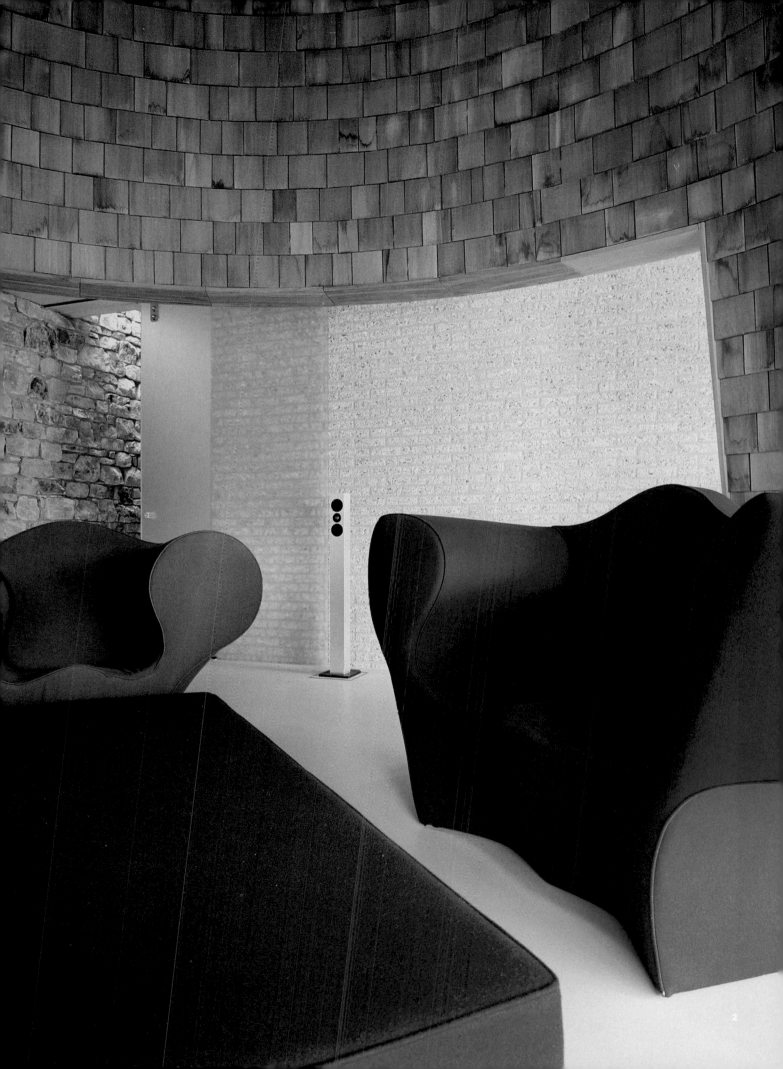

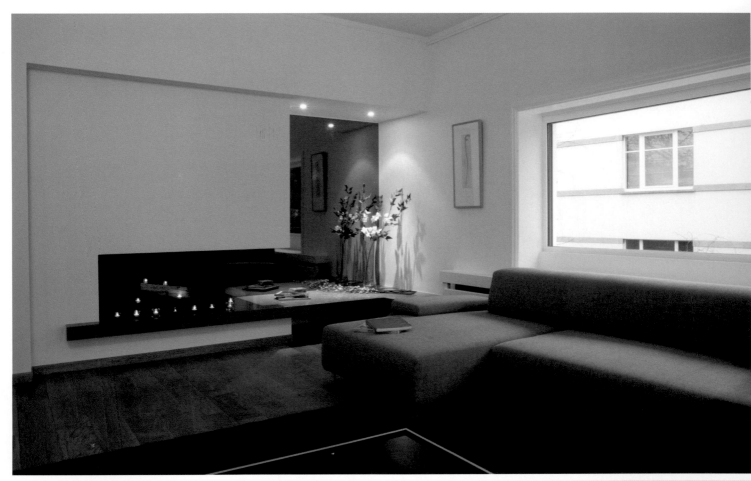

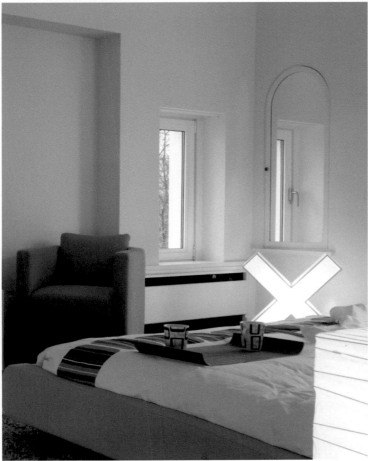

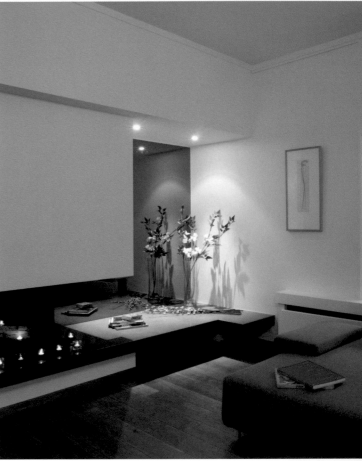

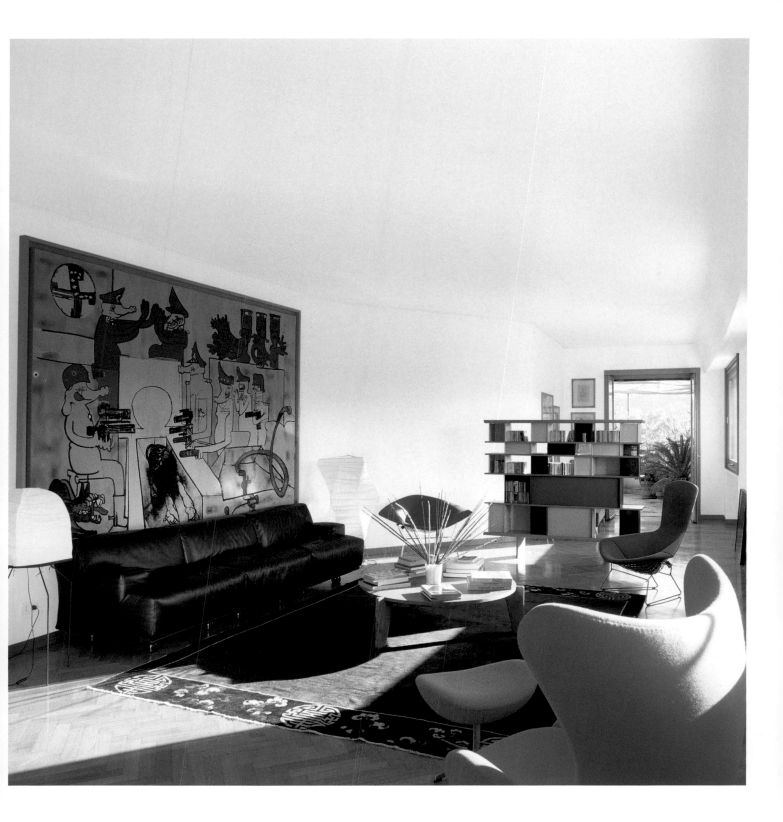

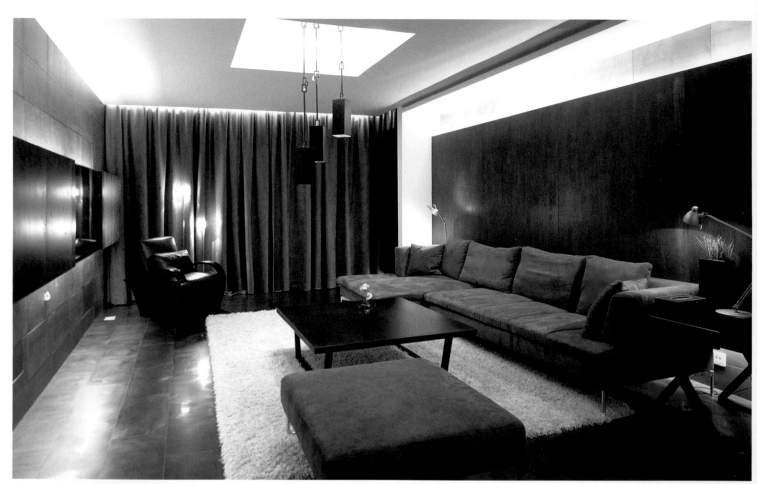

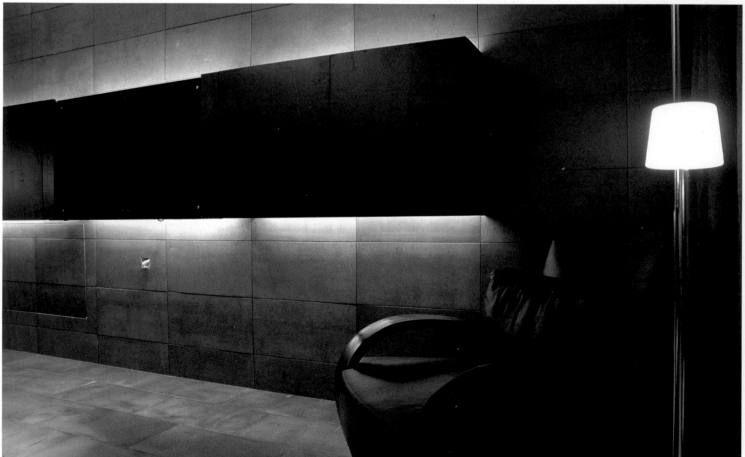

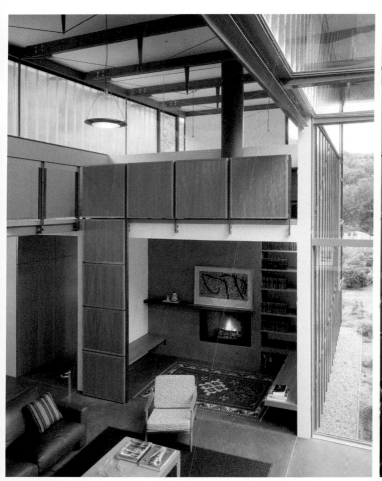
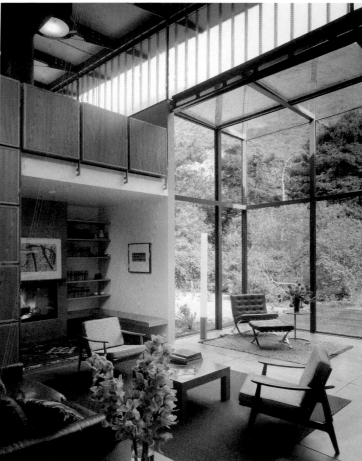
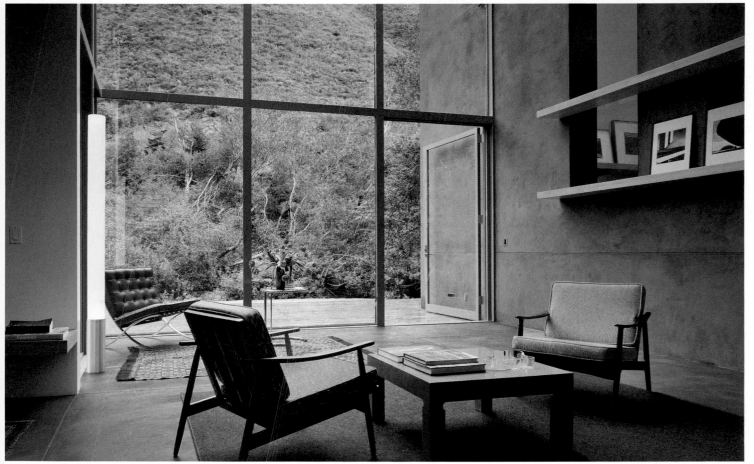

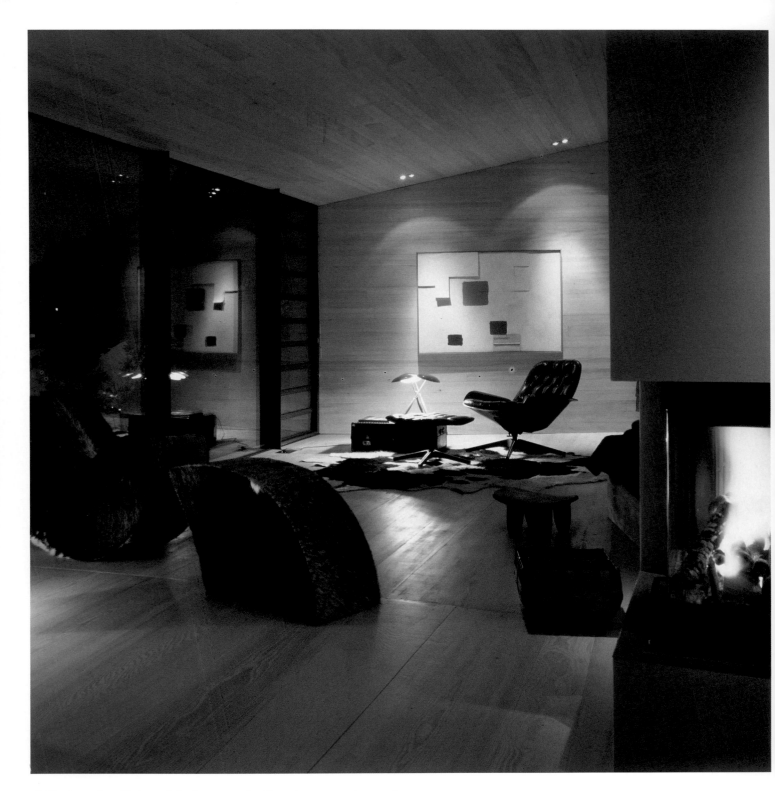

△ The interplay of light and shade creates details and contrasts that mark out the layout, without any need for other elements.

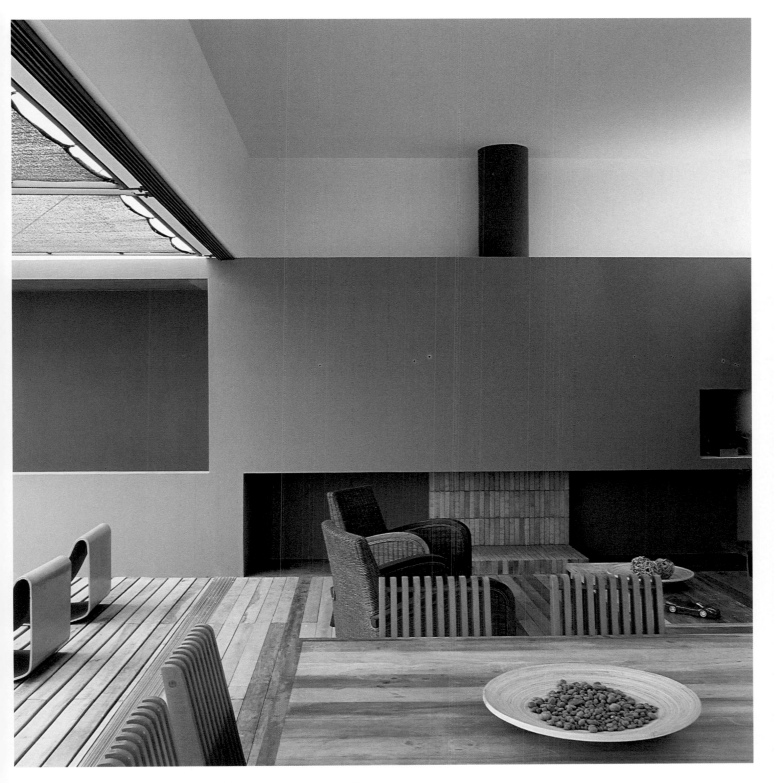

△ Creating a constellation of geometrical forms with furniture precludes
the need for any other decorative elements.

Bedrooms

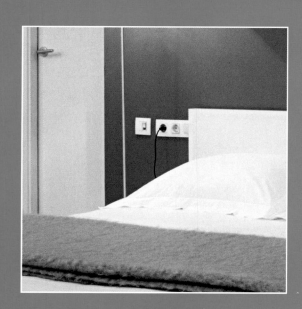

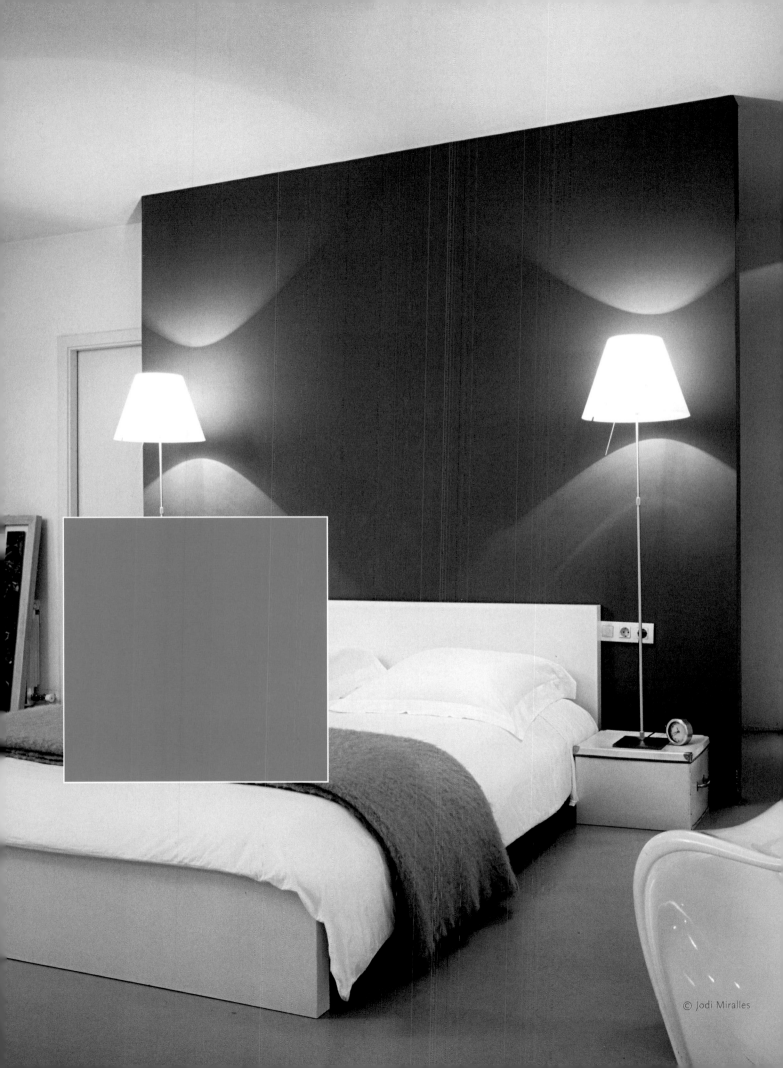

Bedrooms

Sleep can be considered a golden chain that links our body and our health

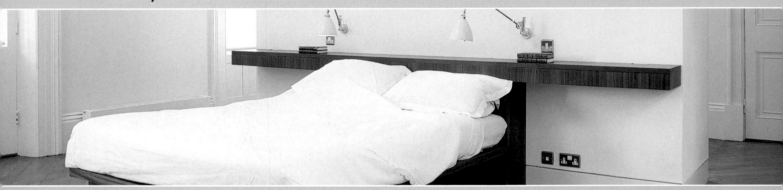

© Carlos Domínguez

"To achieve the impossible dream, try going to sleep." (Joan Klempner) If you want a possible dream to come true, we could add, "Try realizing your dream after you wake." According to this theory, our bedrooms exert a decisive influence over the realization of our dreams, whether impossible or possible.

Sleep can be considered a golden chain that links our body to our health. Asian cultures, especially the Chinese, have appreciated this golden link between sleep and health for centuries. They have made great efforts to enhance this relationship, from the placement of the bed to its colors and materials and surface. Everything is taken into consideration when it comes to designing a bedroom, which is thought to be decisive in improving the quality of sleep and, therefore, the quality of life.

Developments in technology have minimized the effects of climate, making it possible to adapt techniques and formats that once belonged to other cultures and that were impracticable in ours. They can be adapted for use in interior design, including materials that were previously unavailable or too expensive.

Furthermore, globalization continues to educate us in aesthetic parameters far more wide reaching than those of previous generations. Canons of beauty and harmony can vary as we encounter other cultures; some of these cultures have a deep knowledge of the human body, in ways previously neglected by our society, particularly in needs arising from new lifestyles.

In short, the bedrooms seen here present the features of a society that are becoming increasingly sensual and global, yet individualistic. You will see a mixture of styles and materials, designs from many periods that respond more to personal needs and the expression of personality than to fashion, and, most of all, a respect for both body and mind.

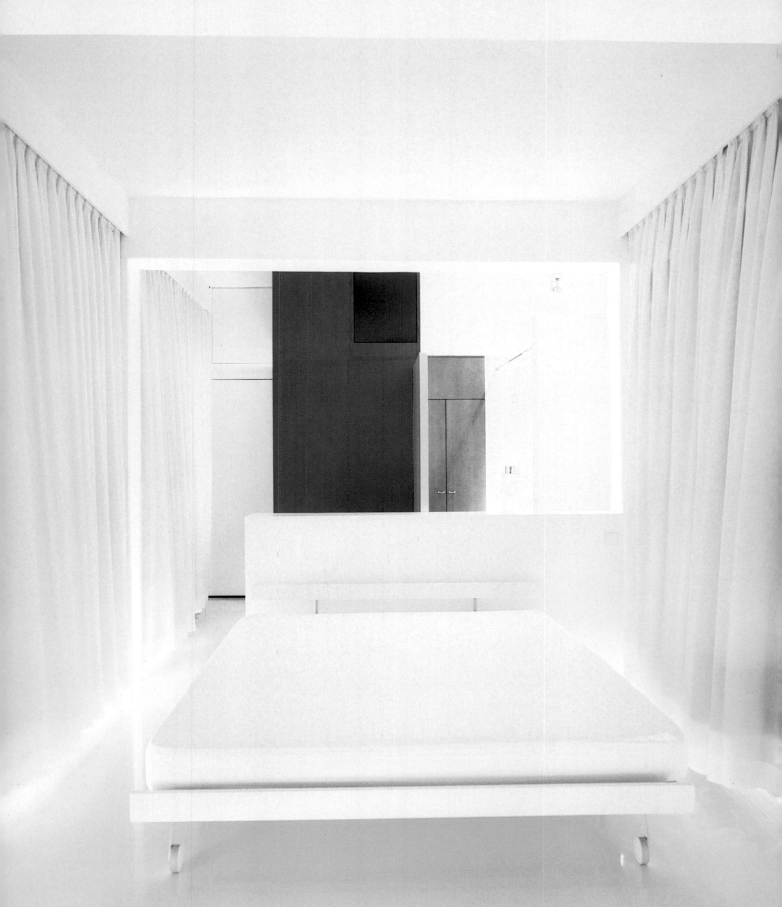

© Almond Chu

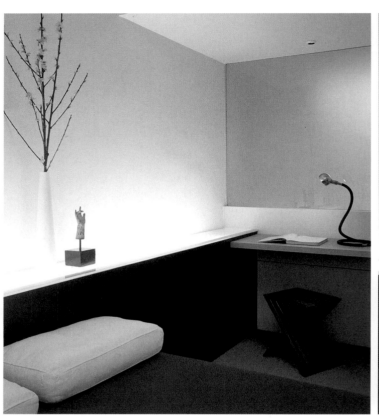
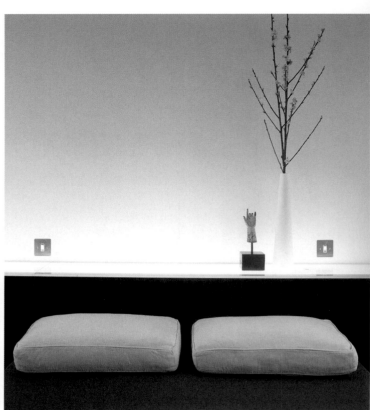

Minimalism focuses on simple, pure forms, bestowing great
importance on space and ecological materials. The maximum
effect is sought using the minimum number of elements.

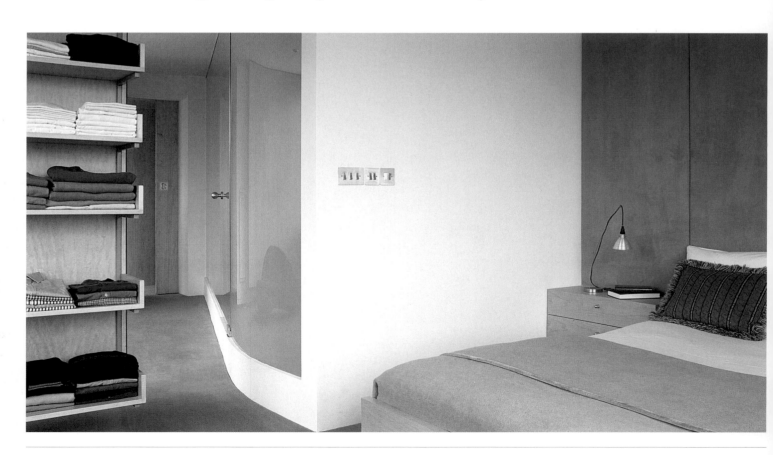

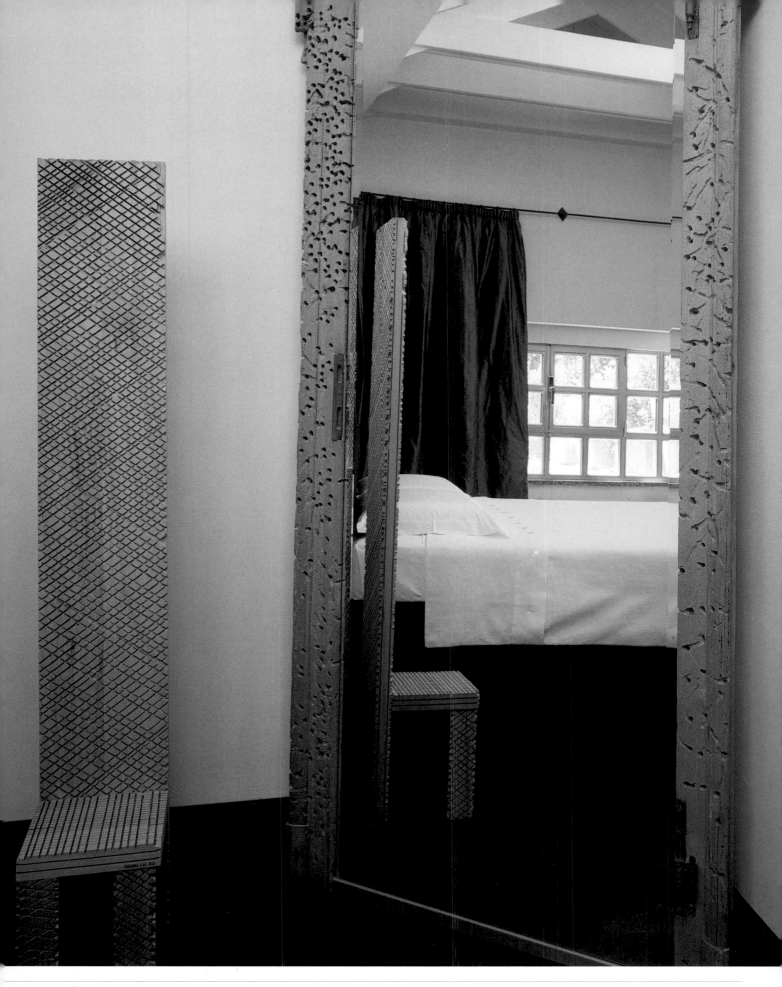

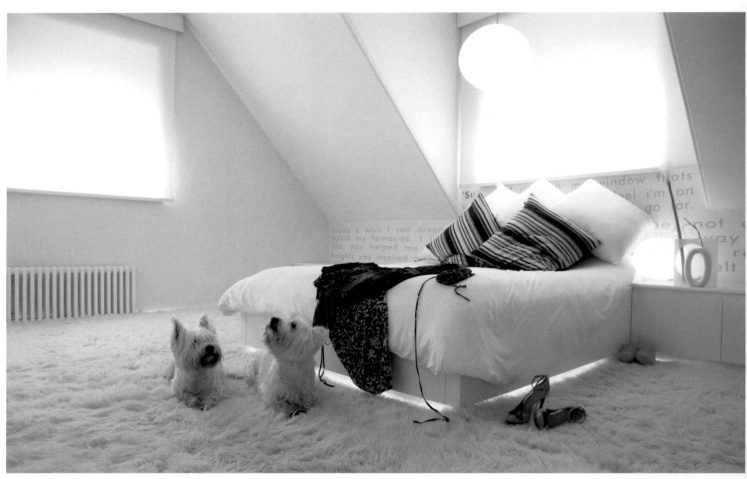

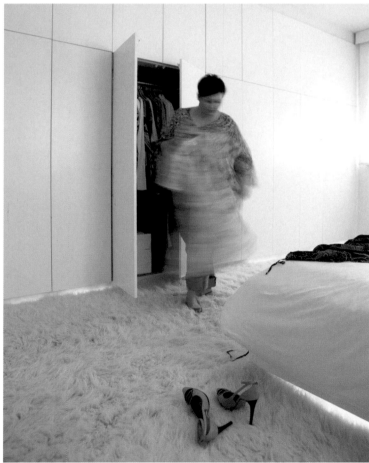

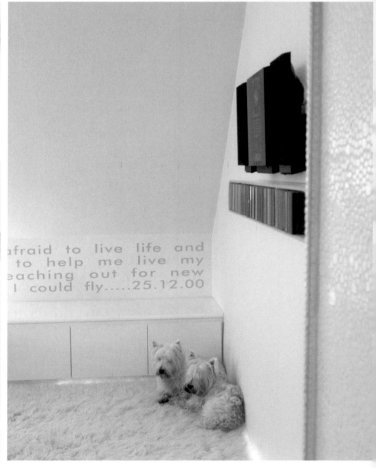

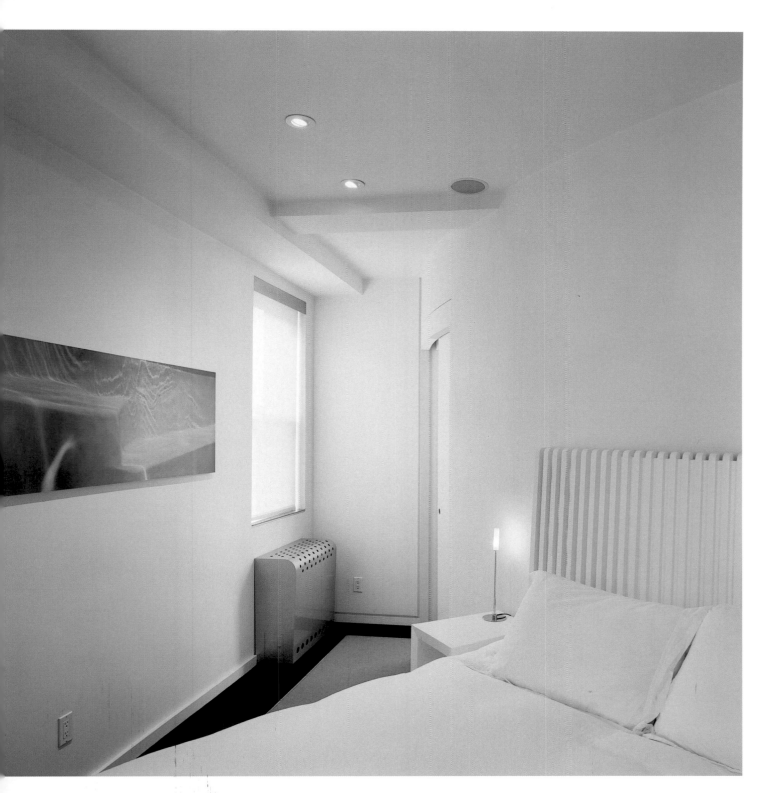

△ Minimalism plays with the sensations aroused by the "minimum": homogeneity, balance, and light. The integration of light sources into furniture reduces the intrusion of extraneous elements on to the smooth, white surfaces.

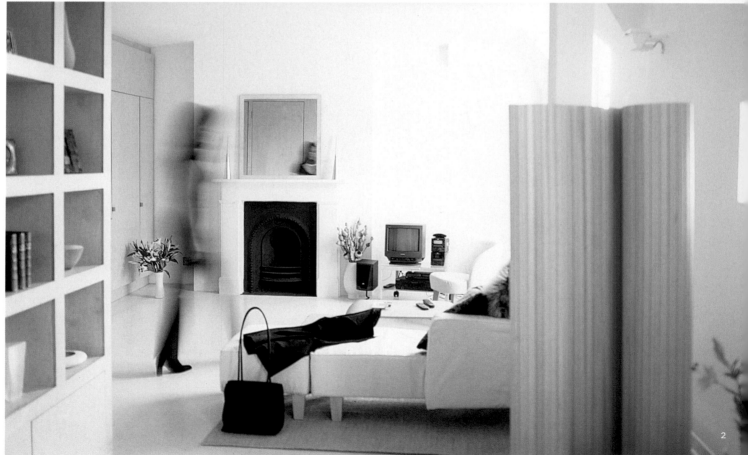

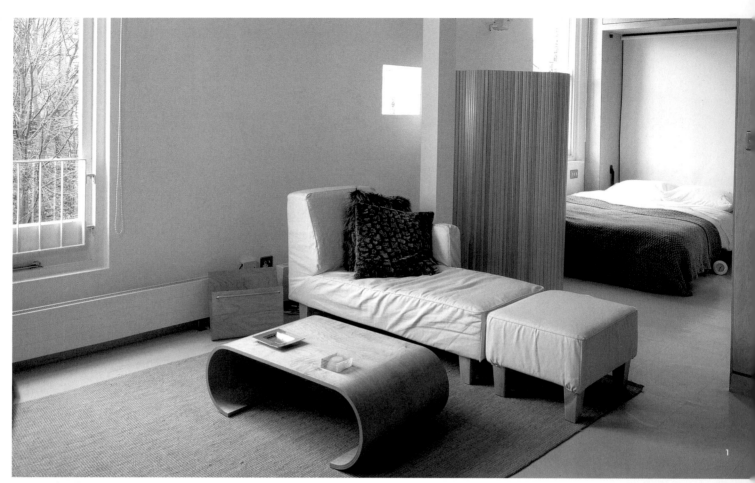

1, 2 © Ed Reeve/Red Cover   3 © Yael Pincus

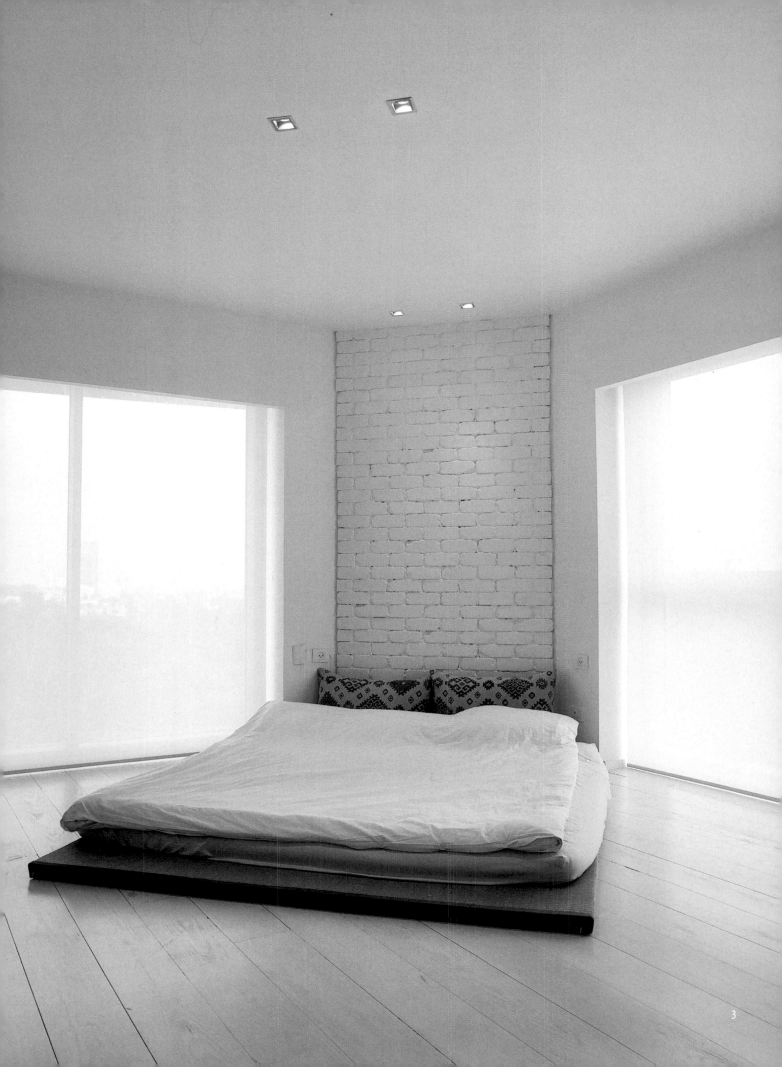

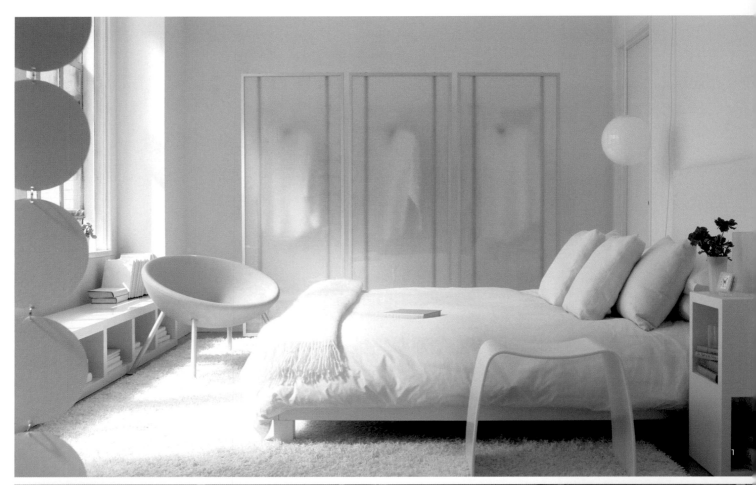

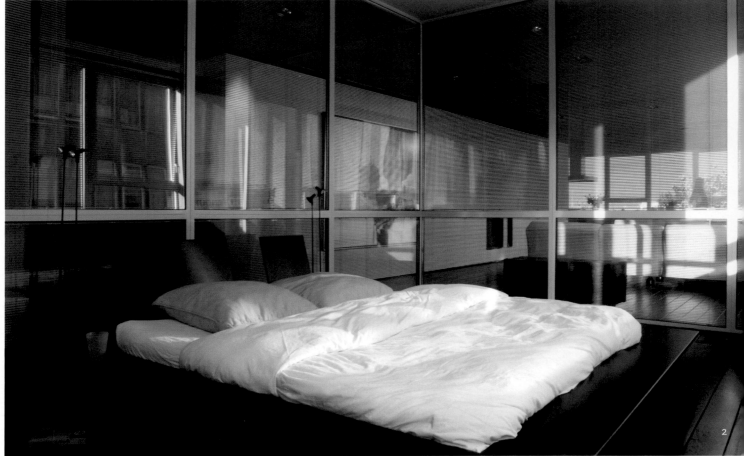

1 © Dominique Vorillon   2 © Laurent Brandajs

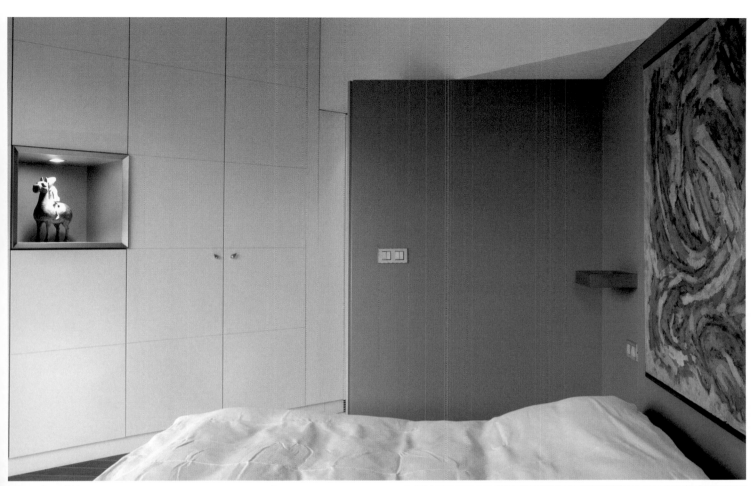

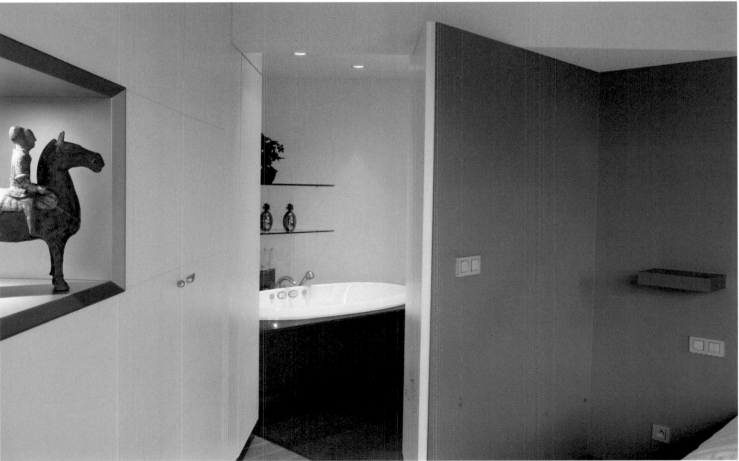

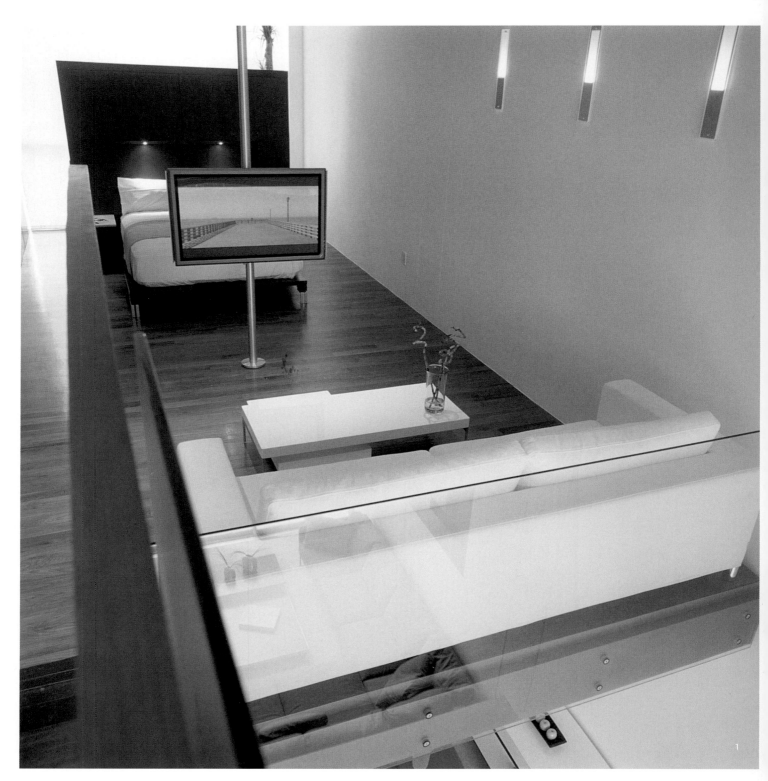

△ Simple lines provide a license for a dramatic touch, as in the case of this home-cinema screen set in the middle of the room, at the foot of the bed.

▷ On the opposite page, a bedroom shows the influence of the Japanese, aesthetic. It does not use prints, but rather smooth textiles. The result is a fresh, relaxed, and very contemporary atmosphere.

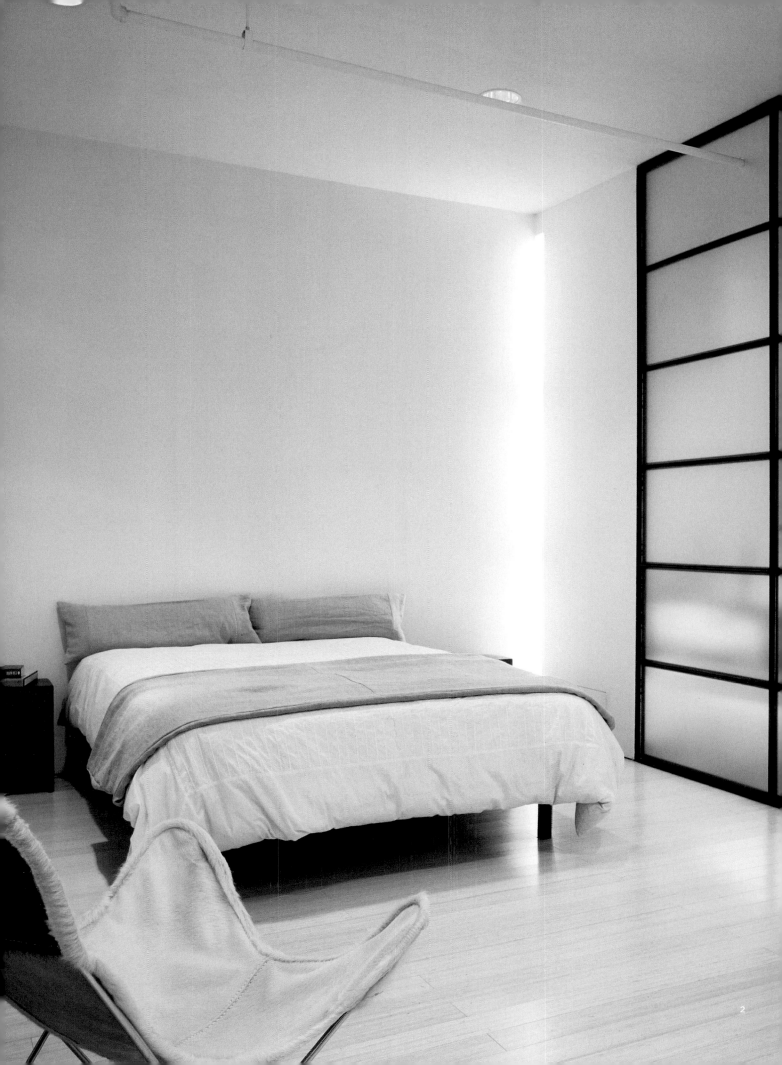

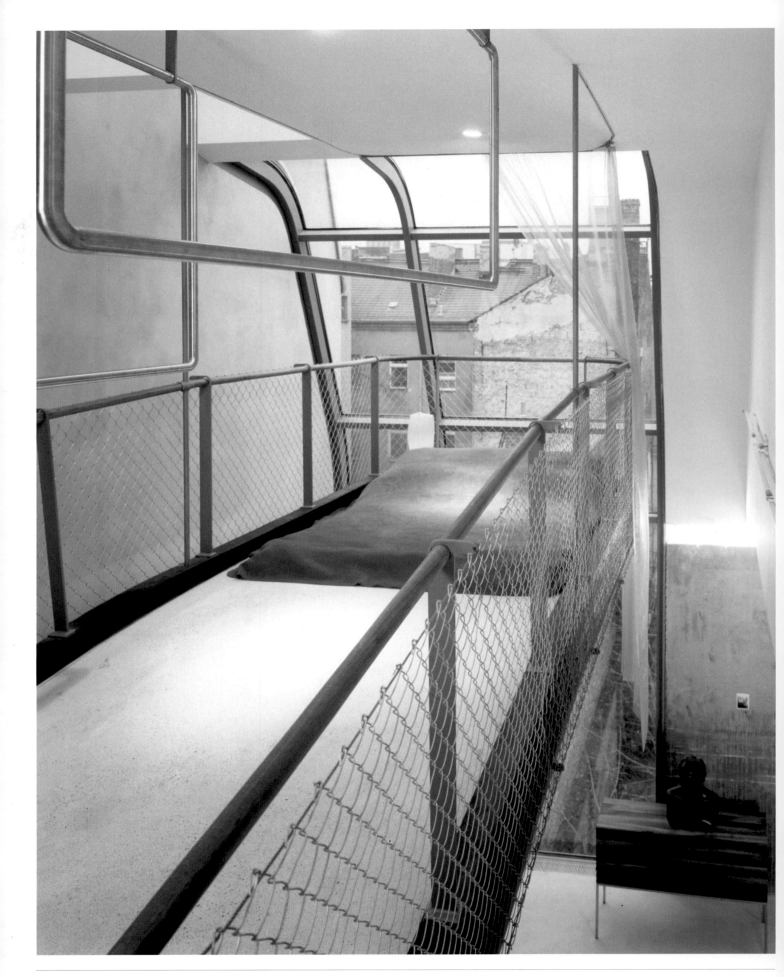

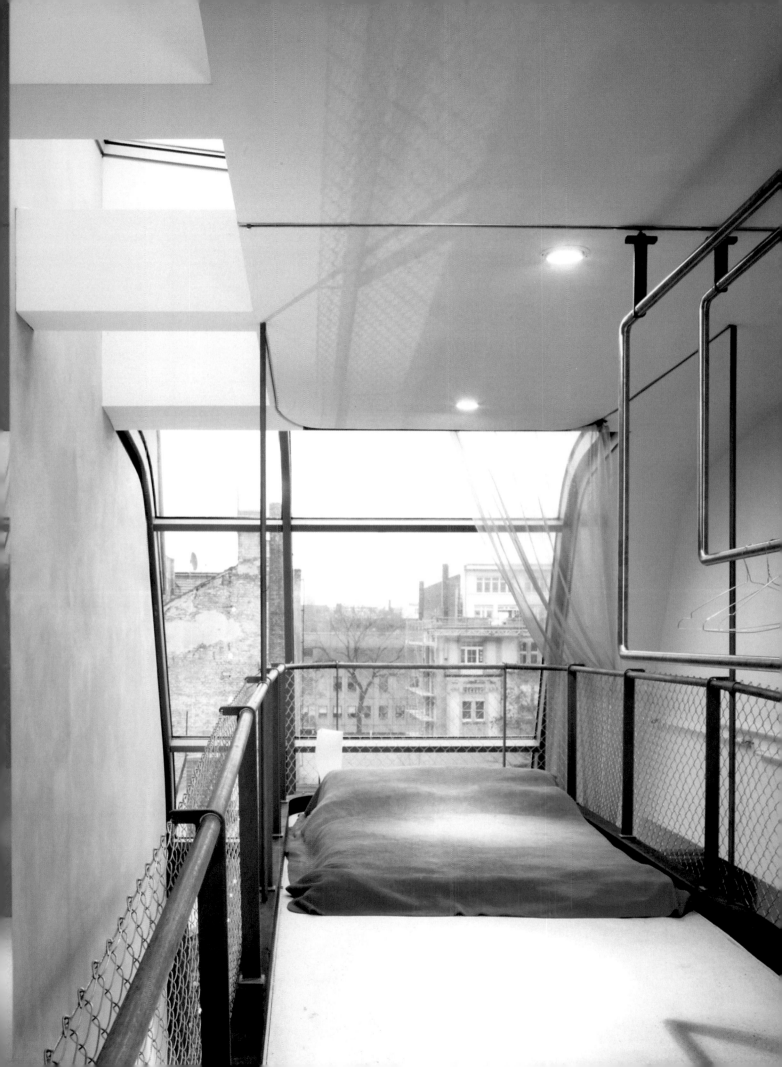

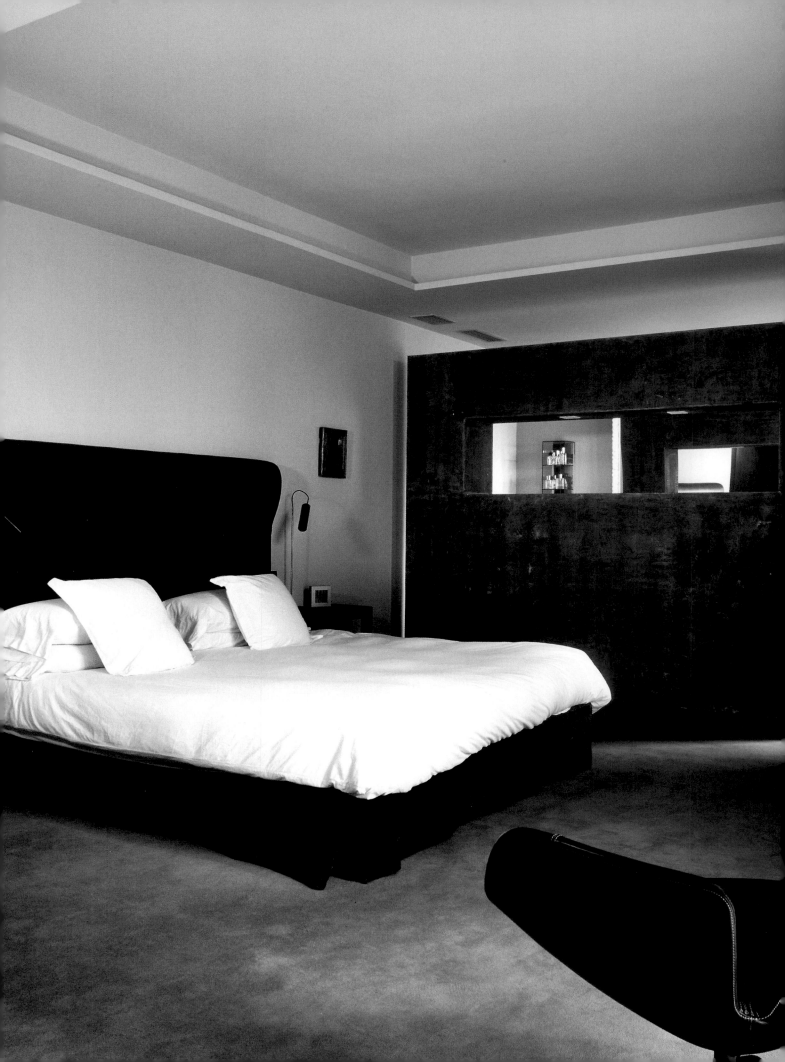

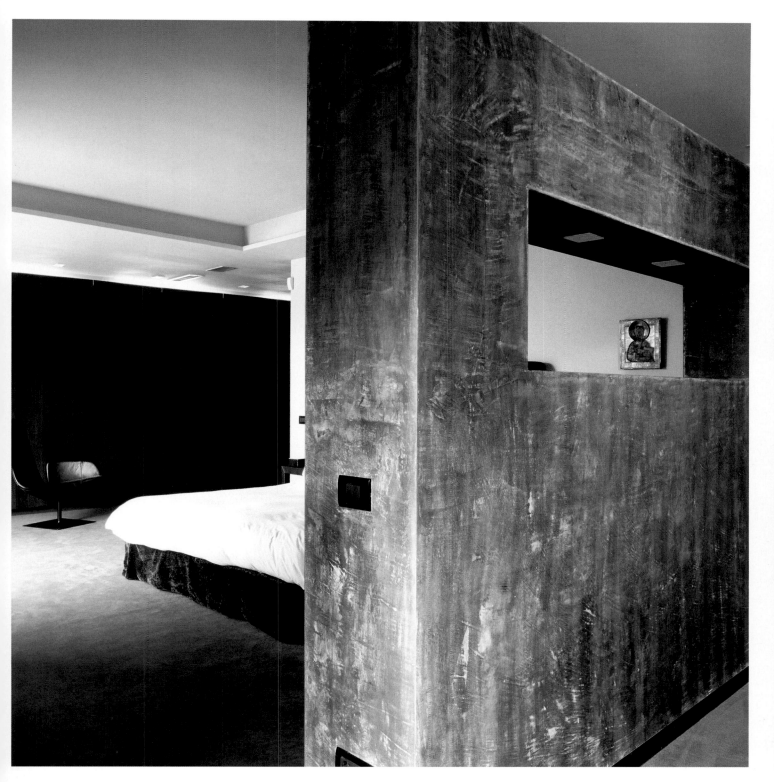

Minimalism welcomed the use of elements with an industrial look, such as metal and concrete. In this case, various styles are mixed to create a personal impression: concrete contrasts with a retro-style chair and heavy velvet.

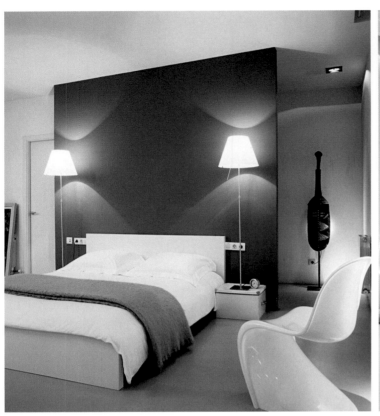
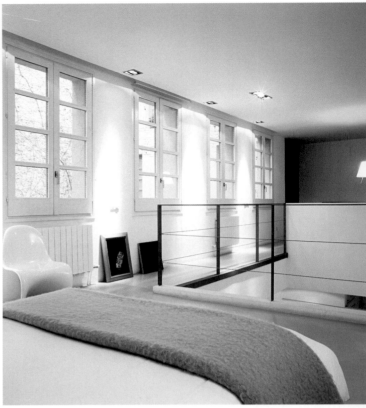

In the top two photos, a Werner Panton chair bestows character
on the bedroom, along with two white lamps set off by a colored
background.

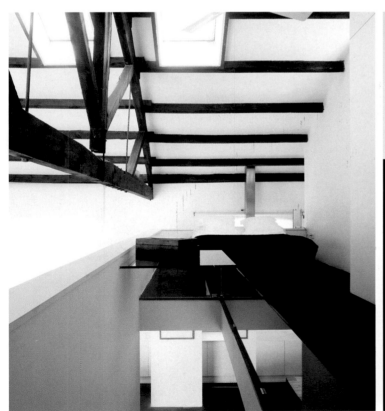
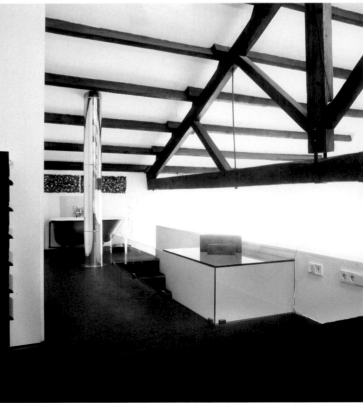

© Jordi Miralles

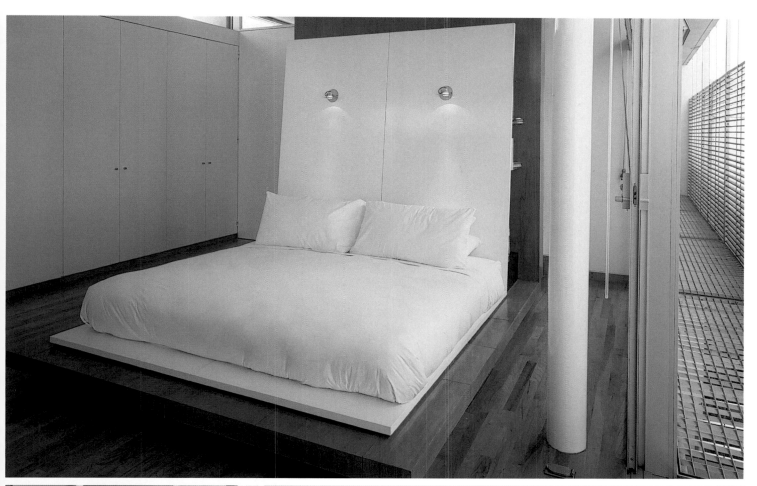

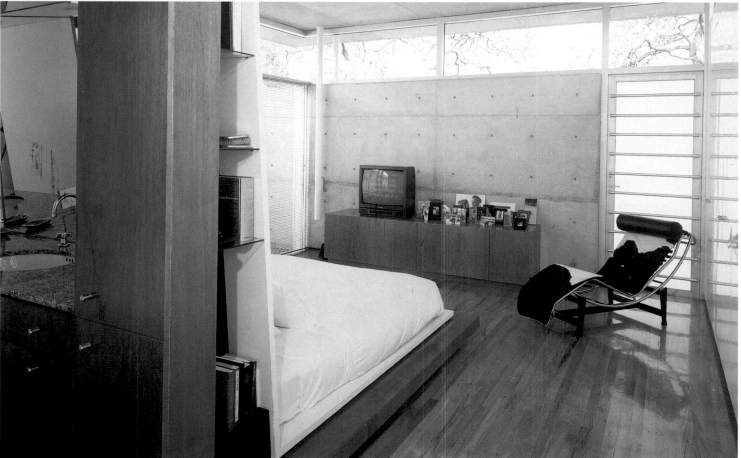

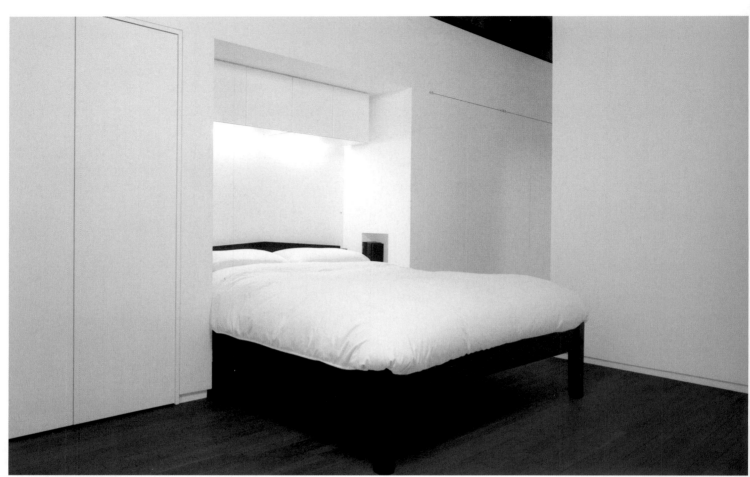

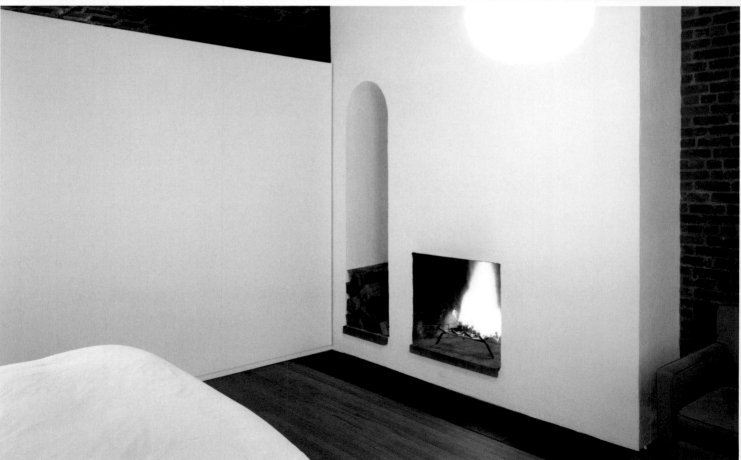

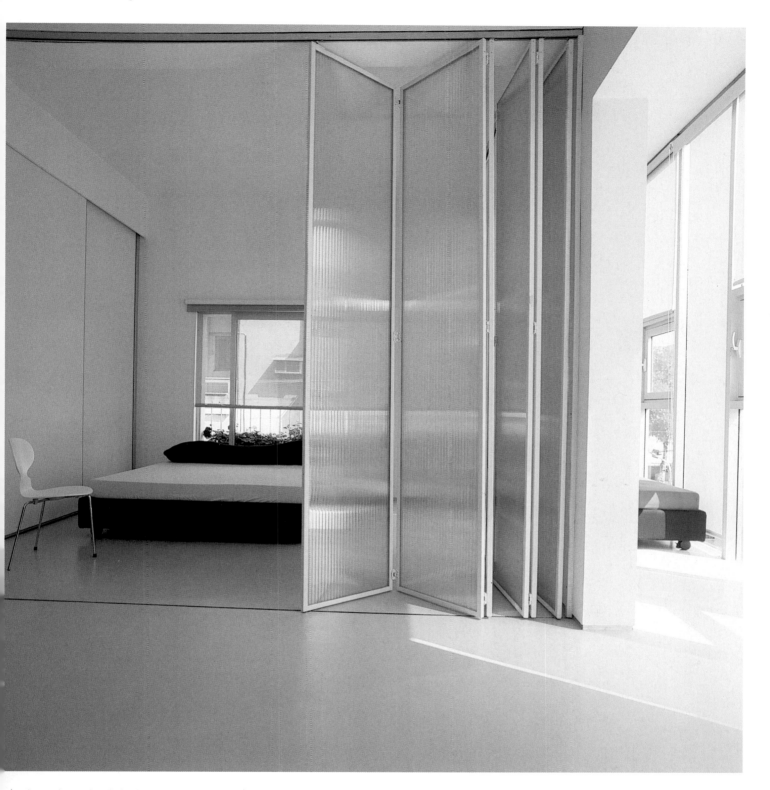

△ This industrial-style bedroom is the work of Itzai Paritzki and Paola Liani.

© Yael Pincus

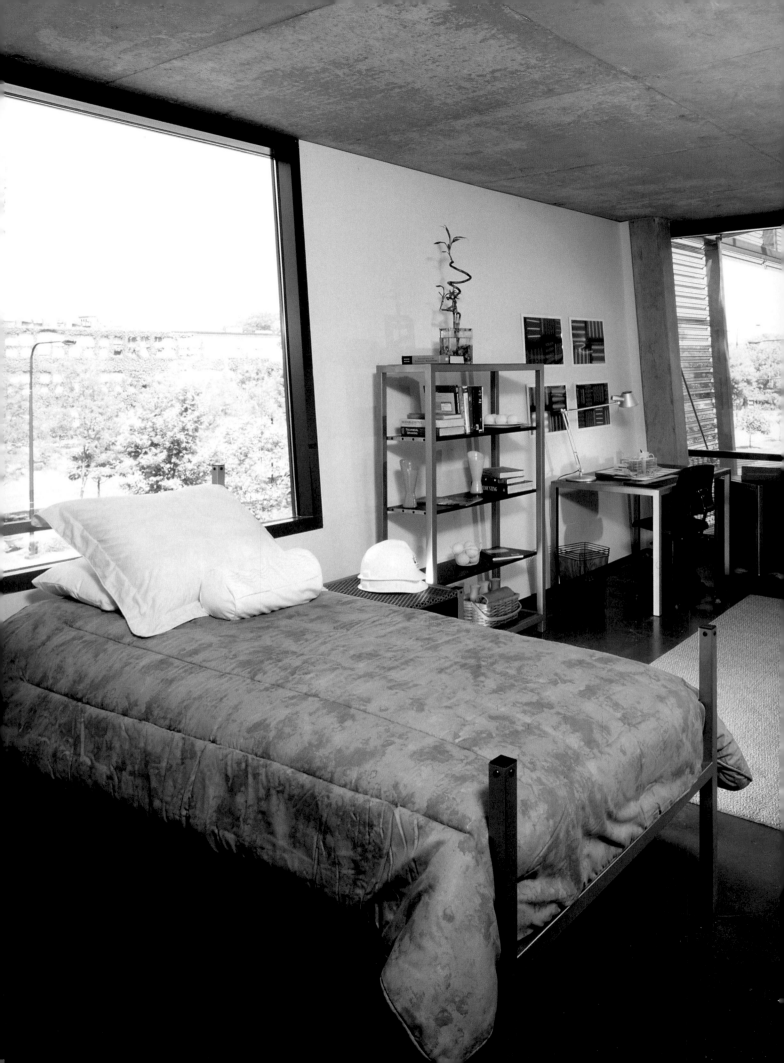

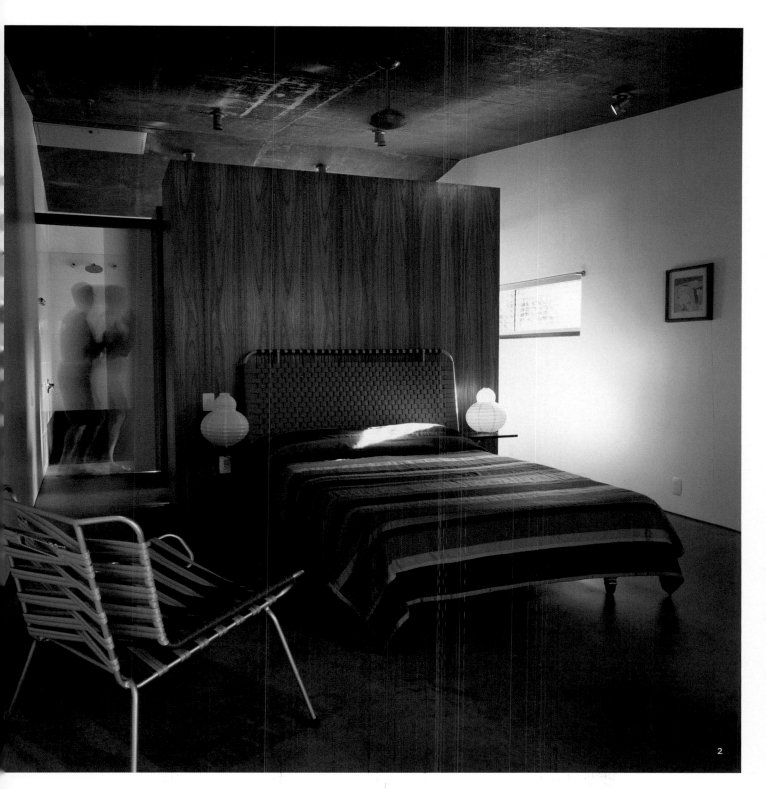

☐ Leaving surfaces unclac, as with these ceilings that reveal the structure's original concrete, makes it possible to save on materials while creating an upbeat look.

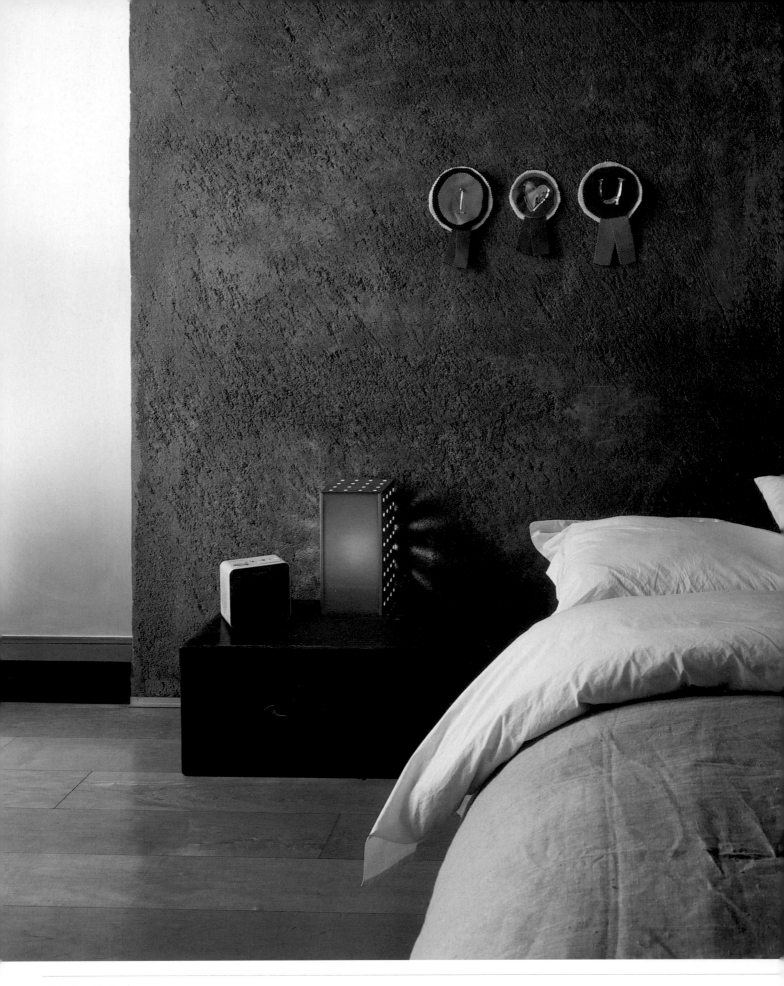

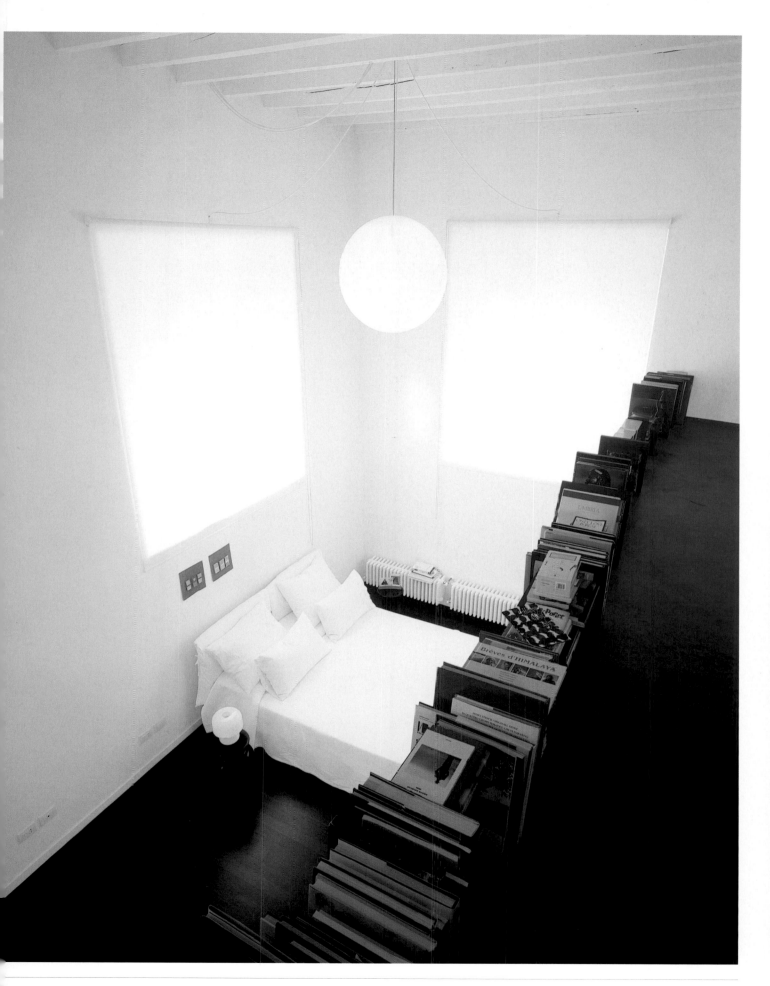

© Andrea Martiradonna

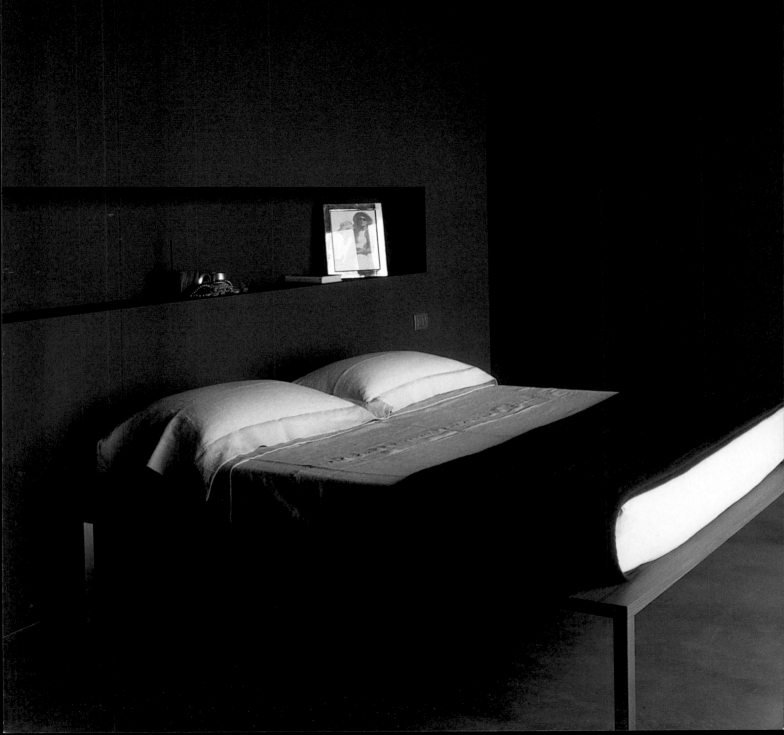

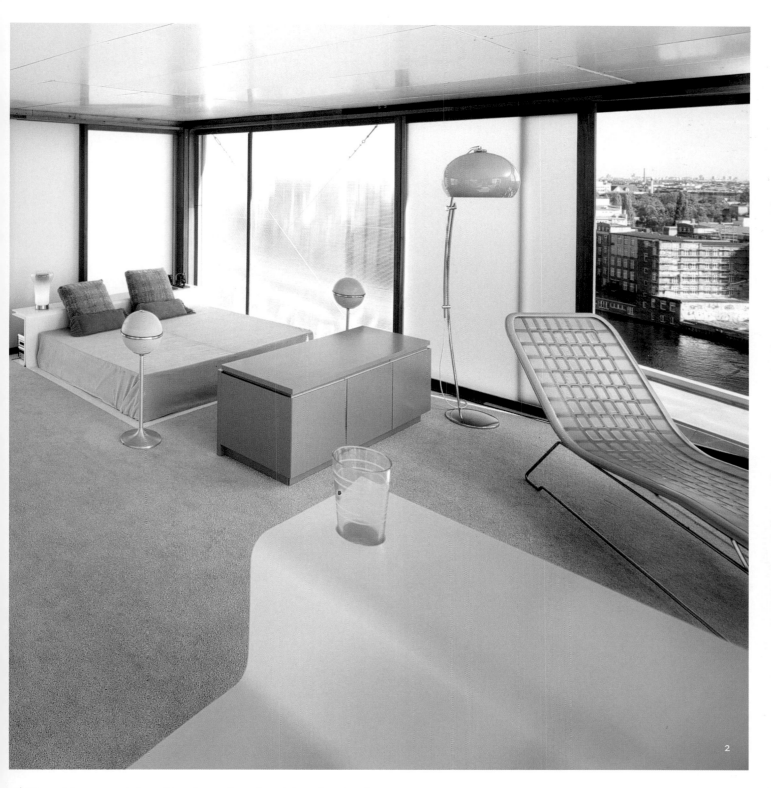

◁ "Something can only be said to be perfect when it is reduced to its essence." Interlübke, German designers.

1 © Gianni Basso/Vega MG   2 © Steffen Jänicke

EMMAUS PUBLIC LIBRARY
11 EAST MAIN STREET
EMMAUS, PA 18049

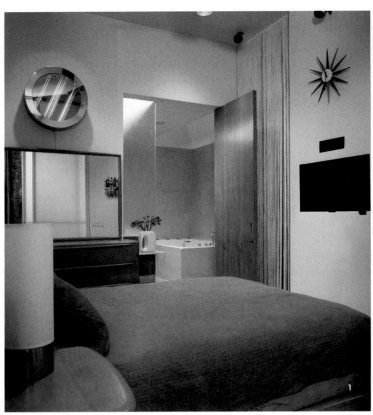

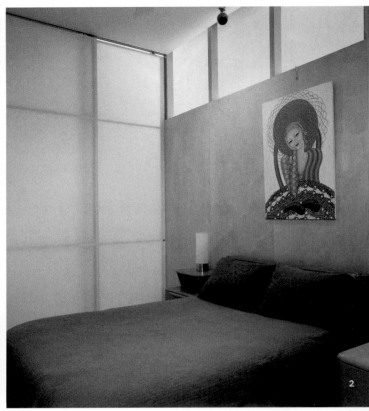

*The retro look is characterized by the use of geometrical forms
(mainly circles and rectangles) and striking colors.*

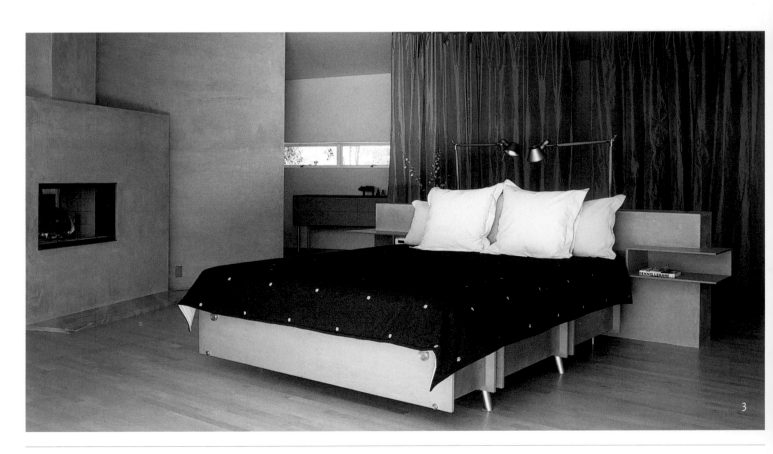

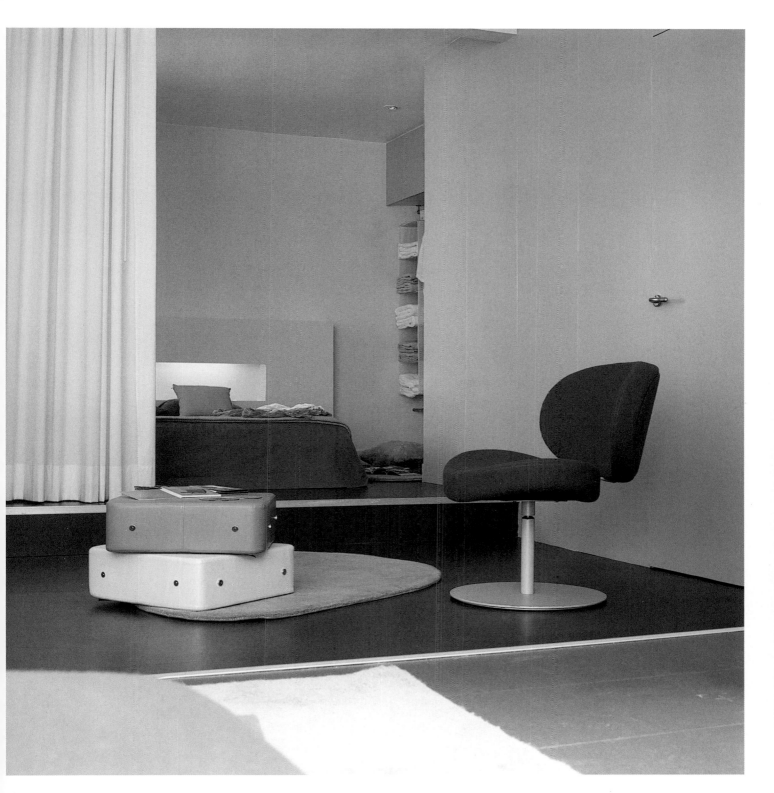

△ In this apartment by Ellen Rapellius, a wall has been eliminated and the bedroom is set apart by means of a curtain, which creates the appearance of a stage set.

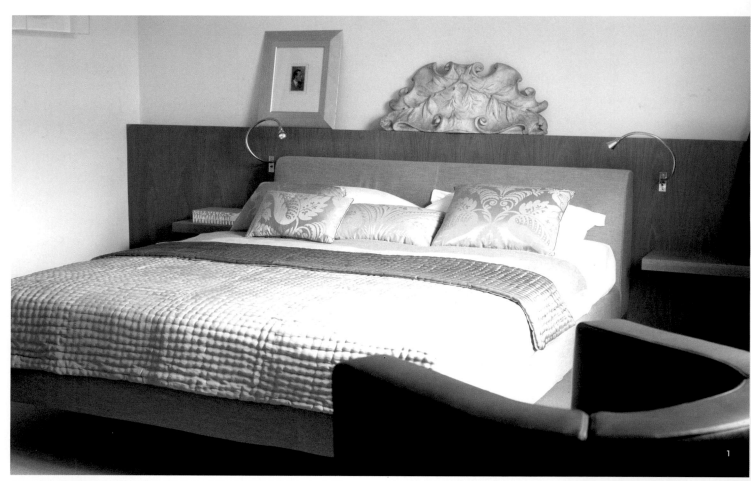

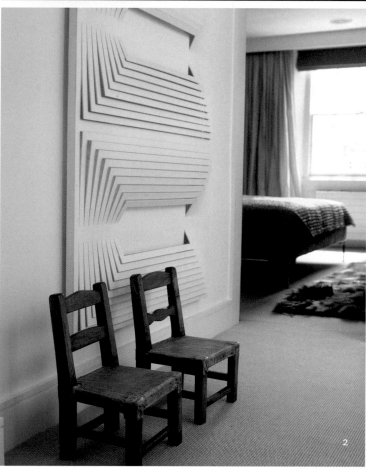

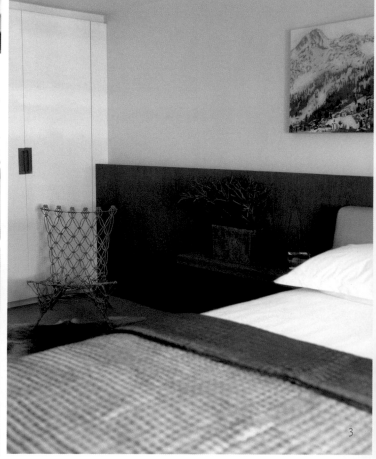

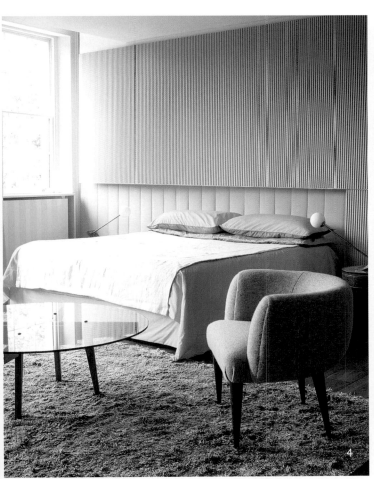
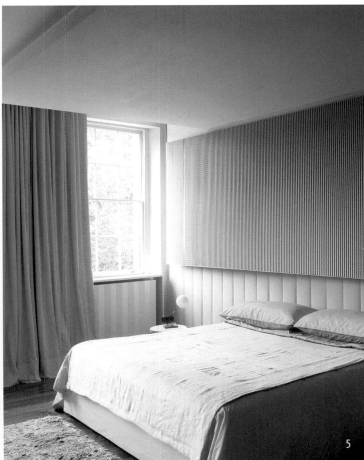
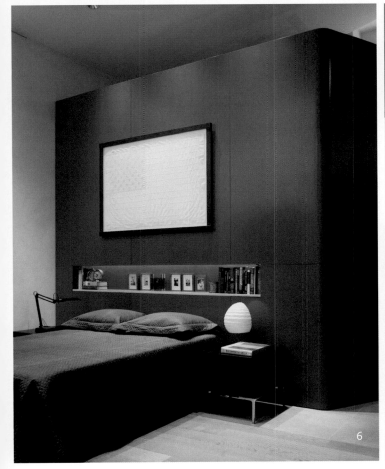
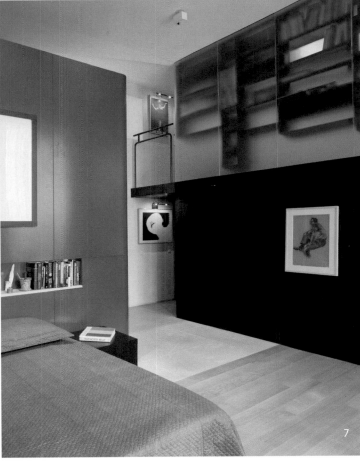

4, 5 © Tim Evan Cook/Red Cover   6, 7 © Gregory Goodes Photography

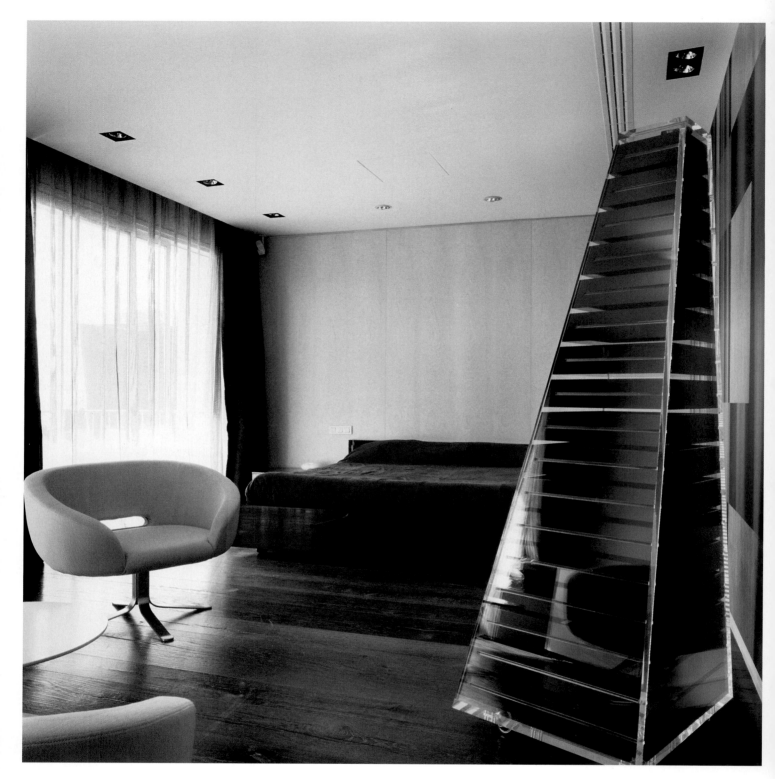

☐ The retro style is characterized by an excess of colors, forms, and sizes. Minimalism emerged as a response to this and is characterized by diametrically opposite attributes.

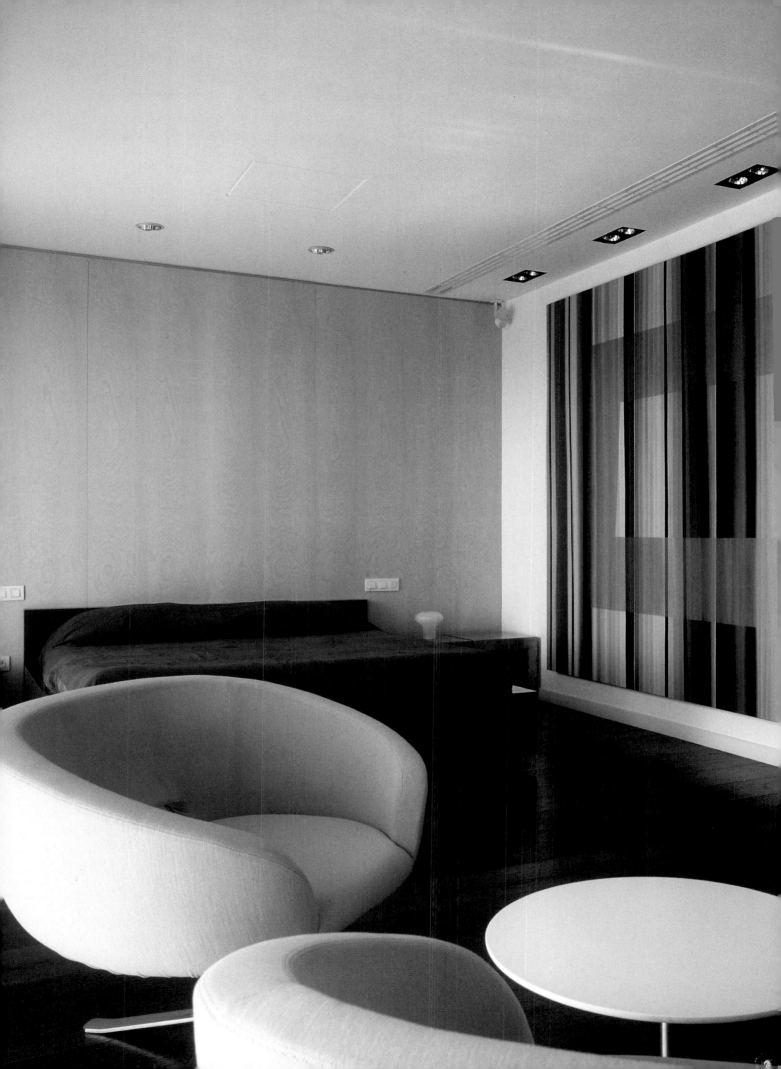

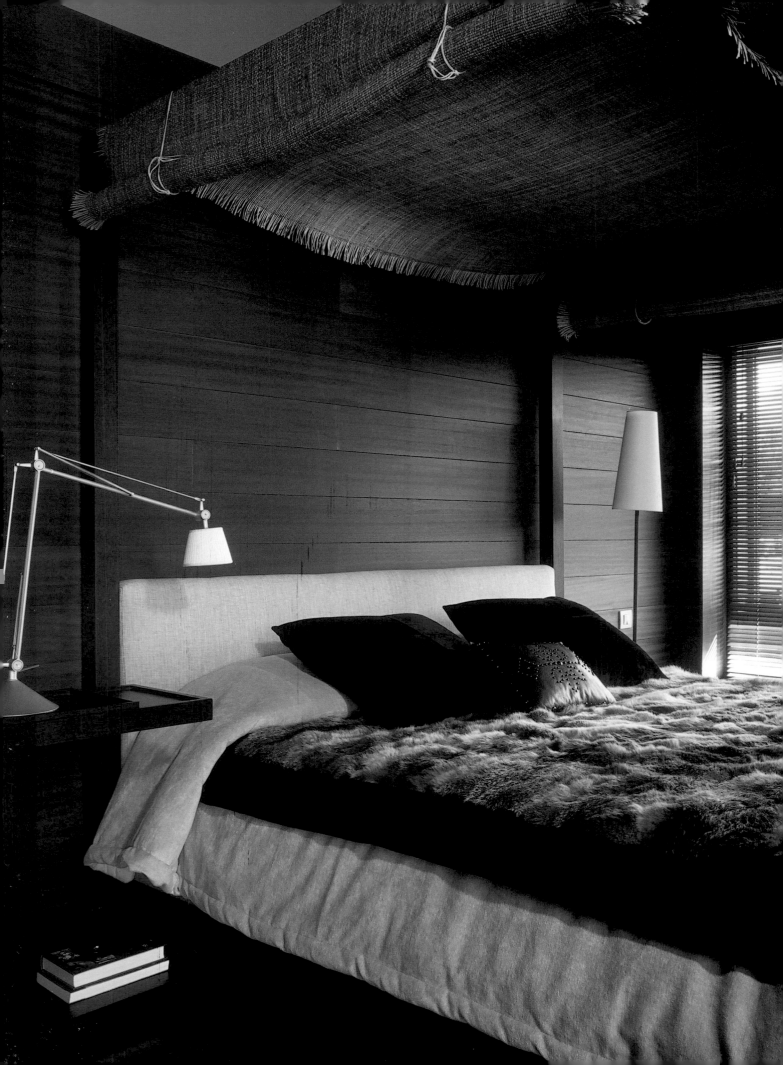

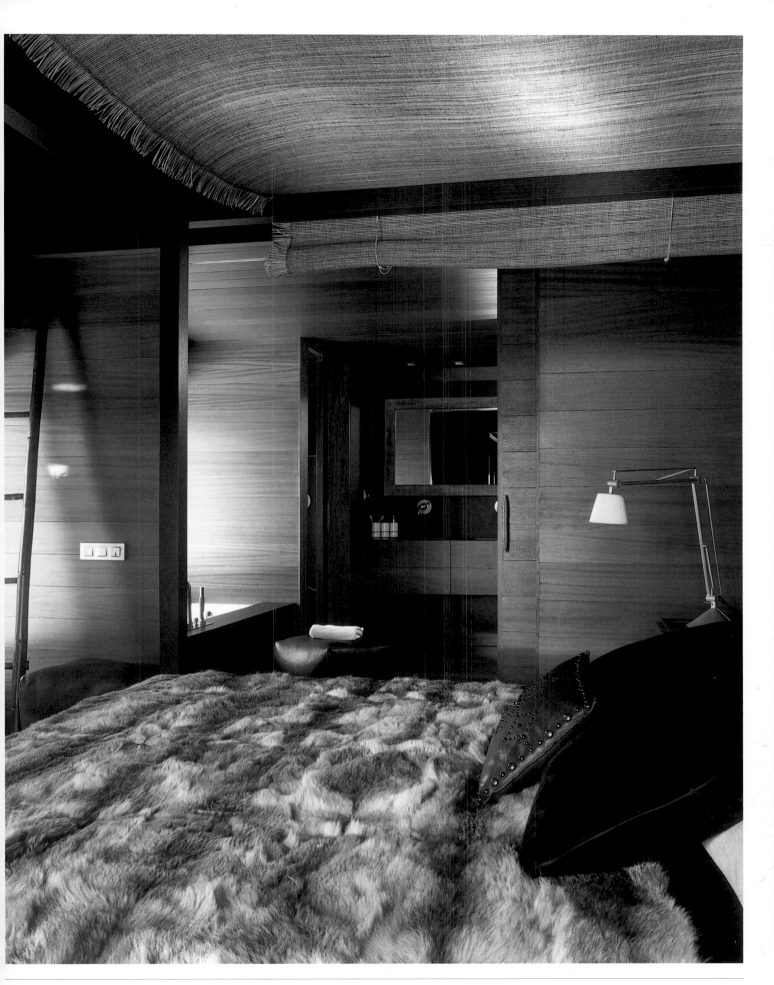

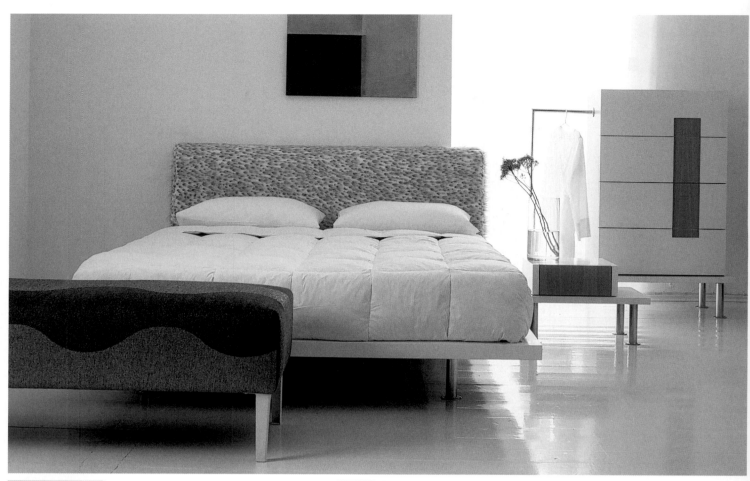

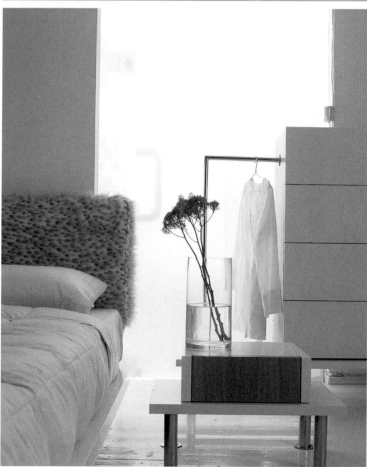

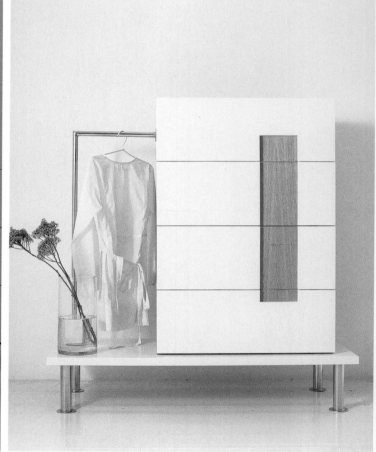

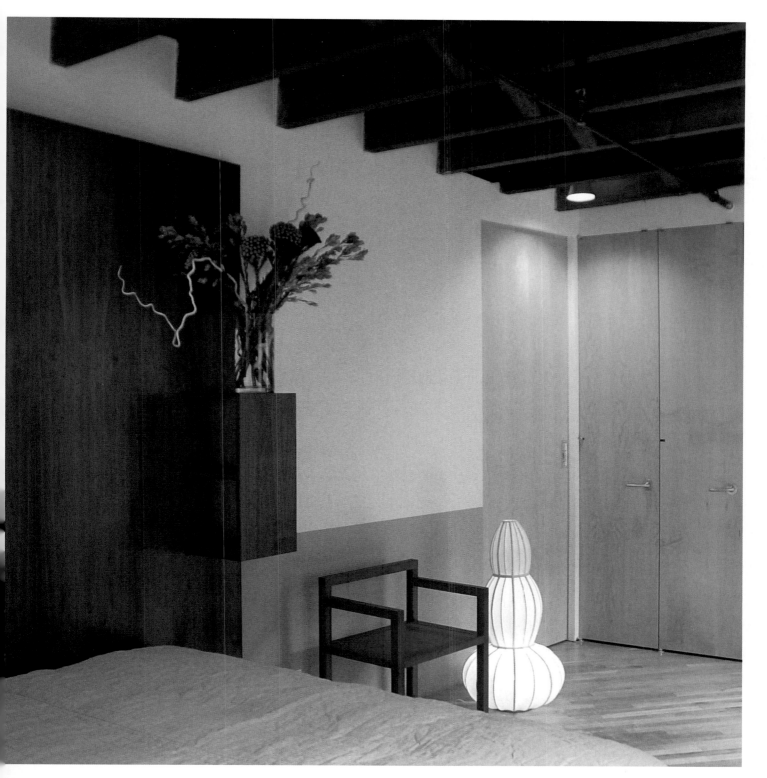

△ Wood, along with other natural materials, has experienced a boom thanks to the revival of ethnic and rustic styles. Cha & Innerhofer produce an interior architecture characterized by the use of wood.

◁ The forms, accessories, textiles, and colors evoke nature. A headrest upholstered with feathers adds a personal touch to this project by Titan Design, Tel Aviv.

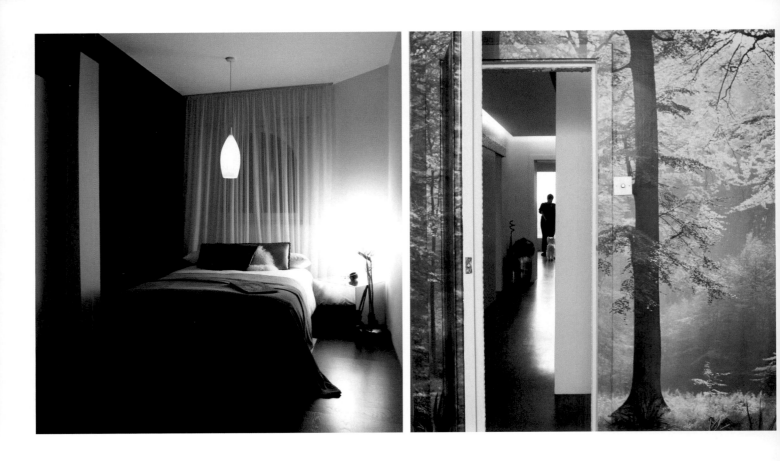

Jo Warman wanted to transform this guest bedroom into a "nature refuge". The wall, covered with a poster of a wood, is intended to break up the apartment's monochromatic color scheme.

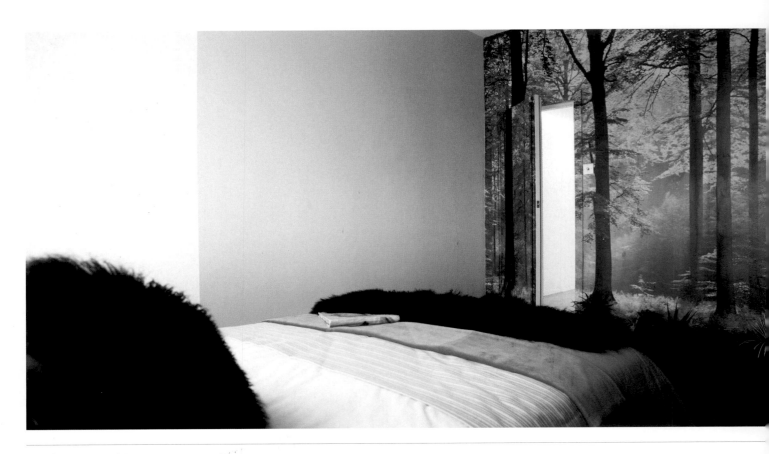

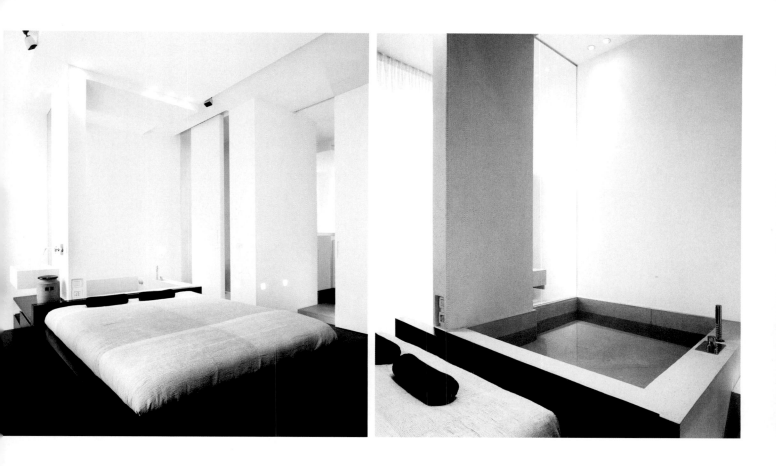

Zen-like sobriety and body care are integrated into the design of bedrooms that combine aesthetically innovative and functionally practical concepts.

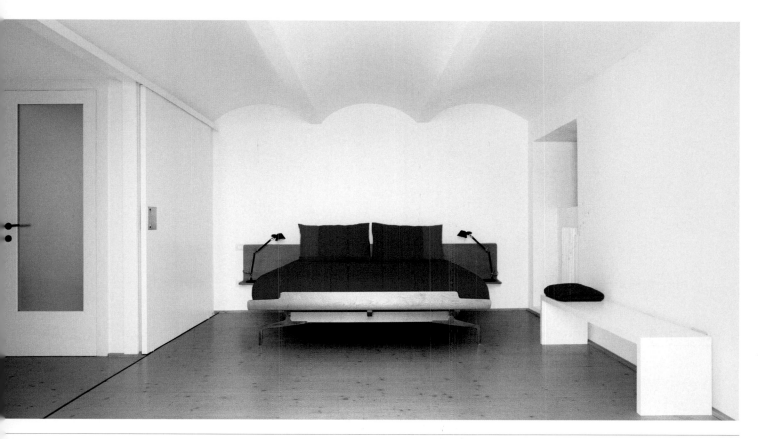

© Matteo Piazza

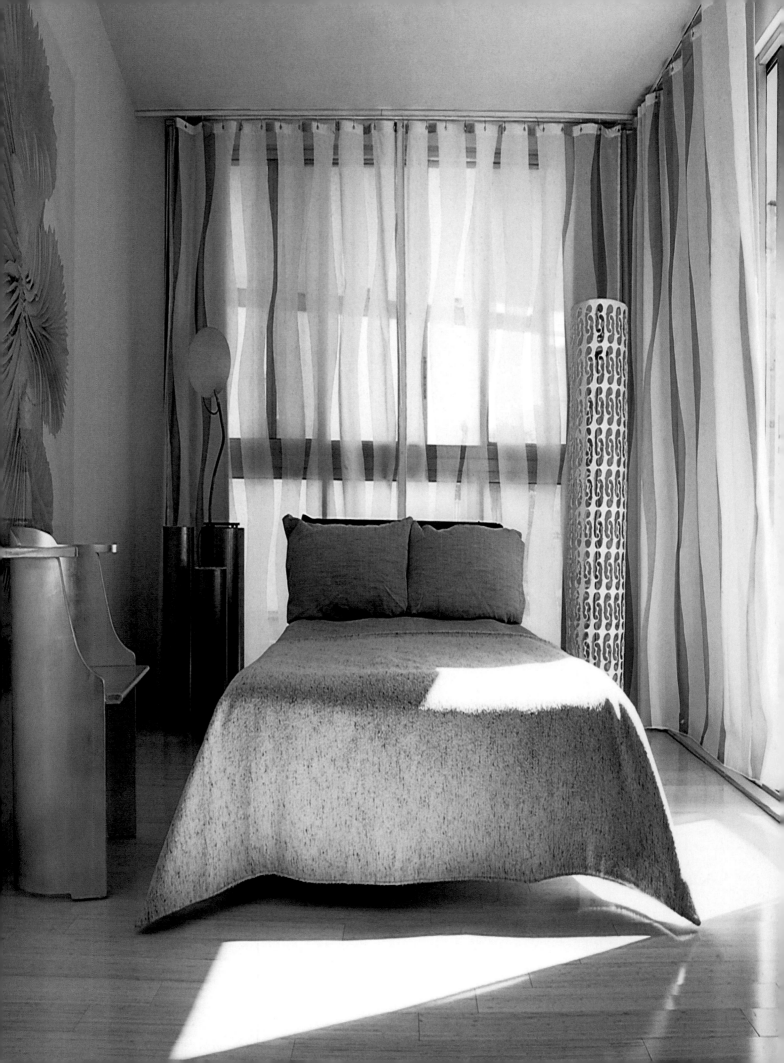

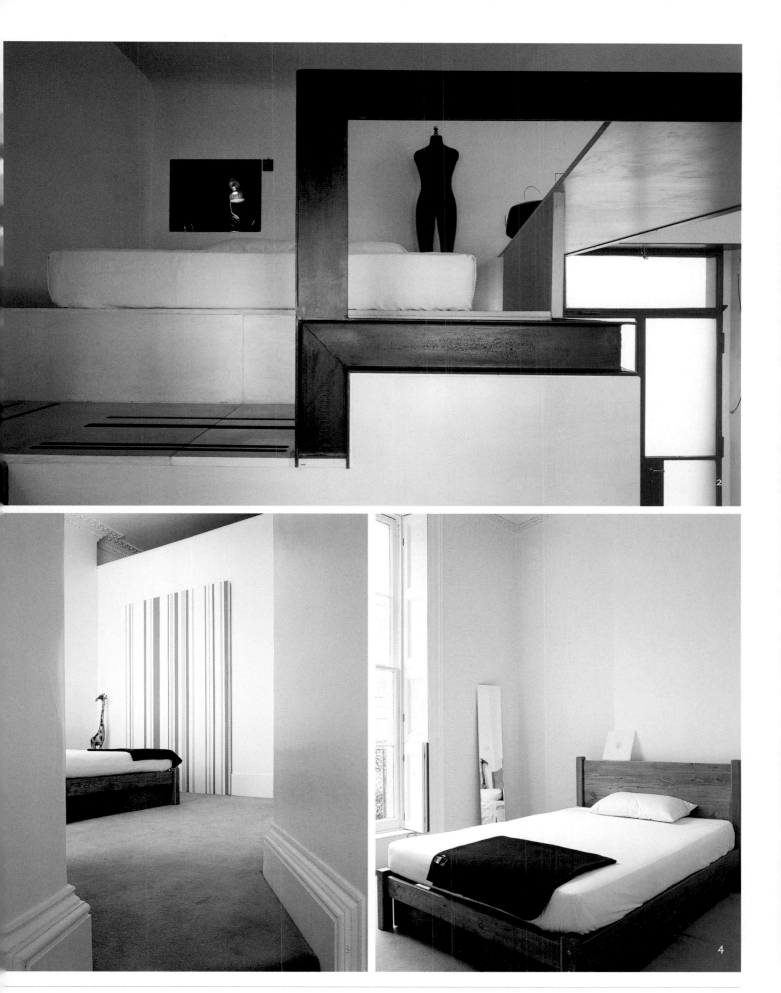

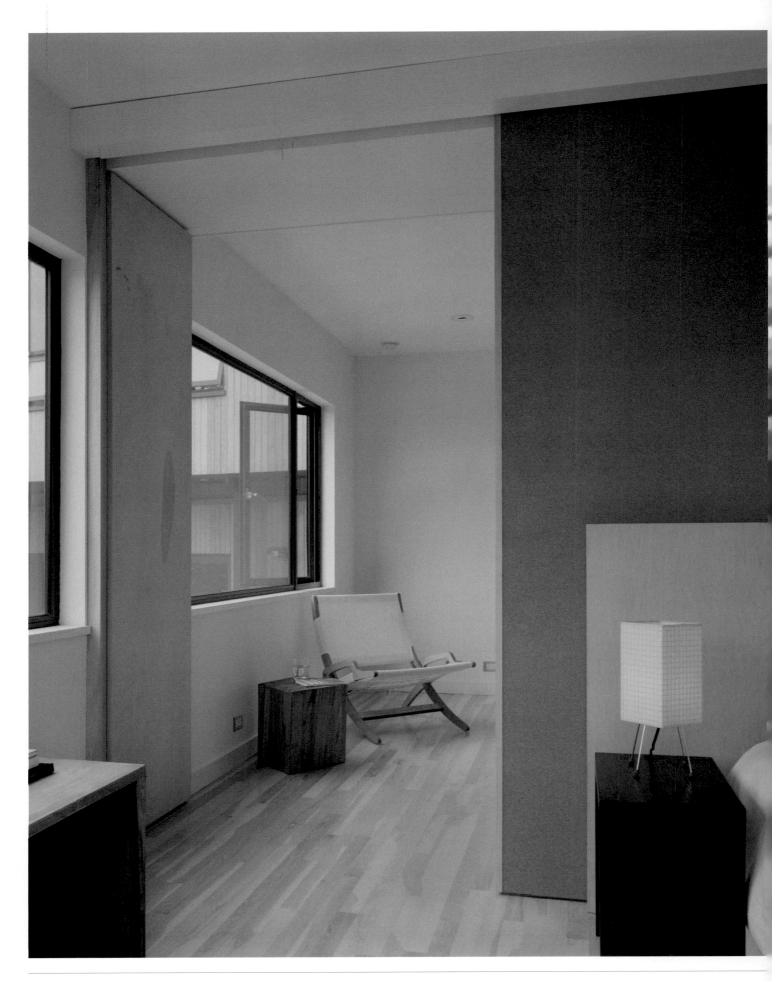

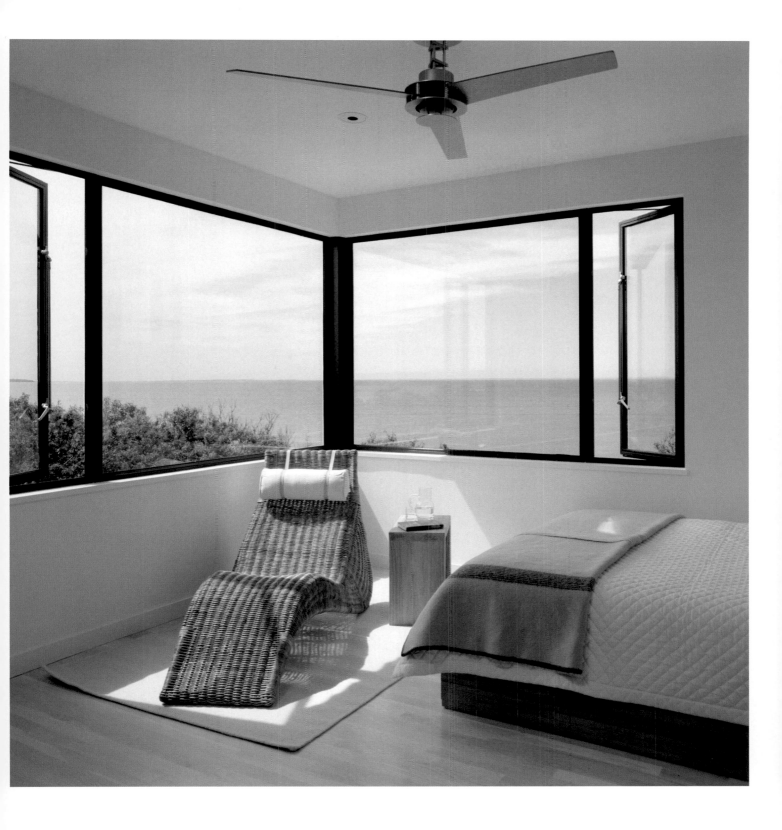

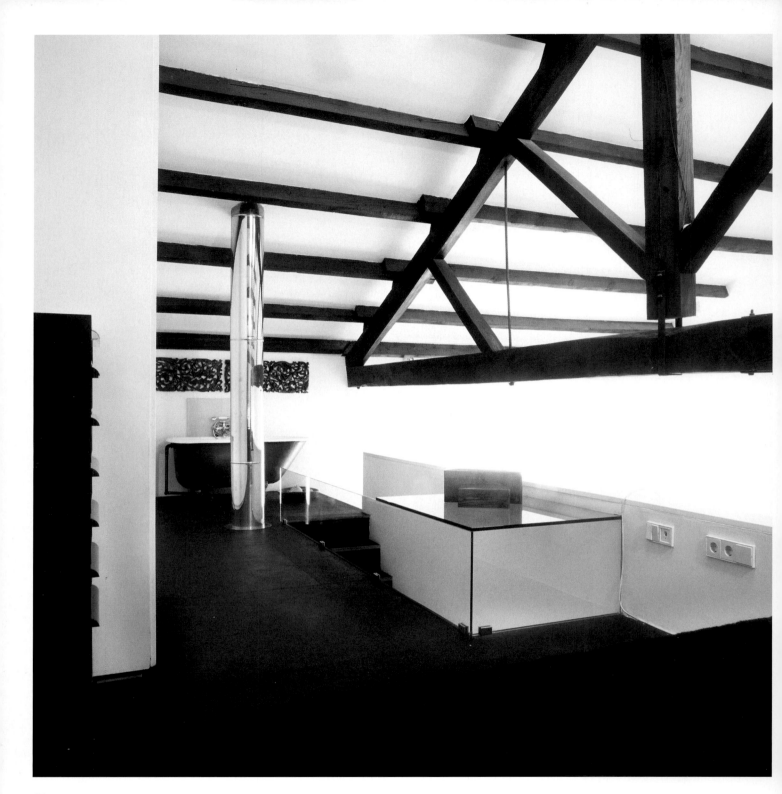

☐ Following the line marked by the ceiling of this attic, the bedroom plays with the wood and the combination of white and dark brown to create a dialogue between the wooden structure of the beams and the rest of the interior.

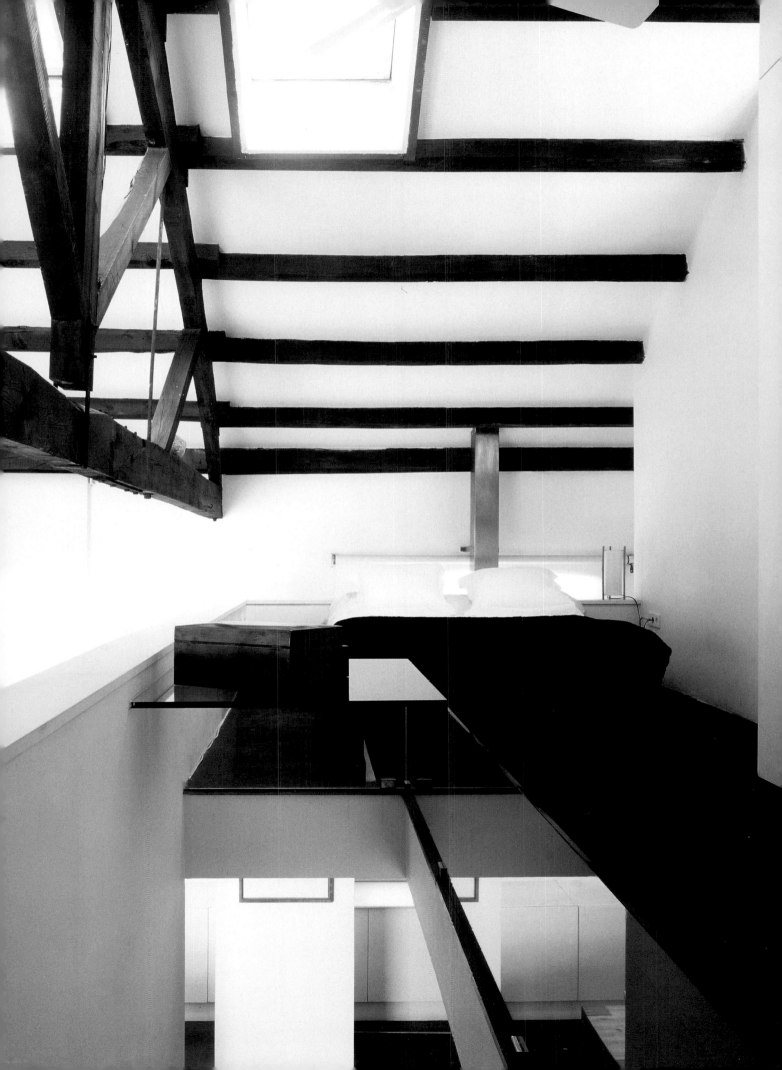

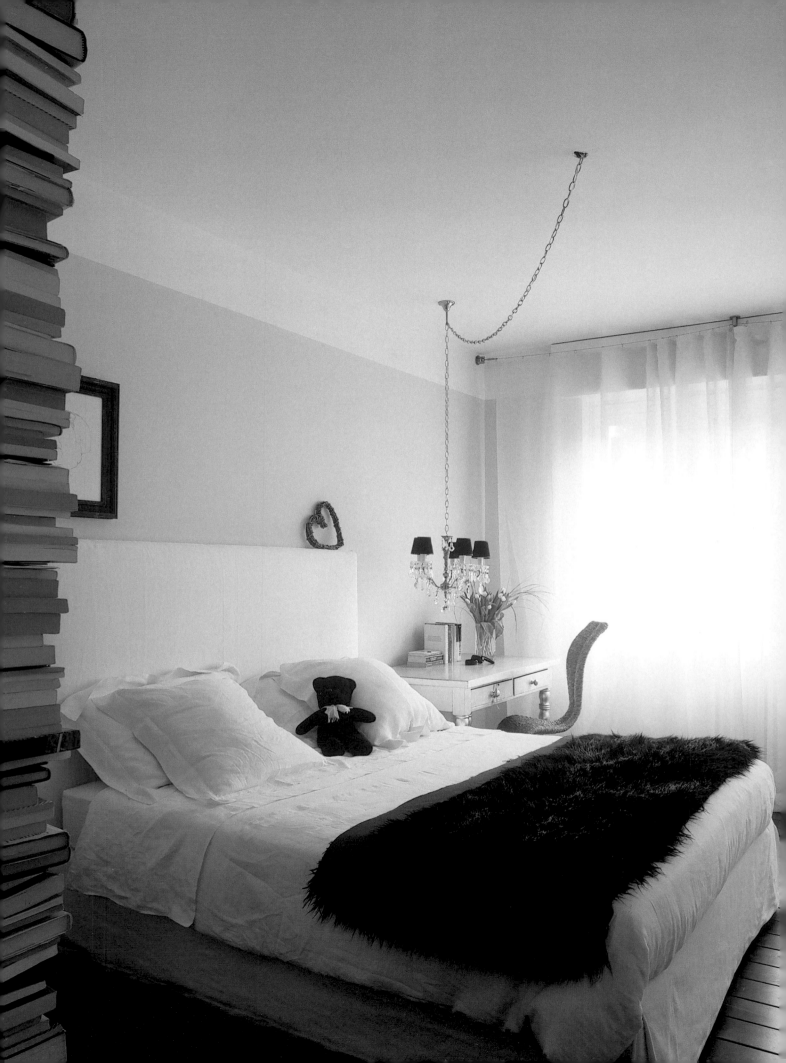

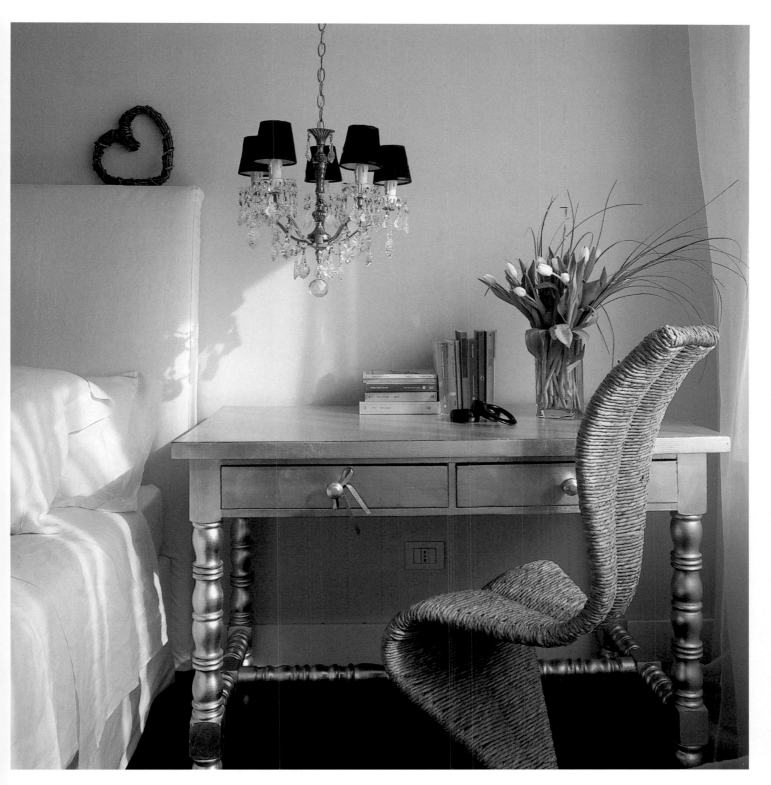

☐ This bedroom, which draws inspiration from the romantic New Rococo style, combines restored period furniture, glass lamps, and sheer fabrics with avant-garde elements to create an atmosphere that is both classical and modern.

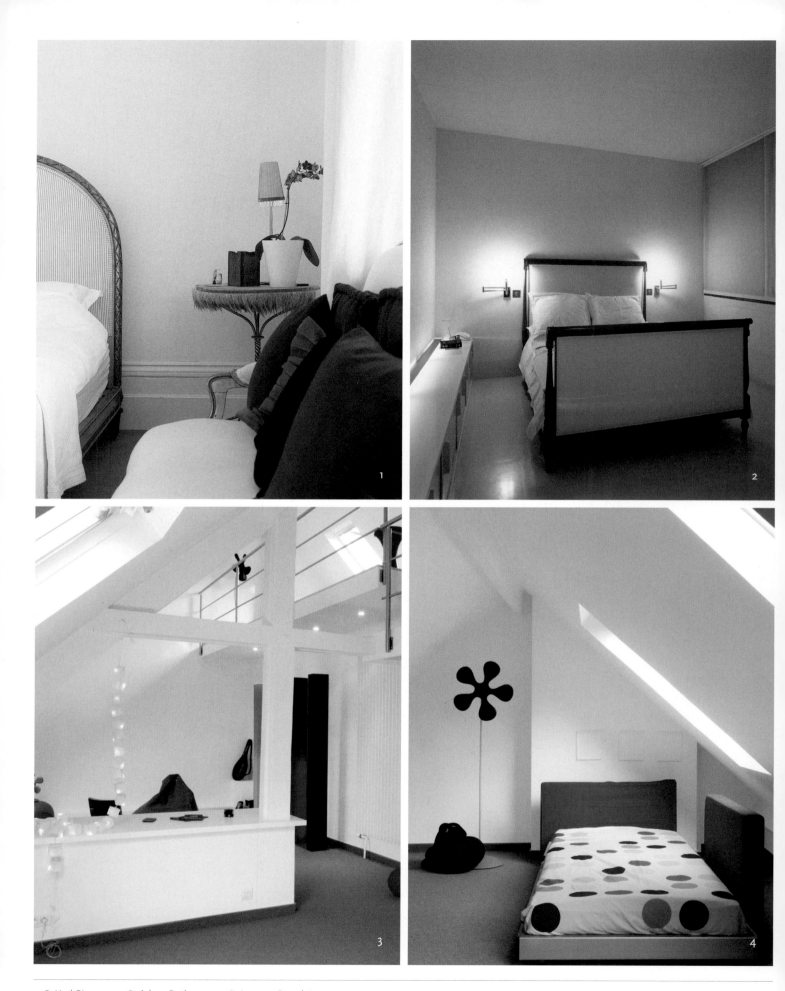

1 © Yael Pincus   2 © Adam Butler   3, 4 © Laurent Brandajs

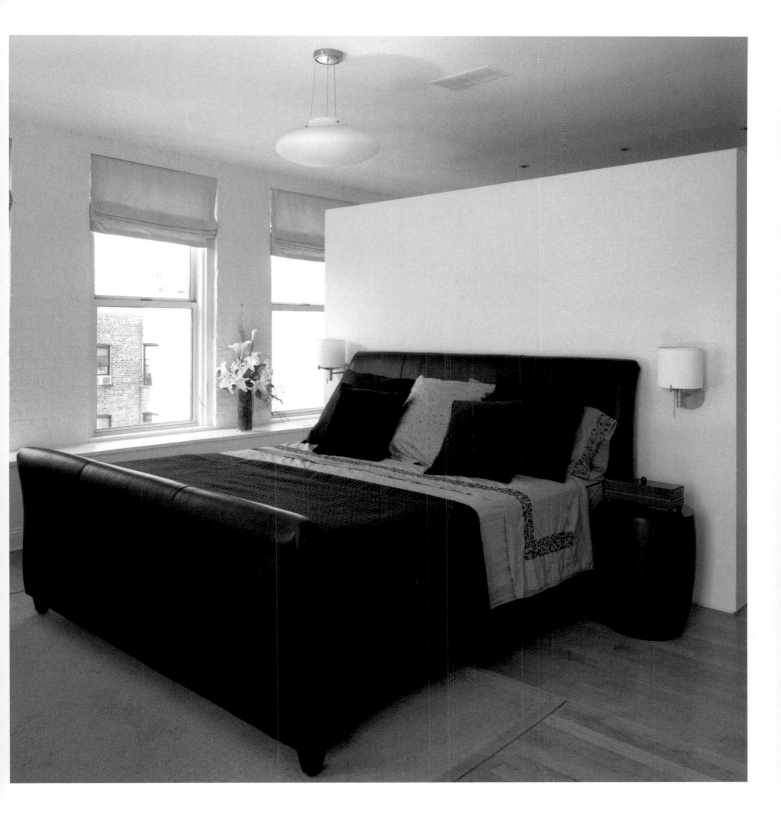

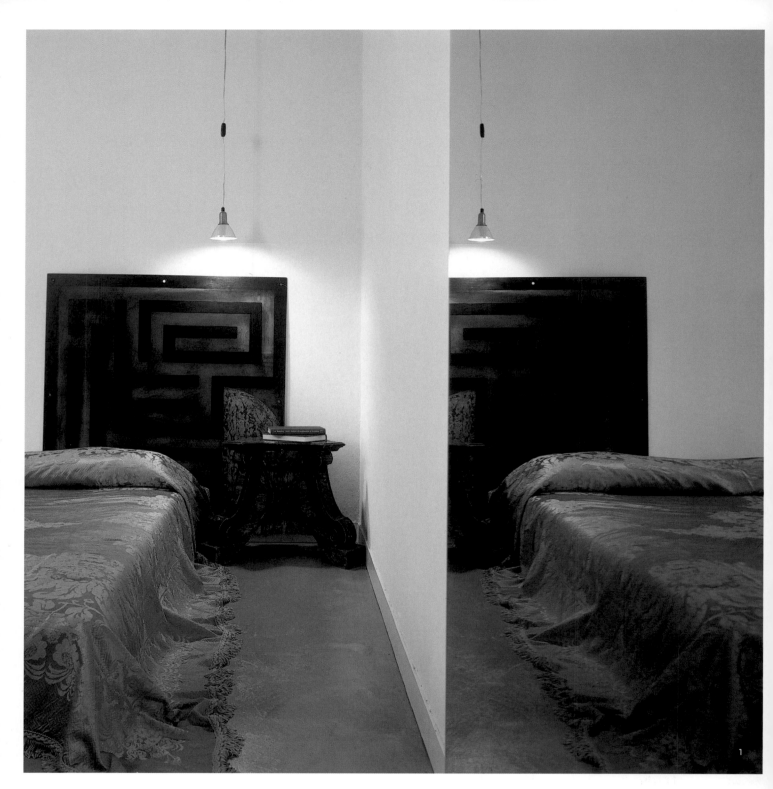

The use of mirrors is still an effective device for increasing the feeling of space and light. Another option is covering the walls with photographs of outdoor scenes.

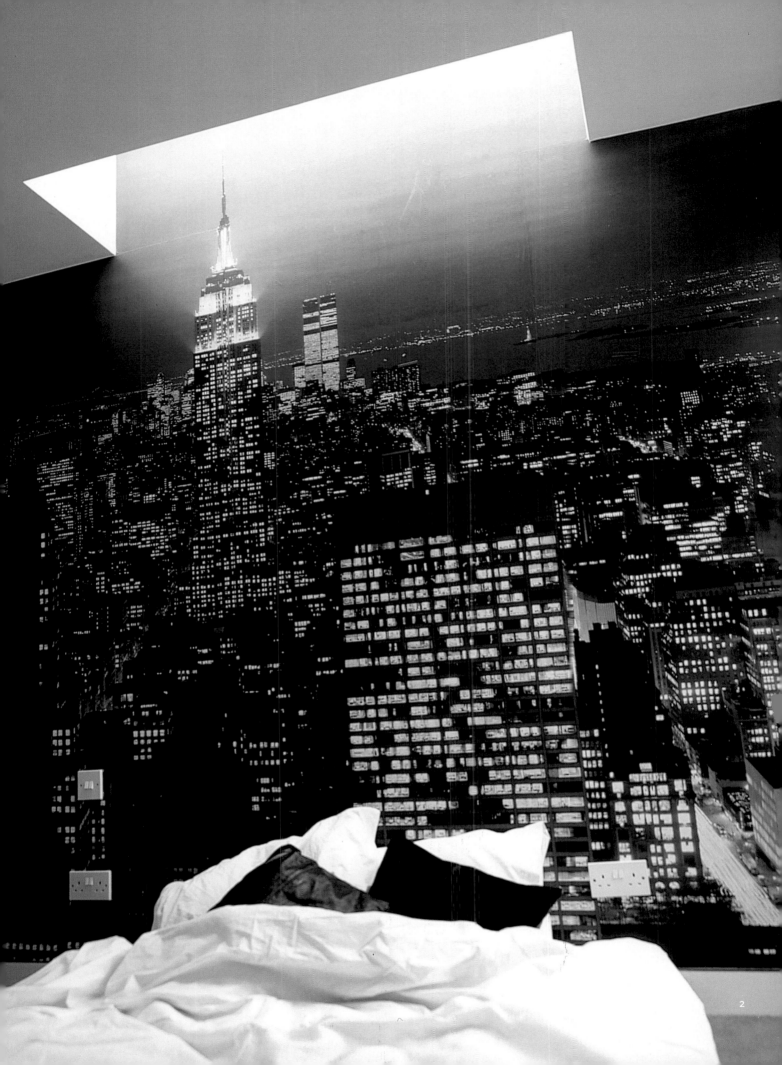

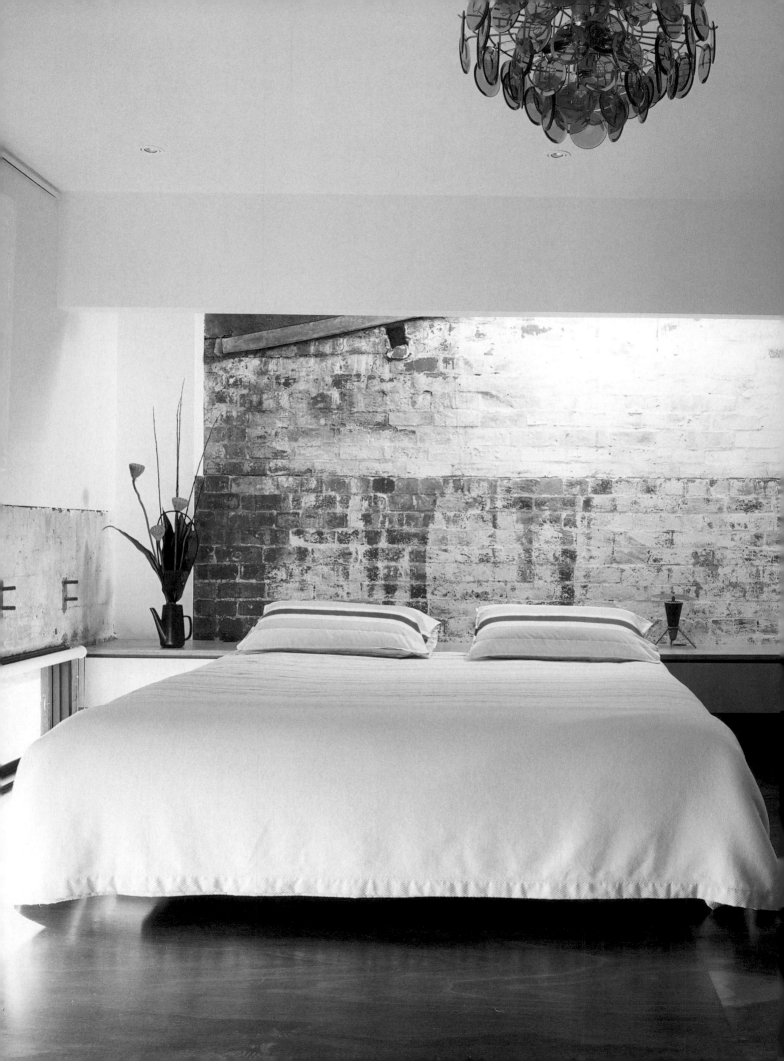

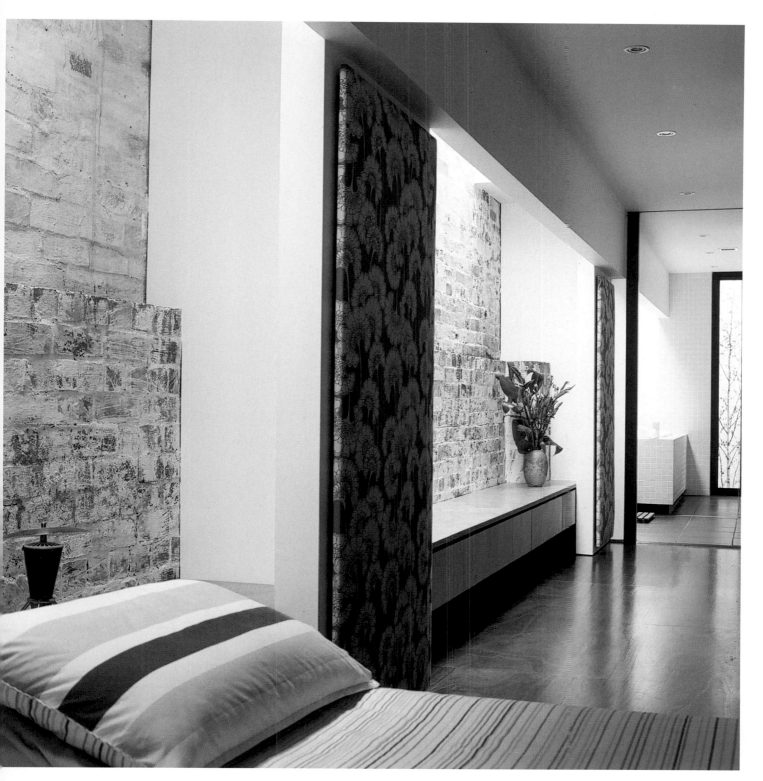

☐ In this project by the Australian firm Six Degrees, false partitions that
do not reach the floor were inserted to hide light sources and to create a
warm atmosphere with indirect lighting.

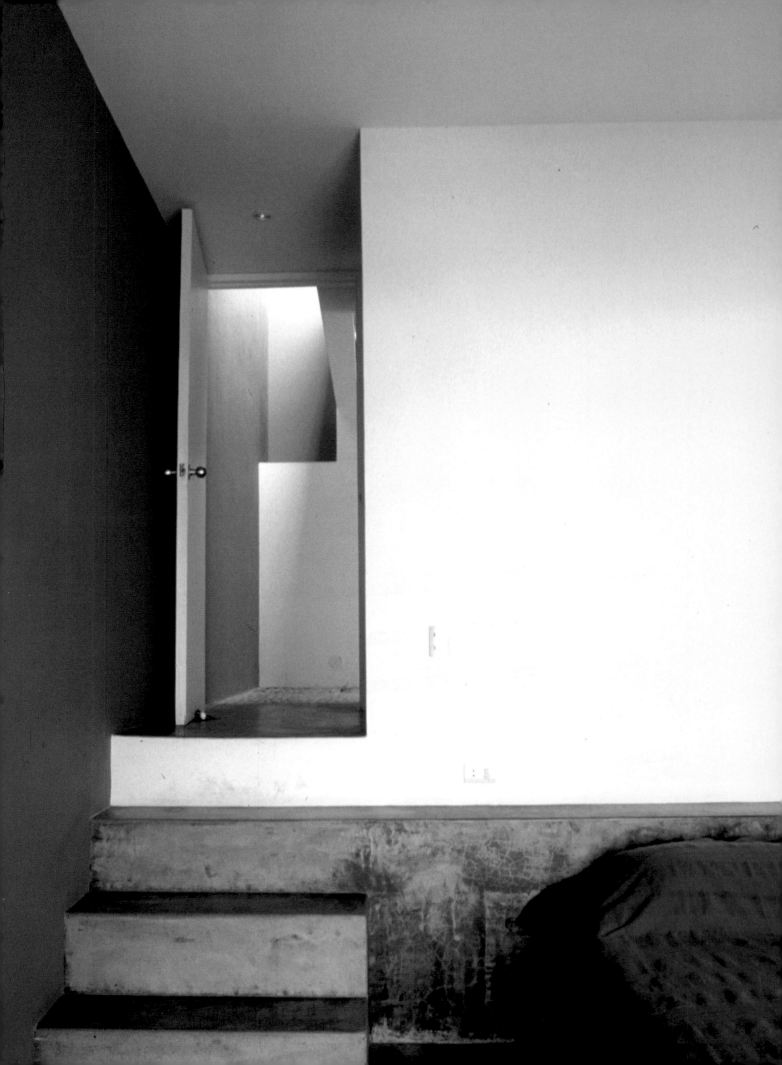

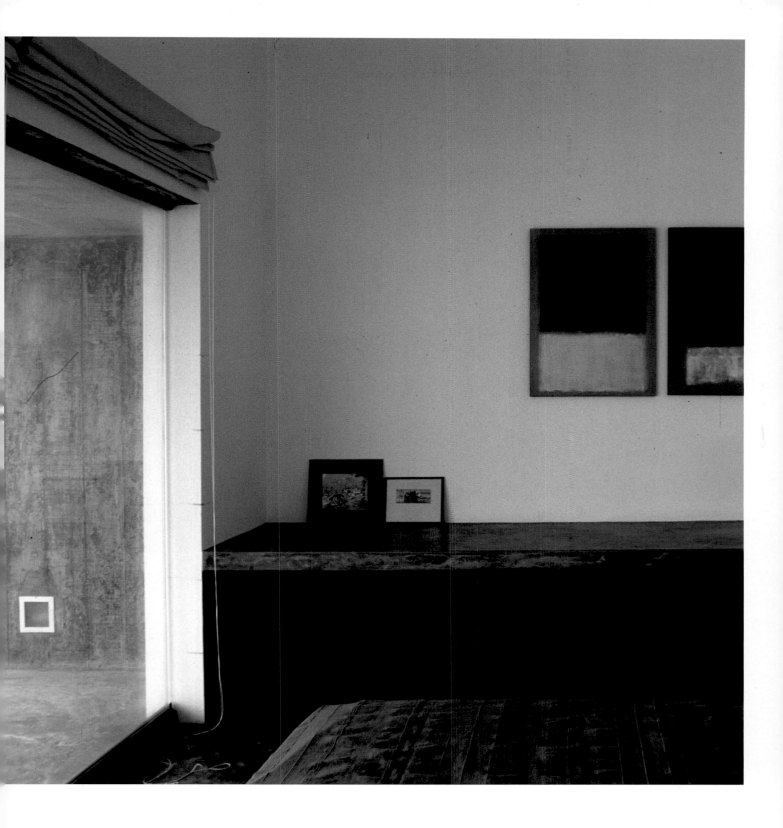

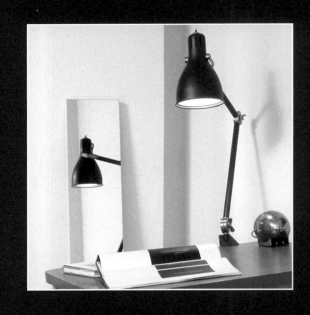

Home Offices

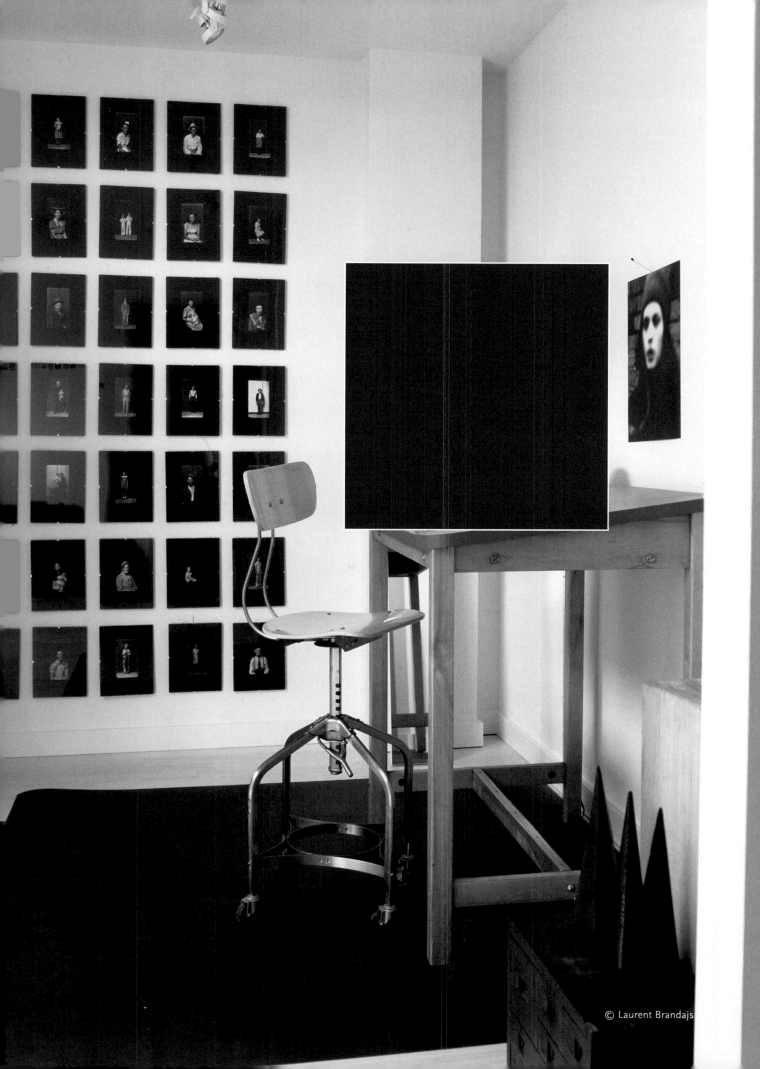

Home Offices

Light, space, and silence are the three indispensable requirements for a home office

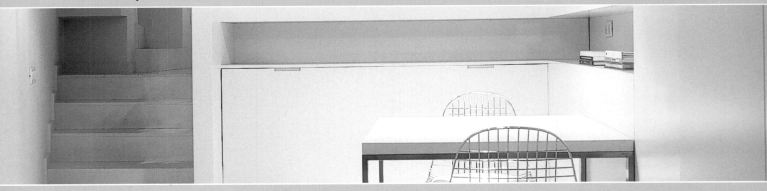

© Eugeni Pons

Sooner or later we almost all end up working at home to some extent. It can be as simple a chore as paying bills, or, thanks to communication technology, we can actually turn our home into our office.

Light, space, and silence are the three indispensable requirements for a home office, just like a professional one.

In a home office we can decide on all the other elements for ourselves, perhaps endowing a workspace with everything we missed in places where we found ourselves working for hours on end, but were designed by other people.

In designing a home office, there are two basic starting points. There may be a readymade space or there may not—this chapter offers ideas for both circumstances. Even when a readymade space is available, certain points must be taken into account to help optimize not only the space but also the effect it can have on our work.

Aside from observing the basic rules of interior design, special attention must be paid to ergonomics and the balance between forms, colors, and materials, all of which can influence our capacity to concentrate and work effectively.

Should there be insufficient space available to devote a room exclusively to work, this chapter provides solutions, such as convertible furniture units and the imaginative use of walls. These can create an office where one would not be expected. Multifunctional spaces that can also be used for other purposes—not simply as offices—are another solution.

Special emphasis is placed on the exploitation of space, on how to turn supremely functional items like bookshelves into decorative objects, on how to imbue an intrinsically austere space with warmth—in short, ways to make working at home as pleasant as possible.

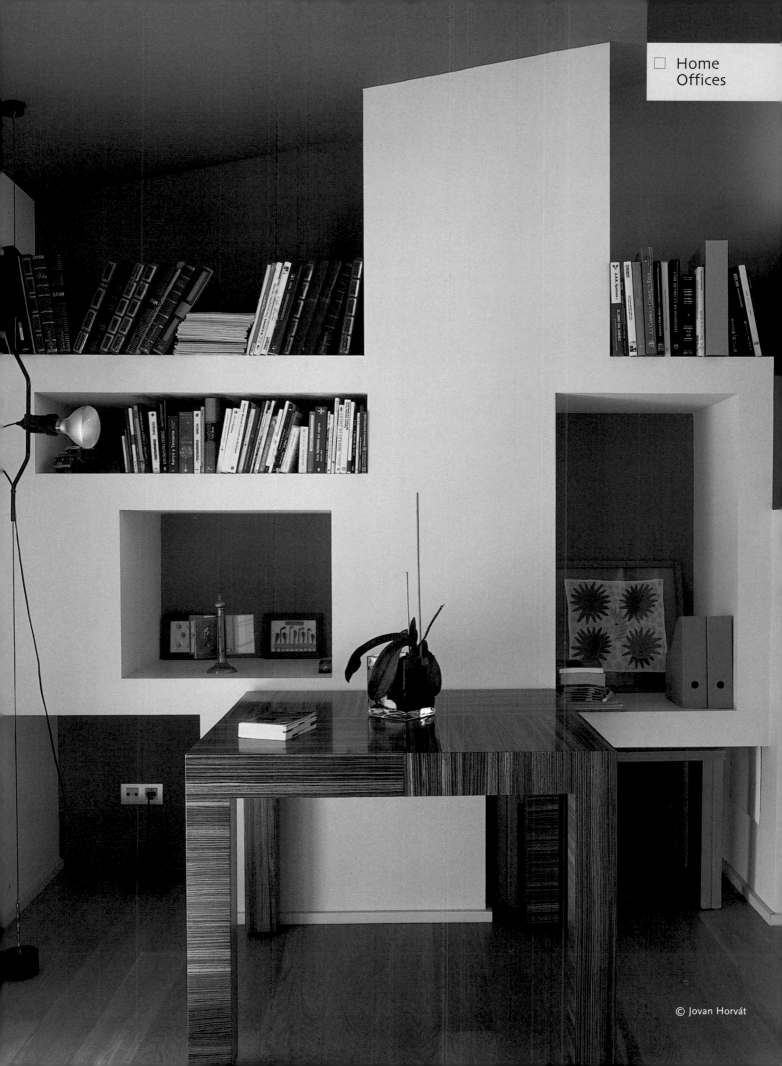

© Jovan Horvát

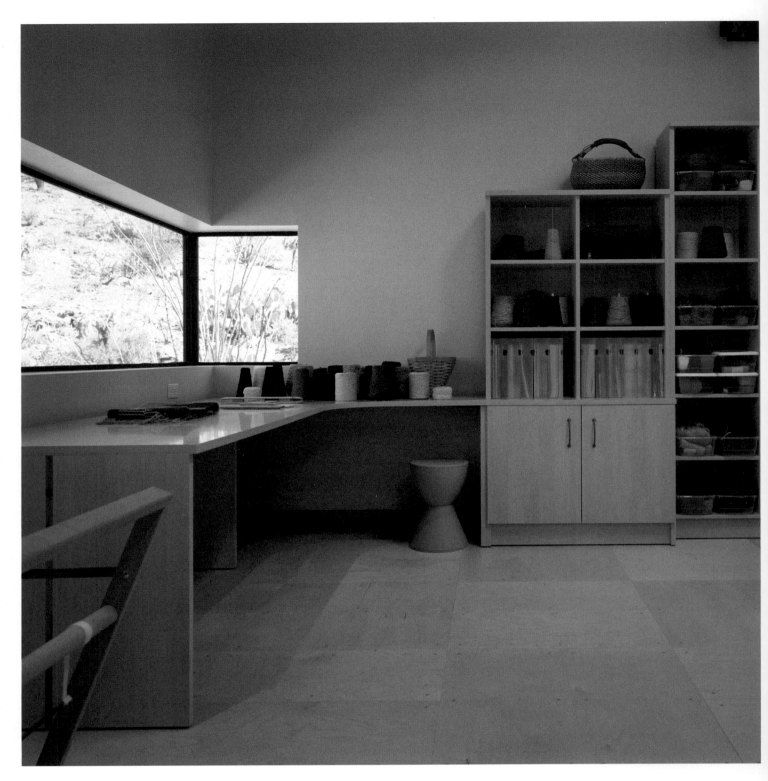

△ Ibarra Rosano Architects is one of the busiest firms in Arizona. Their
work is based on the premise that architecture is space.

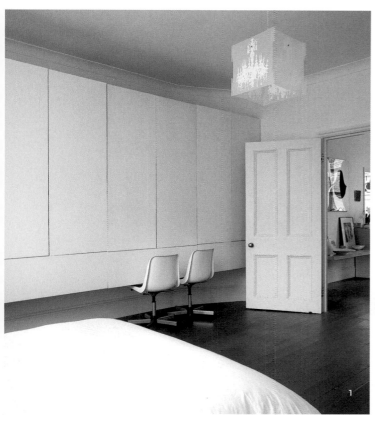

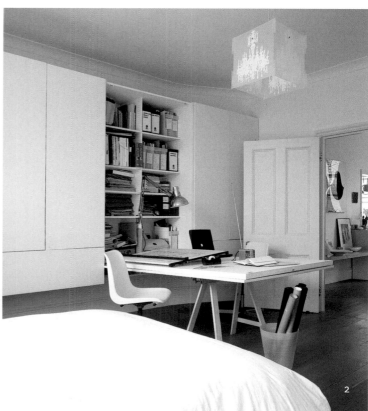

The challenge in interior architecture is to master construction techniques and layout to create useful spaces, even when this seems an impossible task.

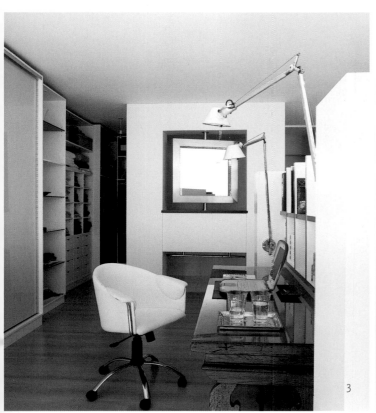

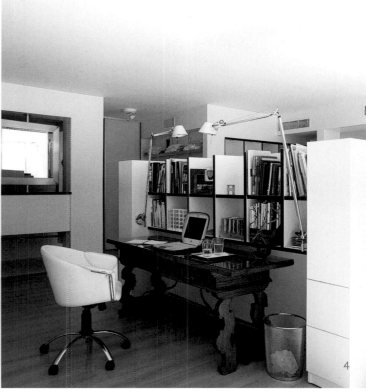

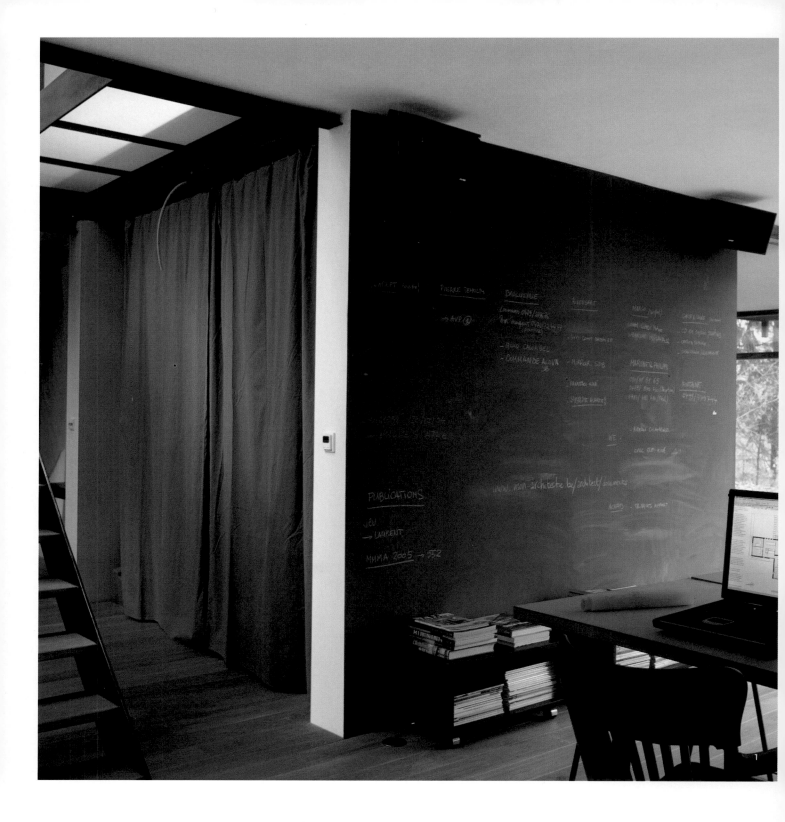

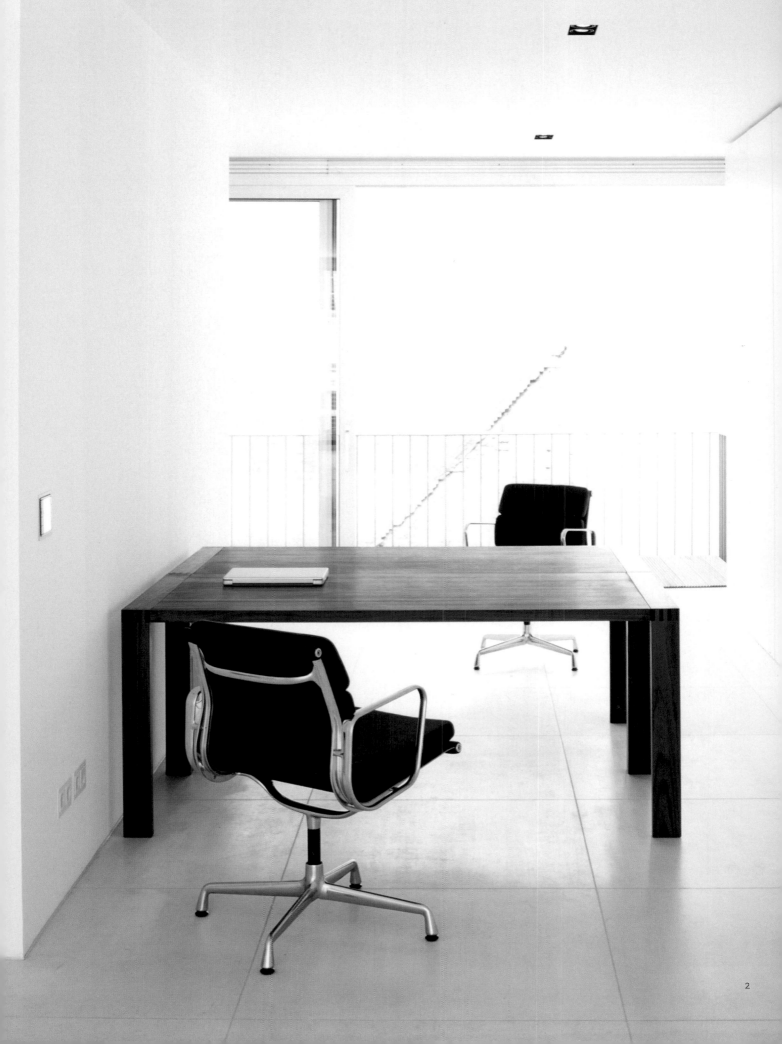

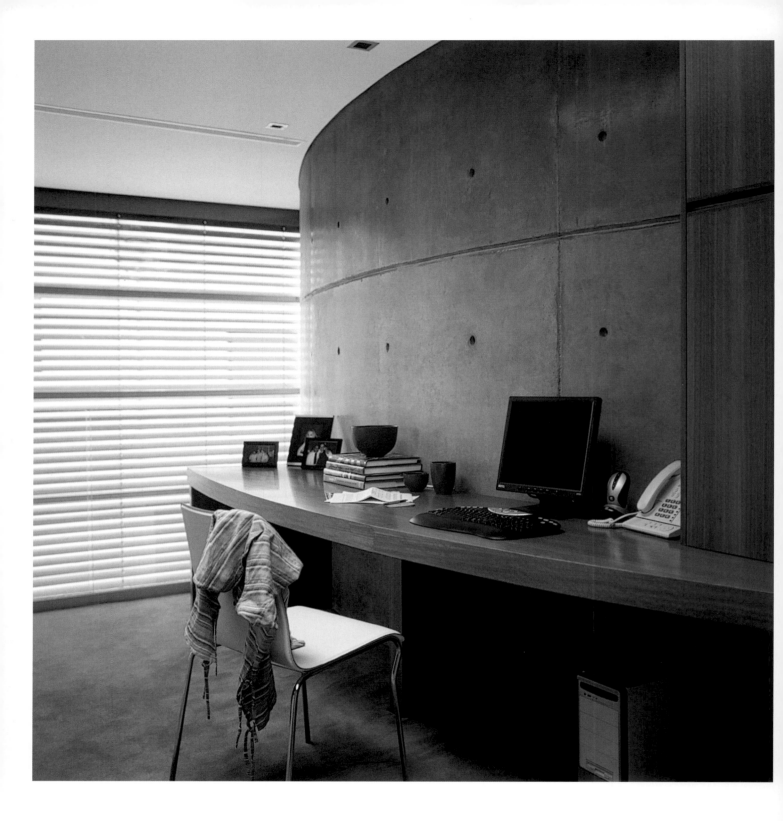

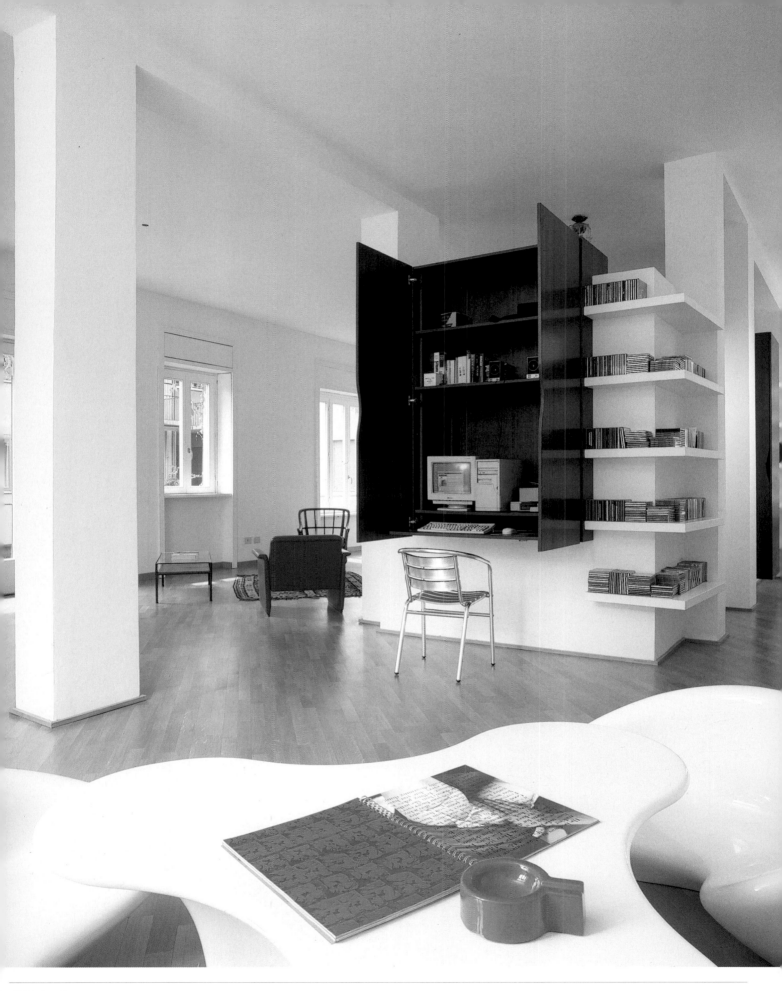

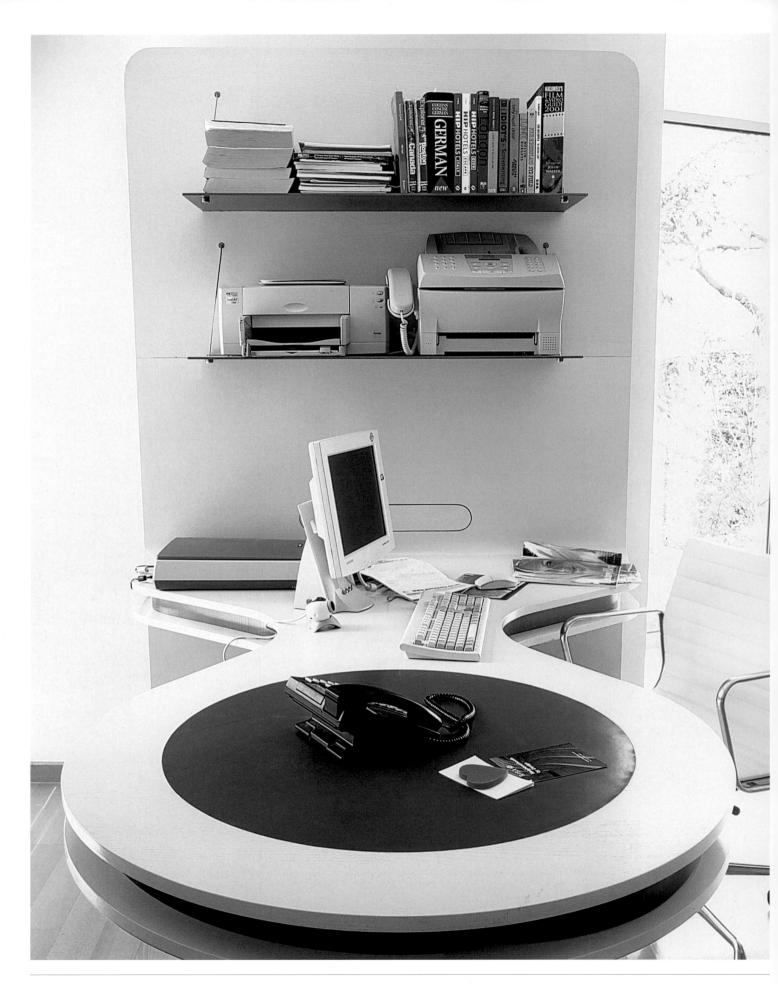

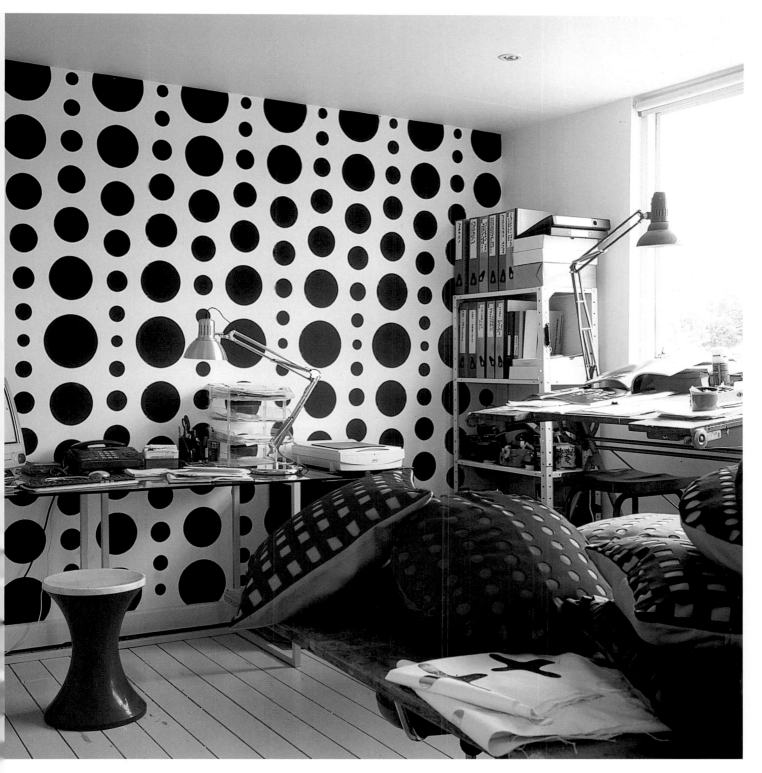

△ Fabrics and wallpaper can create interesting optical effects in rooms
with conventional architecture.

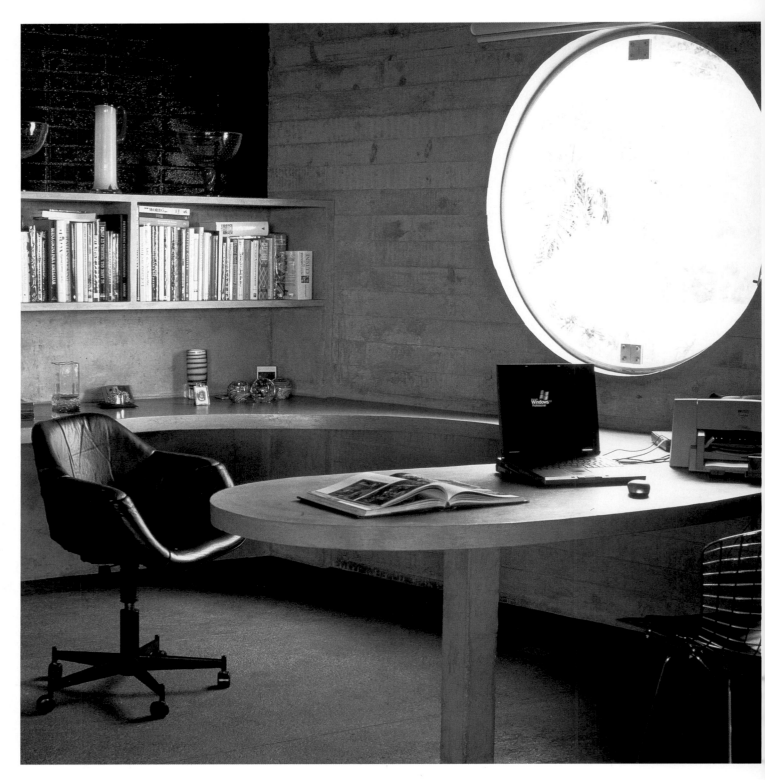

△ Taking advantage of natural light is basic in the design of home offices.

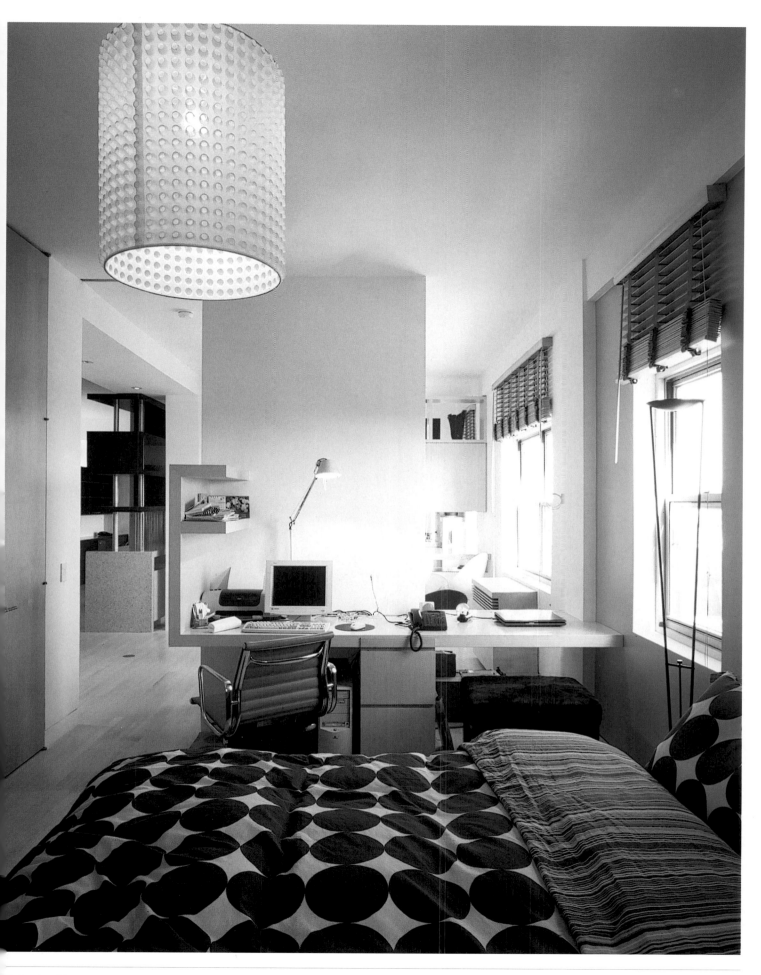

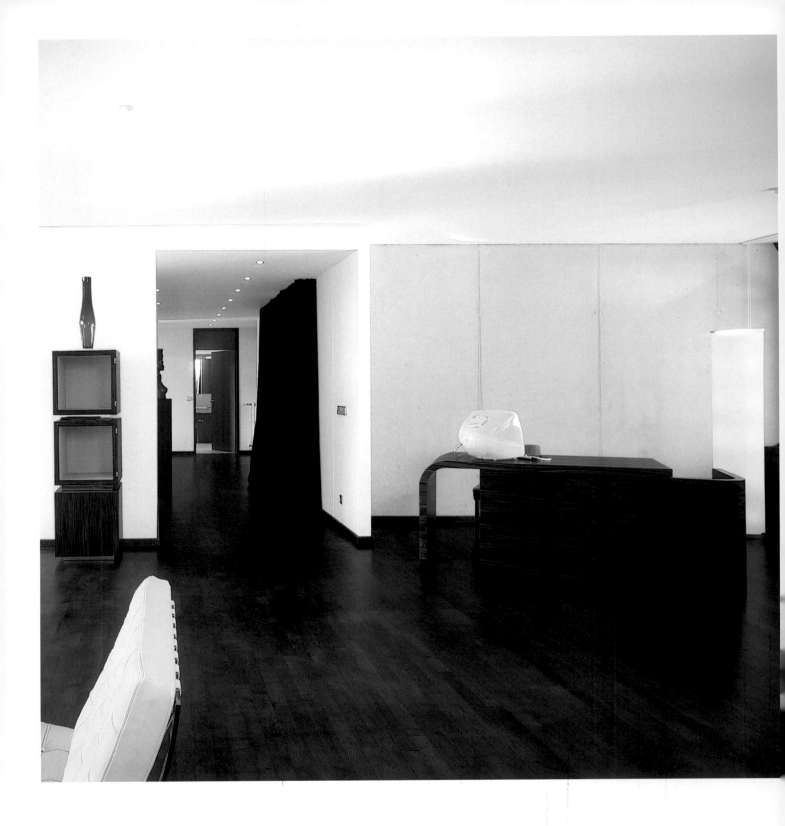

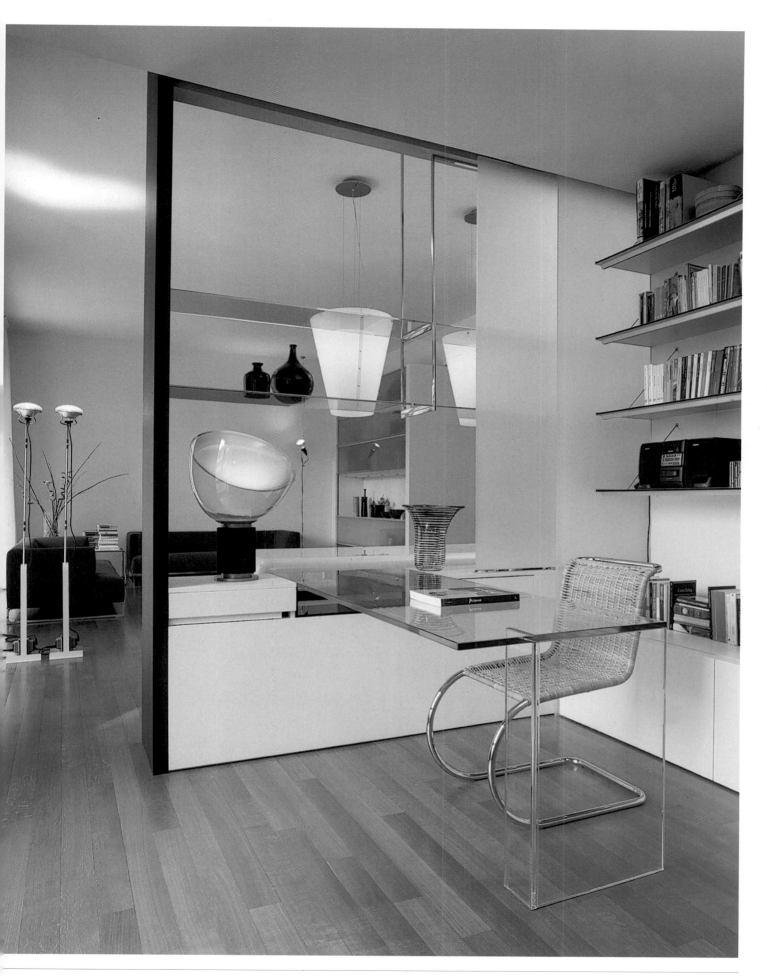

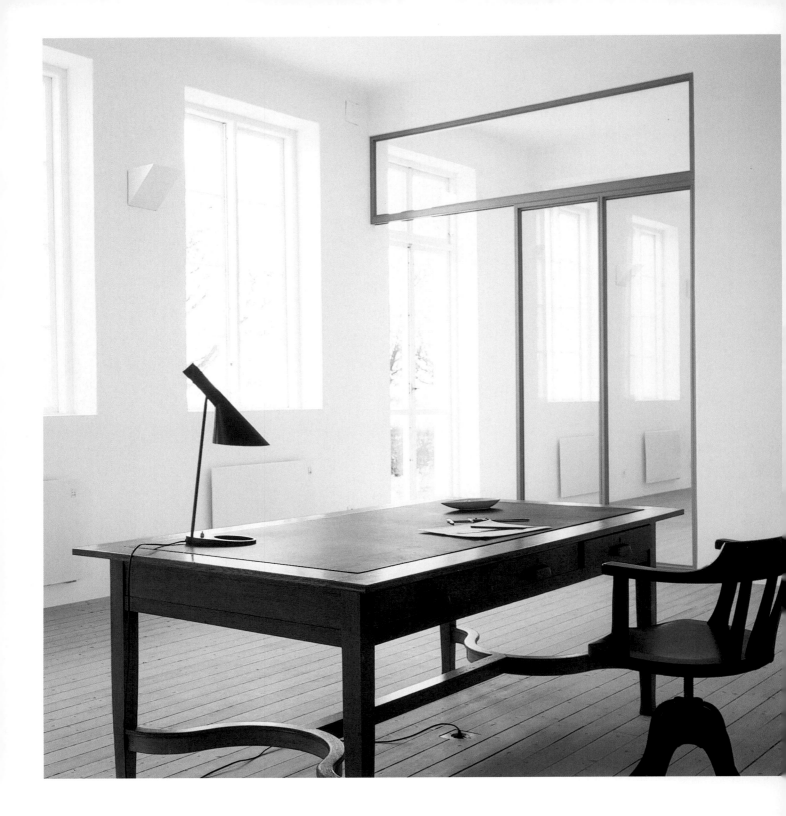

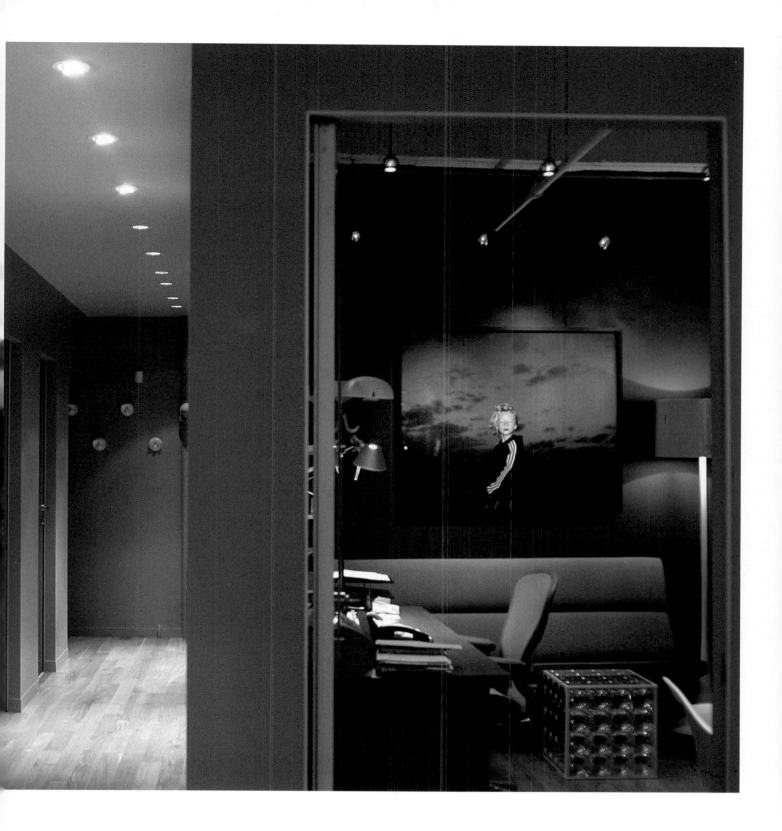

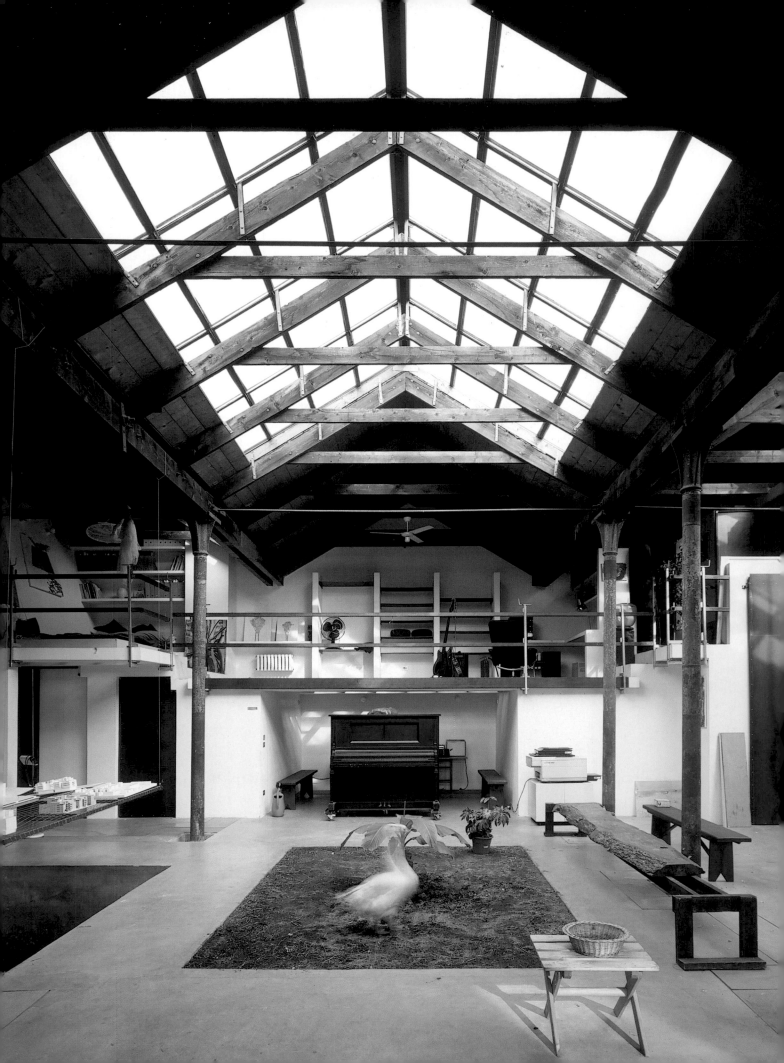

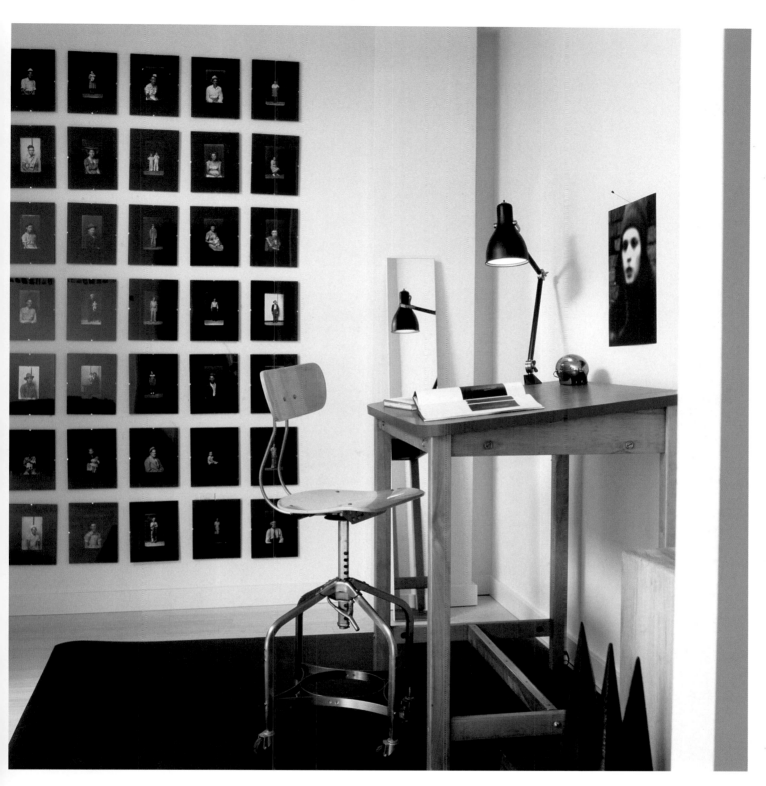

◁ The Oca Loft by the Italian architect Donatti. He decided to preserve the rural spirit of this old goose farm when he converted it into a home and architecture studio. The latter dominates the space as if it were a stage setting.

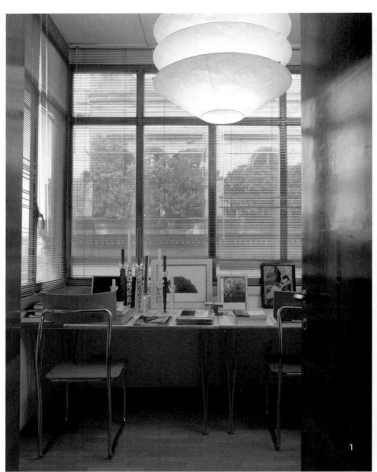

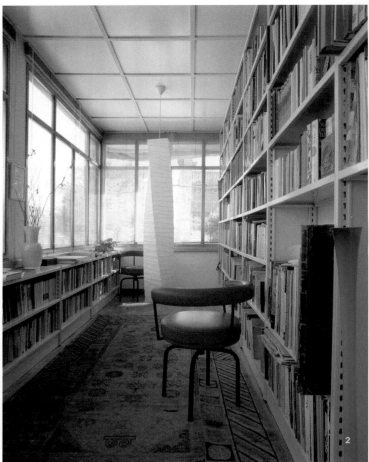

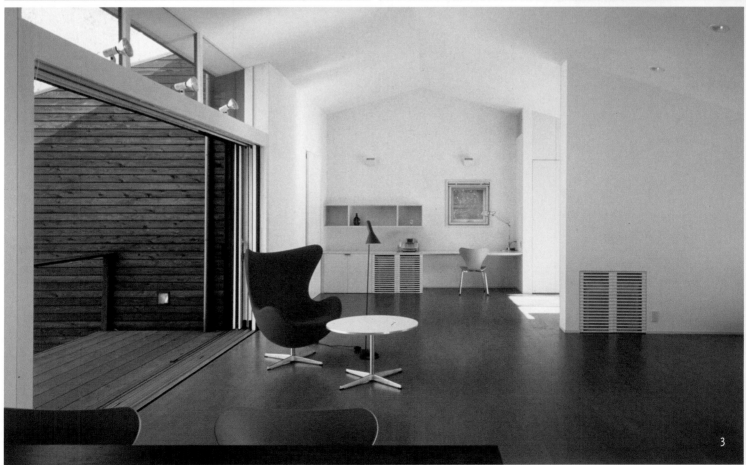

1, 2 © Giovanna Piemonti   3 © Luuk Kramer

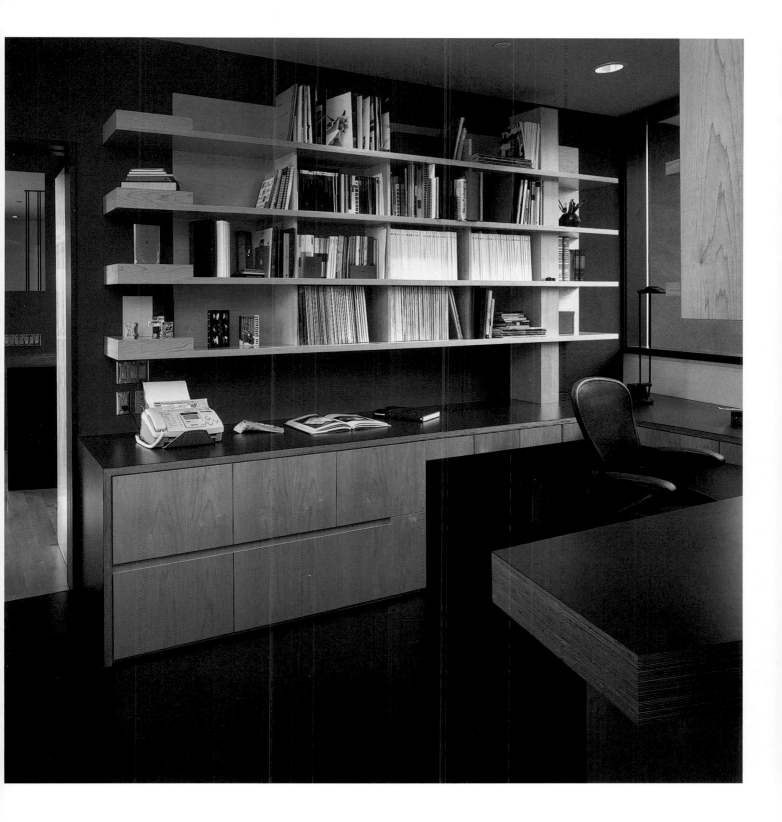

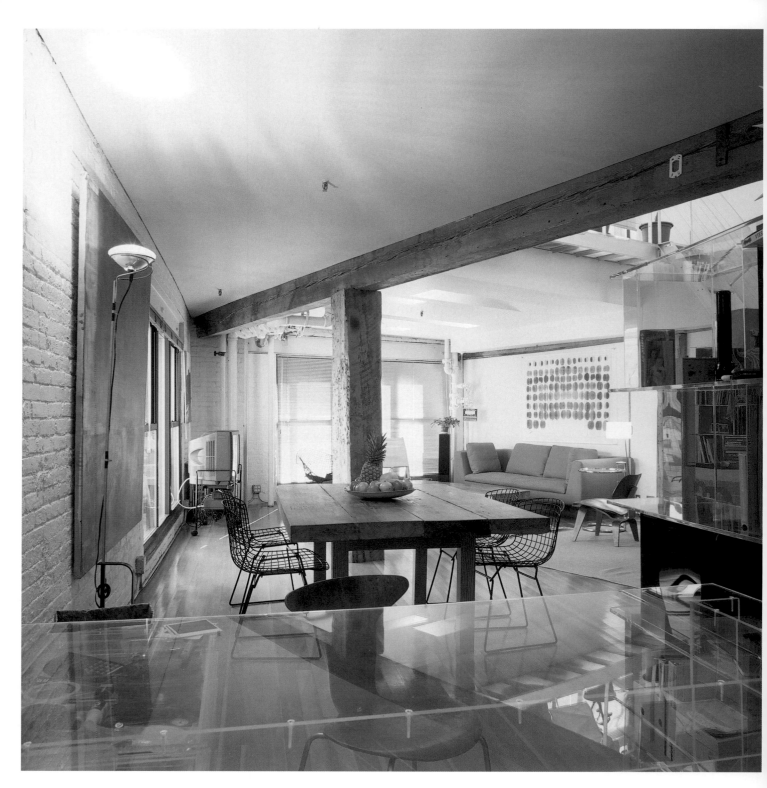

☐ Retro reminiscences for a studio integrated into a sitting room set apart from the rest by its use of color. The translucent surfaces help to preserve the sensation of space.

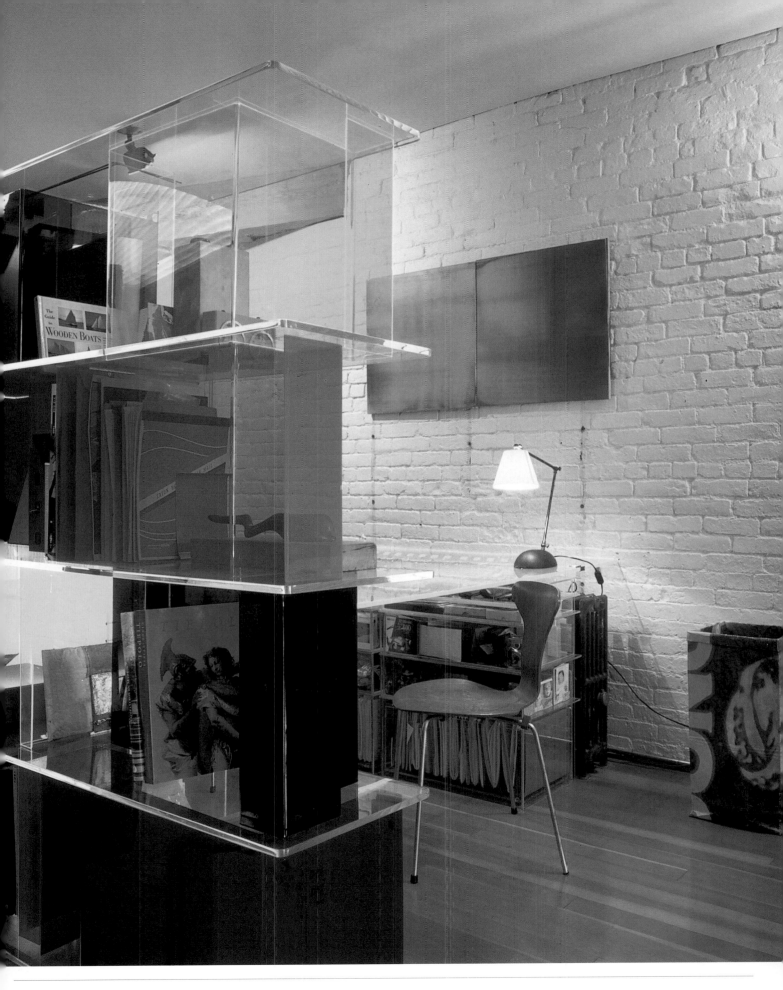

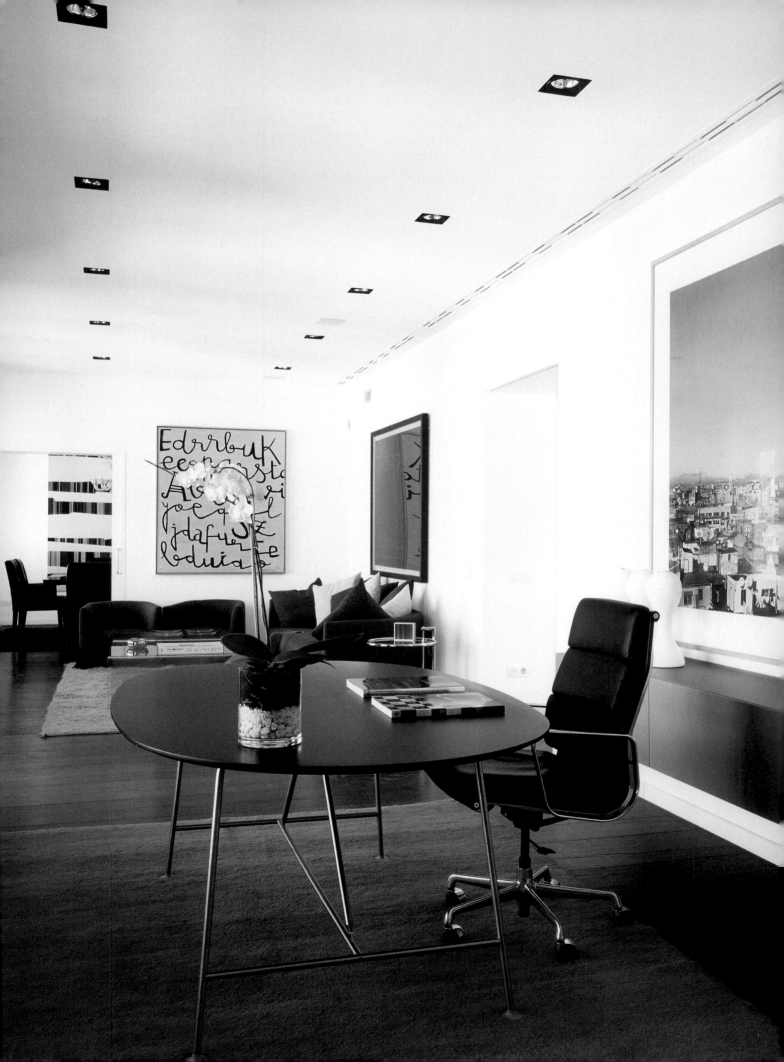

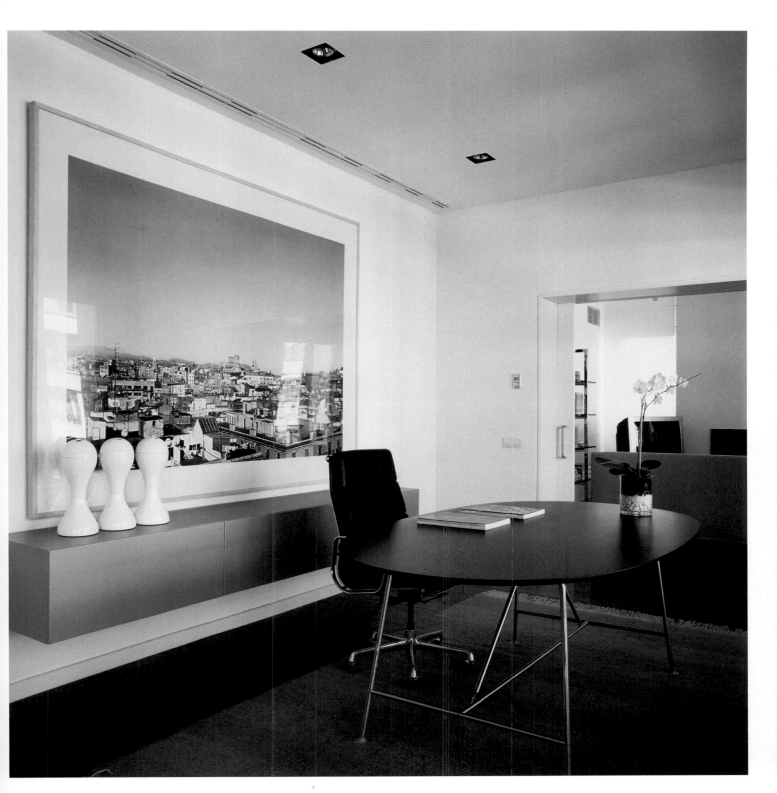

☐ This studio area in the lounge of a house in Barcelona is characterized by its flexibility, achieved by a module that camouflages the closets behind the table.

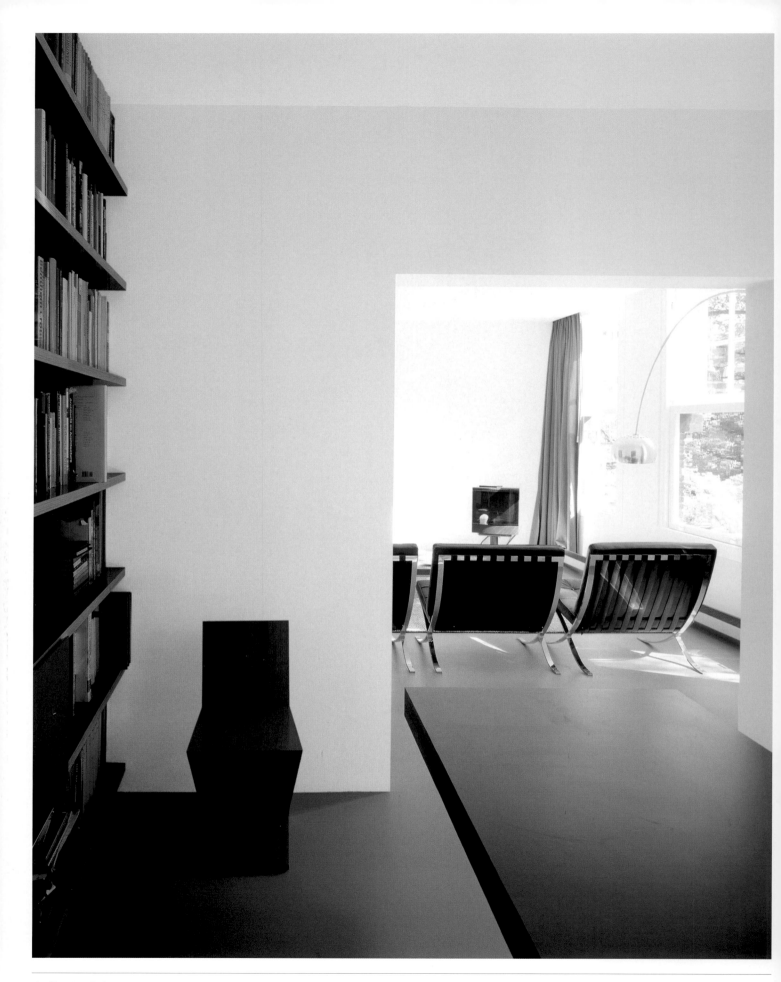

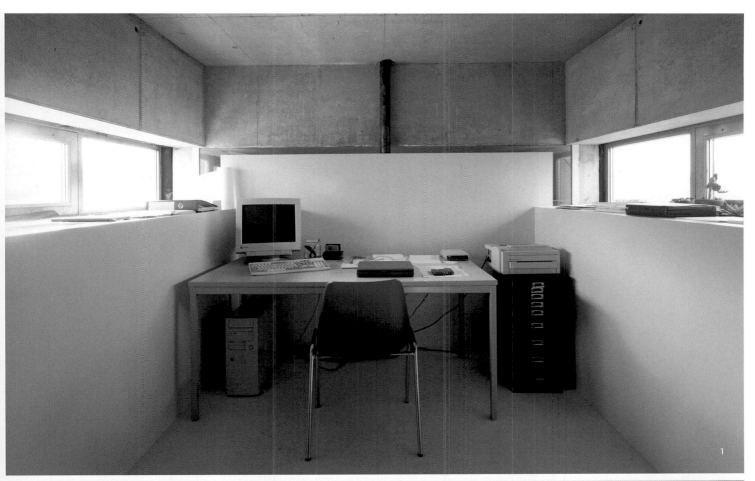

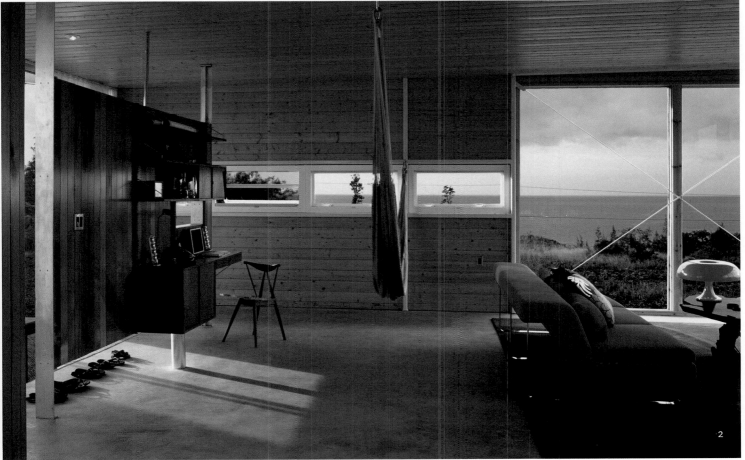

1 © Bruno Klomfar   2 © JD Peterson

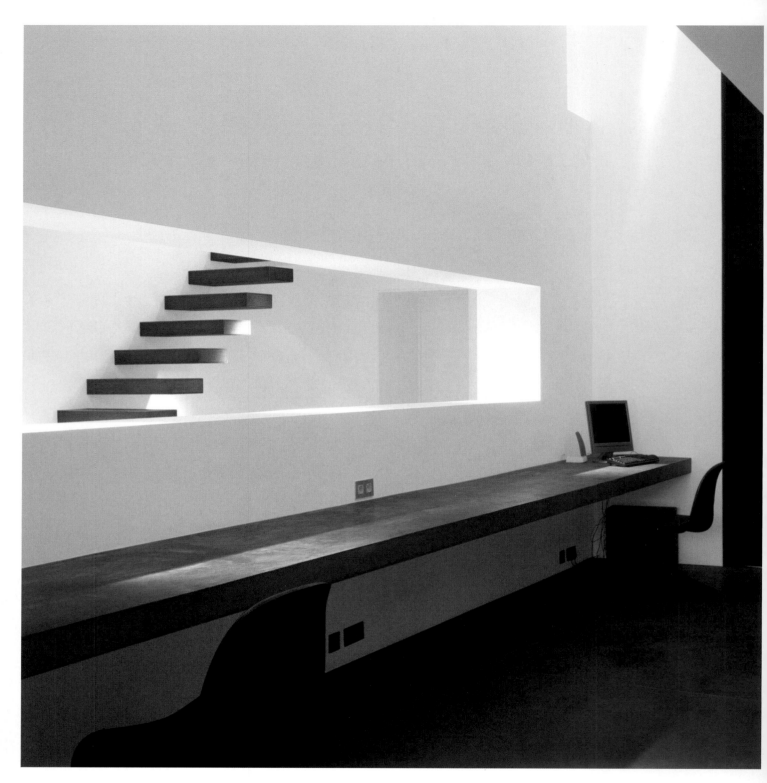

▷ The articulating axis of this studio in a home in Brussels is the bookcase that covers the entire double-height wall.

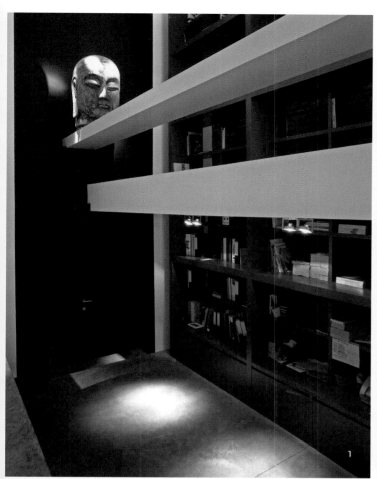

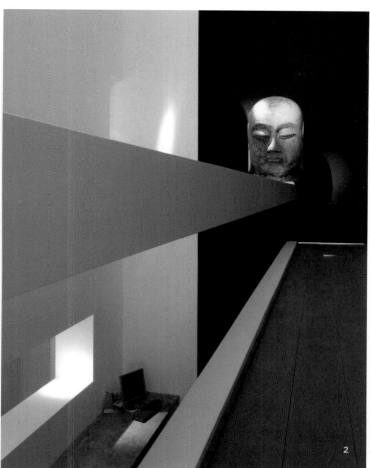

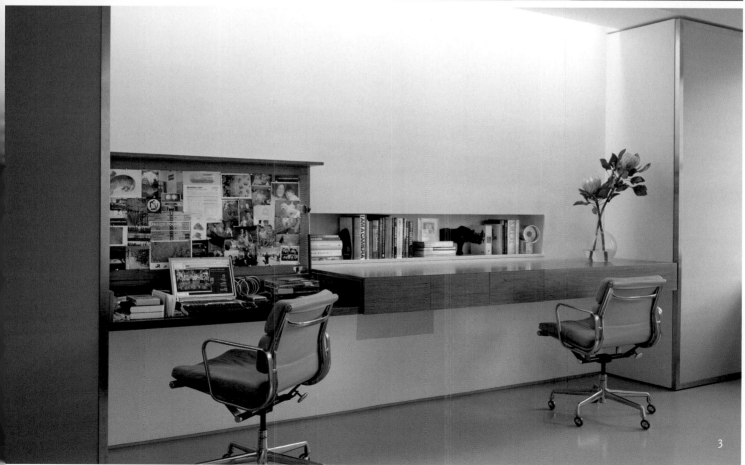

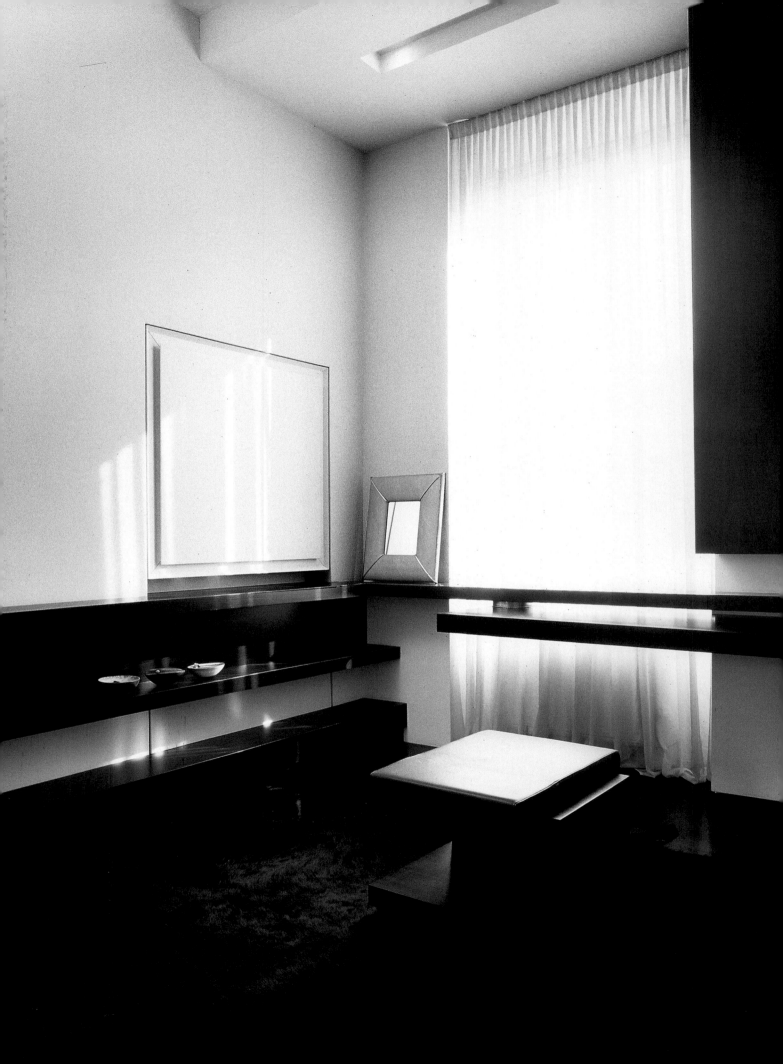

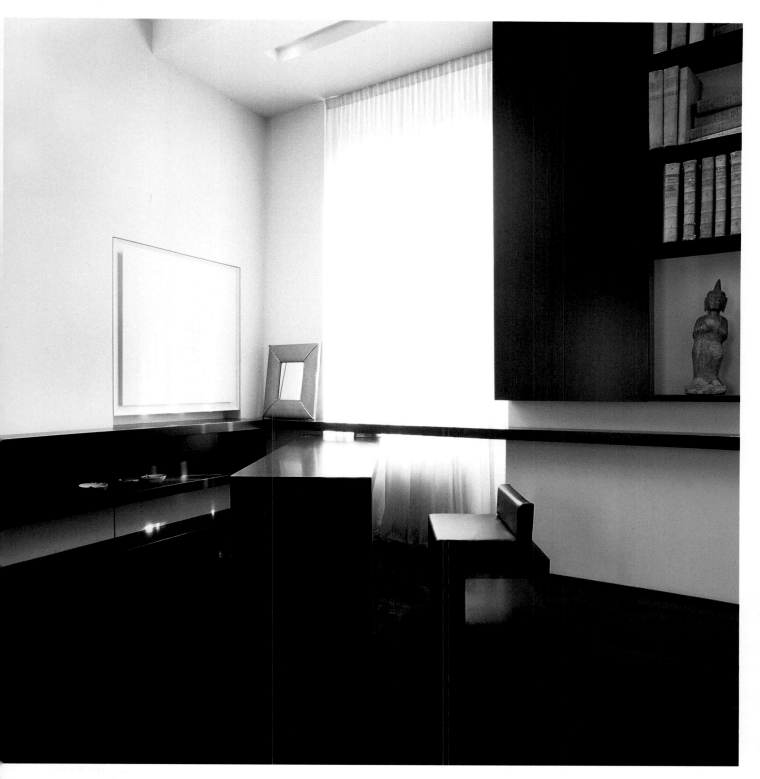

A Zen-style studio with articulating modules by the Italian designer
Marco Savorelli.

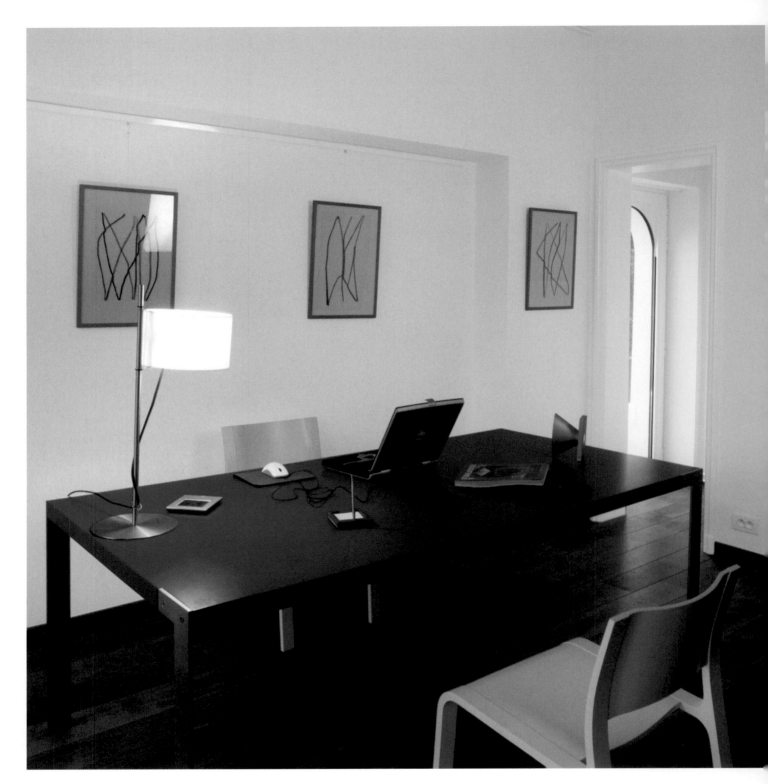

A colorful table bestows character on what is basically a conventional studio. On the right, a practical solution to a clear problem of space.

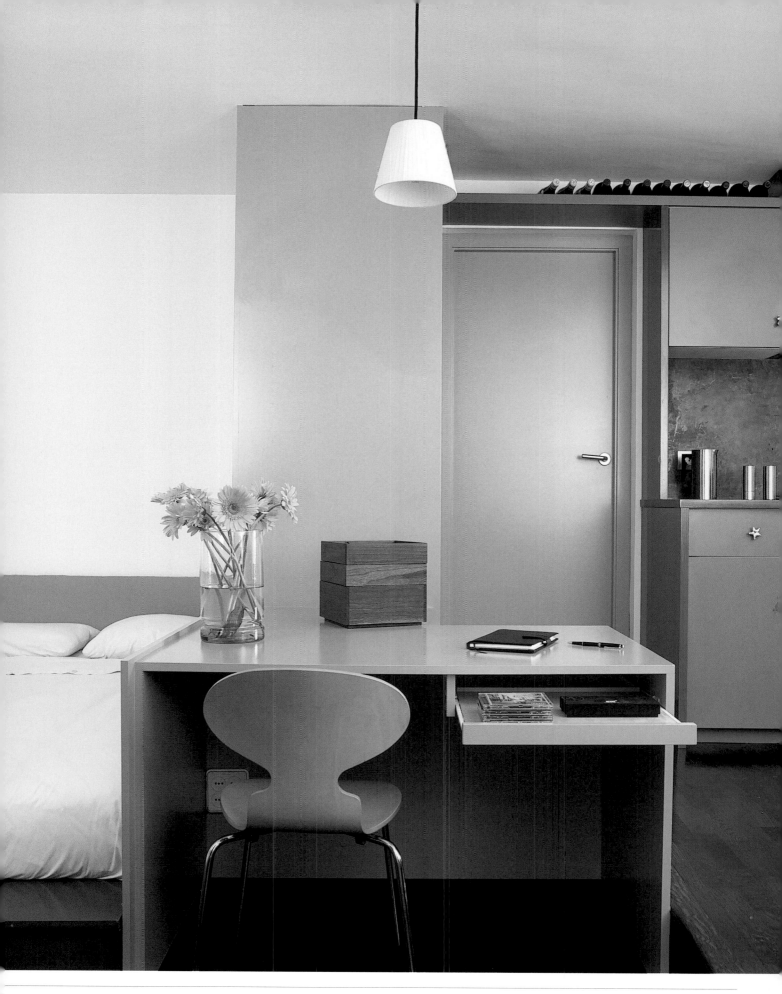

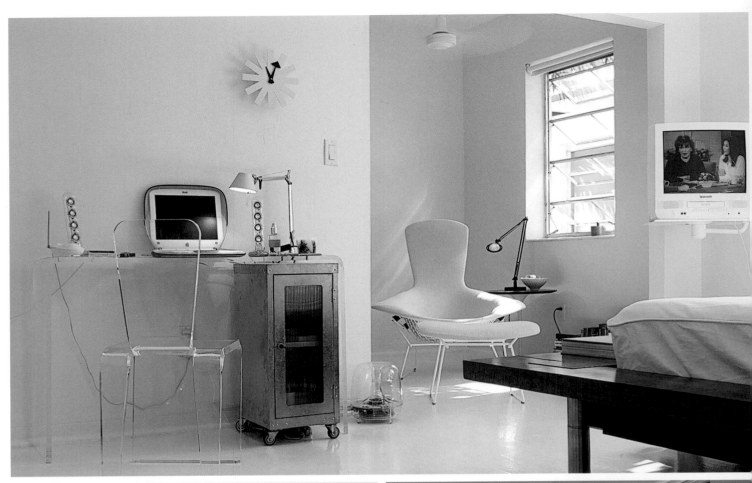

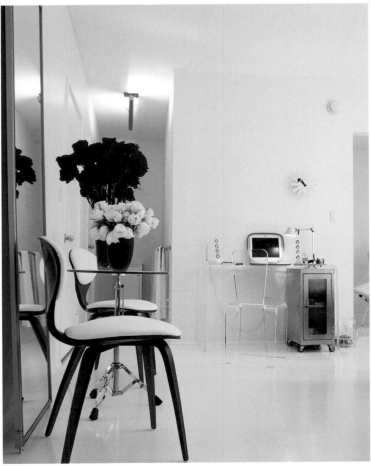

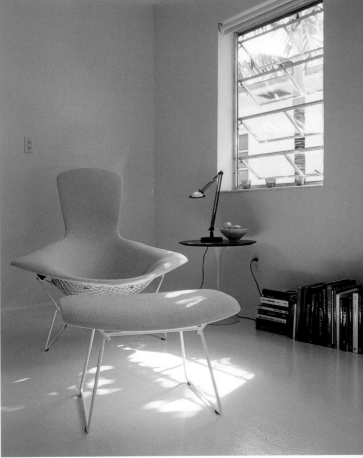

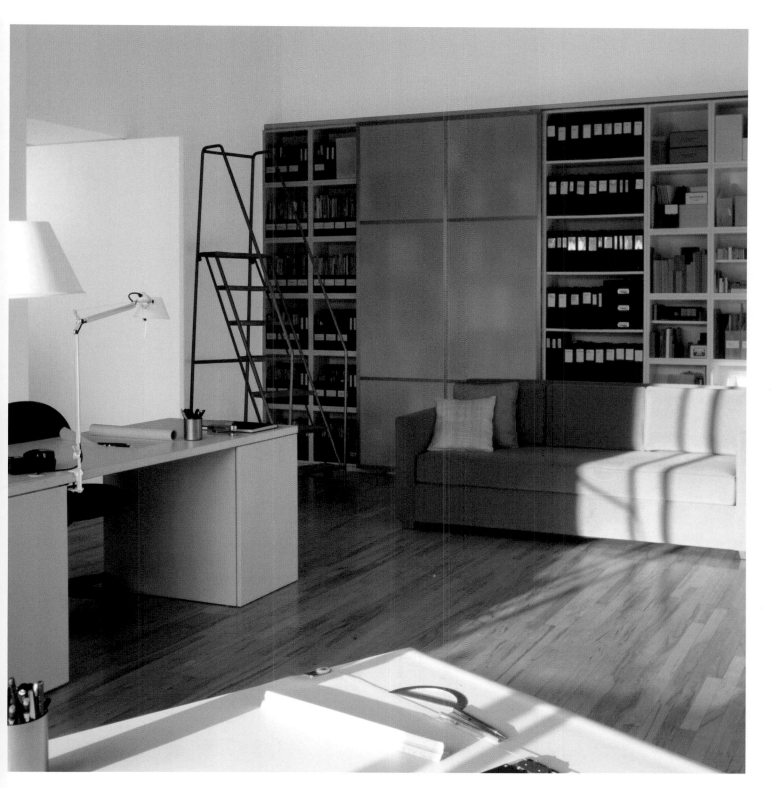

◁ An original design for a mini-studio: a recycled metal closet has been augmented with a mass of metacrylate (the material also used for the chair). The translucent elements do not occupy any visual space.

Bathrooms

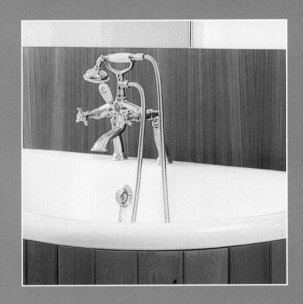

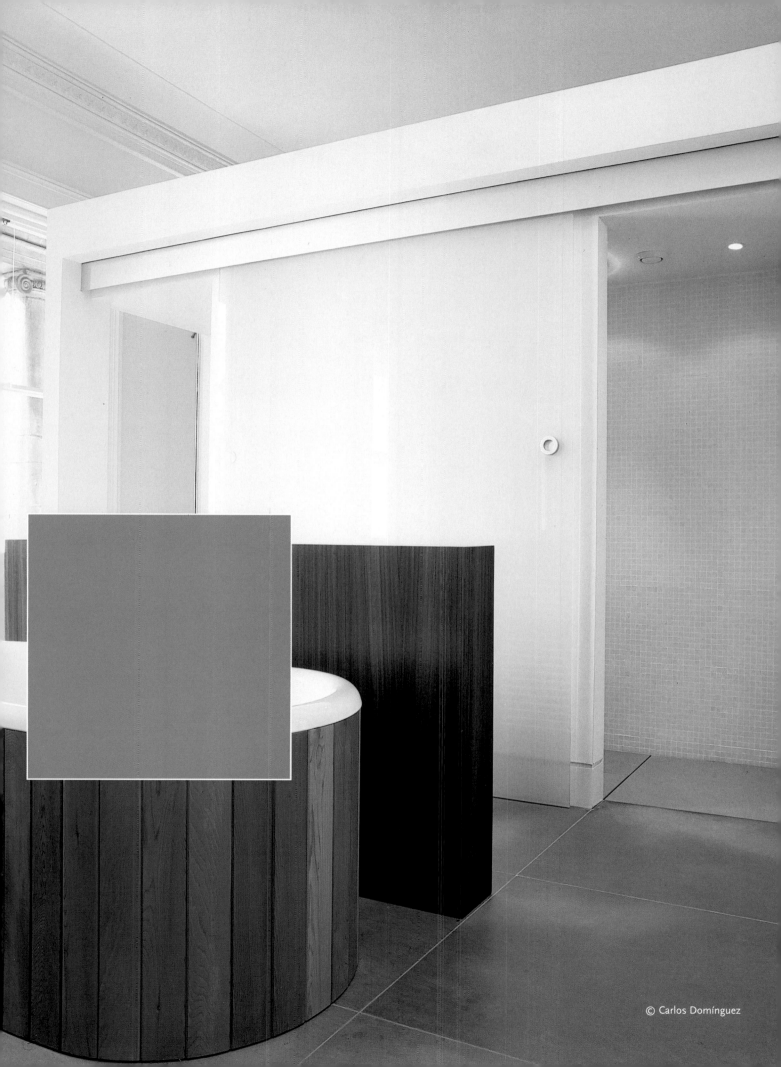

Bathrooms

The concept of the bathroom as an individual room is not so old

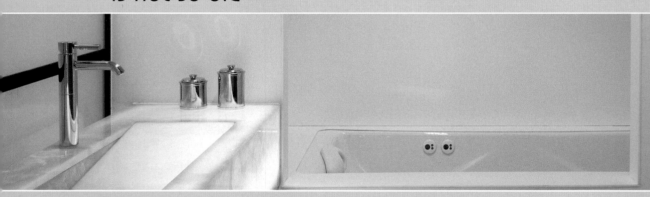

© Jordi Miralles

When Sir John Harrington's friends mocked his seemingly ridiculous invention of a "water closet" in 1596, they could never imagine that its use would have spread all over the world by the 21st century and that it would be an indispensable object for modern society.

Sir John was so affected by the reaction in his immediate circle that he never invented anything else ever again. Although his powers of invention were not rewarded with success and recognition, at least he and his godmother could relieve themselves comfortably in a seated position.

The version closest to today's interpretation of the "water closet" was that of Thomas Twyford, dating from 1885. It was based on one that had been patented by Alexander Cummings, which already included the crucial pitch valve, but substituted metal for porcelain—a change that proved so convincing that it has been respected to the present. Similarly, one of the first showers on record made little impression. It was invented in 1810 and probably belonged to an English estate;

it was little copied, however, as it was seen as bizarre and even suspicious. Nevertheless, the path towards the shower had been laid, and soon after other prototypes appeared. By the end of the 19th century, showers had developed to resemble something close to present-day models.

Although the main elements of the bathroom have been in existence for some time—as we have seen with the shower and toilet, not to mention the bathtub, which goes back to ancient times—the concept of the bathroom as an individual room is not so old, and it could even be said that we are still in a test phase. Proof of this can be seen in the subtle changes that have taken place in bathrooms in response to users' needs: two sinks in place of one, bathtubs with headrests, etc.

In this chapter we shall see how different bathroom designs can provide very different responses to functional needs and to the expression of the spirit of each particular house.

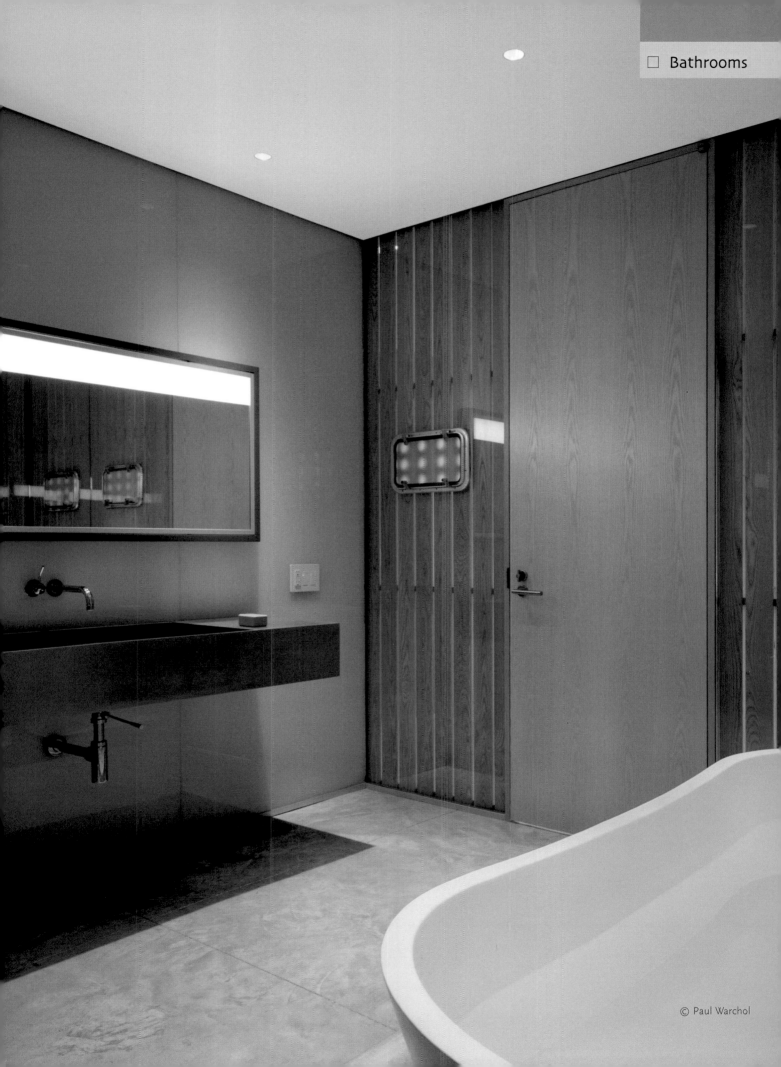

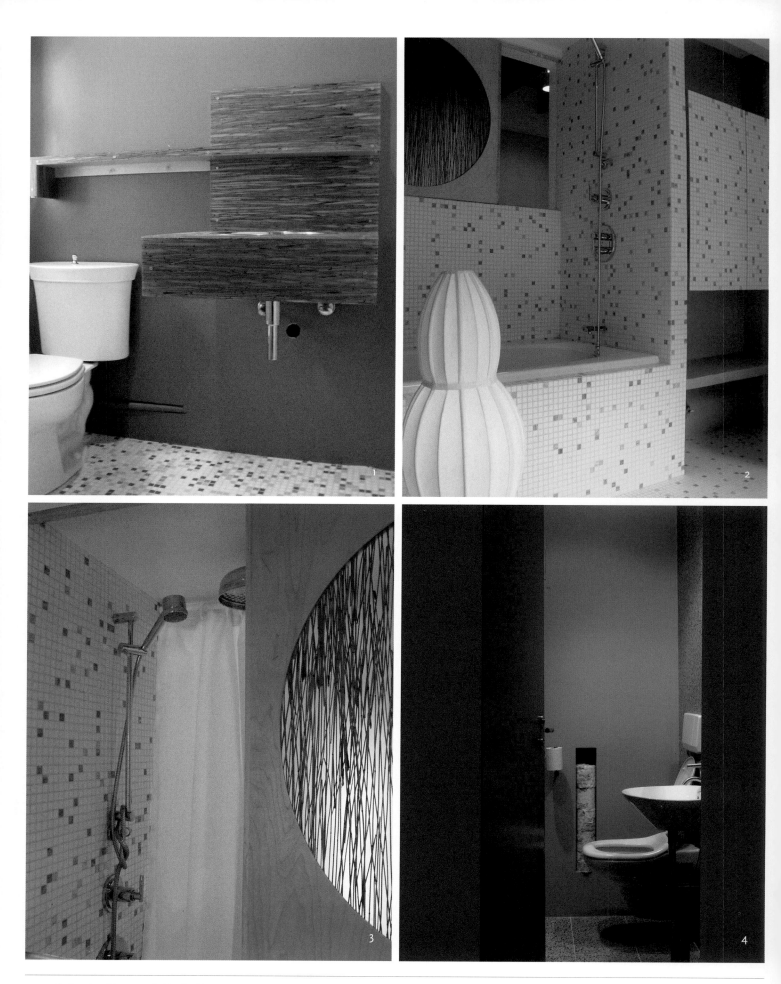

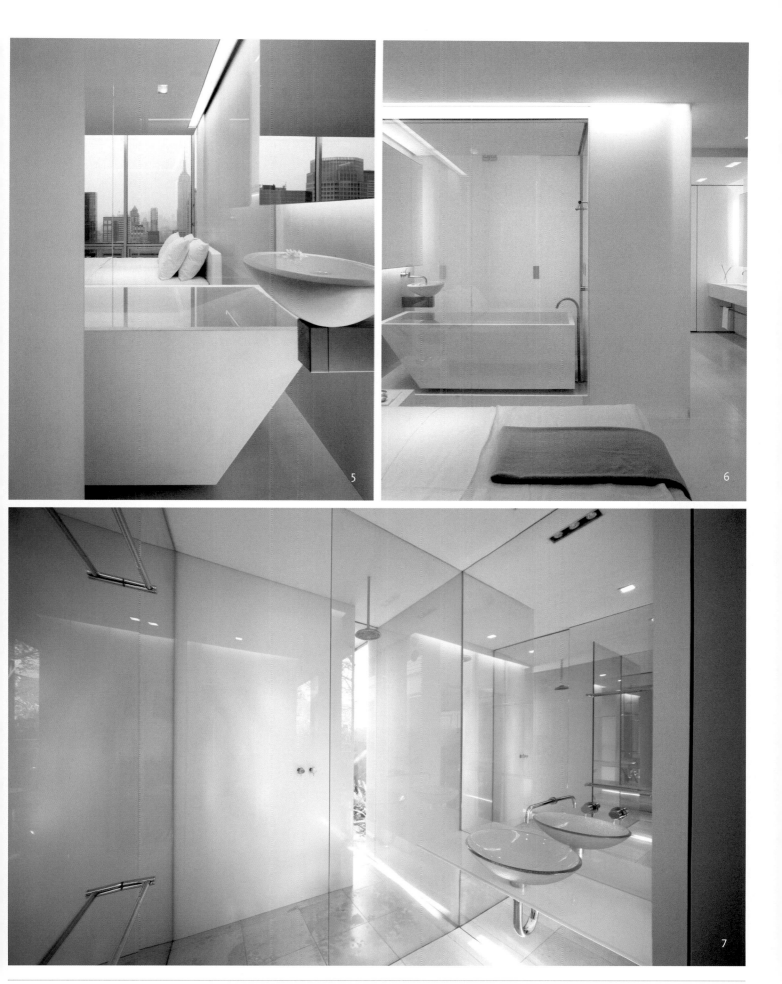

5

6

7

5, 6 © Paul Warchol   7 © John Gollings

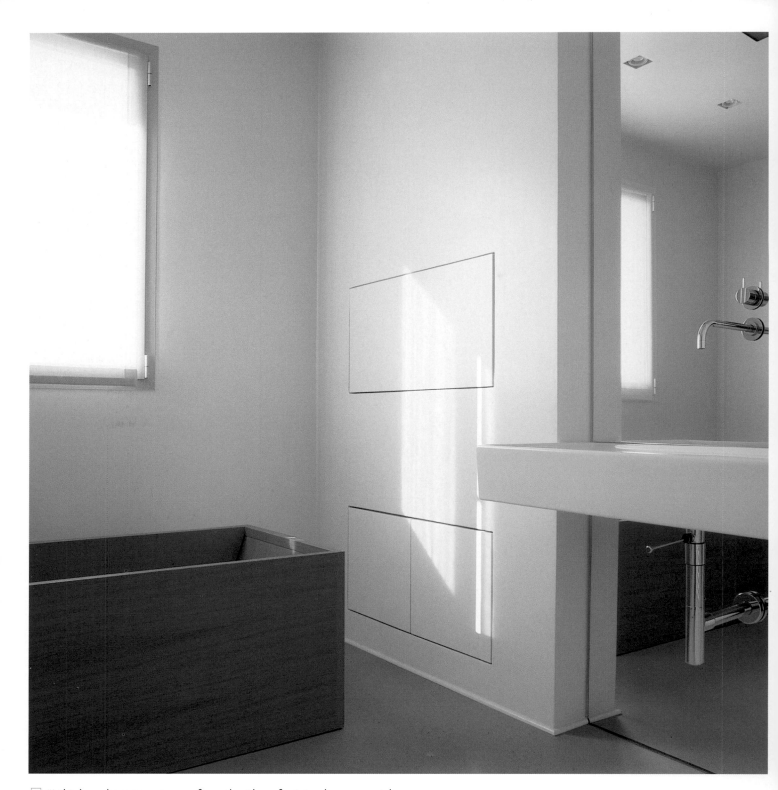

☐ "I think we have to get away from the idea of minimalism as a style and instead understand it as a way of thinking about space—its proportions, surfaces, and the fall of light. The vision is comprehensive and seamless, a quality of space rather than forms, places not things. This is why, in its fullest and most satisfying expression, it is not something which you can readily acquire a piece of." John Pawson, "Minimalism," *The Guardian*, April 2004

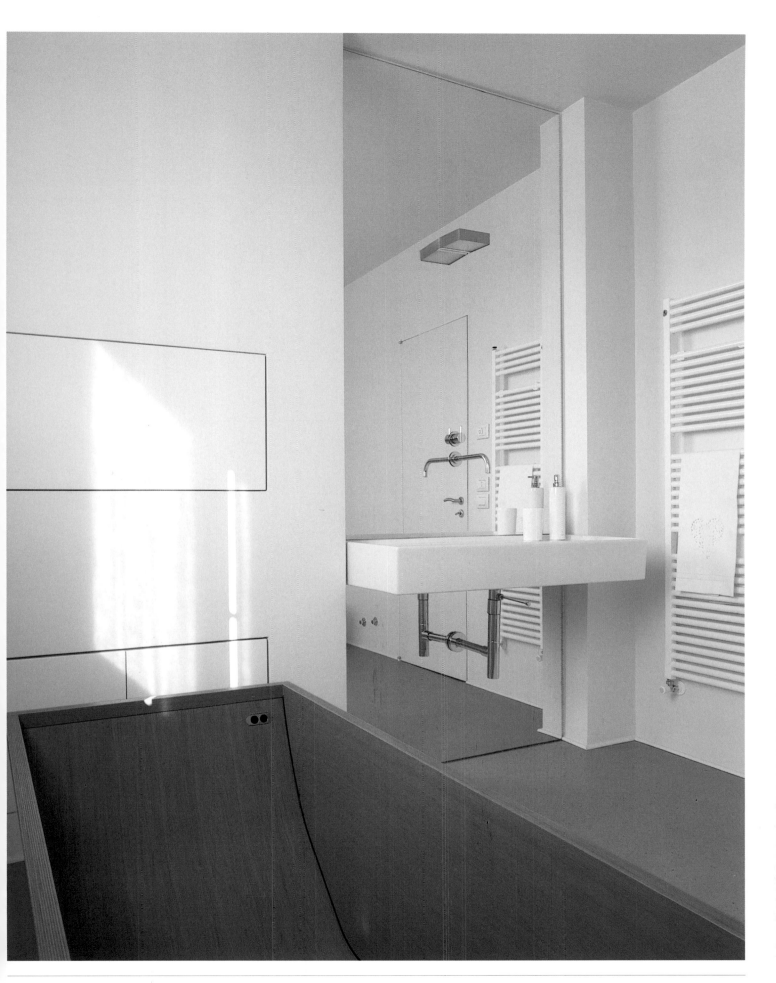

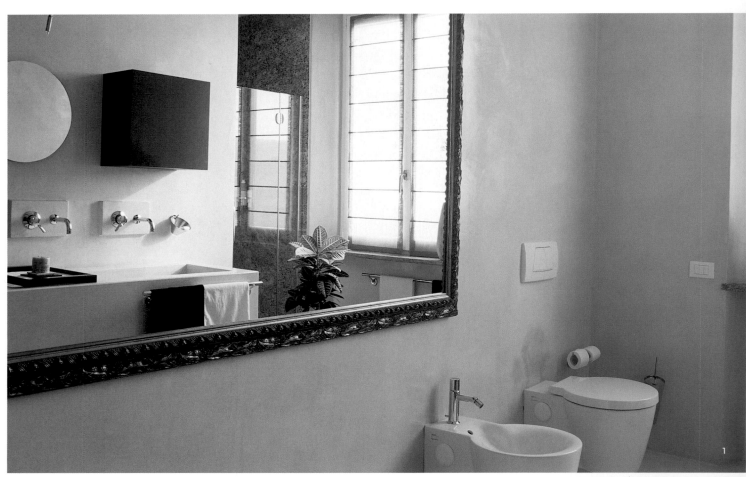

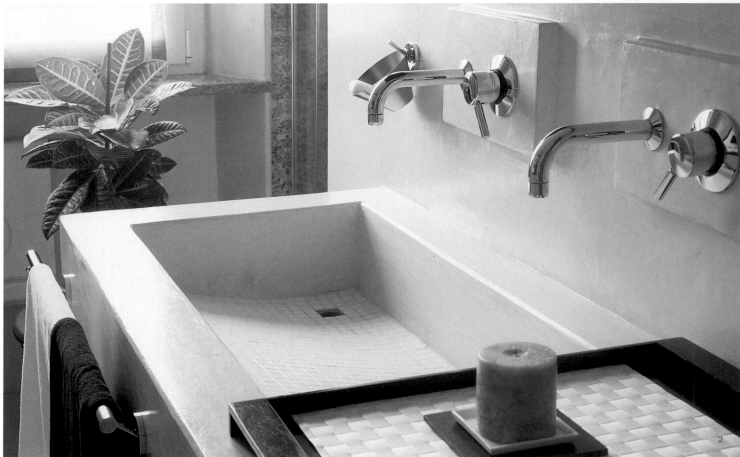

1, 2 © Linda Vismara/Vega MG

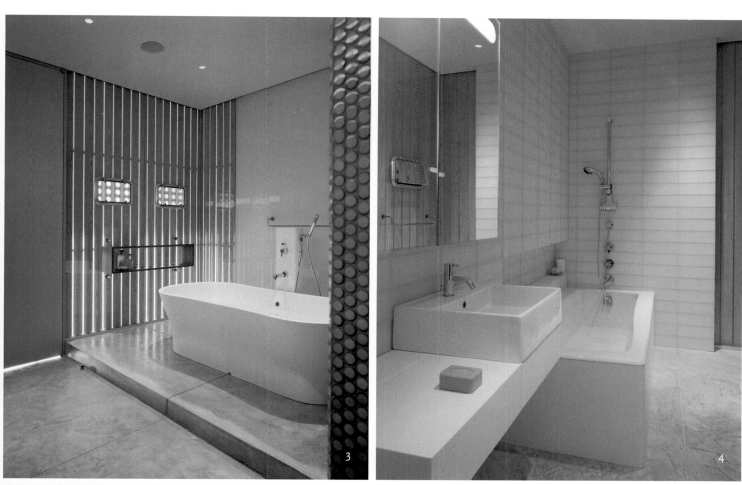

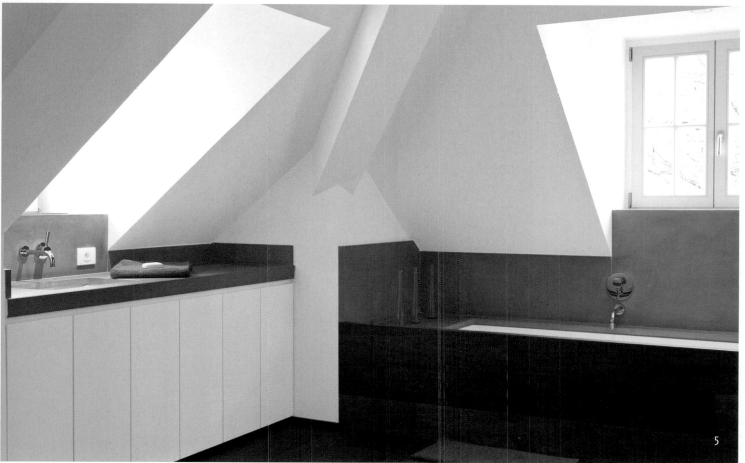

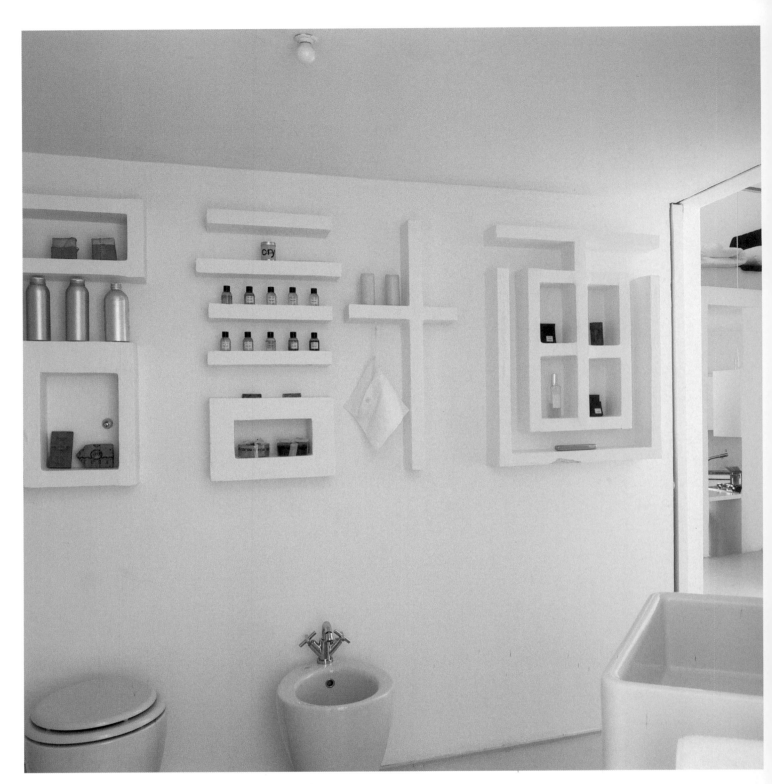

A bathroom can be designed with an emphasis on its functionality and harmony, or it can go one step further by approaching every element as an art object, with the idea of not only optimizing its functionality but also in making it something that expresses the spirit in which it was conceived.

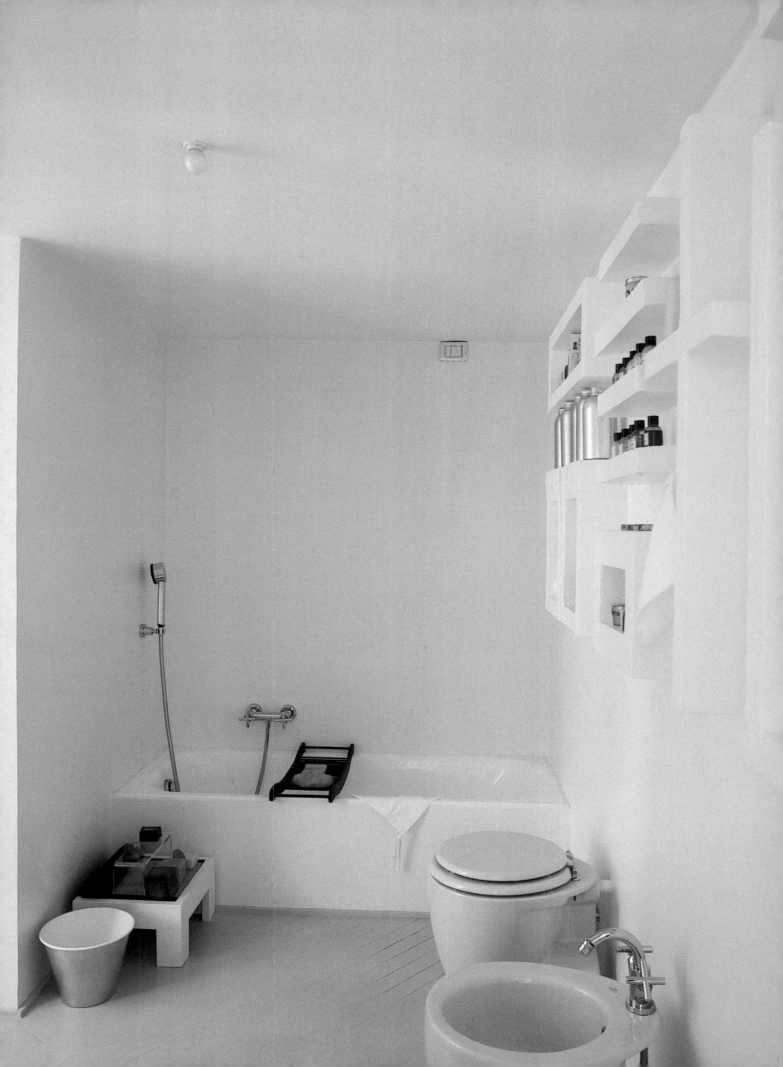

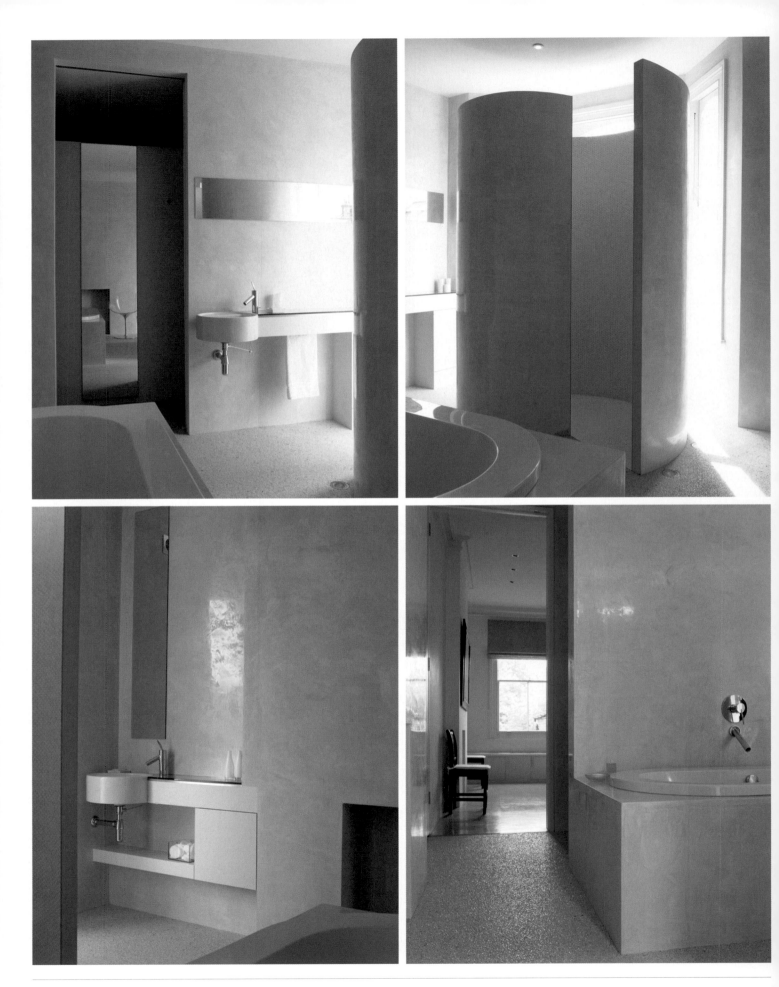

© Cristóbal Palma

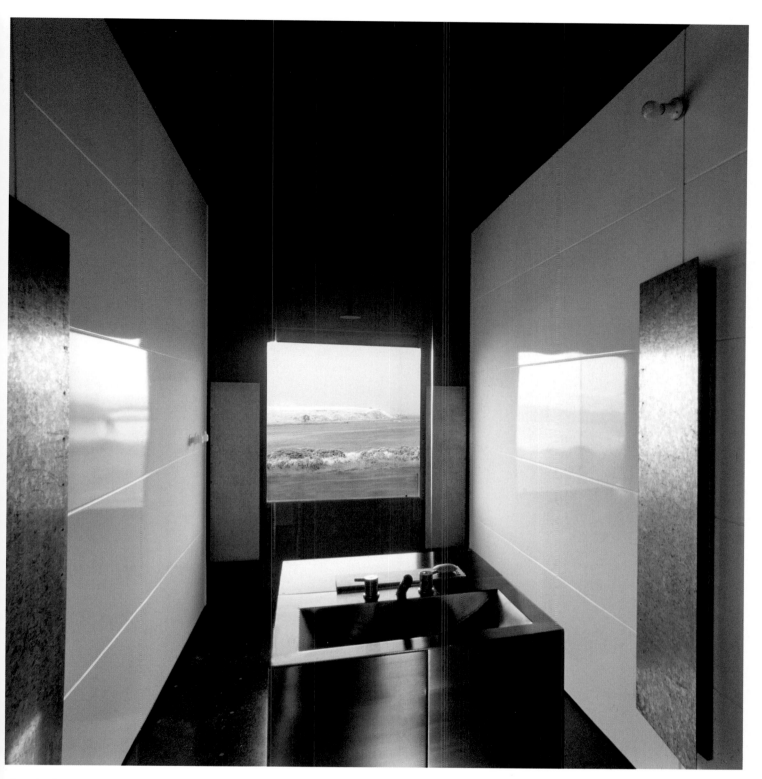

△ "The house in no way connotes residence or domesticity." Denton Corker Marshall wanted to create a subversive, hidden refuge; through its color, forms, and materials. this house is a metaphor for rocks.

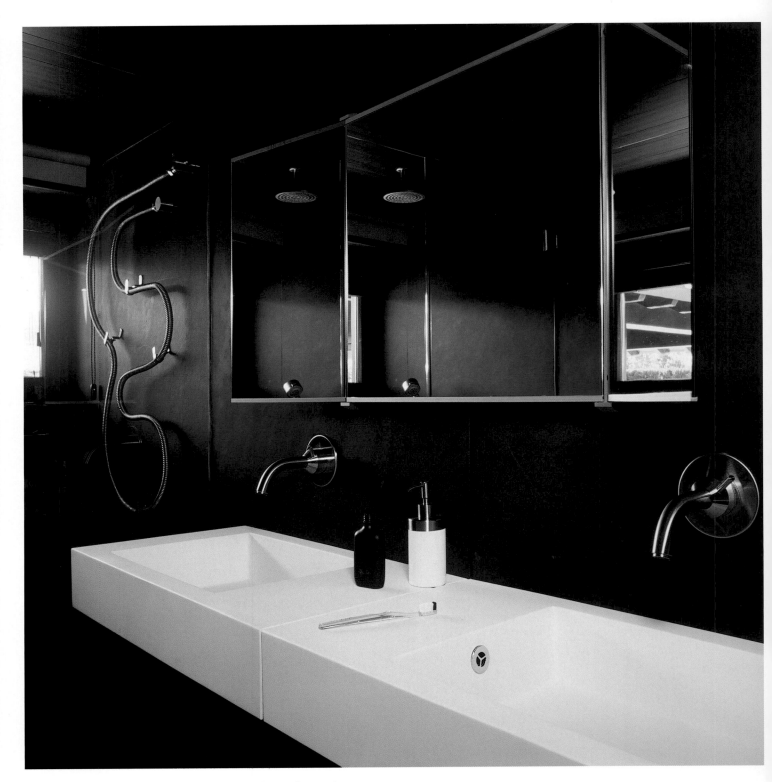

△ A mirror in the form of a triptych and a shower faucet that traces a design—all of the elements in a bathroom can be rethought to achieve decorative effects that preclude any need for other adornments, thereby saving space.

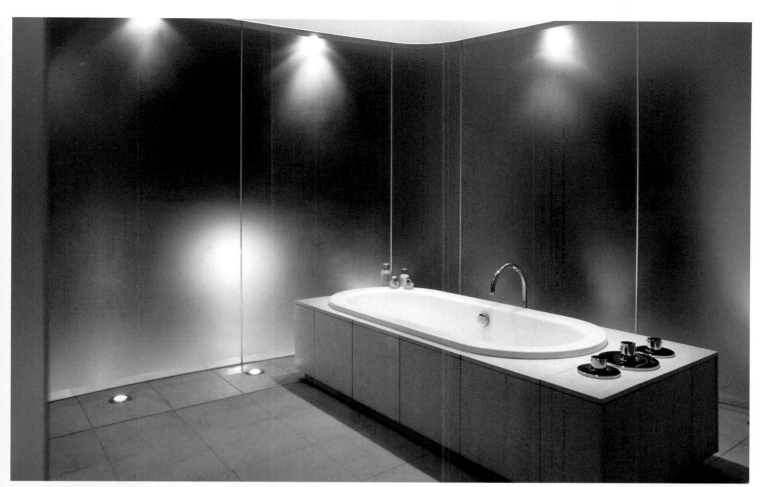

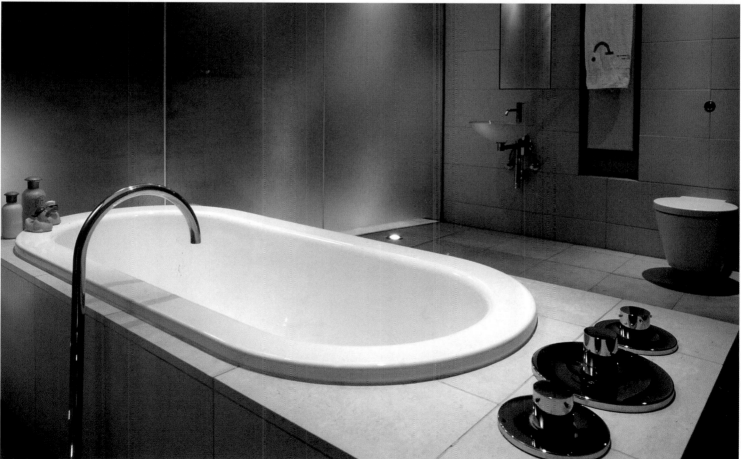

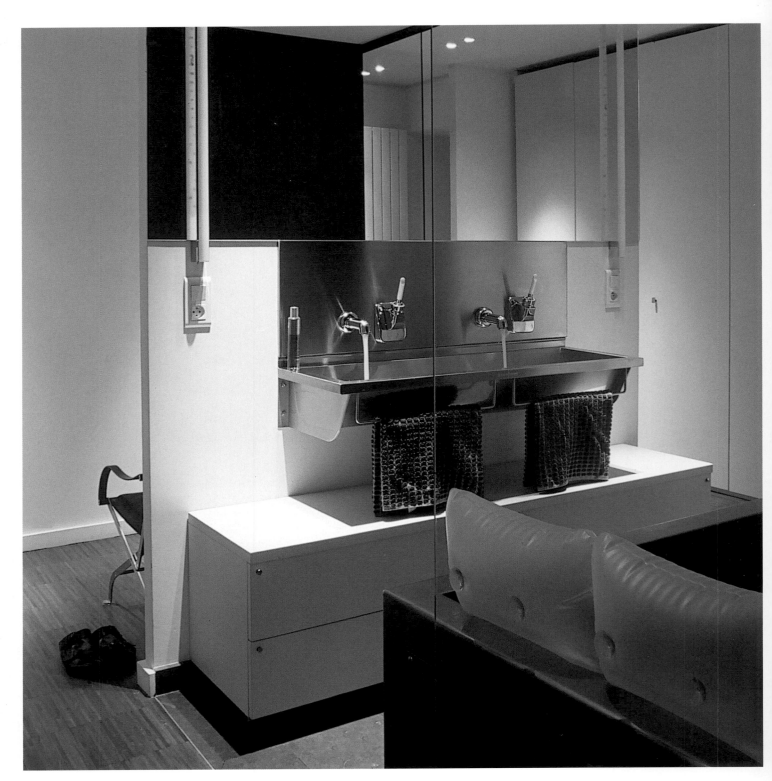

△ The architect Florence Badoux has endowed this bathroom with an industrial austerity by using materials like stainless steel and marble and adopting forms that recall professional installations, as in the case of the sink, which she designed herself and which was manufactured by Fournier Guignard.

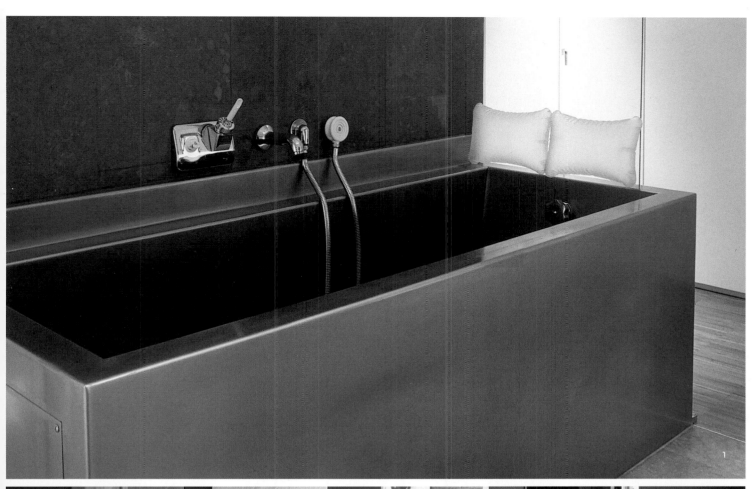

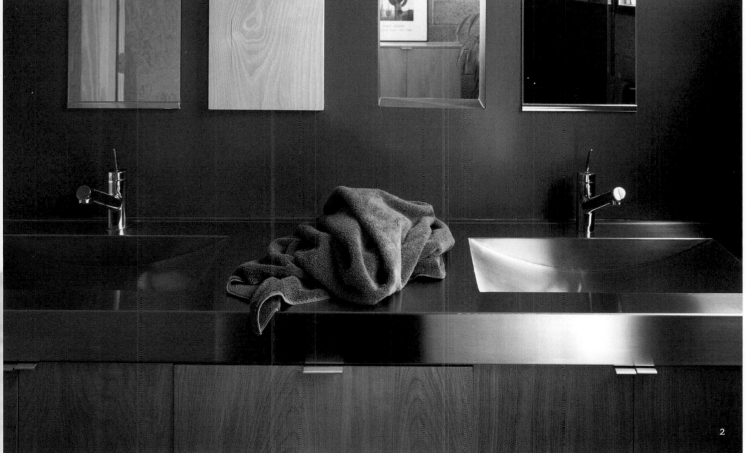

1 © Ricardo Labougle, Ana Cardinale   2 © Bill Timmerman

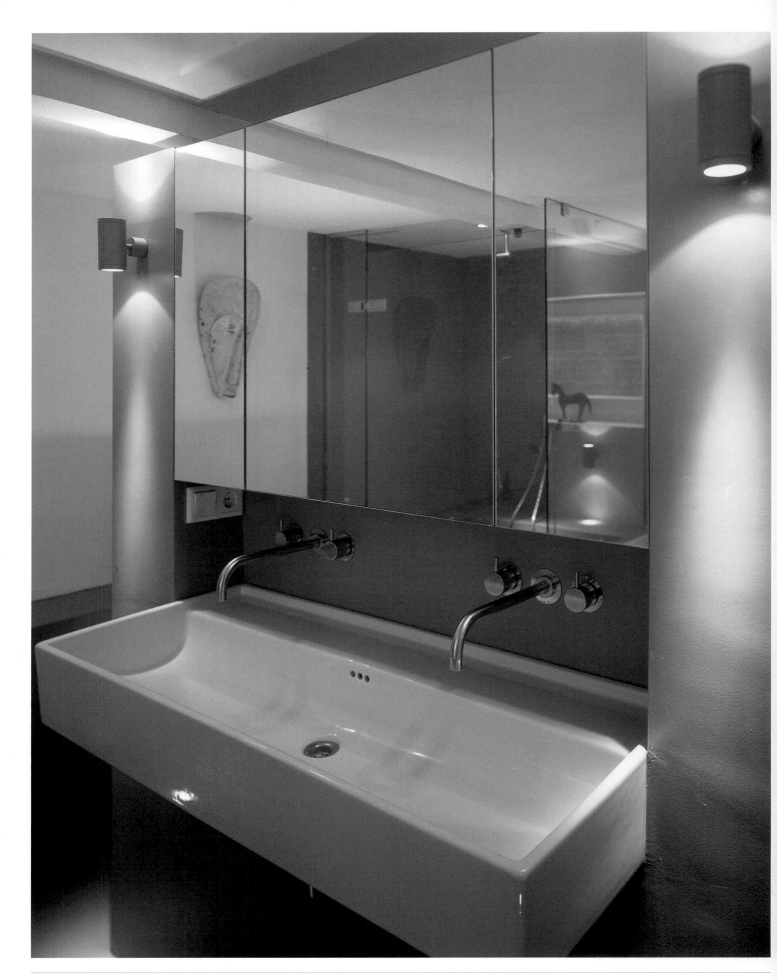

© Luuk Kramer

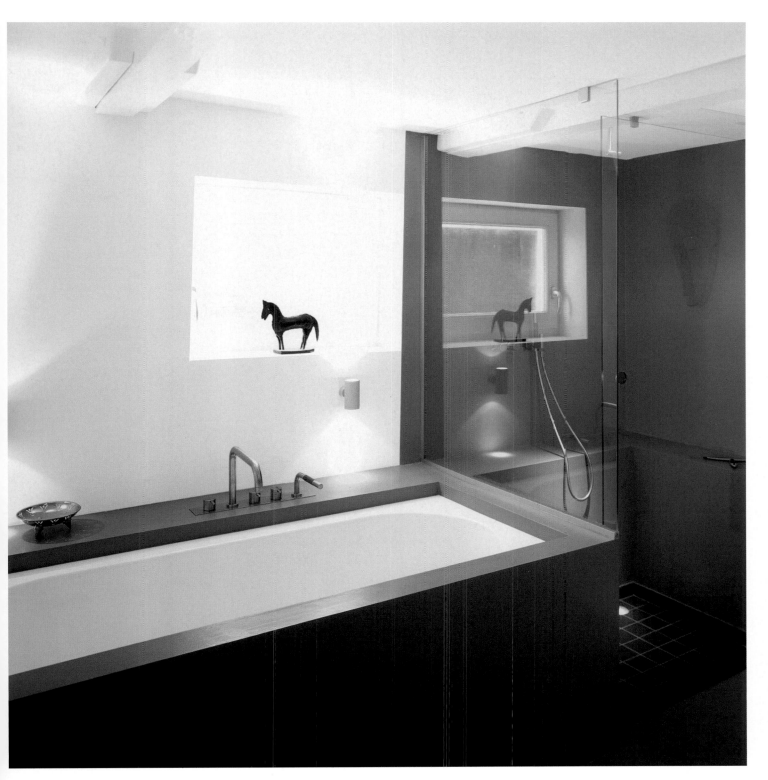

☐ This industrial-style project was designed up by Moriko Kira, a Japanese architect living in Holland. A picture with a figure, painted with light, softens the severe look of the metal and glass.

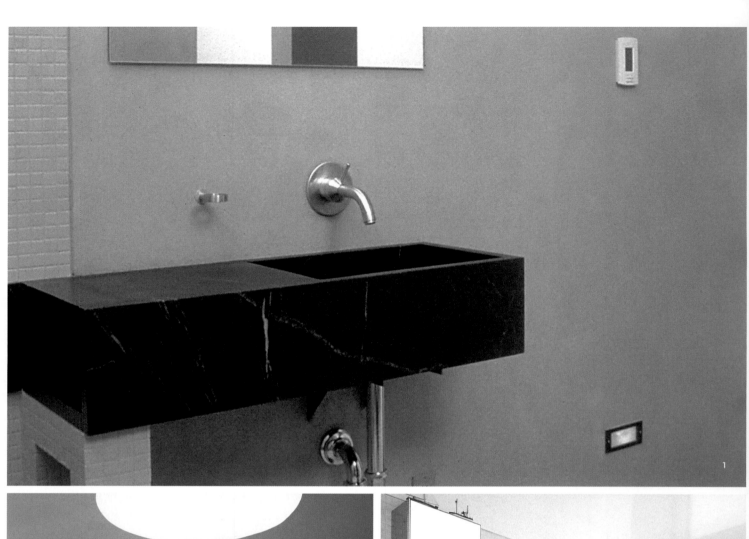

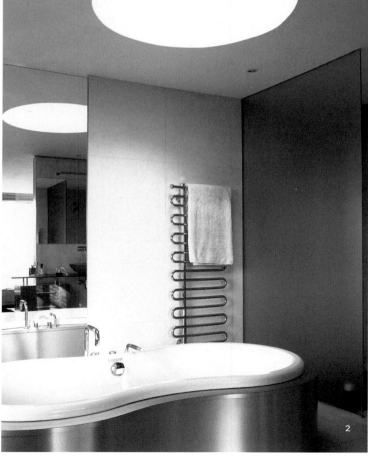

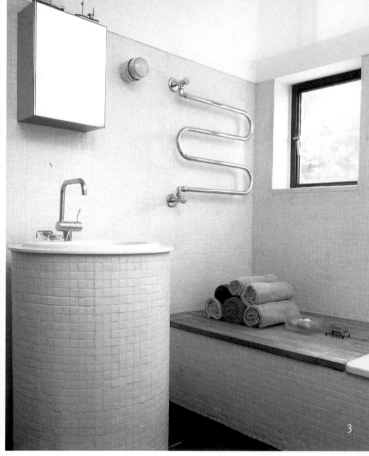

1 © Jack Kucy   2 © Mark York/Red Cover   3 © Henry Wilson/Red Cover

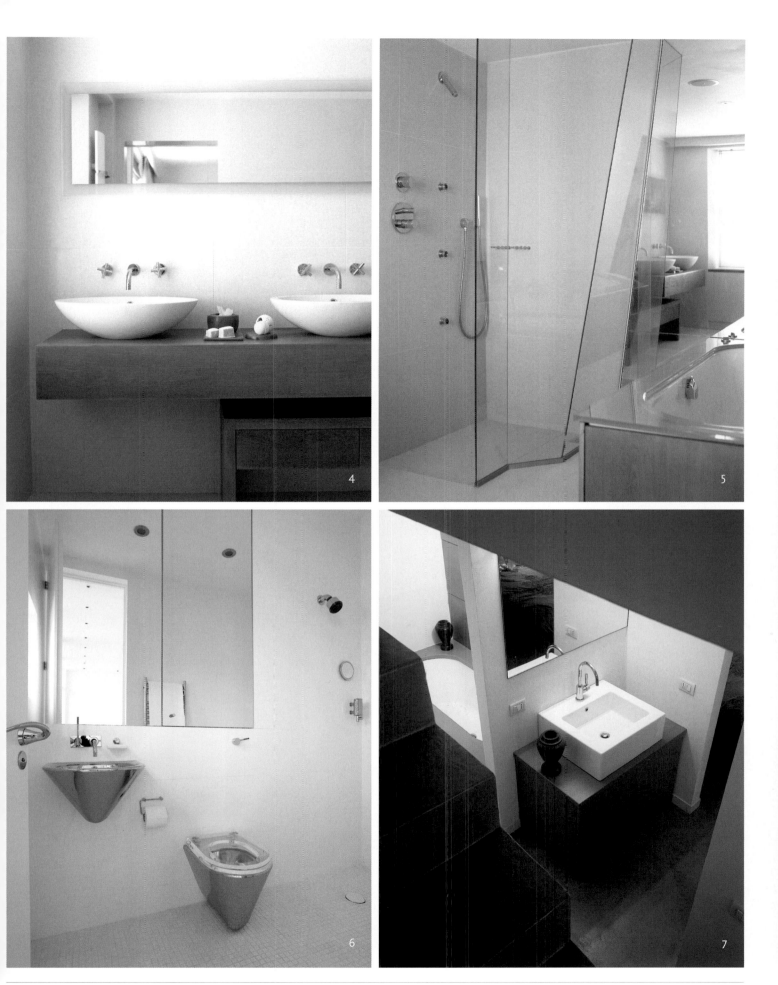

4, 5 © Graham Atkins-Hughes/Red Cover   6 © Ken Hayden/Red Cover   7 © Andrea Martiradonna

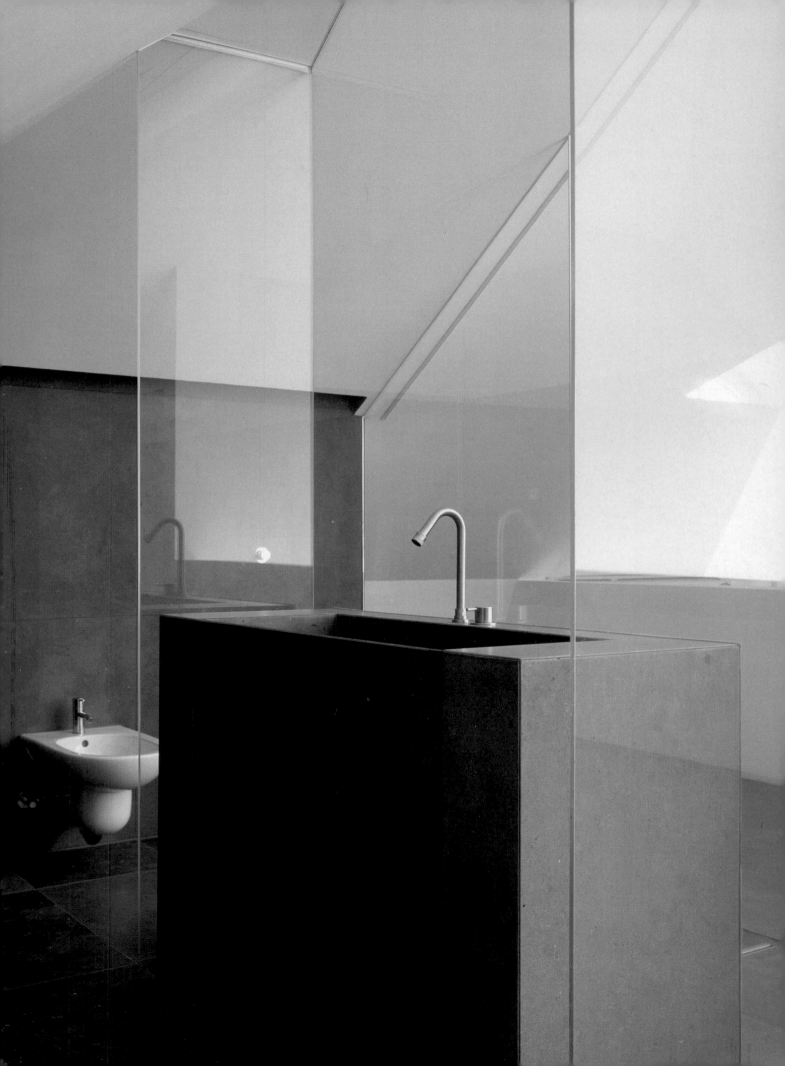

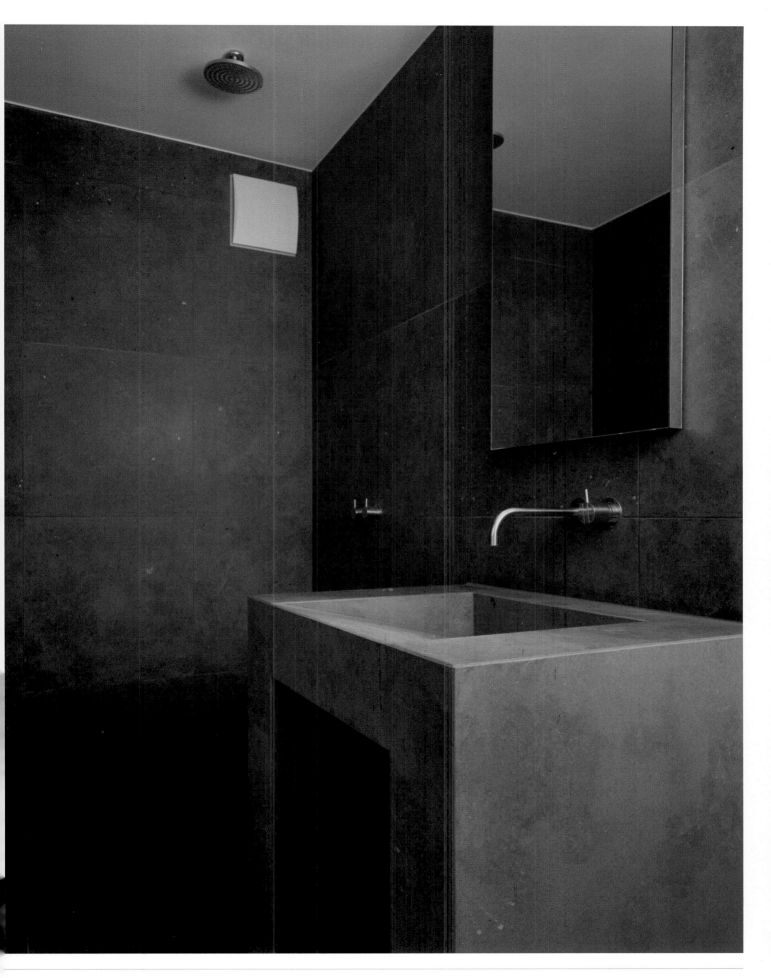

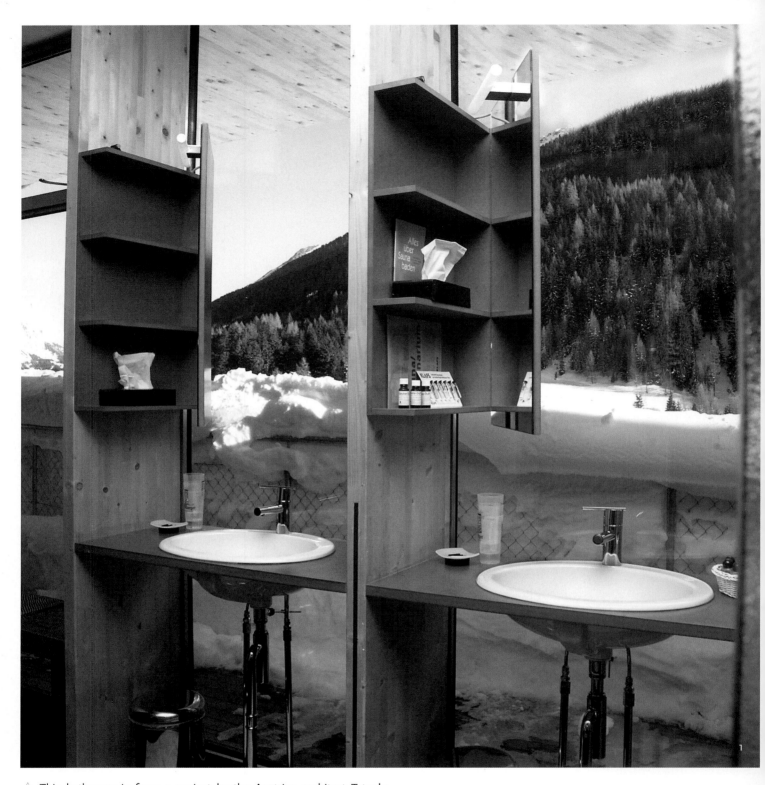

△ This bathroom is from a project by the Austrian architect Tatanka Ideenvertriebgesellschaft. Both the bathroom and the rest of the house benefit from the technical qualities of modern construction materials.

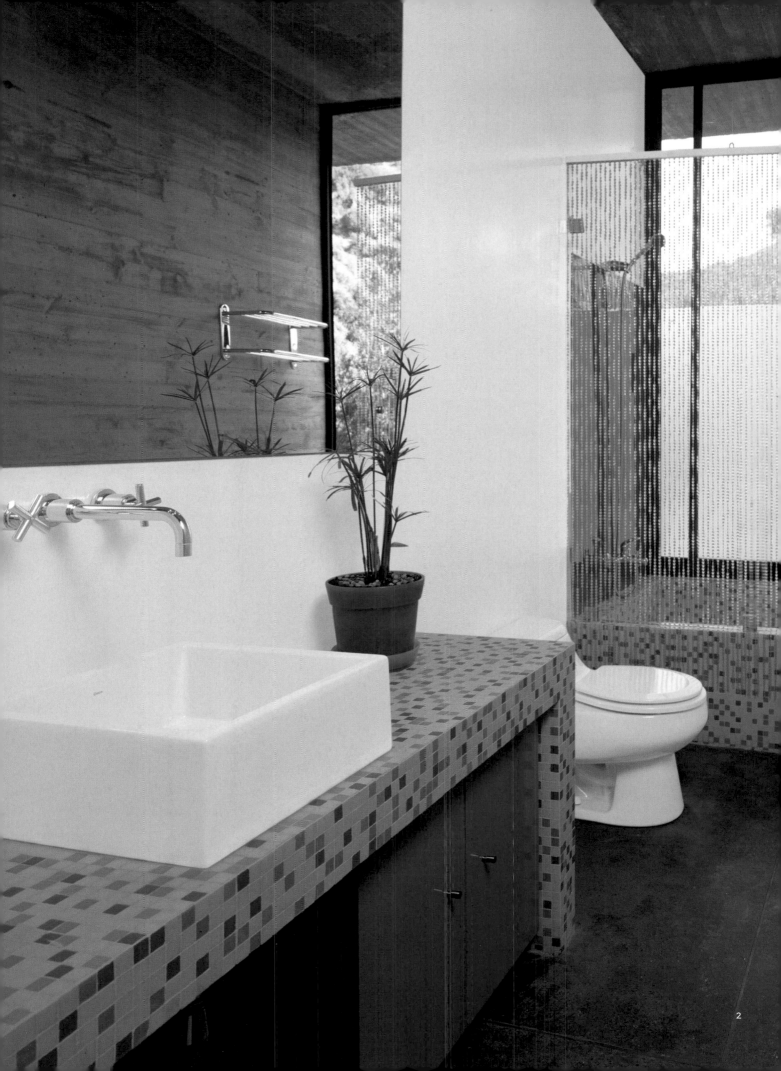

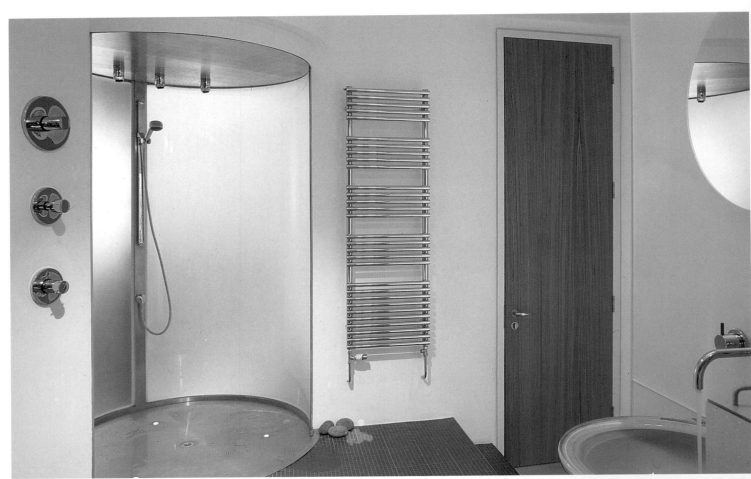

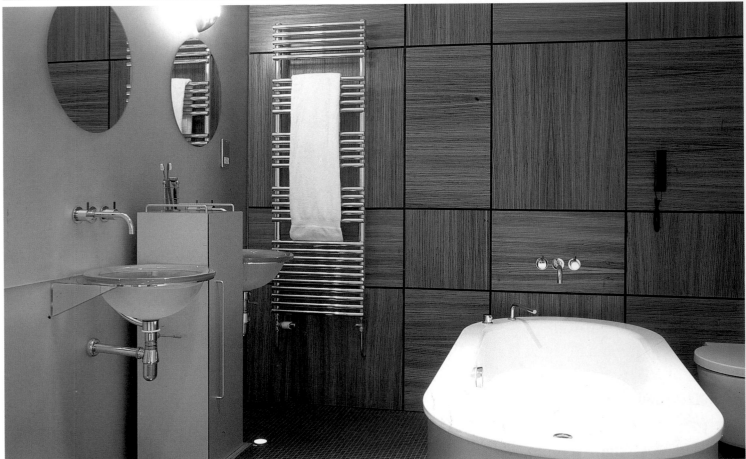

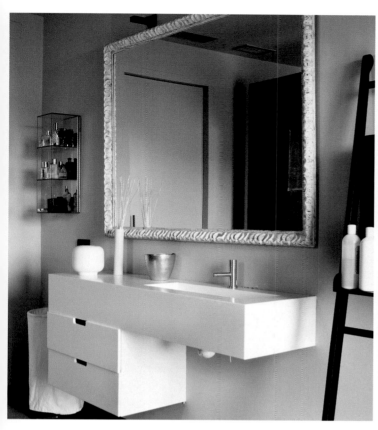
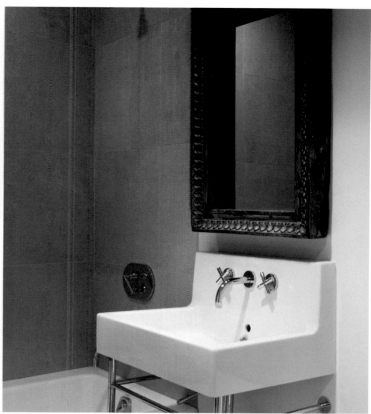

Creating contrasts between classical and ultramodern elements
is a characteristic shared by many of today's designers, including
Philippe Starck. This achieves both impact and personality.

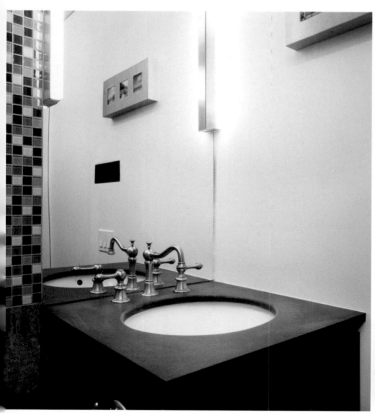
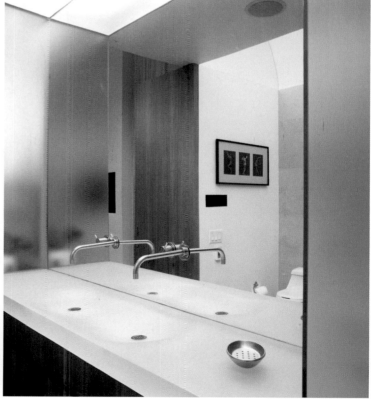

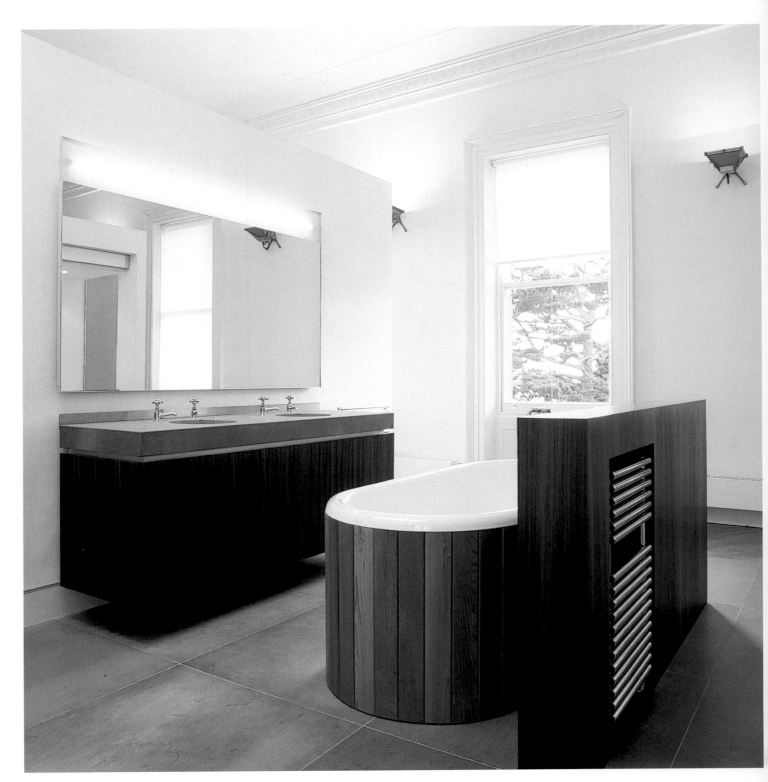

☐ New techniques for treating natural materials—in this case, wood—
mean that they can be used in parts of the house where they were once
banished. Wood has until now been unusual in a bathroom.

© Carlos Domínguez

356

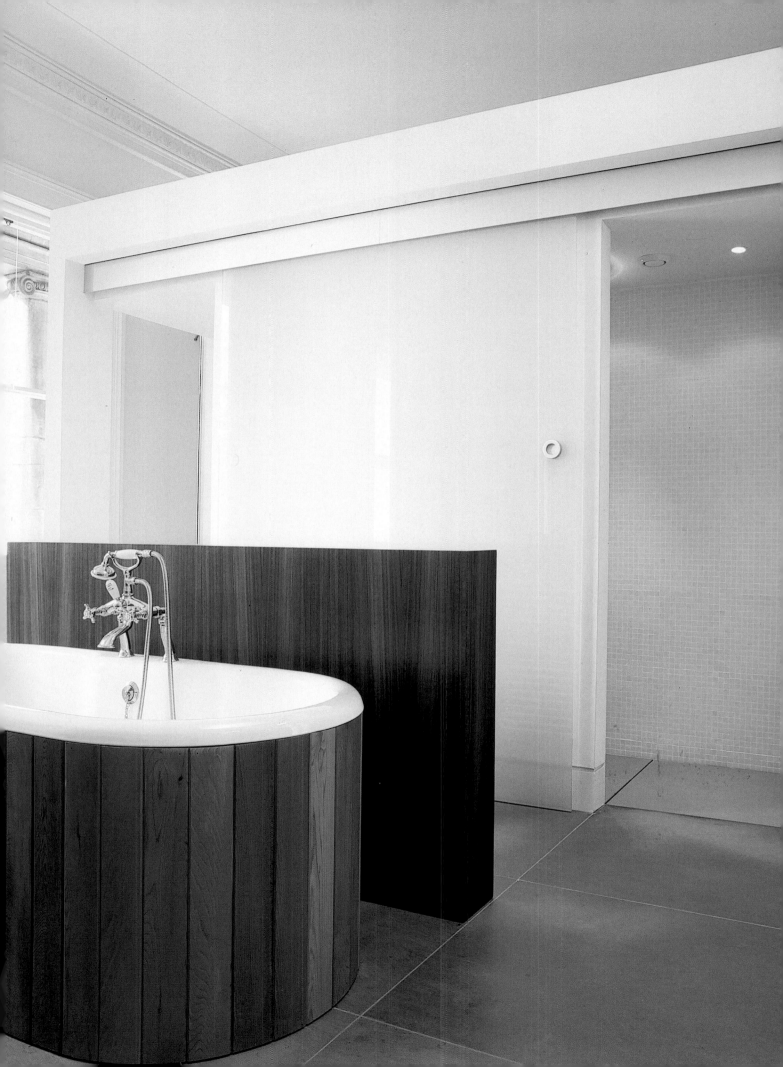

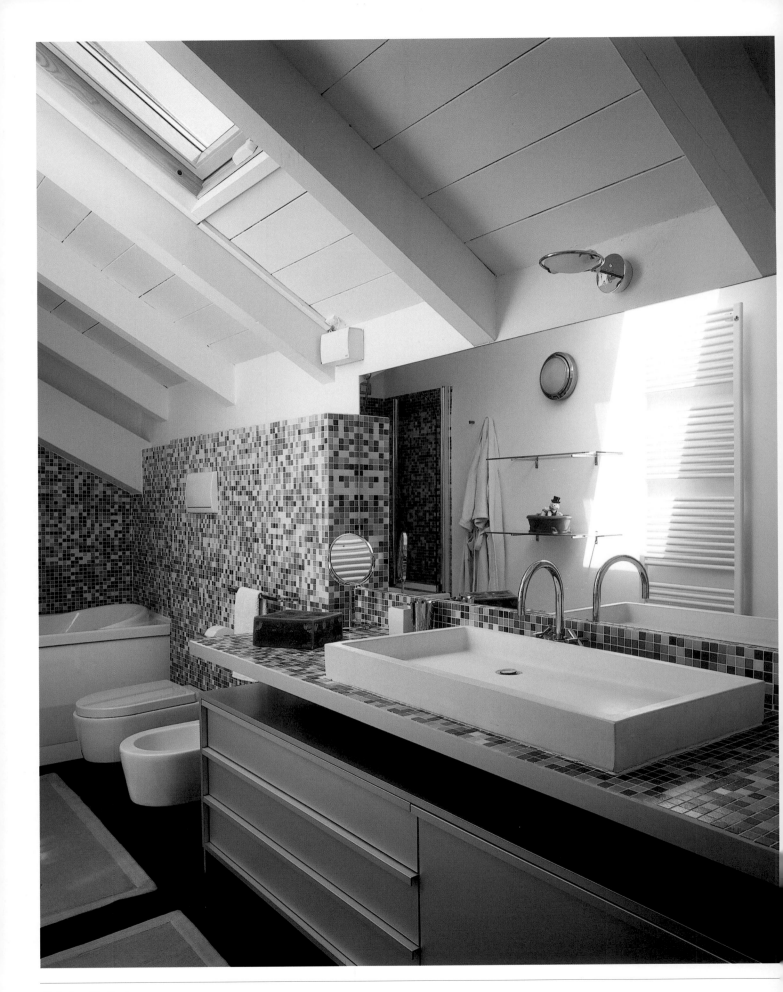

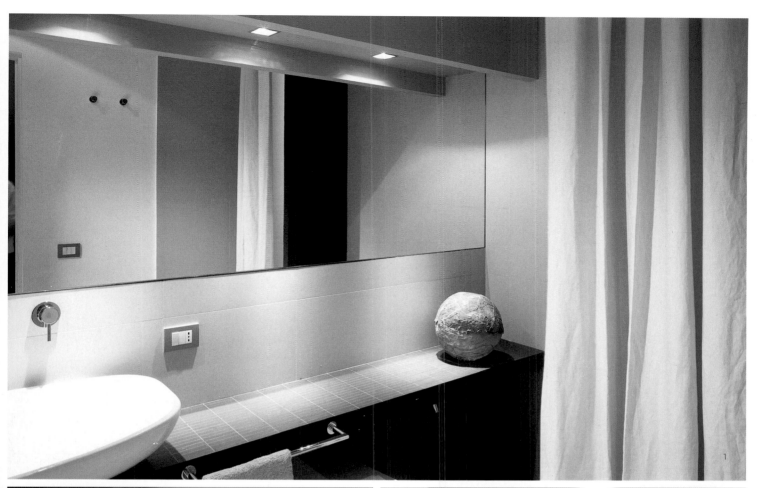

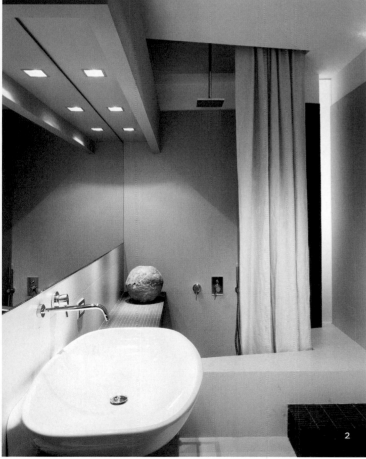

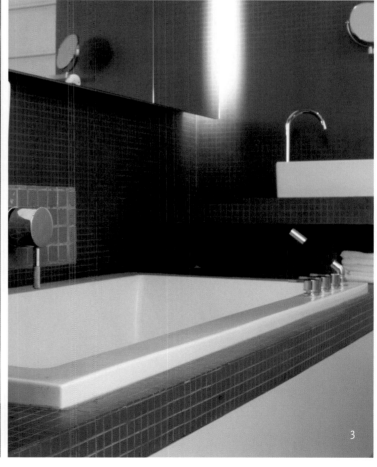

1, 2 © Luigi Filetici   3 © Laurent Brandajs

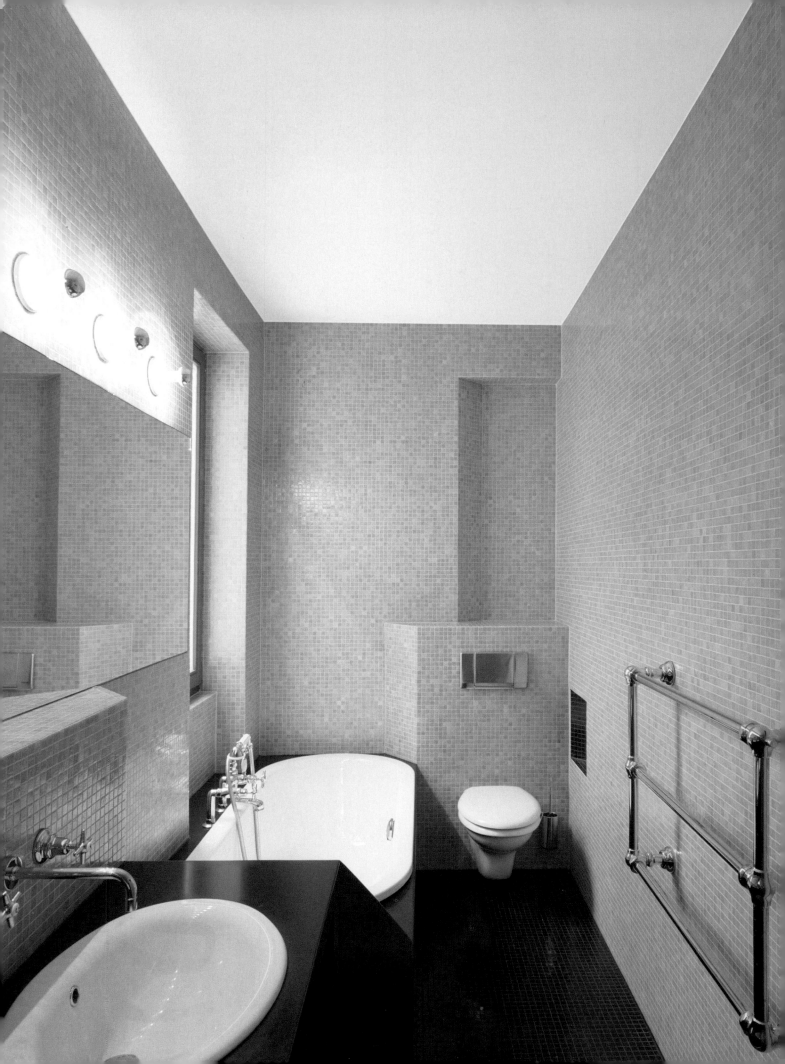

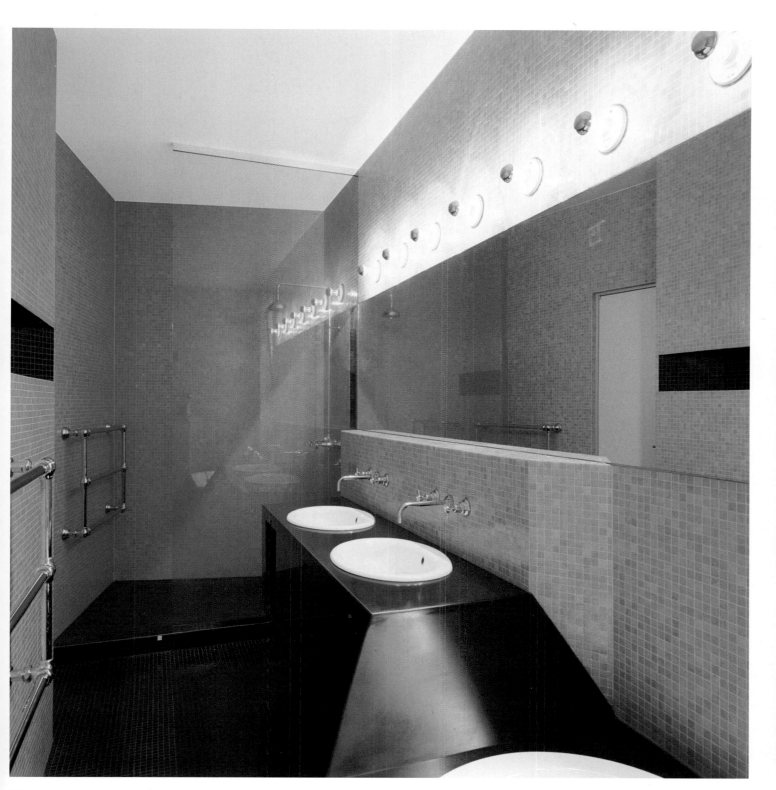

☐ This bathroom by the Berlin-based architects Gonzalez and Haase illustrates the use of color to create specific spatial sensations. Black, pink, and white dominate the lower part of the space, so there is a sense of greater breadth and height as the gaze goes up to the ceiling.

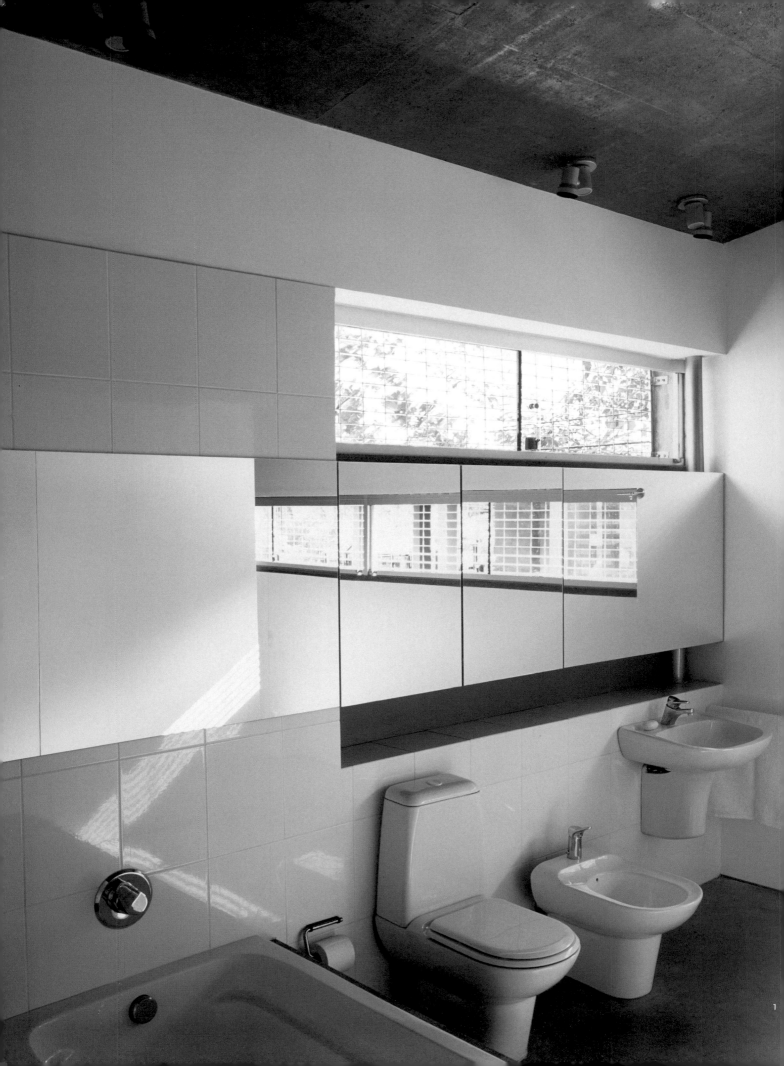

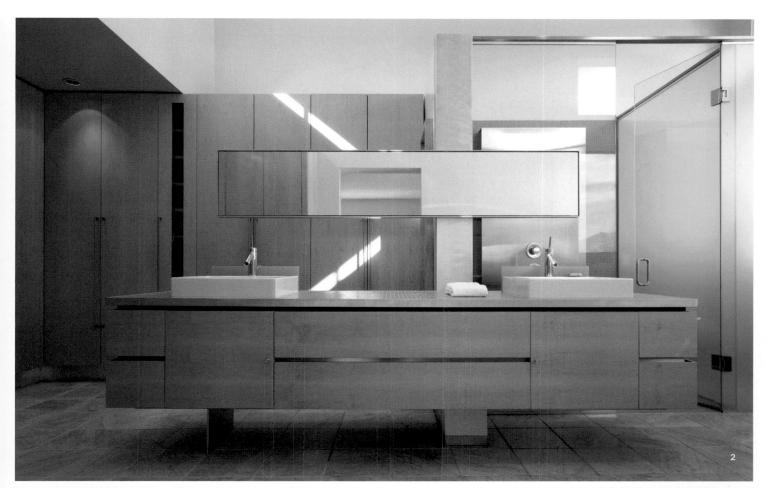

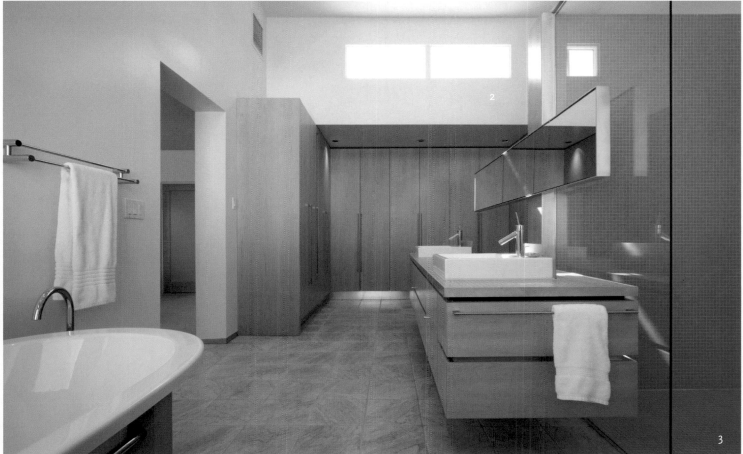

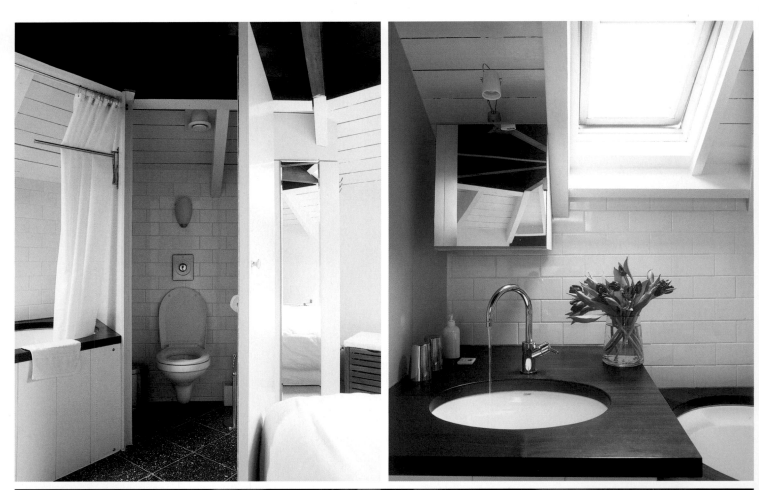

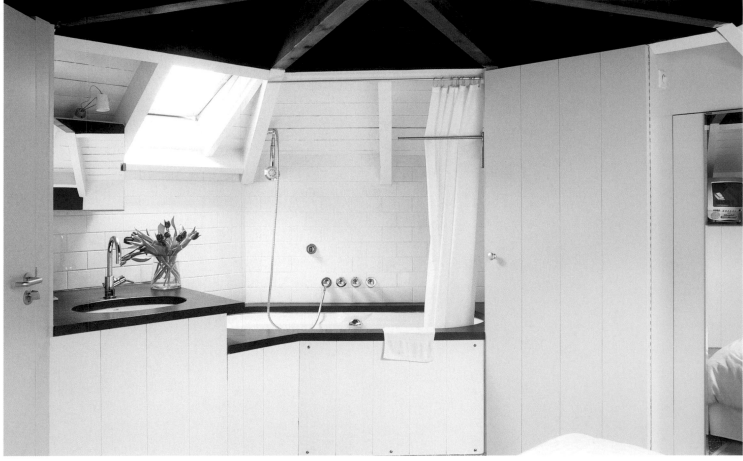

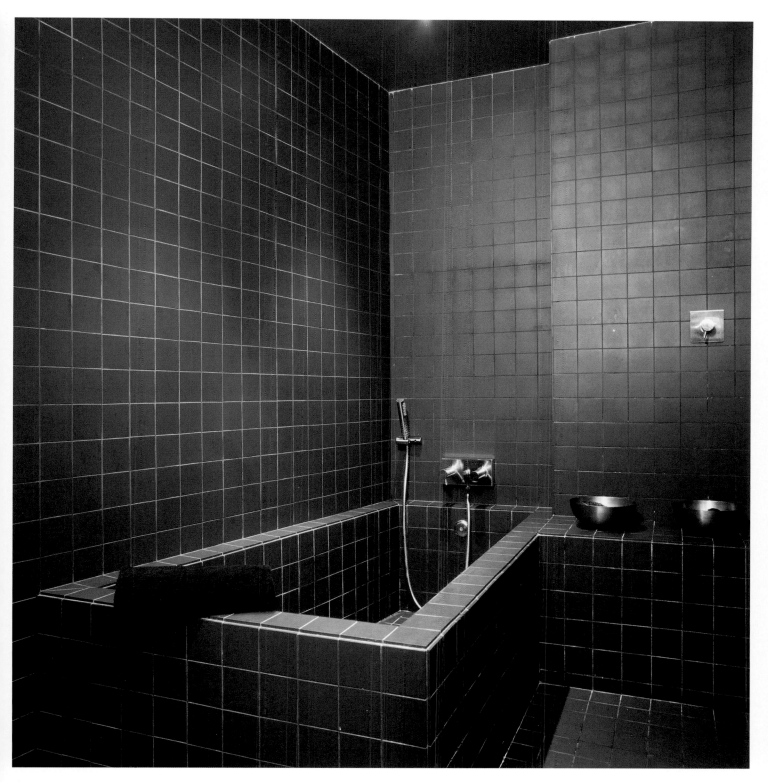

△ This bath exudes a Mediterranean air thanks to the terracotta-colored
tile that has been chosen for both the walls and the floors.

© Jordi Miralles

365

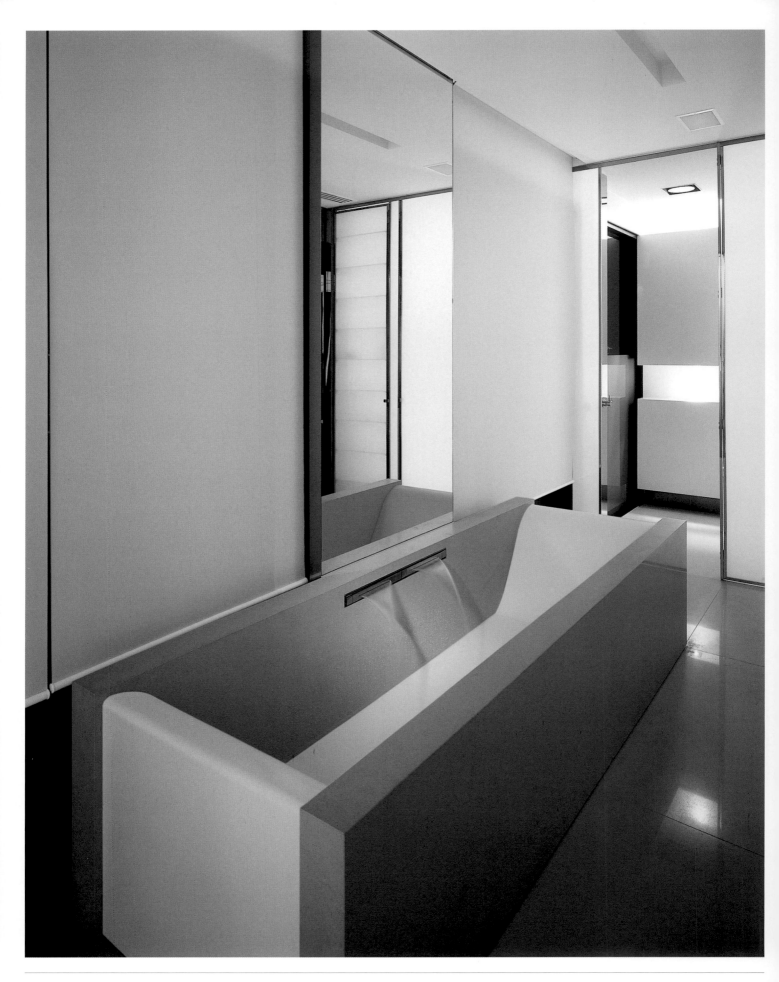

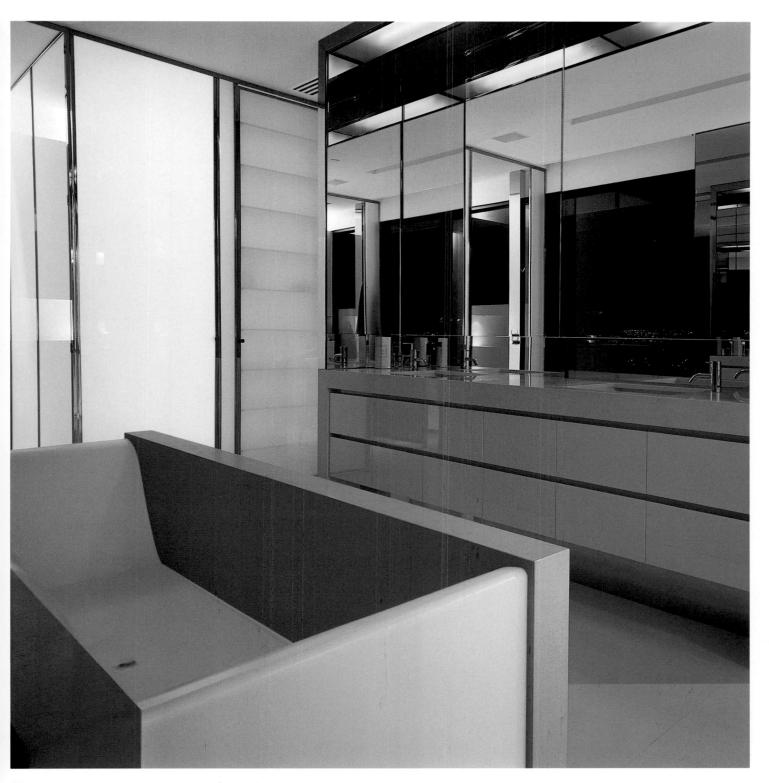

An ultramodern feel for this bathroom from SJB Interiors, in Melbourne, Australia.

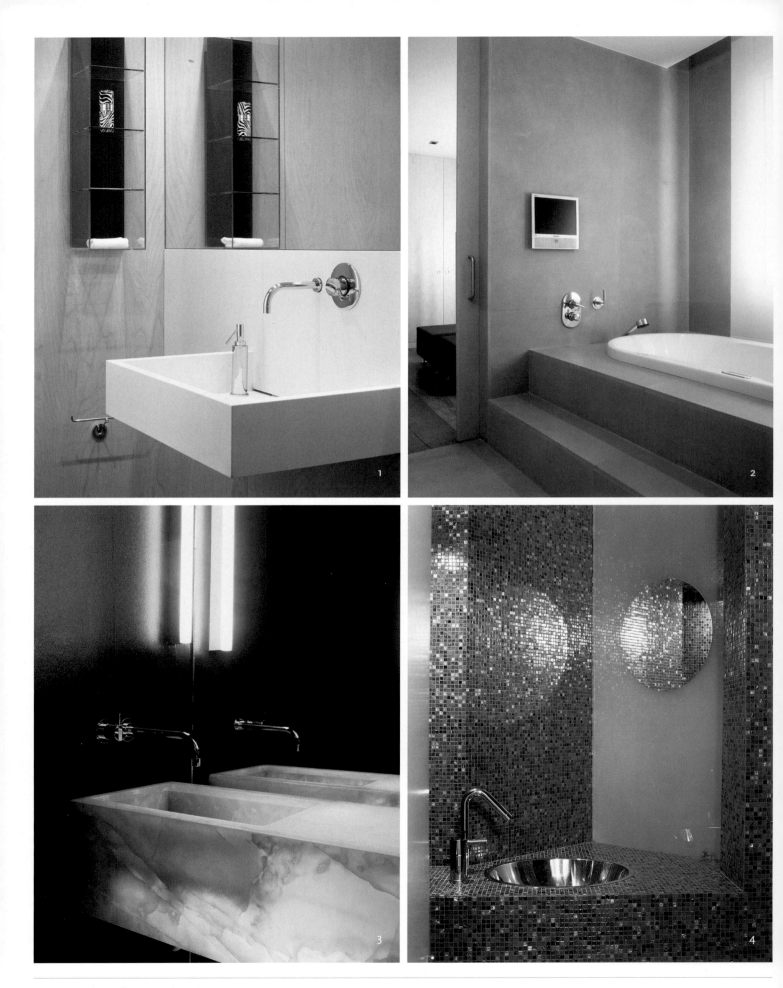

1, 2, 3 © Jordi Miralles   4 © Amit Geron

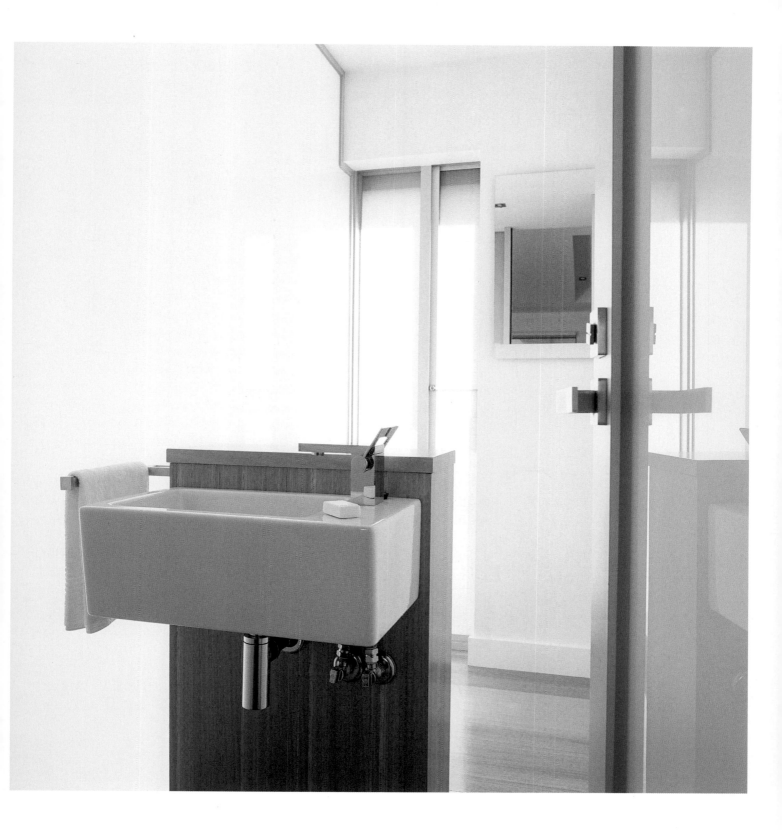

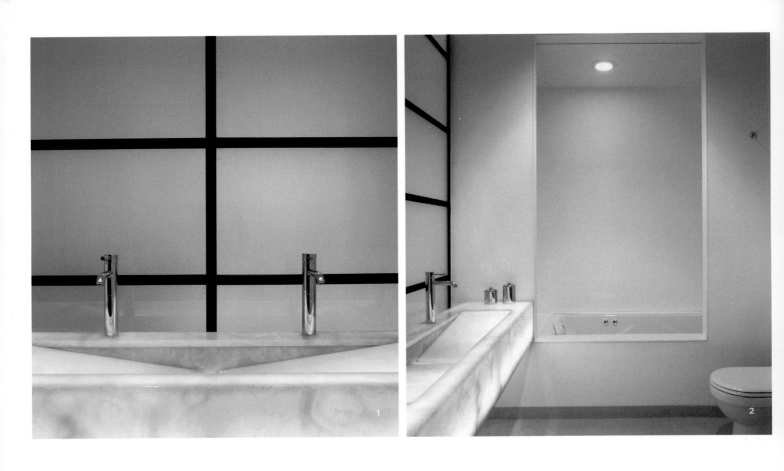

The aesthetics of the Asian bath serve as an inspiration for today's designers.

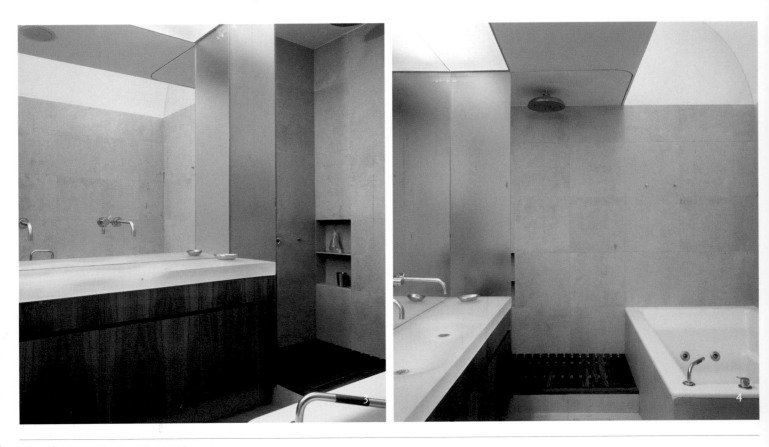

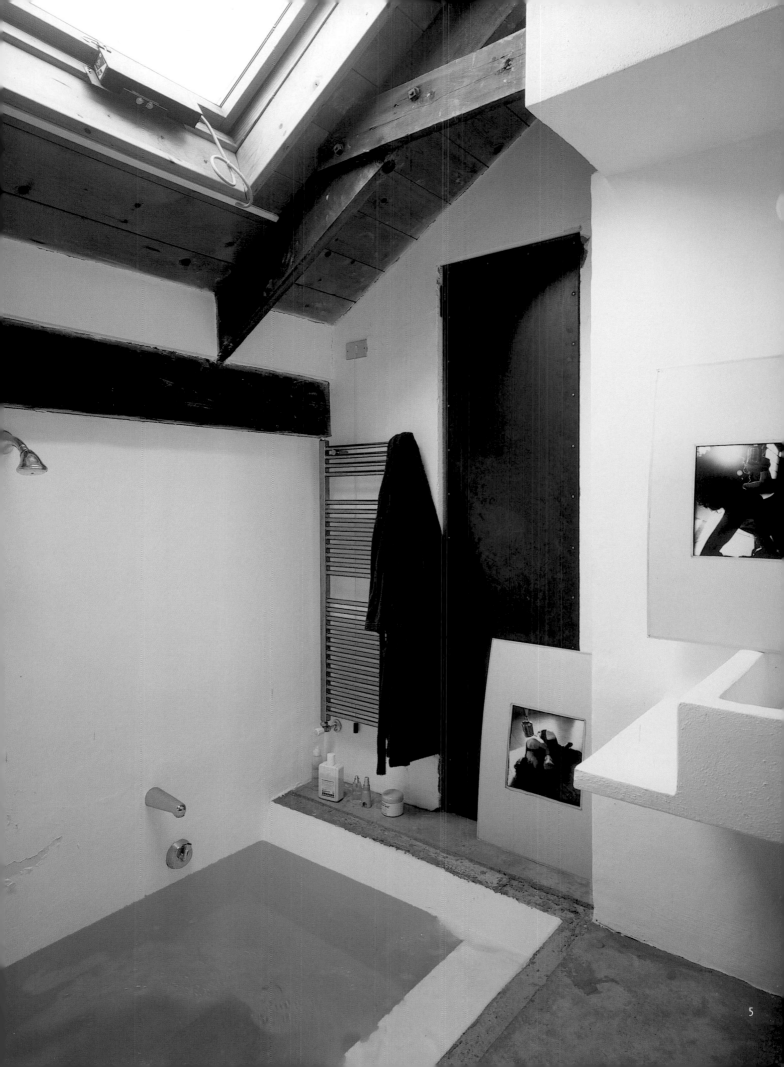

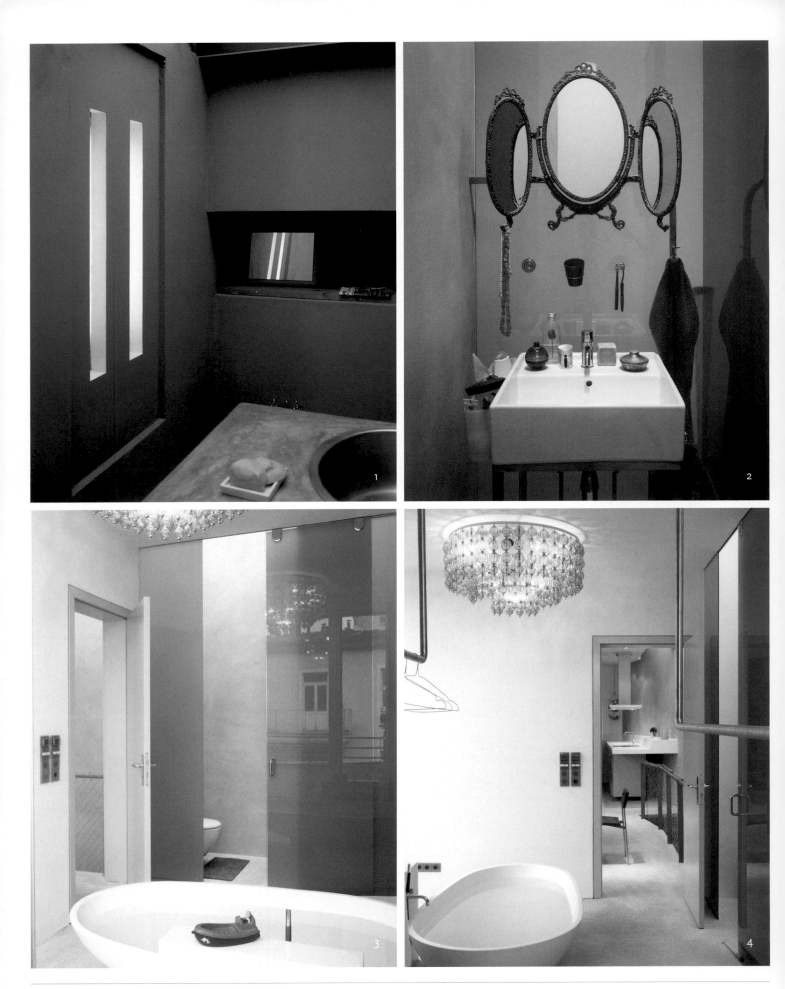

1 © Andrea Martiradonna   2, 3, 4 © Ludger Paffrath

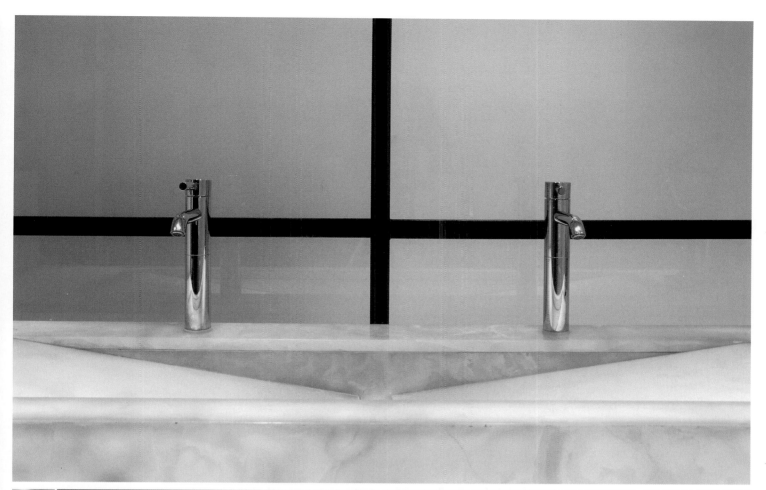

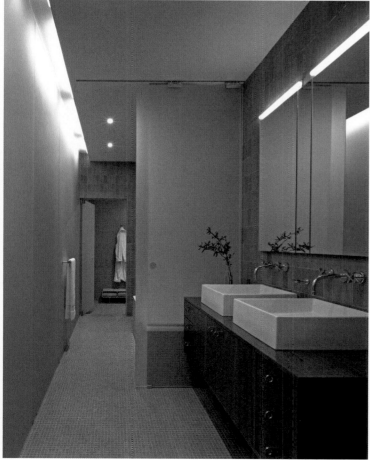

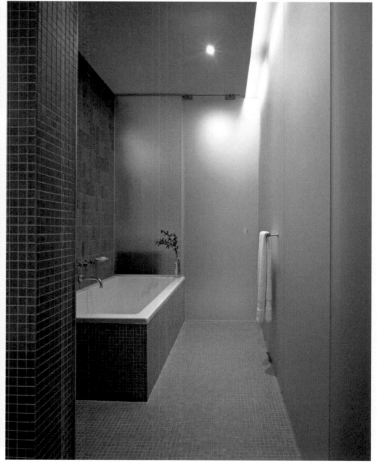

© Jordi Miralles

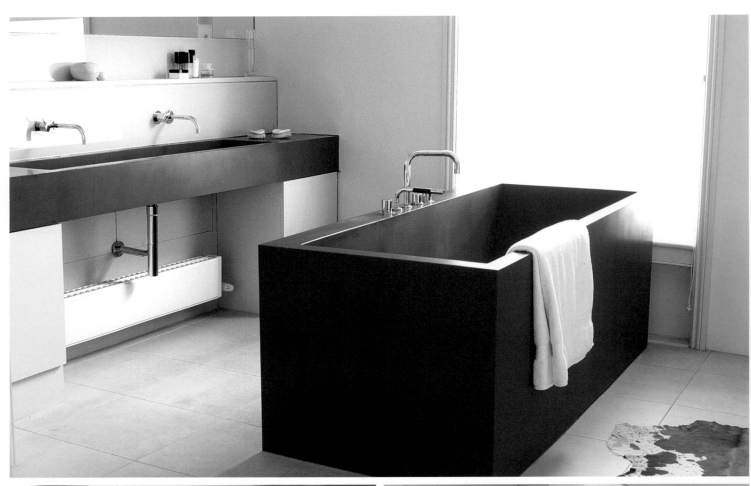

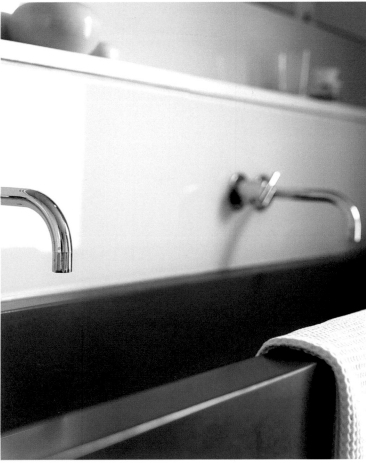

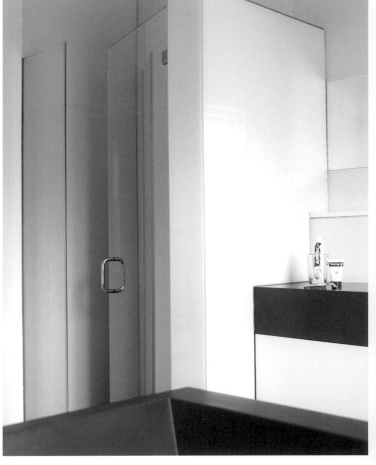

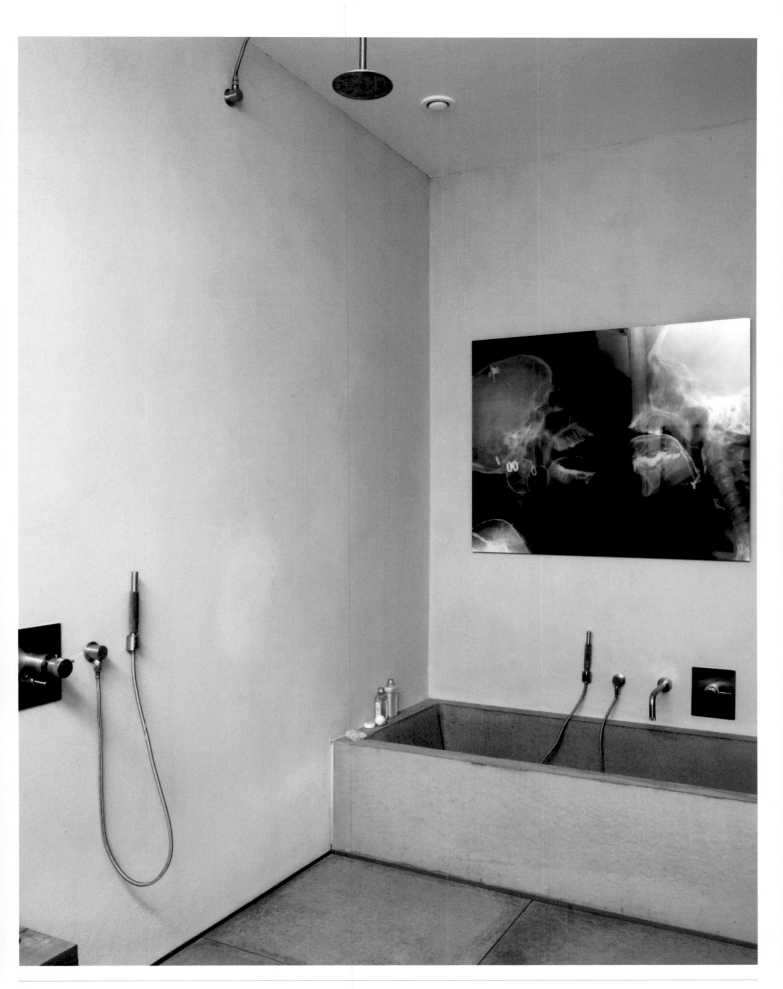

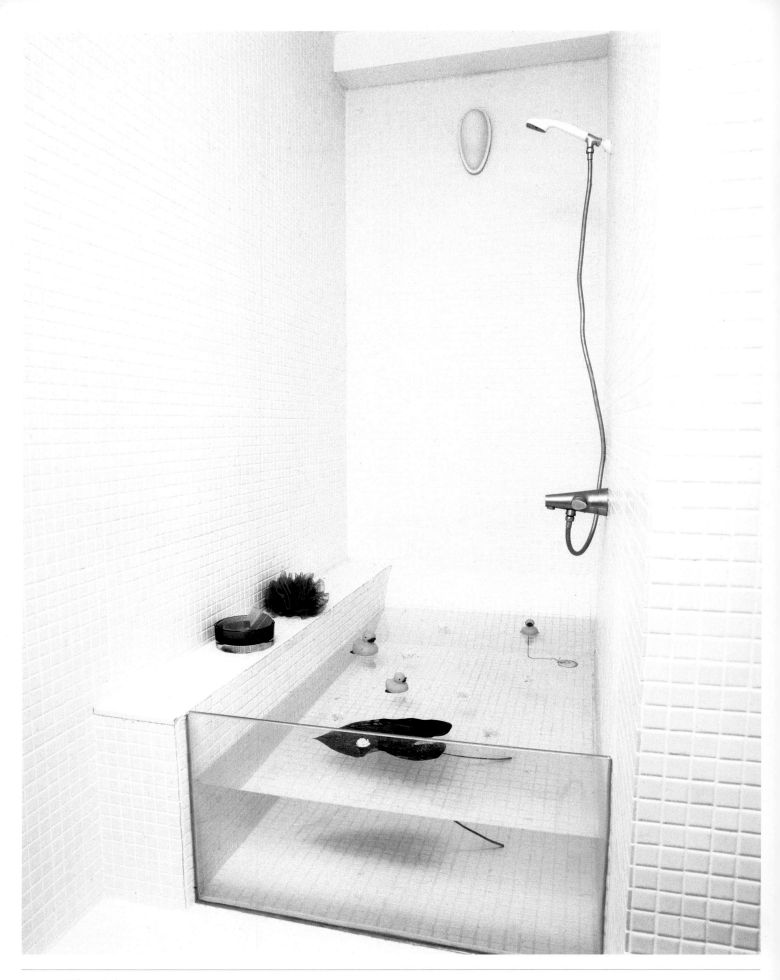

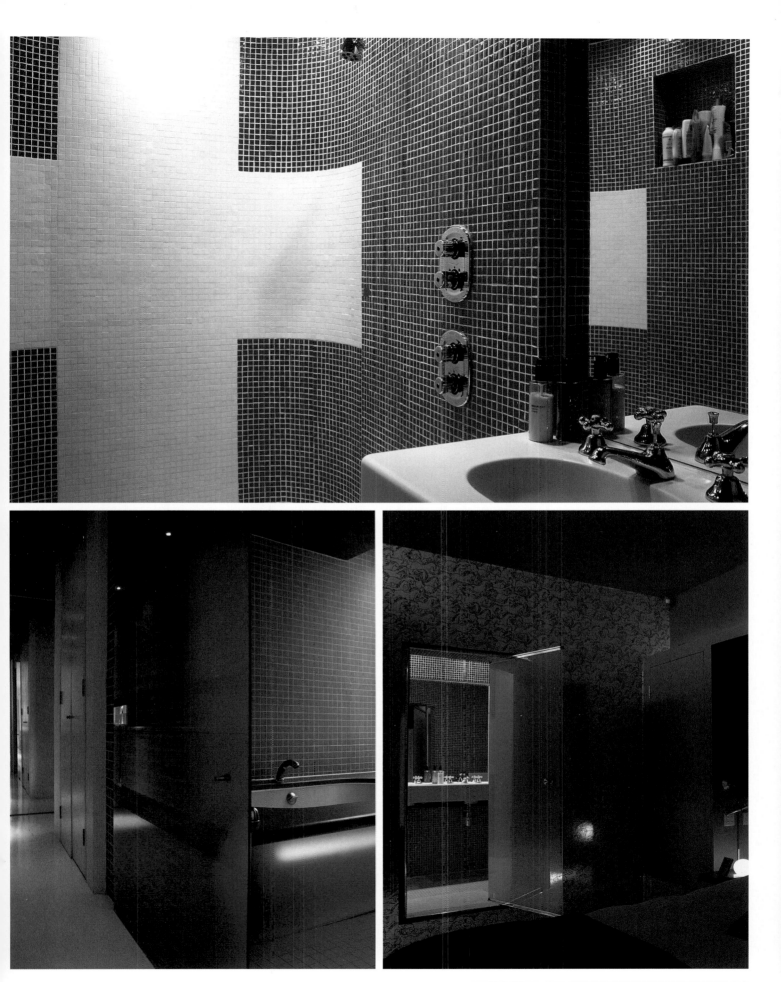

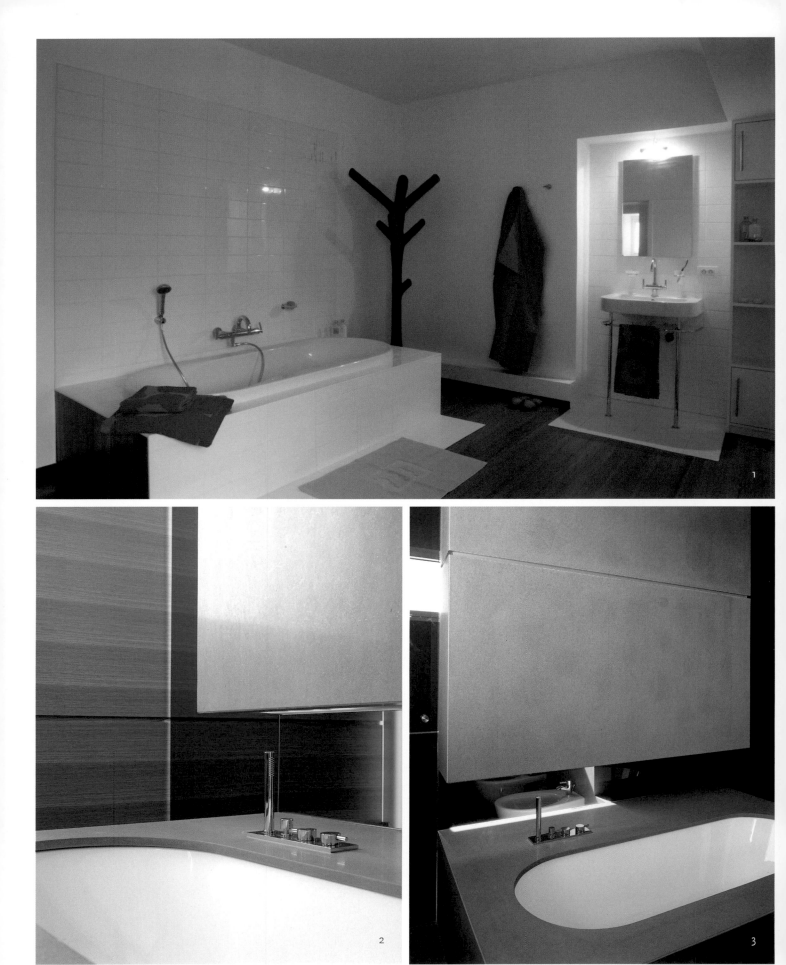

1 © Laurent Brandajs   2, 3 © Ian Chee/Red Cover

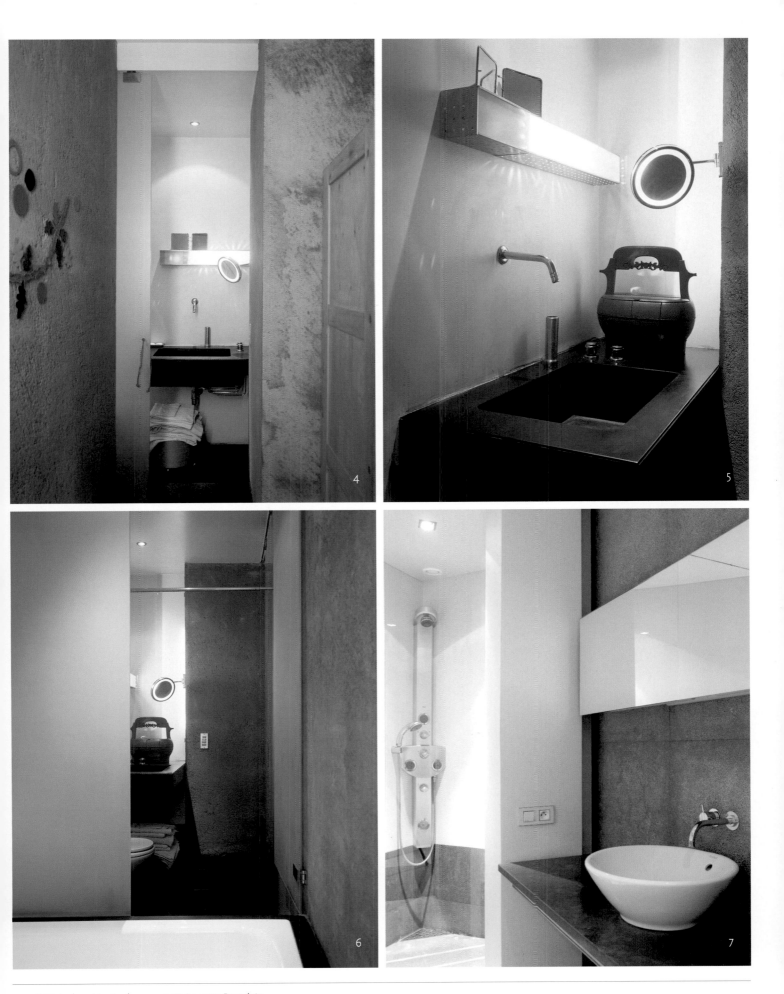

4, 5, 6 © Andrea Martiradonna   7 © Laurent Brandajs

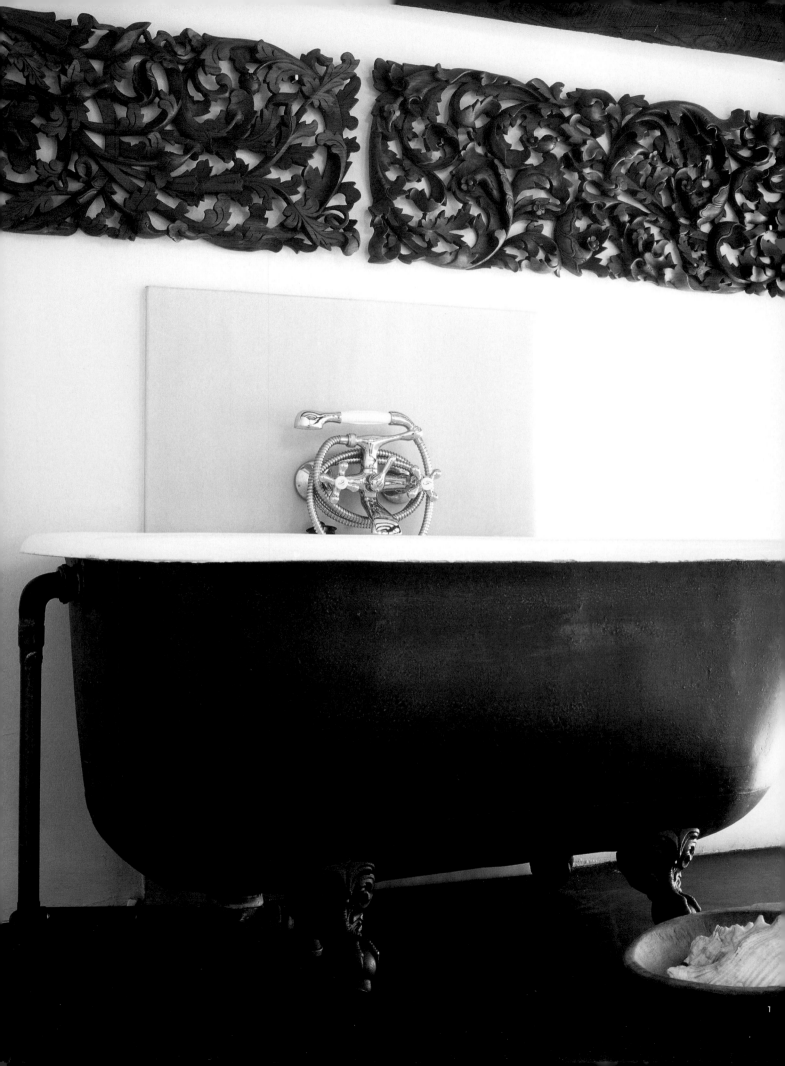

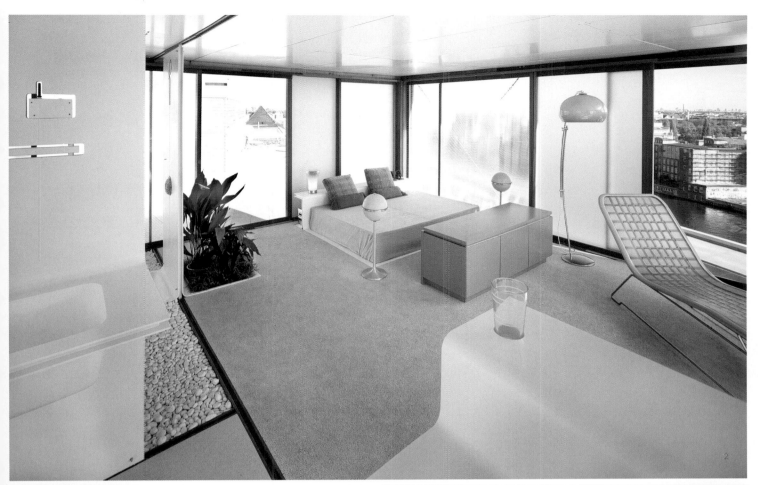

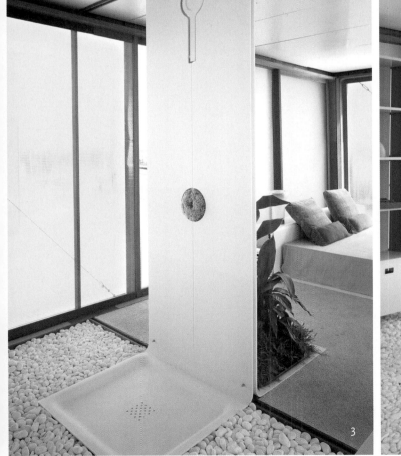

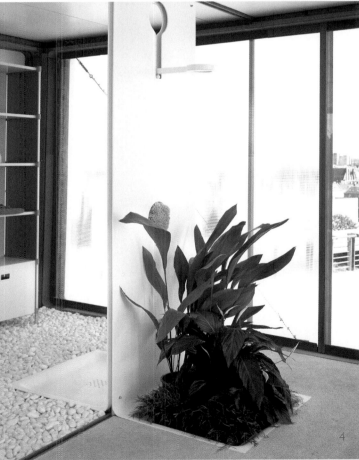

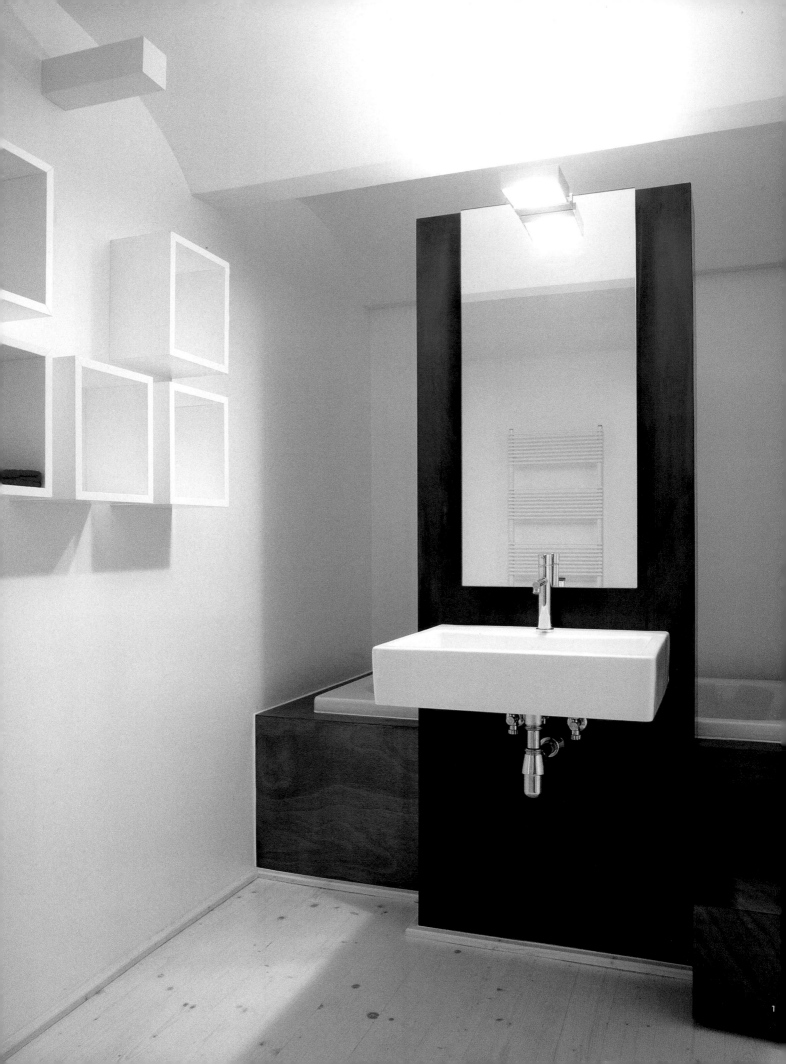

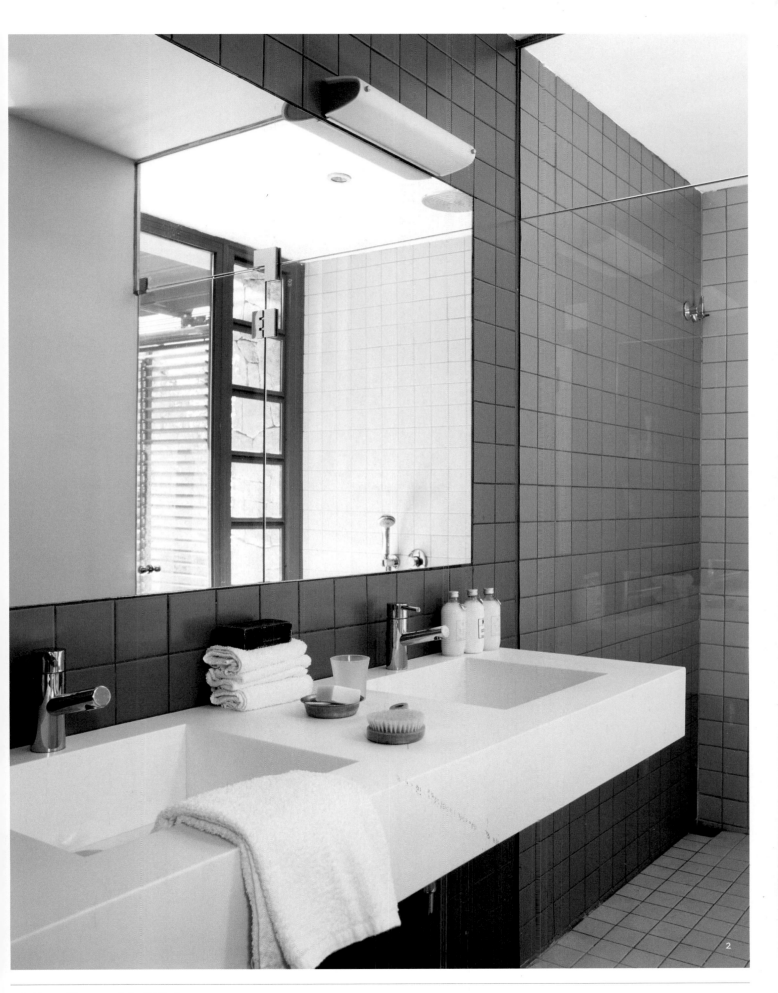